School
Administration

School Administration

Challenge and Opportunity for Leadership

Richard A. Gorton
University of Wisconsin
at Milwaukee

Wm. C. Brown Company
Publishers

Dubuque, Iowa

wcb

Contents

Preface

This book is directed to those individuals who are interested in developing a deeper understanding of the challenges and opportunities for leadership in school administration. The focus of the text is on principles and theories of administering and improving a school; however, many of the chapters are also relevant for other administrative levels. The intended readership includes prospective as well as experienced principals, assistant principals, district administrators, and persons responsible for preparing or working with school administrators.

In the process of preparing the book, the literature on educational administration and leadership was extensively and thoroughly reviewed. The review included relevant literature identified in *Education Index, Reader's Guide, Dissertation Abstracts, Books in Print,* and in Educational Resource Information Center, or, as it is commonly known, ERIC. (ERIC reports will be identified by an ERIC number; such reports are available in most university libraries and can be ordered directly from ERIC Document Reproduction Service, P. O. Box 190, Arlington, Virginia 22210.) Efforts have been made to utilize important ideas from the past (since much that has been recommended, though not yet implemented in many schools, is still sound) as well as more current concepts and data.

At this point it might be well to emphasize that this is *not* a book which extols *present* administrative practices in the schools, but rather one which offers recommendations and suggestions for *improving* current practices. Realistically speaking, school administration is neither as bad as some of its critics have claimed nor as good as many of its defenders would have us believe. However, most people would probably agree that there is room for improvement in school administration, and it is toward meeting that need that this text is addressed.

Finally, it should be mentioned that the major thrust of the book is toward leadership responsibilities and opportunities of the school administrator. Although, as the text indicates, administration should be a team effort and there are others associated with the school who make an important contribution, the proposition is advanced that few problems will be resolved or school improvements initiated unless the school administrator exercises leadership. Given proper administrative leadership, a school can do much to ameliorate its problems and improve educational services; in the absence of appropriate administrative leadership, these goals will seldom be achieved.

It is the author's strong conviction that the way to begin improving education is by improving the administrative leadership of the school. Hopefully, this book will make a positive contribution to that end.

Richard A. Gorton

Acknowledgments

An author of a book is usually indebted to many people. For me, this includes the individuals who reviewed earlier drafts of proposed chapters and offered helpful suggestions, and the students who pilot-tested much of the material in the text. It also includes Grace Hunn, my secretary, who typed those parts of the book that were piloted in classes.

Special appreciation is due my wife, Pat. She has provided essential support, encouragement, and most importantly, love; and it is to her and my sons, John and Jim, that this book is dedicated.

Part I

Purpose/
Direction/
Accountability

1

Role of the School
in a Changing Society

*Cheshire Puss . . . would you tell me,
please, which way I ought to go from here?
That depends a good deal on where you
want to get to . . .*

Lewis Carroll
Through the Looking Glass

The school administrator should not look upon administration as an end in itself, but as a means to an end. That end can be represented by the goals and objectives which the school is trying to achieve. Those goals and objectives give direction and purpose to the people who are associated with a school, and help to identify the various tasks and activities which will need to be accomplished if the school is to be successful in achieving its aims.

An administrator of a school without clear goals and objectives is like a captain of a ship without a rudder. The ship may not sink, but the progress it makes towards its destination will be, at best, uncertain. Therefore, it is in the interest of every administrator to become knowledgeable about the various goals and objectives which have been proposed for the school, and to develop some vision and convictions about the direction that education should, in his estimation, take in the future. A logical way to initiate this process is through the study of various goals and objectives which have been proposed for the school. Too often educators have ignored the wisdom of the past and have, as a result, wasted time and energy reinventing the educational wheel. We will therefore begin our study by considering early concepts of the role of the school and its objectives.

EARLY CONCEPTS OF THE SCHOOL'S ROLE

INITIAL FOCUS

The American school was conceived as an institution the main purpose of which was to teach students to read, write, and "cipher," often with a view toward attending college in preparation for the ministry or one of the other professions.[1] Since the primary function of many schools at that time was to prepare one for college, the students generally received an education which was predominantly classical in nature, with strong emphasis on Latin. "Dame School" was the name commonly applied to the elementary school of that day, while the secondary school was frequently titled "Latin Grammar School." Although other types of school existed, Dame Schools and Latin Grammar Schools were most prevalent during the period, 1647-1750.[2]

In 1751 a new secondary school with a different purpose and title was introduced. The new secondary school, called the "academy," was first chartered in Philadelphia in 1751 by Benjamin Franklin.[3] Its primary objective, as contrasted with the purpose of the Latin Grammar School, was to provide students with an education that would be *practical* as well as college preparatory. In the words of Franklin, "As to their studies, it would be well if they could be taught *everything* that is useful and *everything* that is ornamental; But Art is long and their Time is short. It is therefore propos'd that they learn those Things that are likely to be most useful and most ornamental."[4]

Subsequently, additional academies sprang up in other states. In general, their goals also stressed the practical outcomes of education. Perhaps best typifying this priority was a statement (1781) by the donors of the Philips Academy in Andover, Massachusetts, which indicated that the school's objective was to "lay the foundations of a public free School or Academy for the purpose of instructing Youth not only in English and Latin Grammar, Writing, Arithmetic and those Sciences wherin they are commonly taught; but more especially to learn them the Great End and Real Business of Living."[5] The concept of the academy, with its emphasis on a more comprehensive and practical education, later formed the basis for the early high schools, the first of which was instituted in Boston in 1821.

As the purpose of education was gradually changing at the secondary school level after 1750, so changes were also occurring at the elementary level. Education was becoming more utilitarian, and less emphasis was being given to religion. Certainly, after 1750 emphasis shifted to reflect a greater concern with the educating of all the children, and with providing a broader curriculum than previously. But it should be noted that the curriculum of many of these elementary schools, frequently referred to as "common schools," was still largely college preparatory in nature.[6]

A BREAK WITH THE PAST

Although the academy, the early high schools, and the common schools represented attempts to broaden the function of education, the goals and purposes of many schools continued, until the early 1900s, to emphasize students' preparation for college.[7] In 1913, however, the National Education Association appointed a Commission on the Re-organization of Secondary Education that ultimately issued a series of reports clearly indicating a break with the past, insofar as the goals of the secondary school were concerned. Their main report, entitled, *Cardinal Principles of Secondary Education,*[8] stressed the importance of preparing a person to function in a democracy, rather than in college, as the central focus for secondary education.*

*It should be emphasized at this point that the reports have also greatly affected thinking about the goals of elementary education as well. As Herrick and others have noted, "Although directed towards secondary education, and the 'educated adult,' the *Cardinal Principles of Secondary Education* have affected the elementary school and its practices as much as, if not more than, those of the secondary school." (Virgil E. Herrick et al., *The Elementary School* [Englewood Cliffs, N.J.: Prentice-Hall, 1962], p. 70.)

In deciding which goals were appropriate for secondary education, the Commission analyzed the activities of the individual and found that seven areas were crucial to his existence and should therefore constitute the basic objectives of education, namely, (1) health, (2) command of fundamental processes, (3) worthy home membership, (4) vocation, (5) citizenship, (6) worthy use of leisure, and (7) ethical character.[9]

While most administrators easily recognize a list of *Cardinal Principles of Secondary Education,* many are not familiar with the Commission's discussion and reasoning in support of each objective. For this reason, among others, implementation of the seven principles has not always been as successful or complete as one might have desired. However, since the *Cardinal Principles of Secondary Education* have formed the basis for later attempts to delineate the objectives of American education, and because the principles, for the most part, appear to be as relevant today as at the time of their issuance, a brief summary of their underlying rationale is presented in figure 1.1.[10]

HEALTH

In the area of health, the Commission felt that if the individual was to carry out his other responsibilities—family, vocation, citizenship—he needed to be healthy. Health education, to the Commission, included inculcating health habits in the students, organizing an effective program of physical activities, and cooperating with the home and the community in safeguarding and promoting health.

WORTHY HOME MEMBERSHIP

In regard to worthy home membership, the Commission felt that the school should be trying to develop those qualities that would make it possible for the individual to contribute to and derive benefit from membership in a family. These qualities included, for girls, interest and ability in the proper management and conduct of a home, and for boys, appreciation and skill in budgeting for and maintaining a home. Developing wholesome attitudes and relationships between boys and girls, and developing proper attitudes on the part of students toward their present home responsibilities were also considered important aspects of the objective of worthy home membership.

VOCATION

In the area of vocational education, the Commission took the position that the school should help the student to secure those understandings, attitudes, and skills which would make it possible for him to secure a livelihood for himself

(continued)

Figure 1.1. Cardinal Principles of Secondary Education.

and those dependent upon him, and to serve society. It specifically stated that vocational education should help the student to find in his future vocation his own best development.

CITIZENSHIP

To achieve the citizenship goal, the Commission felt that the school should develop in the individual those qualities which he would need to function properly as a member of a neighborhood, town, city, state, or nation. The particular qualities which the Commission believed were essential were: "A many-sided interest in the welfare of the communities to which one belongs; loyalty to ideals of civic righteousness; practical knowledge of social agencies and institutions; good judgment as to means and methods that will promote one social end without defeating others; and, as putting all of these into effect, habits of cordial cooperation in social undertakings."

WORTHY USE OF LEISURE

In regard to worthy use of leisure, the Commission believed that education should see to it that an adequate recreation program is provided both by the school and by other appropriate agencies in the community so that the individual could recreate his body, mind, and spirit, and enrich and enhance his personality. The Commission also asserted that education should attempt to foster in each individual one or more special avocational interests which could be used during leisure moments.

COMMAND OF FUNDAMENTAL PROCESSES

This principle included the development of adequate skills in reading, writing, arithmetic, and oral and written expression. This Commission did not look upon the development of these skills as an end in itself, but as an indispensable objective if the individual was to function satisfactorily in school and in later life.

ETHICAL CHARACTER

The final objective the Commission recommended was that of building ethical character. The Commission indicated that education for ethical character should include developing on the part of the student a "sense of personal responsibility and initiative and, above all, the spirit of service and the principles of true democracy which should permeate the entire school. . ." The Commission felt that no other objective was as important as the development of ethical character for, in a real sense, achieving all of the other objectives was dependent on the student's possessing ethical character.

Figure 1.1. Continued.

Promulgation of the *Cardinal Principles of Secondary Education* was a landmark event in American education.* While implementation of the Principles in the different classrooms across the country has been and continues to be uneven and less than complete, it is nevertheless true that their publication established a new direction for American education. The influence of the Cardinal Principles can be seen by examining other statements of goals for secondary as well as elementary education.

ADDITIONAL EFFORTS TO DEVELOP SCHOOL GOALS

Since the publication of the *Cardinal Principles of Secondary Education,* numerous attempts have been made to define the goals of American education. These efforts indicate the continuing concern of educators and other Americans about the outcomes of education. This concern seems to reflect the periodic need to establish or, perhaps more accurately, to reaffirm the aims of education, and thus to provide direction and focus in times of turmoil or uncertainty in the larger society. Since one of the purposes of this book is to help the administrator to formulate ideas and convictions about objectives which the school should adopt, four important proposals for goals in education will be presented for consideration. Although these proposals are in a sense historical documents, they deserve the thoughtful consideration of any administrator who hopes to benefit from the wisdom of the past in his efforts to develop school objectives.

THE PURPOSES OF EDUCATION IN AMERICAN DEMOCRACY

The first major proposal for school goals following the issuance of the *Cardinal Principles of Secondary Education* was entitled, *The Purposes of Education in American Democracy.* This proposal, authored by the Educational Policies Commission in 1938, advanced four basic objectives for American education: (1) self-realization, (2) human relationship, (3) economic efficiency, and (4) civic responsibility.[11] Each of these general objectives was divided by the Commission into subobjectives, examples of which

---

*For example, in 1932, a special Committee for Elementary Education, appointed by the New York State Department of Education, adapted the Cardinal Principles for the elementary school. They proposed that the primary function of the elementary school was to help every child to (1) understand and practice desirable social relationships, (2) discover and develop his own desirable individual aptitudes, (3) cultivate the habits of critical thinking, (4) appreciate and desire worthwhile activities, (5) gain command of common integrated knowledge and skills, and (6) develop a sound body and normal mental attitudes. (*Committee for Elementary Education, Cardinal Objectives in Elementary Education*—A Third Report. [Albany: University of the State of New York Press, 1932], pp. 9-16.)

are presented in figure 1.2 so that the reader may better understand and evaluate their merits.

The Purposes of Education in American Democracy builds and elaborates upon the *Cardinal Principles of Secondary Education.* Its value derives largely from the fact that it specifies in greater detail and depth the seven areas of school objectives which had been initially formulated in the Cardinal Principles. Its major limitation, like that of the Cardinal Principles, is that the terms used in stating the purposes frequently fail to lend themselves to precise interpretation of meaning, or are stated in such a man-

---

1. **The Objectives of Self-Realization**
   The Inquiring Mind. The educated person has an appetite for learning.
   Reading. The educated person reads the mother tongue efficiently.
   Writing. The educated person writes the mother tongue effectively.
   Esthetic Interests. The educated person appreciates beauty.
   Character. The educated person gives responsible direction to his own life.
2. **The Objectives of Human Relationship**
   Respect for Humanity. The educated person puts human relationships first.
   Friendships. The educated person enjoys a rich, sincere, and varied social life.
   Cooperation. The educated person can work and play with others.
   Courtesy. The educated person observes the amenities of social behavior.
   Appreciation of the Home. The educated person appreciates the family as a social institution.
3. **The Objectives of Economic Efficiency**
   Occupational Information. The

educated producer understands the requirements and opportunities for various jobs.
   Occupational Appreciation. The educated producer appreciates the social value of his work.
   Work. The educated producer knows the satisfaction of good workmanship.
   Consumer Judgment. The educated consumer develops standards for guiding his expenditures.
   Consumer Judgment. The educated consumer takes appropriate measures to safeguard his interests.
4. **The Objectives of Civic Responsibility**
   Social Justice. The educated citizen is sensitive to the disparities of human circumstance.
   Social Activity. The educated citizen acts to correct unsatisfactory conditions.
   Tolerance. The educated citizen respects honest differences of opinion.
   Conservation. The educated citizen has a regard for the nation's resources.
   Political Citizenship. The educated citizen accepts his civic duties.

Used with the permission of The National Education Association.

Figure 1.2. The Purposes of Education in American Democracy

ner as to make evaluation of the achievement of the purposes difficult. Still, the 1938 statement by the Educational Policies Commission deserves the consideration of the administrator even today. Certainly the statement can be used as a basis for the development or revision of a school's educational objectives. However, for such use, efforts should be made to define terms more precisely so that meaning will be clearer and evaluation of achievement more attainable.

THE IMPERATIVE NEEDS OF YOUTH

Probably one of the most influential documents dealing with the goals of secondary education was published in 1944 by the National Association of Secondary School Principals and was entitled, *The Imperative Needs of Youth of Secondary School Age.* [12] The proposed objectives in the document were based on several assumptions:

1. that education should be planned for all youth
2. that education should be free
3. that all youth have certain educational needs in common, and that education should be adapted to personal and social needs
4. that education should be continuous. [13]

Based on the above assumptions, the Association set forth ten important needs of youth to which it felt education should address itself. They are as follows:

The Imperative Needs of Youth of Secondary School Age [14]

1. All youth need to develop saleable skills and those understandings and attitudes that make the worker an intelligent and productive participant in economic life. To this end, most youth need supervised work experience as well as education in the skills and knowledge of their occupations.
2. All youth need to develop and maintain good health and physical fitness and mental health.
3. All youth need to understand the rights and duties of the citizen of a democratic society, and to be diligent and competent in the performance of their obligations as members of the community and citizens of the state and nation, and to have an understanding of the nations and peoples of the world.
4. All youth need to understand the significance of the family for the individual and society and the conditions conducive to successful family life.
5. All youth need to know how to purchase and use goods and services intelligently, understanding both the values received by the consumer and the economic consequences of their acts.

6. All youth need to understand the methods of science, the influence of science on human life, and the main scientific facts concerning the nature of the world and of man.
7. All youth need opportunities to develop their capacities to appreciate beauty in literature, art, music, and nature.
8. All youth need to be able to use their leisure time well and to budget it wisely, balancing activities that yield satisfactions to the individual with those that are socially useful.
9. All youth need to develop respect for other persons, to grow in their insight into ethical values and principles, to be able to live and work cooperatively with others, and to grow in the moral and spiritual values of life.
10. All youth need to grow in their ability to think rationally, to express their thoughts clearly, and to read and listen with understanding.

Publication of the document, *The Imperative Needs of Youth of Secondary School Age,* was an important contribution to the sharpening of the focus of secondary school education at the end of World War II, and was undoubtedly useful to many administrators and school groups who were seeking direction at that time.* The educational objectives implied in this statement of the needs of youth were comprehensive, covering many facets of student development. The statement also was visionary in its recommendation that education and the educational objectives set forth should be planned for *all* youth.

Unfortunately, like many statements of proposed goals, implementation has been uneven or lacking in important respects. For example, school groups have had considerable trouble determining which ethical values and principles the committee referred to in Imperative Need #9, and agreement on moral and spiritual values has frequently been difficult to achieve. Also, many secondary schools, if not most, have chosen to ignore the premise that *all* youth possess the ten needs identified and have provided only an elective program for certain of the needs, such as #1, #4, #5, and #7. In addition, it seems clear that, inadvertently or by design, most schools have either rejected or ignored the educational objective implied in #8, that all students need to develop understandings, skills, and attitudes in regard to using their leisure time wisely.

Despite the less than complete implementation of *The Imperative Needs of Youth,* the document nevertheless stands as a useful reference for any

*A similar document was published for the elementary school: *Education for All American Children* (Washington D.C.: Educational Policies Commission 1948). The document proposed that elementary schools attempt to develop fully the capabilities of each child by helping the student to acquire a basic health education; a high degree of skill in reading, writing, and arithmetic; habits of good workmanship; skills of critical thinking, constructive discussion, social responsibility; and cooperative skills (p. 58).

administrator who wishes to help establish or revise the educational objectives of a school. It is true that the statement and many of its terms need further definition and elaboration, and cannot be simply transplanted into a new school situation. However, the basic outline, orientation, and thrust of the document provide guidelines which are as valuable and relevant today as they were in the mid-forties.

THE QUESTION OF VALUES

In the proposals on educational aims presented to this point, reference has been made to developing ethical or moral values. The *Cardinal Principles of Secondary Education* referred to education for ethical character. *The Purposes of Education in American Democracy* mentioned "character" and "respect for humanity." *The Imperative Needs of Youth* stated that all youth need to develop insight into ethical, moral, and spiritual values. One problem, however, is that proposals on school goals have not been very specific in stating *which* ethical, moral, or spiritual values the school should attempt to develop in students. To this omission there has been one notable exception.

In 1951, the Educational Policies Commission published an essay entitled, "Moral and Spiritual Values in the Public Schools," which is still probably the best statement available on this very difficult subject. The most important parts of the essay developed by the Educational Policies Commission are presented in figure 1.3.

(Educational Policies Commission, 1)
   The basic moral and spiritual value in American life is the supreme importance of the individual personality.

1. Each person should feel responsible for the consequences of his own conduct.
2. Institutional arrangements are the servants of mankind.
3. Mutual consent is better than violence.
4. The human mind should be liberated by access to information and opinion.
5. Excellence in mind, character, and creative ability should be fostered.
6. All persons should be judged by the same moral standards.
7. The concept of brotherhood should take precedence over selfish interest.
8. Each person should have the greatest possible opportunity for the pursuit of happiness, provided only that such activities do not substantially interfere with the similar opportunities of others.
9. Each person should be offered the emotional and spiritual experiences which transcend the material aspects of life.

Used with permission of The National Education Association.

Figure 1.3. Moral and Spiritual Values
in the Public Schools.[15]

While it is true that the moral and spiritual values proposed by the Educational Policies Commission are not stated in behavioral or operational terms, they do offer an administrator rough benchmarks on the basis of which further refinements can be achieved.

One problem, however, that will confront schools which attempt to include values in their aims or objectives is that everyone does not subscribe to the same values. For example, Nash sees a conflict between the traditional values accepted by many older adults and the emergent values espoused by many young people, as identified in figure 1.4.

---

1. Puritanism versus enjoyment
2. Self-righteousness versus openness
3. Violence versus creativity
4. Politeness versus honesty
5. Bureaucratic efficiency versus human relationships

6. "Objective truth" versus personal knowledge
7. Ideology versus existential decision making and action
8. Authority versus participation
9. Tradition versus change

Figure 1.4. Traditional Versus Emergent Values [16]

The problem of conflict between traditional and emergent values can not easily be avoided by the school. This problem and the questions of how and whether values can or should be fostered will be more fully discussed in chapter 2.

THE CENTRAL PURPOSE OF AMERICAN EDUCATION

In none of the proposals on educational objectives presented thus far has any *priority* of importance been stated or implied. In 1961, the Educational Policies Commission apparently decided that the lack of priority in statements of objectives was a serious omission which needed to be corrected, so the Commission published a document entitled, *The Central Purpose of American Education.* In its statement the Commission took the position that the central purpose of American education " . . . is the development of the ability to think." [17]

It should be noted, as the Commission pointed out, that singling out the development of the student's thinking abilities does not imply that this should be the school's sole objective or that it should be the most important objective in *all* cases. Nevertheless, it is clear from examining the language of the Commission that it considered the achievement of this objective worthy of receiving the highest priority of the school.

The Commission's statement, while accorded general approval by educators, has been attacked in some circles for its failure to address itself to the question of the *purpose* for which the student should use his rational power. Bramheld, for example, criticized the document soon after publication because it did not face squarely the key issue of " . . . whether these powers [thinking abilities] should be used to achieve values and institutions appropriate to an age undergoing, as ours is undergoing, lightning-like change—values and institutions that represent the widest, deepest aspirations of the greatest number of human beings everywhere on earth." [18] While Bramheld's position on the central purpose of education may be that of the minority, the issue has by no means been settled, and it is likely that the debate will continue.

RECENT CONCEPTS REGARDING THE ROLE OF THE SCHOOL

MAJOR EMPHASES

There has seldom been a shortage of proposals from educational leaders, or others outside the field of education, on what the aims of the school should be. [19] Frequently these statements have just reaffirmed positions taken by earlier national groups, but in a number of instances new ground has been broken. Rather than provide an extensive discussion of all of the various recent points of view on school goals, figure 1.5 presents a representative sampling for the reader's consideration and analysis.

Two themes seem to permeate many of the statements presented in figure 1.5: (1) the school should help the student to acquire the knowledge, skills, and appropriate attitudes that will enable him to continue to pursue learning throughout his life in a constantly changing society; and (2) the school should help the student to acquire knowledge, skills, and appropriate attitudes for changing society in the "right" direction. Both of these aims have been proposed for the school at one time or another in the past, but it would appear that there is currently greater emphasis on these aspects of a student's education than ever before. Whether the school should prepare students for a role in a changing society may be debated, but it should be pointed out that there is considerable evidence that such preparation will be needed eventually, if not immediately.*

*For a stimulating discussion of this point, see Alvin Toffler, *Future Shock* (New York: Random House, 1970).

1. *Self-Directed Learner*
   School leaders must strive to produce a better self-directed student who finds information himself, who has clear priorities which enable him to concentrate his efforts, who utilizes feedback from his environment to determine the correctness of his ideas, and who is satisfied by a task well done.[20]

2. *Career Education*
   So what I would hope for is a new orientation of education—starting with the earliest grades and continuing through high school—that would expose the student to the range of career opportunities, help him narrow down the choices in terms of his own aptitudes and interests, and provide him with education and training appropriate to his ambition.[21]

3. *Personality Development*
   When a child leaves our program, depending on his age, does he feel secure? When he leaves us, has he developed a responsibility for himself, does he have a high self-regard; does he recognize his relatedness to other people, regardless of their differences from him in appearance, language, values or anything else?[22]

4. *Cognitive Development*
   . . . the schools should direct their primary efforts toward increases in the pupil's cognitive competency, not towards his personal adjustment . . . toward structure of useful knowledge in various important subjects, not toward the development of general mental abilities.[23]

5. *Continuous Learning*
   With the rapid acquisition of new knowledge, it is no longer possible to give the student in school an adequate command of the facts in each subject which would serve him throughout the balance of his life. . . Hence an important educational aim today is to teach students to learn and to develop in them a strong interest in continued study.[24]

6. *Knowledge to Improve Society**
   An education that is relevant must connect knowledge and social change. Such education should help him [the student] participate in the development of the future by directing him into the mainstream of human events, by giving him experiences in making effective social decisions, and by illuminating the alternative choices and their consequences.[25]

7. *Development of Values*
   I want to see the schools give less emphasis to storing knowledge and give more emphasis to the building of values. It is very important today that the school look for better ways to develop moral and spiritual value concepts into youth as guideposts for decisions they make as free citizens in our society.[26]

8. *Preparation for Change*
   If we indoctrinate the young person in an elaborate set of fixed beliefs, we are ensuring his early obsolescence. The alternative is to develop skills, attitudes, habits of mind, and the kinds of knowledge and understanding that will be the instruments of continuous change. . .[27]

*For an early but still relevant discussion of this point of view, see George S. Counts, *Dare the Schools Build a New Social Order?* (New York: Day Company, 1932.)

Figure 1.5. A Sampling of Proposed School Goals.

(continued)

9. *Cultural Pluralism*

First, in cultural terms, the school must provide each student with a set of relevant cultural experiences so that successful and meaningful cultural adaptations might be made. Second, in educational terms, through a process of individual "cultural worth" the school must establish means for cultural expression in the widest variety of school contexts. . . . Finally, the school must go beyond just becoming a reflection of cultural diversity. It must participate in and prepare youth for a culturally pluralistic life and society. . . [28]

Figure 1.5. Continued.

PUBLIC EXPECTATIONS

As the school administrator considers the question of the role of the school, he should also be aware of public expectations. For example, the Gallup Poll of public attitudes toward education has revealed definite preferences by the public as to what should be the primary functions of the school. Figure 1.6 presents responses to a question about which educational programs should be given more emphasis by the local school.

(In Order of Priority)

Elementary School

1. Teaching students the skills of reading, writing, and arithmetic.
2. Teaching students how to solve problems and think for themselves.
3. Teaching students to respect law and authority.
4. Teaching students how to get along with others.
5. Teaching students the skills of speaking and listening.
6. Teaching students vocational skills.
7. Teaching students health and physical education.
8. Teaching students about the world of today and yesterday (i.e., history, geography, and civics).
9. Teaching students how to compete with each other.

Secondary School

1. Teaching students to respect law and authority.
2. Teaching students how to solve problems and think for themselves.
3. Teaching students vocational skills.
4. Teaching students how to get along with others.
5. Teaching students the skills of speaking and listening.
6. Teaching students about the world of today and yesterday (i.e., history, geography, and civics).
7. Teaching students the skills of reading, writing, and arithmetic.
8. Teaching students health and physical education.
9. Teaching students how to compete with each other.

Figure 1.6. Public Perception of Educational Functions Needing Greater Attention[29]

It seems clear that the ways in which the public perceives the importance of various functions of the school need to be seriously considered. To paraphrase an important observation made in another context, "The question of what should be the primary function or goals of education is too important to be left solely to educational authorities." The school administrator and associates need to become more aware of the public's point of view, and to utilize data from national polls and local surveys of community attitudes in establishing or revising the goals of education in the school.*

EDUCATION AND THE FUTURE

Goal proposals and public expectations are two useful sources of ideas for determining the role of a school. However, the administrator needs to recognize that the students who are now attending school will in all probability be confronted by circumstances and problems when they are adults that will be very different than those faced by adults today. Certainly, if the amount of change which has occurred in the past three decades is any indication, the type of society in which we will be living in the twenty-first century will be much different from that of the twentieth century. Therefore, if one of the functions of the school is to prepare students for the kind of world in which they will be living as adults, then the school administrator needs to become more aware of projections and predictions of what society will be like in the future.

Although there have always been people who have tried to predict the future, it was not until recently that social scientists—particularly those in education—began a systematic effort to project future trends and possibilities and their implications for education. As one might suspect, this has not been an easy task, for as Ziegler has pointed out, " . . . we have no way of validating our predictions until the future becomes present."[30] For this reason and because the field of predicting the future is so new, the predictions advanced by any group or individual are usually very tentative and their implications for education are frequently not specific.† However, based on the author's review of the literature on the subject of the future and its implications for education, it would appear that the school needs to

---

*Since the Gallup Poll is a national survey, school administrators should conduct their own study in the local community if they doubt the national findings.

† A major exception to the latter would be the work of the educational laboratory, Research for Better Schools, which has attempted to address the subject of the future and education in a comprehensive and useful manner. See *The Future of Education: Perspectives on Tomorrow's Schooling,* ed. Louis Rubin (Boston: Allyn & Bacon, 1975). See also, *The 80's: Where Will the Schools Be?* (Reston, Va.: National Association of Secondary School Principals, 1974).

prepare students for a future in which the following abilities will be important:[31]

1. Directing and coping successfully with change in an ever-changing society
2. Conserving the environment and managing resources wisely in a society with increasingly scarce resources and a growing technology capable of destroying larger segments of the environment
3. Pursuing learning continuously in a society in which new knowledge will be coming to the fore constantly and much previously acquired knowledge will become obsolete
4. Utilizing increased amounts of leisure time wisely
5. Developing and maintaining rewarding human relationships in a society becoming increasingly impersonal
6. Developing and maintaining a set of ethical values and philosophy which will provide an individual with purpose, direction, and a basis for decision making in an increasingly pluralistic and valueless society
7. Perceiving the increasing interdependency of the various parts of the world, and supporting attempts to develop cooperative and peaceful solutions to increasingly difficult world problems

It should be noted that many of the abilities which are predicted as necessary in the future, are currently needed and several of them have been recommended for some time. However, if various predictions of the future are correct, then these abilities will be not only desirable but essential for a successful adult life.

Historically, the school has frequently been slow to respond to changes in society and seldom has anticipated change. Generally, the school has tended to *react* to change after it has occurred in the larger society rather than trying to anticipate, plan for, and direct change. As a result, while one could argue that the school has done a good job, its graduates have not been as well prepared as they might have been, had the future and its implications for education been taken into greater consideration.

The school must not only prepare students for current circumstances and challenges but also for their adult life. The school administrator can play a leadership role in achieving that goal by not only considering goal proposals and public expectations for the role of the school, but also predictions, projections, and ideas about the future.*

---

*For the administrator who is interested in a magazine which attempts to report predictions about the future, see *Tomorrow's World,* P.O. Box 43, Babson Park, Mass. 02157 ("a semi-monthly newsletter for those interested in the world of the late 1970s. . . . the 1980s. . . . and beyond. . . ")

Review

1. Why is it in the best interest of an administrator to be concerned about school goals and objectives?

2. In what ways did the purpose and program of the school change between inception and the twentieth century?

3. Discuss the main focus and implications for the school of the following goal proposals:

    a. Cardinal Principles of Secondary Education, or Cardinal Objectives in Elementary Education

    b. The Purposes of Education in American Democracy

    c. The Imperative Needs of Youth of Secondary School Age, or Education for All American Children

    d. Moral and Spiritual Values in the Public Schools

4. Two major themes permeate the goal statements presented in figure 1.6. What are their implications for the school?

5. In deciding the goals and objectives, to what extent should the school consider the expectations of the community?

6. Why is it important for the administrator to become aware of projected future school and societal trends?

Notes

1. Ellwood P. Cubberley, *Public Education in the United States* (Boston: Houghton-Mifflin, 1934), pp. 12-25.

2. Ibid., pp. 27-33 for further detail about these schools.

3. H. G. Good, *A History of American Education* (New York: Macmillan Co., 1956), pp. 72-77.

4. Edgar W. Knight and Clifton L. Hall, *Readings in American Educational History* (New York: Appleton-Century-Crofts, Inc., 1951), p. 76.

5. Quoted in Elmer E. Brown, *The Making of Our Middle Schools* (New York: Longmans, Green & Co., 1903), p. 195.

6. Cubberley, *Public Education*, p. 330.

7. Ibid., pp. 542-44.

8. *Cardinal Principles of Secondary Education,* Bureau of Education, Bulletin no. 35. (Washington, D.C.: Government Printing Office, 1918).

9. Ibid., pp. 5-10.

10. Ibid.

11. Educational Policies Commission, *The Purposes of Education in American Democracy.* (Washington, D.C.: National Education Association, 1938), pp. 50, 72, 90, 108.

12. National Association of Secondary School Principals, *The Imperative Needs of Youth of Secondary School Age*. Bulletin no. 145. (Washington, D.C.: National Education Association, 1947).

13. Ibid., p. 4.

14. Ibid., p. 43.

15. Educational Policies Commission, *Moral and Spiritual Values in the Public Schools.* (Washington, D.C.: National Education Association, 1951), pp. 18-38.

16. Paul Nash, "Student Protest: A Crisis of Values," *Boston University Journal* 18 (Winter 1970):23-31.

17. Educational Policies Commission, *The Central Purpose of American Education.* (Washington, D.C.: National Education Association, 1961), p. 12.

18. Theodore Bramheld, "What Is the Central Purpose of American Education?" *Phi Delta Kappan* 43 (October 1961):12.

19. For several other useful statements of educational goals and objectives in addition to those presented in this section, see *The National Commission on Reform of Secondary Education, A Report to the Public and the Profession* (New York: McGraw-Hill, 1973).

20. Abraham Fischler, "Frontiers in School Leadership: Gentlemen, Start Your Engines," an ERIC publication: Ed-022-261 (January 1968):53-55.

21. Sidney P. Marland, Jr., "Marland on Career Education," *American Education* 7, no. 9 (November 1971):25.

22. Ira J. Gordon, "Success and Accountability," *Childhood Education* 48, no. 7 (April 1972):347.

23. Robert L. Ebel, "Command of Knowledge Should Be Primary Objective of Education," *Today's Education* 60 (March 1971):36.

24. Ralph Taylor, "Purposes for Our Schools," *National Association of Secondary School Principals Bulletin* 51 (December 1968):8.

25. William H. Boyer, "Education for Survival," *Phi Delta Kappan* 52 (January 1971):259-60.

26. Oscar Granger, "Value Concepts in America," *National Association of Secondary School Principals Bulletin* (November 1971):63, 65.

27. John W. Gardner, *Annual Report, Carnegie Corporation of New York* (New York: Carnegie Corporation, 1962), p. 11.

28. Thomas C. Hogg and Marlin R. McComb, "Cultural Pluralism: Its Implications for Education," *Educational Leadership* 27 (December 1969):237-38.

29. George H. Gallup, "Fourth Annual Gallup Poll of Public Attitudes toward Education," *Phi Delta Kappan* 54 (September 1972):35.

30. Warren L. Ziegler, *An Approach to the Future—Perspective in American Education.* (Syracuse, N.Y.: Educational Policy Research Center, Syracuse University Research Corporation, 1970), p. 12.

31. Rather than a list of all the sources consulted by the author, those books which seemed to be most helpful in predicting the future and in provoking consideration about the implications for education are provided below.

　　Robert Theobald, *Future Conditional*. (Indianapolis and New York: Bobbs-Merrill Co., 1972).

　　The Use of Futurism in Educational Planning, (Washington, D.C.: The National Institute of Education, 1973).

　　White House Conference on Children, Learning into the Twenty-first Century. (Washington, D.C.: Department of Health, Education and Welfare, 1970).

Edgar Faure et al., *Learning to Be: The World of Education Today and Tomorrow* (Paris: United Nations Educational, Scientific, and Cultural Organizations, 1972).

Robert R. Leeper, ed., *A Man for Tomorrow's World* (Washington, D.C.: Association for Supervision and Curriculum Development, 1970).

For a good description of methods of forecasting the future, see Charles de Houghton et al., . . . *And Now the Future* (London: PEP-12, 1973).

2

Development of School Objectives

The ideas presented in chapter 1 should be viewed and utilized as conceptual tools for the development of a school's educational objectives. Certainly one of the most significant leadership responsibilities which an administrator and relevant others can perform today is to develop school objectives, including not only the evaluation and revision of current objectives, but also the generation of new objectives. While all of the administrative and leadership activities that will be discussed in this book are important, they will not result in positive contributions to the school if the educational objectives to which they should be related are vague or nonexistent.

In generating school objectives, the administrator and the people with whom he is working will need to understand the context in which, and the process through which school objectives are developed and approved, and they must be prepared to deal with the major issues and problems which can arise during the process. The following sections take up each of these essential aspects.

MAJOR CONSIDERATIONS AND PROCEDURES

ORGANIZATIONAL RELATIONSHIPS AND SOCIAL FACTORS

The development of school objectives does not occur in a vacuum. The school administrator will need to take into consideration certain organizational relationships and social factors as he works with others on this important task.

Organizationally, a school is composed of several subunits and is itself a member of a larger unit, the school district.[1] The relationship between the goals and objectives of these organizational units is depicted in figure 2.1.

The most important organizational fact which an administrator should understand from an examination of figure 2.1 is that a school is not a separate entity but a member of a school district which has a philosophy and set of goals to which it must adhere. Consequently, the administrator and the professional staff of a school are not free to act unilaterally in developing school objectives, but must work within the philosophical and goal framework set by the school district. Usually the district's philosophy and goals will be stated in general terms—general enough to allow the individual

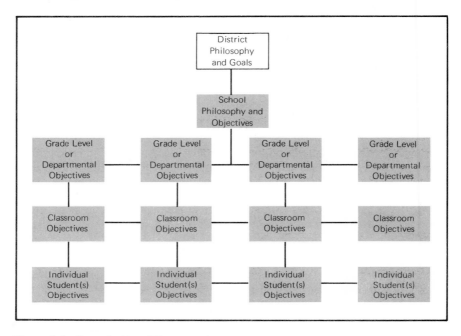

Figure 2.1. Organizational Framework
for School Objectives.

school considerable latitude in developing its own objectives. But regardless of the degree of flexibility in a district's framework, the objectives of an individual school must be compatible with the district's goals.

Secondly, in the development of school objectives the administrator and staff need to be aware of the organizational units within the school and their interrelationships. Most schools are organized according to grade level and, in the secondary school, by department also. Within these organizational units there are individual classrooms. While the emphasis in this chapter and the previous one is on the development of *school-wide* objectives, there should also be objectives for each grade level, department, classroom, and student which are related to the overall school objectives. Therefore, when the school administrator and staff are working on the development of school-wide objectives, they need to consider how these might be implemented at the grade, department, classroom, and student levels. It makes little sense to develop what may appear to be desirable school-wide objectives if, for some reason, they cannot be implemented at more specific levels within a school.

In addition to organizational relationships, the administrator and the staff will need to consider certain major social factors in developing school objectives. These factors are identified in figure 2.2.

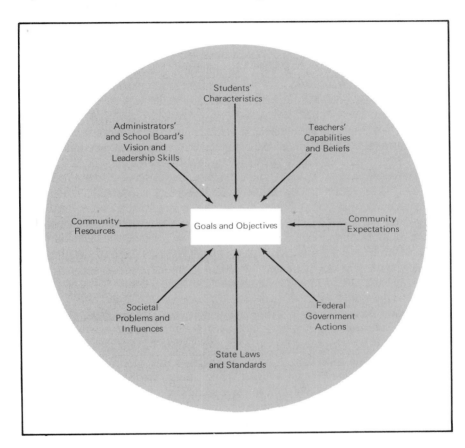

Figure 2.2. Major Social Factors Affecting the Development of Goals and Objectives.

As figure 2.2 shows, many social factors can affect the development of school objectives and need to be taken into consideration by the school administrator and staff. While all of the factors identified are important, five of them merit further discussion.

The characteristics of students enrolled in a school should be an important source of input to the development of the objectives—perhaps the *most* important source. Objectives which do not take into account the backgrounds, capabilities, and aspirations of students in a school will tend to be unrealistic, and the objectives may not be achieved. Consequently, in developing a school's objectives, the characteristics of students in the school should be identified and defined, and that information should be made available to all appropriate parties.

Community expectations and resources are two other important factors which can affect the development of school objectives. For example, a community which believes the school should not become involved in certain innovative aspects of education probably will not support educational objectives which go beyond traditional student learnings. On the other hand, a community that may believe strongly in an enlarged role for the school may lack the financial or human resources to support its commitment.* Of course, community resources and expectations can often be changed. State and federal aid can supplement the resources of a local community, and administrative and faculty leadership (or the lack of it) can affect the expectations of a community. However, it seems clear that, in the development of school objectives, the administrator and staff will need to consider community expectations and resources.

Two additional factors which are especially significant in establishing objectives for a school are the capabilities and beliefs of the faculty, and the vision and leadership skills of the administration and school board. If the faculty lacks the skills for the achievement of particular school objectives, or doesn't value the importance of those objectives, this situation will need to be rectified before they can be successfully implemented. Certainly, unless the teachers possess both the skills for and commitment to achieving whatever objectives are established in a school, their achievement is unlikely. The objectives may look good on paper, but they are not apt to be reached at the level intended.

It should be emphasized, however, that the capabilities and beliefs of the faculty can be influenced by the educational vision and leadership skills of the administration and the school board. The vision and leadership skills of the latter two groups may help the faculty to acquire increased skill and higher aspirations; conversely, the absence of vision and leadership may result in a stagnant situation. In the case of both the faculty and the community, the educational vision and leadership skills of the administration and the school board are extremely important factors in the development of school objectives.

The remaining factors in figure 2.2—societal problems and influences, federal government actions, and state laws and standards—are also significant, and will be discussed in chapter 4.

*For an interesting though somewhat pessimistic view of the influence of resources on the development of school objectives, see Edmond H. Weiss, "An Inverted View of Educational Planning," *Administrators Notebook* 22, (1973).

WHO SHOULD BE INVOLVED IN DEVELOPING EDUCATIONAL OBJECTIVES?

In the elementary and secondary system of education in the United States, the school board or board of directors makes the overall educational policy in a district; and the aims and objectives of a school constitute policy decisions within the province of a school board.[2] But the board's role is generally one of giving final approval to—or disapproval of—proposed educational objectives for a school. The board does not typically take an active role in initiating or proposing new educational objectives for a school, although there are exceptions. Normally, the school board assumes that the professionals in the school system, particularly the school administrators, will assume the leadership in proposing educational objectives, and the board's role will be that of evaluating such proposals and making final decisions. The main point that the school administrator must remember is that he is not free to implement new educational objectives without securing the final approval of the board of education. It would also be in his best interest to keep the board involved in efforts to develop school objectives.

In the process of developing objectives for a school, the administrator should also consider involving several other groups, which include: (1) the central office staff, (2) the faculty, (3) the parents, (4) the community, and (5) the students. Each of these groups can contribute valuable input to the development of educational objectives, and their support and commitment will be required in most cases if the objectives are to be implemented successfully.

Specifically, the central office staff can be helpful in providing time, materials, budgeting, and consultant assistance; and their understanding and support of the educational objectives ultimately proposed to the school board will be essential. The faculty represent the main vehicle for implementing the educational objectives, and without their understanding and commitment, implementation will undoubtedly be hampered, if not resisted. In addition, the educational backgrounds of faculty members, and their daily contacts with the student body, increase the potential value of their contribution to the development of educational objectives.

While some administrators may question whether parents, the community and students should be involved in the development of school objectives, it would seem that each of these groups can offer unique and frequently useful input. All three sources represent the layman's point of view, and that kind of a contribution is probably healthy in any discussion of educational objectives. If a school is to successfully implement its educational objectives, it will definitely need the understanding of parents and students, and such an understanding may be best achieved through their involvement in the process of developing educational objectives. In the case of the community, there are undoubtedly specialized resources such as businessmen, and professional and labor leaders, who could offer valuable insights and whose expertise should be utilized in the development of objectives for a school.

APPROACHES TO THE DEVELOPING OF SCHOOL OBJECTIVES

The traditional approach to the development of school objectives is the establishment of a committee which examines various materials and, after considerable discussion and usually some compromise, arrives at a statement of proposed objectives. The main limitations of this approach are that committee discussions frequently generate more heat than light, and the more influential members of the group tend to dominate the discussion and the decision making.

A recently proposed alternative or adjunct to the traditional approach to the development of school objectives is the Delphi Method. The Delphi Method, which grew out of the work of Olaf Helmer and Norman Dalkey, was originally intended as a tool for the scientific and technological forecasting of the future.[3] It has, however, been adapted for use in generating objectives and in establishing priorities among those objectives.[4] The major steps involved in the method are the following:

1. Identifying those individuals and/or groups whose opinions, judgments, or expert knowledge it would be valuable to obtain in the development of school objectives.
2. Soliciting anonymous recommendations for proposed objectives from those individuals and groups.
3. Compiling a list of the proposed objectives recommended by individuals and groups, and distributing this list to those who participated in step 2.
4. Requesting participants to indicate the importance or priority of each proposed objective on the list, e.g., very important, important, somewhat important, unimportant, no opinion.
5. Summarizing the results of step 4 and distributing data to participants; requesting participants to review the results and indicate any change in their assessment of the importance of certain objectives. The activities of this step are repeated until there is a reasonable consensus on the objectives which a school or school district should try to achieve.

It should be noted that information regarding proposed school objectives and their importance can be gathered and communicated by mailing questionnaires and reports of the data obtained, or the information may be collected and disseminated at a meeting, although the former procedure is more typically used. An important element of the Delphi Method, however, is that in the initial stages particularly, the anonymity of any individual or group proposing a school objective or indicating its priority should be maintained. The basic assumption is that an individual or group whose identity is not made known to the other participants is likely to be more candid in proposing school objectives and more flexible in considering and reconsidering their importance. Of course, in later stages of the process, it may be necessary for participants to discuss their differences openly, in order to compromise or arrive at a consensus.

The Delphi Method is an excellent approach for involving a large number of people in the development of school objectives and for minimizing the importance of status factors in deciding which objectives are most important.* However, there are potential weaknesses and questions associated with this approach which the administrator and staff may need to resolve. [5] One potential limitation is the time element: if mailed questionnaires are used, difficulty may be encountered in securing an adequate number of responses without too much delay. Also, there is the question of whether the responses to the questionnaires should be the sole basis for determining school objectives or whether they should constitute only one of several bases for making decisions about school goals. And finally, there is the question of who should organize the process of generating objectives and attend to its implementation.

To resolve these problems and questions the administrator and staff may need to establish a committee on school objectives which would plan and implement the foregoing process and which would prepare a report to the school board about the proposed objectives which the school would like to adopt. The committee, which might be composed of representatives from the groups mentioned in the previous section, could also be helpful in generating support for the Delphi Method by providing materials and data for the consideration of participants, and in helping them to resolve problems. In working with the committee, as well as with the other participants, the administrator should utilize his leadership skills to make the entire process more productive.

Of course, there are other approaches to the development of school objectives which deserve the administrator's consideration and merit further

*For a description of how the Delphi Method was successfully employed by a school district to develop agreement on educational goals, see Ray L. Sweigert and William H. Schabacker, "The Delphi Technique: How Well Does It Work in Setting Educational Goals?" (Paper presented at the Annual Meeting of the American Educational Research Association, Chicago, 1974).

investigation.* However, regardless of the method that the administrator ultimately employs, he and all other participants should try to adhere to the following principles proposed by the Joint Committee on Educational Goals and Evaluation.[6]

1. The goal setting process should be kept open to all points of view without domination or intimidation by any special interest group.
2. The purpose of bringing people together is not to dwell on past deficiencies or lay blame, but to evolve a philosophy, identify needs, determine goals, goal indicators, or sub-goals and program objectives, and to establish priorities.
3. Participants should not expect to have everything their way; they should come seeking a better understanding of the community, its people, and problems.
4. A spirit of cooperation and trust should be established among individuals and groups involved in the process.
5. Roles of leadership in school-community planning should be earned rather than based on authority.
6. Individuals and groups who are instrumental to the goal setting process should provide for the open flow of information.
7. The individual school should be the base of operation for bringing people together.
8. In the process of determining philosophy, goals and objectives, opinion must be balanced with fact.
9. The interaction process must begin with the concerns which have high priority for the people involved.
10. The governing board should commit the resources necessary to see the goal setting process through to a satisfactory conclusion; board members should be encouraged to participate in the interaction process, not as board members, but as private citizens.
11. Teachers, administrators, and classified employees should honor their responsibility to the community by taking an active part in the goal setting process.
12. A variety of meetings should be held as a part of the goal setting process; mixed groups assist consensus building.
13. Inasmuch as the learning process is recognized as being dynamic and individualistic, any objectives of education that are established should not be so specific or restrictive as to pre-program the learning process for any student.

---

*For example, Phi Delta Kappa's Commission on Educational Planning distributes a manual and materials (produced by the Program Development Center of Northern California) for developing and stating priorities among school goals and objectives which definitely deserve further consideration by the administrator. The manual and materials can be ordered from Phi Delta Kappa, P.O. Box 789, Bloomington, Ind. 47401.

14. To ensure that the philosophy, goals and objectives of public education continue to be relevant, a recycling process should be designed.
15. The goal setting and planning process should result in observable action.

MAJOR ISSUES AND PROBLEMS

WHICH OBJECTIVES SHOULD BE INCLUDED?

Herbert Spencer alluded to the question of which educational objectives should be included in the school's program when he asked in 1880, "What knowledge is of the most worth?"[7] Since that time, and undoubtedly even before then, educators and others have debated the question. Over the years, there has developed rather general agreement that the schools should teach the basic skills of reading, writing, and arithmetic, and the ideas contained in certain subject matter disciplines, such as history and science; but beyond that, there is little consensus, and debate continues. Therefore, an administrator who attempts to broaden the educational objectives in a school will probably encounter issues or problems which will need to be resolved.

One issue which the administrator will face is whether a school's objectives should be limited to developing students' skills and knowledge, or whether the school should try to enlarge its mission to include the teaching of attitudes and values. As the administrator reviews the various proposed goals and roles of the school presented in the previous chapter, he will note that in most instances a broad and comprehensive role and set of objectives are recommended for the school. And yet, the administrator will probably meet resistance and opposition from particular individuals and groups if he attempts to move the school in the direction of teaching attitudes and values.

For example, some people may question whether the school *should* teach values and attitudes to students. Frequently, this inquiry will be raised in the context of doubt as to whether there is a consensus on the values and attitudes which should be taught,[8] but concern may also be expressed about whether the school knows *how* to teach attitudes and values, such as compassion or integrity.[9] These questions raise legitimate issues which require discussion and analysis. However, what needs to be recognized is that the school does teach values and attitudes, whether or not it intentionally sets out to do so. As Charles Silberman notes:

> And children are taught a lot of lessons about values, ethics,
> morality, character, and conduct every day of the week, less by the
> content of the curriculum than by the way schools are organized,
> the way teachers and parents behave, the way they talk to children
> and to each other, the kinds of behavior they approve or reward,

and the kinds they disapprove or punish. These lessons are far
more powerful than the verbalizations that accompany them and
that they frequently controvert. [10]

Silberman's observations suggest that the school *does* teach attitudes
and values to students, regardless of whether or not explicit objectives and an
organized program exist. While there may remain legitimate concerns on the
part of educators about how one can best teach attitudes and values, there is
really no lack of materials and approaches for developing these student
characteristics.*

A more serious objection to the school's teaching of attitudes and values
is the disagreement over which attitudes and values the school should emphasize. For instance, anthropologist George Spindler has found in his
studies of the American culture that a new set of values has begun to surface.
He calls these "emergent values," and sees a possible conflict between them
and the more traditional values that have been espoused in our country. [11]
(See Nash's list of traditional and emergent values presented in chapter 1.)
Spindler has discovered that many communities comprise a mixture of people holding traditional and emergent values, and that such conditions are
responsible for many of the conflicts between the school and the community.

Complicating the problem of achieving agreement on specific attitudes
and values that the school should teach is the diversity of cultures and life-
styles that can be found in any particular community. Differences in ethnic
and racial background, social class, and other personal and social factors all
compound the school administrator's difficulty in trying to secure consensus
on the attitudes and values that the school should teach to students. [12]

In attempting to resolve these problems the administrator and staff
would appear to have available at least four main alternatives. [13] (1) They
may choose to resolve the problems and issues by focusing on those values
which represent dominant values in the local community, ignoring the
possibility that a number of students may not stay in the local community;
(2) the choice may be made to focus on more generalized values which
transcend the local community; (3) they may choose to involve students in an
analysis of a variety of values for the purpose of helping students to select
those values which are best for them, or (4) the administrator and staff may
choose to do nothing.

While each of these alternatives needs to be examined carefully for its
consequences and implications, the administrator cannot avoid a decision in
this matter. Even deciding to choose alternative four is a decision to maintain
the status quo. This probably means that, although the school will not focus

*For example, The Human Values Series, published by Steck-Vaughn Co., P.O. Box 2028,
Austin, Texas 78767. Also Science Research Associates and the National Education Association
publish many materials for use in this area.

in any explicit way on attitudinal or value objectives, it will continue to "teach" attitudes and values in the ways Silberman noted. Whichever decision is made, it would seem that the question of whether or not a school should concern itself with values and attitudes cannot easily be avoided.

HOW SHOULD SCHOOL OBJECTIVES BE STATED?

In recent years, the question of how school objectives should be stated has become an issue in American education. Ideally, they should be stated clearly and in terms which facilitate the evaluation of progress or achievement. This means that school objectives should be operationalized and defined in behavioral terms as suggested by Mager. [14] And yet, the administrator needs to be aware that there continues to be debate on the part of some people about the issue of behaviorally-stated objectives. [15]

Those opposed to behaviorally-stated objectives usually put forth the following arguments:

1. Some objectives are impossible to state in behavioral terms. (The examples used are typically in the affective learning domain.)
2. There are certain objectives that, even if they could be stated in behavioral terms, could not be measured because there are no evaluation techniques available. (Again, the examples used are typically from the affective learning domain.)
3. By emphasizing behaviorally-stated objectives, which are usually developed prior to interaction with the learner, the educator fails to utilize the interests and insights of the learner in developing the objectives, and may easily overlook or ignore objectives which arise spontaneously out of a learning situation for which there was no previously stated goal.
4. The process of operationalizing an objective, i.e., stating it in behavioral terms, is a sterile, mechanistic approach which tends to focus one's efforts on measurable aspects of learning at the cost of ignoring humanistic elements of education.

A careful examination of the first two objections to behaviorally-stated objectives would suggest that they are based, for the most part, on inadequate skill or knowledge. While there may be exceptions, the vast majority of objectives in education can be stated behaviorally, and progress or accomplishment can be measured in some reasonable manner.*

---

*For help in this area see D.R. Krathwohl et al., *Taxonomy of Educational Objectives, Handbook II: Affective Domain* (New York:David McKay, 1964). Also see Oscar K. Buros, ed., *The Mental Measurement Yearbook* (Highland Park, N.J.: Gryphon Press, 1972).

Therefore, the first two arguments against behavioral objectives should not be posed by an administrator as insurmountable obstacles to defining school objectives in behavioral terms.

Possibly the strongest argument against the use of behavioral objectives is the potential problem resulting from lack of student involvement. Although there is no reason why behavioral objectives could not be developed with the involvement of the learner, this has generally not been the case. Most behaviorally-stated objectives are developed by educators with little or no involvement of the learners who will be expected to achieve the objectives. It should be noted, however, that this characteristic is not unique to behaviorally-stated objectives; it is true of most school goals and objectives, whether or not they are stated in behavioral terms. Whether students *should* be involved in the development of school goals and objectives is a separate issue. However, there is nothing inherent in the behavioral objectives approach which precludes student input in their development.

Finally, it may be true that, by developing a behaviorally-stated objective, the achievement of which can be measured, there may be a tendency to overlook or ignore important outcomes which might arise spontaneously from a learning situation for which there were no previously stated goals. It is also possible that the operationalizing of objectives may tend to focus one's efforts on the more measurable aspects of learning to the neglect of education's more humanistic elements. These are not inevitable or predictable consequences of behaviorally-stated objectives, but they are potentialities which the administrator and staff must consider. The resolution of these problems, however, does not lie in the rejection of behaviorally-stated objectives, and reliance on objectives which *cannot* be measured or that arise spontaneously out of a classroom situation (since they may not arise spontaneously). Instead, there should be an awareness by the administrator and staff of the limitations inherent in behavioral objectives, and a flexibility that will permit the adjustment of goals when problems occur.

The basic case for behaviorally-stated objectives is that, in contrast to non-behaviorally-stated objectives, the accomplishment of the former can be more easily evaluated while the latter frequently cannot be evaluated at all, or only with great difficulty. Therefore, rather than engaging in nonproductive arguments about whether objectives should or can be stated in behavioral terms, it would appear that the essential task for administrators and others is to address themselves to the process of trying to operationalize school objectives. In pursuing this essential task the administrator should work closely with the professional staff, who (it should be noted) may be ambivalent about the need to develop behaviorally-stated objectives.[16] Still, there are effective ways of working with the staff on this matter, and the school administrator should utilize whatever resources are available.[17]

SHOULD THE SCHOOL BE HELD ACCOUNTABLE FOR ACHIEVING ITS OBJECTIVES?

Accountability may be the most controversial and explosive issue concerning school objectives. Simply defined in the context of school objectives, accountability means that the school should be held responsible for achieving its educational aims. [18] For example, it is not sufficient for the school administrator and staff to develop behavioral objectives; both should also be responsible for *achieving* those objectives. A humorous but pointed example of the thrust of the concept of accountability is presented in figure 2.3.

The movement for school accountability developed in the late 1960s, stemming from dissatisfaction on the part of an increasing number of people about the kind of product (i.e., the student) emerging from the school. [19] Although the movement reached a high point in the early seventies, in terms of widespread attention, the issue of school accountability is still an important one in American education. The issue has raised three questions in the minds of many administrators: (1) Who is accountable? (2) for what? and (3) to whom?

RECALLED FOR REVISION

By William C. Miller

Many of us who own recent model automobiles have received a communication from the factory, asking us to return the vehicle to the dealer so that defects can be corrected. Although I have gotten used to call-backs initiated by car manufacturers, I must admit I was startled to receive the following letter from my son's high school:

EDSEL MEMORIAL HIGH SCHOOL

. . . . Anywhere, U.S.A.

August 1, 1971

Dear Parents of our Graduates:
    As you are aware, one of your offspring was graduated from our high school this June. Since that time it has been brought to our attention that certain insufficiencies are present in our graduates, so we are recalling all students for further education.
    We have learned that in the process of the instruction we provided we forgot to install one or more of the following:

(continued)

Figure 2.3.

. . . at least one salable skill;

. . . a comprehensive and utilitarian set of values;

. . . a readiness for and understanding of the responsibilities of citizenship.

A recent consumer study consisting of follow-up of our graduates has revealed that many of them have been released with defective parts. Racism and materialism are serious flaws and we have discovered they are a part of the makeup of almost all our products. These defects have been determined to be of such magnitude that the model produced in June is considered highly dangerous and should be removed from circulation as a hazard to the nation.

Some of the equipment which was in the past classified as optional has been reclassified as standard and should be a part of every procuct of our school. Therefore, we plan to equip each graduate with:

. . . a desire to continue to learn;

. . . a dedication to solving problems of local, national, and international concern;

. . . several productive ways to use leisure time;

. . . a commitment to the democratic way of life;

. . . extensive contact with the world outside the school;

. . . experience in making decisions.

In addition, we found we had inadvertently removed from your child his interest, enthusiasm, motivation, trust, and joy. We are sorry to report that these items have been mislaid and have not been turned in at the school Lost and Found Department. If you will inform us as to the value you place on these qualities, we will reimburse you promptly by check or cash.

As you can see, it is to your interest, and vitally necessary for your safety and the welfare of all, that graduates be returned so that these errors and over-sights can be corrected. We admit that it would have been more effective and less costly in time and money to have produced the product correctly in the first place, but we hope you will forgive our error and continue to respect and support your public schools.

Sincerely,

P. Dantic, Principal

Reprinted by permission of Phi Delta Kappa, Inc., December 1971.

Figure 2.3. Continued.

While several answers might be given to the first question, it should be clear in the administrator's mind that the school in general and the administrator in particular can and should be held accountable. In the American system of education the local school is a creation of the state, which has delegated certain broad responsibilities and authority to the local school board, elected by the community. In order to accomplish the objectives of the school district, the school board delegates certain responsibilities to the administrators of the district. Therefore, in a real sense, a school administrator can and should be held accountable to the members of the school board, who in turn can and should be held accountable to their constituents, and to the state that gave them a charter and form of organization.

The question of *what* the school (or more specifically, the administrator and the staff) is accountable for is less easily answered. It could be asserted that the staff and the administrator should be held accountable for achieving the educational objectives which the school has set forth. However, this position has been challenged on two grounds: (1) that there are many variables over which the staff and the administrator have little or no control, e.g., home environment of the student, which may affect the achievement of the school's educational goals, and (2) that the accomplishment of many of the school's objectives is a shared responsibility with other agencies or institutions in society, such as the family, and that the staff and administrator should not be held totally accountable for the achievement of school goals.[20]

Although both of these arguments are valid to a point, they leave unresolved the basic issue of the degree to which the administrator and staff should be held accountable. If, in fact, the achievement of school objectives depends on many variables over which the administrator and staff have little or no control, does this mean that neither should be held accountable at *all* for the achievement of school objectives?* Obviously not, but researchers and educational theorists have not been very helpful in identifying *the extent* to which the administrator and staff should be held accountable.

And if the achievement of many educational objectives is a shared responsibility, what *specifically* is the staff's and school administrator's share, as compared to that of other agencies of society? All too frequently when the argument of shared responsibility is advanced, the end result is that *no one* takes responsibility for achieving a particular objective. The concept of shared responsibility has merit if it leads to efforts to coordinate resources and activities. But too often, when proposed, it fails to affix a specific degree of responsibility to the parties who are responsible for achieving the objective.

Although a definitive answer has not been developed by the education profession to the question of *what* the school should be held accountable for,

---

*It should be noted that recent evidence has been developed which seems to suggest that the school may have more significant impact on student learning than was asserted several years ago. See David Wiley and Annegret Harnischfeger, "Explosion of a Myth: Quantity of Schooling and Exposure to Instruction, Major Educational Vehicles," *Educational Researcher* 3, no. 4, (April 1974).

it is important that the educators in a school think through their own position. In general, it would appear that if the administrator and staff are going to establish certain educational objectives, they should be held accountable for their achievement. If particular conditions will affect the degree to which those objectives can be achieved, then the staff and the administrator have the responsibility of taking this into consideration in stating the objectives.

In regard to the school administrator's own accountability, it would seem that, in addition to being responsible for carrying out the typical duties assigned, he should also be held accountable for:

1. Identifying and clearly defining, with the help of others, the educational objectives of the school.
2. Specifying which teaching, supervisory, or administrative procedures and resources are needed in order to achieve those objectives.
3. Developing and implementing a plan for evaluating the extent of progress or achievement of the school's objectives.
4. Informing the school board and the community periodically about the degree to which objectives have been achieved, and the reasons for problems, if they occur.

The entire issue of school and school administrator accountability is an emotionally charged one. Undoubtedly, several significant factors should be considered in limiting the degree of the staff's and the school administrator's accountability. However, these factors should not be weighed so heavily that they become an argument for avoiding accountability completely or for avoiding the responsibility of making explicit the *extent* to which the staff or the school administrator should be accountable. In a true sense, the extent to which one is willing to be held accountable for achieving an objective is a valid indicator of the degree to which he has a real commitment to achieving that objective, as opposed to merely giving lip service to its importance.*

EVALUATING EFFORTS TO ESTABLISH AND IMPLEMENT SCHOOL OBJECTIVES

The end product which should result from consideration and resolution of the various issues and problems discussed in this chapter is the establishment of a set of educational objectives or aims to which the school is committed

---

*For excellent guidelines on how to organize a Planning Accountability Team at the school level, see Richard L. DeNovellis and Arthur Lewis, *Schools Become Accountable* (Washington, D.C.: Association for Supervision and Curriculum Development, 1974).

and which it is prepared to implement. To aid the administrator in evaluating the strengths and weaknesses of the school's educational objectives and plan for implementation, specific criteria stated in question form are presented as follows:

Criteria for Assessing the School's Efforts in Establishing, Implementing, and Evaluating School Objectives

1. Do the school's objectives reflect and maintain an appropriate balance between the needs of the individual and those of society?
2. Are the school's objectives comprehensive, rather than restricted to knowledge and skill outcomes? Is the development of student interests, attitudes, and values also included in the objectives of the school?
3. Does the school make clear which objectives are its sole or primary responsibility and which objectives it shares with other institutions? If the school shares a responsibility with other institutions, does it make explicit the *extent* to which *it* is responsible?
4. Do the school's objectives focus on *student outcomes* rather than school functions, activities, or processes?
5. Are the school's objectives stated clearly and in terms which facilitate the evaluation of progress or achievement?
6. Does the statement of each school objective indicate
   a. the proposed *level* of performance?
   b. *when* the objectives will be achieved?
7. Do the school objectives take into consideration individual differences among students as to backgrounds, abilities, interests, and aspirations?
8. Is there a school plan for the continuous development of understanding of and commitment to the objectives on the part of students, teachers, parents, and important others?
9. Is there a formal plan for periodic and systematic evaluation of progress toward or achievement of the school's objectives?
10. Are the objectives re-examined periodically (every two or three years would be desirable) to see whether modification, elimination, or the addition of new objectives is needed?

In too many schools, objectives are developed, published in the school district's or teacher's handbook and remain there year after year, without critical examination as to their relevancy or accomplishment. Utilization of criteria presented in the statement above should help the school administrator maintain a set of relevant objectives whose achievement is evaluated.

A FINAL COMMENT

It should be emphasized that the administrator must take the initiative to utilize the criteria (in cooperation with others associated with the school, e.g., teachers, parents) if the formulation and evaluation of achievement of school objectives are to be improved. It will be easy for an administrator to feel that he is too busy to engage in such efforts and that there are other priorities which demand attention. Certainly, the school administrator's job is a demanding one, and there are many problems and issues that compete for his time. However, the development and evaluation of school objectives may very well be the most important task which the administrator can perform, since the objectives chart the direction that education should take in a school.

Review

1. What are the main organizational and social factors an administrator needs to take into consideration in the development of school objectives?
2. Identify the groups an administrator should involve in the development of school objectives. What contribution can each group be expected to make?
3. How can the Delphi Method and the principles proposed by the Joint Committee on Educational Goals and Evaluation be utilized in the development of school objectives?
4. What are the major factors that an administrator needs to consider in resolving the issue of whether or not the school should include in its objectives the teaching of values and attitudes?
5. State the arguments for and against behaviorally defined school objectives.
6. To what extent should the school and the school administrator be held accountable?

Notes

1. Stephen J. Knezevich, *Administration of Public Education* (New York: Harper & Row Publishers, 1975), p. 213.
2. Edgar L. Morphet et al., *Educational Organization and Administration* (Englewood Cliffs, N.J.: Prentice-Hall, 1974), p. 311.
3. Olaf Helmer and Norman Dalkey, "An Experimental Application of the Delphi Method to the Use of Experts." *Management Science* 9 (April 1963):458-67.
4. "Exploring the Potential of the Delphi Technique by Analyzing Its Application" (Symposium of the American Educational Research Association, Minneapolis, Minn., March 1970).

5. Robert C. Judd, "Delphi Applications for Decision-Making," *Planning and Changing* 2 (October 1971):155.

6. Joint Committee on Educational Goals and Evaluation, *Education for the People* 1, "Guidelines for Total Community Participation in Forming and Strengthening the Future of Public Elementary and Secondary Education in California" (Sacramento: California Legislature, 1972):21-26.

7. Herbert Spencer, *Education.* (New York: D. Appleton and Co., 1880), p. 32.

8. Roger D. Abrahams, "Cultural Differences and the Melting Pot Ideology" *Educational Leadership* 29, (November 1971):118-21.

9. See, for example, Celia B. Stendler, "Class Biases in the Teaching of Values," *Progressive Education* 27, no. 2 (February 1950):123-26. See also Richard L. Gortush, "Value Conflict in the School Setting." An ERIC Report: Ed-057-410, 1971.

10. Charles Silberman, *Crisis in the Classroom* (New York: Random House, 1970), p. 9.

11. George D. Spindler, "Education in a Transforming American Culture," *Harvard Educational Review* 25, no. 3 (Summer 1955):145-56.

12. Edward G. Ponder, "Educational Pluralism," *Educational Leadership* 29 (November 1971):99-101.

13. For an excellent and still relevant discussion of the problem and these four alternatives, see George E. Artelle, "How Do We Know What Values Are Best?" *Progressive Education* (April 1950):191-95.

14. Robert Mager, *Preparing Instructional Objectives* (San Francisco: Fearon Publishers, 1962).

15. For example, see James D. Raths, "Teaching without Specific Objectives," *Educational Leadership* 28 (April 1971):714-20; and W. James Popham, "Must All Objectives Be Behavioral?" *Educational Leadership* 29 (April 1972):605-8.

16. See, for example, Hans P. Guth, "The Monkey on the Bicycle: Behavioral Objectives on the Teaching of English," *English Journal,* September 1970, pp. 785-92.

17. For example, see *Educational Goals and Objectives: A Model Program for Community and Professional Involvement* (Bloomington, Ind.: Phi Delta Kappa, Commission on Educational Planning, 1973).

18. Stephen M. Barro, "An Approach to Developing Accountability Measures for the Public Schools," *Phi Delta Kappan* 52, no. 4 (December 1970): 196.

19. Leon M. Lessinger, "Accountability for Results: A Basic Challenge for American Schools," *American Education* 5 (June/July 1969).

20. For a description of these and other arguments against school accountability, see Edythe J. Gaines, "Accountability: Getting Out of the Tangled Web," *Nation's Schools* 88 (October 1971): 55-58.

Part 2

Elements of Administration

3

The School Administrator: Tasks and Processes

The goals and objectives discussed in chapters 1 and 2 represent the desired outcomes of education in a school. However, these outcomes are not likely to materialize without the organization and administration of human and physical resources. The essential job of the administrator is to organize and administer these resources efficiently and effectively so that the school objectives can be successfully achieved. This will involve the administrator in the performance of many administrative tasks and in the employment of certain administrative processes. The following sections will present an introduction to these tasks and processes.

ADMINISTRATIVE TASK AREAS

One way to look at the job of the school administrator is to examine the various administrative tasks which are typically assigned to him to perform. Figure 3.1 presents an overview of the administrative task areas and examples of their component activities, based on a synthesis of several studies concerned with identifying the major activities of the school administrator.[1]

I. **Staff Personnel**

A. Help formulate staff personnel policies.
B. Recruit staff personnel; attract able people to the school staff.
C. Select and assign staff personnel.
D. Schedule teachers' assignments.
E. Communicate the objectives of the school program to the faculty.
F. Observe teachers in their classrooms.
G. Diagnose the strengths and weaknesses of teachers.

H. Help resolve the classroom problems of teachers.
I. Evaluate the performance of teachers.
J. Improve the performance of teachers.
K. Coordinate the work of teachers.
L. Stimulate and provide opportunities for professional growth of staff personnel.
M. Maximize the different skills found in a faculty.
N. Develop *esprit de corps* among teachers.

(continued)

Figure 3.1. Major Task Areas in School Administration

43

II. **Pupil Personnel**

A. Provide guidance services.
B. Institute procedures for the orientation of pupils.
C. Establish school attendance policy and procedures.
D. Establish policy and procedures for dealing with pupil conduct problems.
E. Establish policy and procedures in regard to pupil safety in the building and on the school grounds.
F. Develop and coordinate the extracurricular program.
G. Handle disciplinary cases.
H. Arrange systematic procedures for the continual assessment and reporting of pupil performance.
I. Confer with juvenile court, police agencies, etc.

III. **Community-School Leadership**

A. Develop and administer policies and procedures for parent and community participation in the schools.
B. Confer with parents.
C. Handle parental complaints.
D. Assist PTA and other parent groups.
E. Represent the school in participation in community organizations.
F. Cooperate with other community agencies.
G. Make possible the continual reexamination of acceptable plans and policies for community improvement with particular reference to the services which the schools are rendering.

IV. **Instruction and Curriculum Development**

A. Help formulate curriculum objectives.
B. Help determine curriculum content and organization.

C. Relate the desired curriculum to available time, physical facilities and personnel.
D. Provide materials, resources, and equipment for the instructional program.
E. Provide for the supervision of instruction.
F. Provide for in-service education of instructional personnel.

V. **School Finance and Business Management**

A. Prepare school budget at local school level.
B. Provide for a system of internal accounting.
C. Administer school purchasing.
D. Account for school monies.
E. Account for school property.
F. Keep the school office running smoothly.

VI. **School Plant**

A. Determine the physical plant needs of the community and the resources which can be marshalled to meet those needs.
B. Develop a comprehensive plan for the orderly growth and improvement of school plant facilities.
C. Implement plans for the orderly growth and improvement of school plant facilities.
D. Develop an efficient program of operation and maintenance of the physical plant.
E. Supervise the custodial staff.

VII. **General Tasks**

A. Organize and conduct meetings or conferences.
B. Handle delicate interpersonal situations.
C. Direct the work of administrative assistants.
D. Publicize the work of the school.

Figure 3.1. Continued.

(continued)

E. Diagnose the strengths and weaknesses of the school program.
F. Attend school functions, such as assemblies, plays, athletic contests.

G. Respond to correspondence.
H. Prepare reports for the district administration.
I. Attend principals' meetings.
J. Keep school records.
K. Schedule school programs.

Figure 3.1. Continued.

It should be pointed out that in most situations one administrator is not solely responsible for carrying out all of the activities listed in figure 3.1. Many of these responsibilities are shared between two or more administrators at the building level, or with other administrative or supervisory personnel at the district office. However, the school administrator is either actually involved in carrying out most of the activities in figure 3.1, or is responsible for making sure the tasks are implemented if the activities have been delegated to someone else. Because the task areas of school administration are so important, an in-depth examination of each of them will be taken up in later chapters.

ADMINISTRATIVE PROCESSES

In order to carry out the different activities listed under the task areas, the school administrator will need to engage in certain kinds of administrative *processes*. Administrative processes are simply the methods which an administrator utilizes to achieve specific tasks or objectives. By thoroughly understanding these processes and by appropriately applying them, an administrator will be able to accomplish administrative tasks more effectively, and should experience greater success in achieving objectives.

While many writers have attempted to identify the various administrative processes which an administrator employs, it would appear that most if not all of them fall into the thirteen categories shown in figure 3.2.

1. Problem Identification
2. Diagnosis
3. Setting Objectives
4. Decision Making
5. Planning
6. Organizing
7. Coordinating
8. Delegating
9. Initiating
10. Communicating
11. Working with Groups
12. Problem Solving
13. Evaluating

Figure 3.2. Administrative Processes.

Although there is some conceptual overlap among several of the administrative processes identified in figure 3.2, a case can be made that each of these processes contains one or more unique characteristics. Rather than trying to discuss all thirteen administrative processes in detail, since entire books have been devoted to most of them, a brief discussion of each will be presented for the purpose of establishing its functions and use. [2] These processes will also be discussed further as they apply to the task areas examined in later chapters.

PROBLEM IDENTIFICATION

There is no shortage of problems for which an administrator will be expected to provide solutions. In fact, some administrators—those on the "firing line" particularly—may feel that they need not concern themselves with identifying problems; other people, such as students, teachers, and parents will identify or present them with more problems than they may care to think about. These administrators' motto is, in essence, "Why seek trouble where none exists?" or, "Let sleeping dogs lie!"

Nevertheless, if an administrator wants to avoid going from crisis to crisis, he must begin to identify those underlying problems which will eventually manifest themselves in troublesome behavior, and he must begin to identify potential problem areas which, if not corrected, could ultimately lead to serious consequences for the school. The administrator who fails to engage in this kind of problem identification will probably continue to be besieged with crises which seem to come upon him suddenly and from which there appears to be no respite.

Although much has been written about the process of problem solving, comparatively little attention has been given to the process of problem identification. [3] Generally, theorists and writers have assumed that a problem already exists, and the main question is how to solve it. However, the author's position is that the school administrator should actually spend some of his time trying to *identify* problems of the nature described above.

To identify problems, the administrator needs to ask questions. Asking the right questions is the key to uncovering potential problems which, if left uncorrected, could lead to serious consequences. It should be pointed out, however, that whether the "right" questions are raised depends, at least in part, upon one's criteria for satisfaction or success, and on whether an assessment is made of performance in a specific area.

For example, if only 35 percent of the parents show up for parent-teacher conferences, the level of attendance may not be perceived as a problem by anyone unless one of the criteria for judging the success of parent-teacher conferences is attendance greater than 35 percent. In addition, if no attempt is made (by the administrator or someone else) to ascertain the percentage of parents who participate in parent-teacher conferences, people will have no basis for determining whether a problem exists. Therefore, before a problem can be identified, criteria must be established for determining whether objectives have been attained, and information must be collected to establish the degree to which the criteria were met. This will involve the administrator in asking value and evaluative questions in order to identify problems.

Sample questions which illustrate the kinds of inquiries that an administrator, in cooperation with teachers, students, and parents, might pursue in attempting to identify problems are presented in figure 3.3.

Criteria Questions	Assessment Questions
A. Students	
1. What *should* be the attitude of students toward the value and usefulness of their school program?	1. What *is* the attitude of students toward the value and usefulness of their school program?
2. What *should* be the level of performance achieved by the students in the school?	2. What *is* the level of performance achieved by students in my school?
3. To what extent *should* students be developing a positive self-concept, self-initiative, and problem-solving skills?	3. To what extent *are* students developing a positive self-concept, self-initiative and problem-solving skills?
B. Teachers	
1. To what extent *should* teachers know and understand the home background and learning strengths and disabilities of their students?	1. To what extent *do* teachers know and understand the home background and learning strengths and disabilities of their students?
2. To what degree *should* teachers individualize instruction and adapt the curriculum to meet the individual needs of students?	2. To what extent *do* teachers individualize instruction and adapt the curriculum to meet the individual needs of students?
3. To what extent *should* teachers go beyond teaching skills and subject matter to developing student attitudes and values?	3. To what extent *do* teachers go beyond teaching skills and subject matter content to developing student attitudes and values?

Figure 3.3. Sample Problem—Identification Questions

(continued)

C. Parents

1. To what degree *should* the parents understand clearly and accurately the objectives of the school and the programs and activities offered in order to reach those objectives?
2. What *should* be the extent and nature of parent participation and involvement in the school?
3. What *should* be the attitude of parents toward the school program and the professional staff?

1. To what degree *do* parents understand the objectives of the school and the programs and activities offered to reach those objectives?
2. What *is* the extent and nature of parent participation and involvement in the school?
3. What *is* the attitude of parents toward the school program and professional staff?

Figure 3.3. Continued.

To identify potential problems, then, an administrator should ask two kinds of questions: (1) How well *should* we be doing? and (2) how well *are* we doing? Of course, these questions frequently are not easy to answer, nor are the answers always pleasing to the administrator. The easiest thing for an administrator to do—at least temporarily—is to *refrain* from asking basic questions or seeking their answers, and instead proceed through the school year, hoping that nothing serious erupts, and delaying any response to a situation until trouble actually develops. Unfortunately, the consequences of this type of behavior is that the administrator seldom deals with problems until they manifest themselves in ways which are frequently difficult to resolve and, as a result, the school fails to function as well as it might.*

DIAGNOSIS

Why are some students underachieving? Why don't more parents participate in school affairs? Why don't some teachers seem to carry out their responsibilities fully? To answer any of these questions adequately, the administrator must engage in the process of diagnosis—investigating the basic causes of a problem.[4] Diagnosis is concerned with ascertaining the underlying roots of a problem and distinguishing these from its mere symptoms or manifestations. It includes careful, thorough, and objective investigation into the conditions which have led to or created the problem. The process of

*The process of problem identification is quite similar to the process of needs assessment. Both involve identifying the discrepancy between what is and what should be. For a good description of the needs assessment approach and how it relates to problem identification, see *Needs Assessment in Education* (Trenton, N.J.: Department of Education, 1974).

diagnosis, like that of problem identification, begins with the formulation of questions.

For example, an administrator who is confronted by a growing student attendance problem, might begin his investigation by asking, "Why do so many students skip school?" One immediate response to that question could be that "these students are lazy, or they don't have good habits of attendance." Some administrators would stop at this point, satisfied that they have answered the question, and begin to try to change the students. Other administrators would continue to ask questions, seeking more fundamental causes of the students' misbehavior: "*Why* are the students lazy? *Why* don't they have good habits of punctuality? What is the home situation of these students? Is it possible that the attendance behavior of some or many of these students is affected by learning disabilities, e.g., reading problems, and would the school's cumulative records or diagnostic testing be helpful in checking out this possibility? Is the educational program that the school offers perceived by these students as relevant? Is there anyone in the school with whom these students relate well?"

These are all examples of diagnostic questions seeking the basic causes for the students' misbehavior. Whether these specific questions will uncover the root causes of the problem or whether, perhaps, other questions will need to be raised is not at the issue. The main point is that, if the school administrator is to avoid dealing with only the symptoms of problems, then he must raise questions which attempt to identify the underlying and basic causes of a situation.

The school administrator should engage in the process of diagnosis before he attempts to solve any problem or implement any task. In a sense, the administrator is asking a fundamental question: "What is *really* involved here?" Unless an administrator employs appropriate diagnosis in solving the problems of a school and carrying out his administrative tasks, he is not likely to be successful.

SETTING OBJECTIVES

Anyone who wishes to be reasonably productive must set objectives, which represent the outcomes that we want to achieve, and the targets at which we are aiming. [5] The function of objectives is to give an individual or group a direction, purpose, and reason for action.

Objectives may be categorized as individual, group, or program. If, for an example, an administrator is to be productive, he must set *individual* objectives for himself. If the faculty or PTA are to capitalize on their potentialities, then the administrator should work with them in establishing *group objectives*. If the various programs or services which the school offers are to meet the needs of those who they are designed to serve, the administrator should work with the personnel who are involved in the program, helping them to define *program objectives*. Each individual, group, and program in the school should have well-defined objectives of a short and long-range nature.

The administrator needs to ask two basic questions in establishing objectives: "What should we be trying to accomplish?" and, "Have we clearly defined what we want to accomplish?" The first question is designed to stimulate thinking about what the objectives of an individual, group or program should be. The second question is intended to focus efforts on the precise specification of objectives for an individual, group, or program. In essence, the administrator should be trying to arrive at more appropriate and more sharply defined objectives, which can be clearly communicated and can subsequently serve as standards against which progress or achievement will be measured.*

DECISION MAKING

The administrator engages in decision making perhaps more often than in any other process. In fact, some authors have even taken the position that it is the single most important process in school administration. [6]

Decision making is basically the process of choosing among alternatives. In most situations there exist two or more alternative courses of action, and an administrator must decide which alternative to pursue. Before making a decision, however, the administrator should engage in diagnosis in order to better understand the nature of the situation calling for a decision, and the alternatives available to him as well. Then he should assess the advantages and disadvantages of each alternative and the probabilities of success in each case. During the process of reaching a decision, an administrator should involve teachers, parents, students, central office supervisors, or others as appropriate, in order to capitalize on any special insights and expertise which they may be able to contribute. [7]

Once a decision has been made, the administrator will need to concentrate on such other administrative processes as planning, organizing, and coordinating the implementation of the decision.

PLANNING

Like decision making, planning partially overlaps into several other administrative processes. However, much of the planning process occurs *after* goals have been established and decisions made.

*Goal setting is also treated in chapter 2.

Planning is concerned primarily with the question of *how* a goal is to be achieved or a decision implemented.[8] Consideration of the following questions is involved:

1. What kinds of activities or actions must occur in order to achieve the goal or decision?
2. What kinds of resources—personnel, facilities, supplies—must be utilized to achieve the objective or decision?
3. How should activities be sequenced to best advantage, and resources most efficiently coordinated, to achieve the goal or decision?
4. What kind of time schedule should be followed in implementing the plan of action?

In an oversimplified sense, the administrator who engages in the planning process is attempting to answer the questions, "Who does what, with whom, and over what period of time, in order to accomplish what purpose?" Without adequate planning, the performance of the school administrator will be impaired and the implementation of individual, group, or program goals and decisions will be hampered.

ORGANIZING

Organizing can be considered a component of planning, yet there is value in analyzing it separately.

The administrator engages in the process of organizing whenever he wants to accomplish a task or achieve an objective. He may be involved in organizing his own activities or those of others. However, whenever the administrator employs the process of organizing, he is typically concerned with defining and arranging in some logical and systematic manner, people's activities, time, and resources. [9]

When the administrator attempts to so organize, he generally will try to establish formal structures of responsibility, authority, supervision, and communication. In doing this, the administrator should ask himself the following questions: [10]

1. What needs to be done? — *Task definition.*
2. What resources are needed to do the job, and within what period of time? — *Definition of resource needs and time parameters.*
3. Who is competent, interested, and available to do the job? — *Selection of personnel.*
4. What responsibilities need to be assigned to whom? — *Definition and assignment of responsibility.*

5. Which tasks and people need to be related to each other in some manner?	*Identification of coordination needs.*
6. Who should be in authority over whom?	*Specification of authority relationships.*
7. Who should supervise whom and in which areas?	*Specification of supervisory relationships.*
8. Who should communicate with whom and about what?	*Specification of communication relationships.*
9. What standards will determine effectiveness?	*Establishment of evaluation criteria.*

The process of organizing should begin with a definition of the tasks or activities needed to achieve previously approved goals and decisions, and should conclude with the determination of criteria which will be used to evaluate the extent to which the goals are achieved, or the decisions successfully implemented. Intermediate steps include specifying authority, supervisory, and communication relationships between people, and defining the resources which will be required to carry out specific tasks within a certain period of time.*

COÖRDINATING

The school administrator engages in the process of coördinating when he attempts to relate people, tasks, resources, and/or time schedules in such a way that they are mutually supplementary and complementary.[11] A potential need for coördination exists whenever two or more people, activities, resources, and/or time schedules either operate in conjunction with each other or *should* operate in conjunction with one another. The need for coördination is particularly evident when personnel with different specializations work toward the same or similar objectives. For example, when guidance counselors, nurses, social workers, psychologists, and other pupil personnel specialists are working in the school there is usually a need for coördination. All of these individuals, along with the teachers, are trying to help the student; for total effectiveness, their efforts should be coördinated.

The process of coördinating should occur not only during the organizing process, but may also be needed as a plan or decision is being implemented. It is at the latter stage that the blueprint for action starts to take form. People begin to perform tasks, use resources, and interact with each other, based on some kind of a time schedule. While in many situations prior planning and

*Related concepts and associated problems and issues are discussed in chapter 6, "Organizing the School."

organizing for a task or program may obviate the necessity for further coördination, in other instances the administrator may need to become actively involved in the process of coördinating after a program has been introduced.

For example, the administrator may have to redefine roles so that they complement each other better. He may need to restructure tasks so that they do not conflict with or overlap each other; new lines of communication may need to be designated so that there is better coördination of activity or use of resources, and time schedules may need to be rearranged so individuals or groups can work together more easily. In all of these activities the administrator is engaged in the process of coördinating. He is reorganizing people, tasks, resources, and time so that functions proceed more smoothly. As a result the administrator can increase the extent to which an activity or program will be carried out efficiently and effectively.

DELEGATING

No administrator can effectively perform *all* of the various administrative functions and tasks within a school. Therefore, some duties must (or at least, should) be delegated to other people. In certain cases, the administrator may be faced with the problem that, because of financial constraints in hiring assistants or additional staff, there is no one to whom responsibilities can be delegated. However, in many situations, an administrator doesn't delegate responsibilities to an assistant or another person on the staff simply because he either doesn't know how to delegate or has reservations about relinquishing some of the duties.

According to Heyel, who has studied the latter problem, an administrator may be reluctant to delegate responsibility to others when he should, for one or more of the reasons identified below. [12]

1. He has a strong need to be involved in every aspect of administration, and cannot bear to delegate any of his responsibilities to others.
2. He is concerned that others may begin to wonder if he is really capable of handling the job if he attempts to delegate some of the responsibilities to other people.
3. He is not confident that others will do a good job if he delegates certain responsibilities, or at least doubts whether they could do as good a job as he would in carrying out a task.
4. He has a strong need to be recognized as *the* leader in the organization, and is concerned with the possibility that delegation of some of the responsibilities will necessitate the sharing of leadership recognition.

5. He is concerned that by delegating responsibility to someone else, he may be facilitating the advancement of that individual to the point at which the situation could become competitive.

The extent to which an administrator may be influenced by one or more of the considerations suggested by Heyel can be determined only by objective self-analysis. Certainly many, if not most of these factors would affect him in a subconscious way that might be difficult to ascertain. At any rate, it seems reasonable to assume that in many instances the lack of additional staff due to financial constraints is not the only factor which would account for the administrator's failure to delegate responsibility.

For some administrators, uncertainty about when or under what circumstances to delegate responsibility may also be a problem. Figure 3.4 presents four general guidelines which should be of assistance to an administrator.

1. When someone else can do the task as well as or better than you can.

2. When you don't have the time to do the job or you have other important priorities.

3. When someone else could do the job adequately, if not as well, but at less expense.

4. When you are attempting to provide orientation and training to someone else who is preparing for a similar position.

Figure 3.4. When to Delegate Responsibility

In delegating a task or responsibility the administrator should ask himself, "What would I want to know if my superior were delegating the same kind of responsibility to me?" To answer this question adequately, the administrator should define in considerable detail the nature and scope of the responsibility being assigned, the degree of authority that the individual should be given over others, the extent to which there are supervisory responsibilities associated with the assignment, and the people with whom the individual should communicate in carrying out his new assignment. As a result of carefully defining these factors, an administrator can avoid, or at least minimize uncertainty and unsatisfactory performance on the part of the person to whom an assignment has been delegated.

INITIATING

Administrators engage in the process of *initiating* when they reach the point at which they are ready to take some kind of action individually or with a group.

The school administrator attempts to initiate action on the part of other people in a variety of ways. He requests, instructs, directs, commands, motivates, or tries to persuade others to initiate desired action or activity.[13] In selecting the manner in which he attempts to initiate action, the administrator needs to examine the assumptions he may be making about his authority and power, other people's perception and acceptance of that authority and power, and the kind of an initiating approach that is most likely to be successful in bringing about the desired results.[14] For example, is the administrator merely *assuming* that he has the authority or power to direct, command, or instruct people to do what he wants done in particular circumstances? Or has the authority or power upon which he is basing his attempts to initiate action been explicitly delegated to him through school board action or a directive from his superior?

In addition to examining his own assumptions about whether he has actually been delegated the authority to initiate action on the part of other people, the administrator should also attempt to ascertain the extent to which other people perceive and accept the fact that he does indeed possess such authority and power. Even though he may, in fact, validly derive his authority and power from the organization in which he serves, the administrator will undoubtedly experience difficulty in initiating action if the people from whom he is attempting to elicit action don't accept this fact.

And finally, the administrator needs to consider all feasible alternative methods for initiating action. Although he may feel that it is easier simply to issue directives, give commands, and instruct others what to do, there may be additional approaches to initiating action which will be ultimately more successful, particularly in specific situations with certain types of people. For example, requesting or asking others to do something is frequently a productive approach to initiating action. Also, trying to persuade people of the value of taking a particular action is often desirable and may be essential.

Although some administrators may recoil at the notion of trying to *persuade* someone to take action rather than directing him to do it, circumstances can arise in which the former approach is the only viable one, particularly if the administrator's authority or power is lacking or rejected. In addition, if people are persuaded of the merits of taking certain actions, they may be more likely to perform these actions with greater commitment than if they are merely responding to the administrator's authority or power. In any case, the administrator will want to give serious consideration to the advantages and disadvantages of the various approaches he might use in attempting to initiate action on the part of others.

COMMUNICATING

The school administrator is probably engaged in the process of communicating more often than in any other process, with the possible exception of decision making. In order to persuade, instruct, direct, request, present, stimulate, or develop understanding, the administrator must communicate. In order to communicate, he must deliver a *message* via a *medium* which reaches a *receiver* (another person or group) and registers a desired response, e.g., action, understanding. [15]

For example, an administrator may wish to bring to the faculty's attention that there has been too much noise in the hallways during the week, and that the professional staff should increase their efforts to keep noise to a minimum. This, then, is the *message* the administrator wants to deliver to the staff. In delivering the message, he has a choice of several different media for communication. He could write a memo, present the message over the public address system, announce it at a faculty meeting, or have an administrative assistant "pass the word" to teachers. Each of these communication media may possess advantages and disadvantages for delivering this particular message, depending on the administrator's skill in communicating, the type of group to whom the message is delivered, and the nature of the circumstances surrounding the message.

But actual transmission of the message by some means, is not the end of the communication process. The message also *must register* with the receiver(s), in this instance the faculty, before the communication can be judged to be effective. They must, first, become more aware of the noise problem in the hallway, and second, that the administrator wants them to take action to reduce the noise level. If, after the message is delivered, the faculty isn't any more aware of the noise problem, and the administrator's expectation that they take action to reduce the level of noise in the hallways, then the administrator hasn't communicated effectively. He may have *attempted* to communicate, but unless the message has registered, communication hasn't really taken place.

Whether the faculty *will* take action to reduce noise in the hallway, depends, of course, on factors beyond that of whether the administrator has communicated effectively with them. The faculty may clearly understand what the administrator wants and yet not accept it. On the other hand, if the purpose of the administrator's communication was to *initiate* action on the part of the faculty, then he hasn't "successfully communicated" with them unless they take such action.

Communicating is one of the most important administrative processes. By the very nature of his job the administrator communicates with a variety of people, including students, teachers, parents, and central office personnel, about a wide range of items during the course of a school year. The administrator's success in working with these people and in productively carrying out his other responsibilities will be greatly influenced by the extent to which he is an effective communicator. [16]

WORKING WITH GROUPS

Most school administrators spend a considerable amount of their time working with various groups in different types of group settings. Administrators interact with the faculty, the parent organization, and the student body, as well as with other kinds of smaller groups, ranging from student clubs and organizations to the individual departments or grade units within a school. These groups differ in many important respects, particularly in size and degree of organizational structure and purpose, but they all possess certain basic characteristics in common which the administrator needs to recognize. These characteristics are presented in figure 3.5.

Formal Characteristics	Informal Characteristics
1. A group is originally organized to accomplish a particular objective(s).	1. The objective(s) which the members of the group presently feel to be important may not be the same as the one(s) for which they were originally organized.
2. A group has an appointed or elected leader.	2. There is usually one or more individuals in a group to whom the members of the group look for informal leadership.
3. A group has formally defined roles and tasks.	3. A group generally develops norms and expectations for what constitutes appropriate behavior for its members and others who interact with the group.
4. A group has a prescribed and defined system of communication among its members and its leader.	4. An informal system of communication usually develops within a group which is not readily apparent to those who are not accepted members of the group.

Figure 3.5. Common Characteristics of Most Groups [17]

Since most school administrators are aware of the formal characteristics of the groups with whom they have contact, the informal characteristics are the ones to which administrators need to become more sensitive. If an administrator, in working with a group, proceeds only on his knowledge of its formal characteristics, real problems could result.

For example, he may assume that a group has a certain organizational objective, the original one for which it was organized, when in reality the group may have developed a different kind of objective. Or the administrator may assume that the appointed leader of a group, such as a department head, is the actual leader of the department, when in reality there is another individual in the department to whom the members actually look for leadership. In another situation, an administrator may determine the tasks for a group to perform, but if he fails to understand group norms and expectations toward the accomplishment of these tasks, they may not be performed well or may not get done at all. Knowledge of the informal characteristics of a group can facilitate the administrator's efforts with that group; lack of such knowledge can constitute a major handicap for him. [18]

In addition to being knowledgeable about the informal characteristics of a group, the school administrator will need to be competent in functioning as a group leader and in helping a group to work together effectively, since he will be the appointed leader in many situations. How the administrator performs as a group leader will be influenced in large part by his own conception of how a leader should behave, and his perceptions of the needs of a group. If the administrator sees his leadership role in working with the members of a group as that of instructing, directing, or ordering them, he will probably tend to play a very dominant, perhaps authoritarian, leadership role. In response to this type of leadership, the behavior of the group may tend to be either passive, restive, or perhaps hostile to his efforts to lead. [19]

If, on the other hand, the administrator sees his leadership role as being a consultant, resource person, or facilitator of group discussion and decision making, he is more likely to work with the group as one of its members than as the individual in charge. Under this kind of leadership there is apt to be greater participation on the part of the members and more group cohesion and *esprit de corps.*

In working with a group the school administrator needs to be aware of the fact that most groups when first formed go through certain stages in their development and enact particular behavior at their meetings, characteristic of their stage. These various stages are described in figure 3.6.

During the first two stages the members of a group do not really function very well together, and the cause can be detected from the nature of the comments which are made. In the last two stages group members begin to perform better as they develop greater purpose and focus, become better acquainted with each other, resolve major differences, and define more functional relationships.

1. *The "Groping" Stage.* It is characterized by comments such as "What are we supposed to be accomplishing?" "Who is supposed to do what? "Who is really in charge here?"
2. *The Griping Stage.* This is a period during which the members of a group find it difficult to adjust to the task of the group or the role which has been assigned to them.
3. *The Consolidation Stage.* This is the stage during which efforts are made to develop group harmony and avoid conflict. Members of the group begin to be more comfortable with each other and their roles in the group.
4. *The Solidifying Stage.* The group is now functioning well, and all members are performing their roles and cooperating easily with each other.

Figure 3.6. Stages in Group Development. [20]

As an administrator interacts with a group, he should attempt to behave in ways which will tend to help the group to work cooperatively together and to accomplish their objectives. These behaviors, revealed in a study of group leadership, are enumerated and identified as follows.[21]

Group Leadership Behavior

1. Help members of the group to define their goals and delineate their problems.
2. Establish a cooperative, permissive atmosphere which puts the participants at ease so that they contribute their best thinking to the solution of the group's problems.
3. Utilize the various talents and knowledge of the members of the group in arriving at decisions.
4. Show a genuine regard and appreciation for the worth of each individual and a willingness to understand and accept each one at his own level of growth.
5. Enlist the help of outside resources. Don't always give answers but help to provide experiences through which teachers and lay groups can find their own answers.
6. Plan the procedures, the timing, and the situation so that the group members will be comfortable, have sufficient time, and have opportunity to participate.
7. Allow sufficient time for group thinking so that the participants do not have too many hurdles to surmount at one time.
8. Practice the technique of acceptable group procedures by becoming a listener, teller, questioner, and silent partner as your leadership and expertness merge with the best interests of the group.

9. Instill in others the desire to belong, to participate, and to take responsibility for and pride in the work of the group.
10. Discover skills, competencies, interests, and abilities so that each individual, while taking part in group processes, gains the maximum security which results from having a part to play and a contribution to make.
11. Relinquish leadership to other members of the group when appropriate, but continue to serve as consultant and adviser, to clear obstacles, and revive flagging enthusiasm.
12. Provide materials and resources and make available research studies and data to aid the group in their work.
13. Evaluate yourself continually to see that your purposes are valid, that human relationships are observed, that the steps in group processes are followed, that you are not moving too fast for the group, and that the work of the group is in keeping with the overall program of the school.
14. Be sensitive to group techniques and to human relationships between teachers and administrators, among teachers, administrators, and supervisors.

The behaviors of an effective group leader which are identified in the preceding enumeration need not be restricted to the school administrator. These are behaviors which can be initiated by any member of a group and should be so encouraged by the administrator. The important factor is not *who* enacts the behavior but that it is initiated by someone in the group and at the appropriate moment. Stimulating other people in the group to engage in leadership-type behavior may be the most important group process skill which an administrator can exercise.

PROBLEM SOLVING

The position has been advanced elsewhere by the author that problem solving is the most important administrative process. [22] The school administrator may participate more frequently in decision-making and communicating processes, but if he is not an effective problem solver, especially in light of the problems facing educators today, it is unlikely that he will be a successful administrator.

It should be noted that administrators differ in their approaches to problem solving. [23] Some administrators respond to a problem by immediately "jumping at a solution," while others take considerable time to seek information which will enable them to define more adequately the nature of the problem as a basis for deciding on possible alternative solutions. Administrative styles in problem solving also differ and can range from authoritarian to democratic to laissez-faire.

While there may be no one "best" approach to problem solving which would cover every problem, circumstance, and individual, the effective problem solver bases his actions on the following principles, extracted from a review of the educational and social science literature:

1. Doesn't wait for problems to manifest themselves. Tries to *anticipate* problems or identify potential problem areas which, if not given attention, may result in significant trouble.
2. When faced with a problem, seeks more information about its causes, nature, and severity. Avoids leaping to quick or easy solutions.
3. Searches for more than one or two alternative solutions to a problem. Avoids settling on the first possible solution that is apparent, or viewing any proposed solution as the only one possible.
4. Evaluates carefully the consequences—both positive and negative—of each of the alternative solutions under consideration.
5. Utilizes the insights, perceptions, and assistance of relevant others throughout the problem-solving process. Avoids the assumption that the administrator possesses all the wisdom and/or expertise for solving a problem successfully.
6. Recognizes that adopted solutions to a problem must be thoughtfully implemented and eventually evaluated. Evaluation is particularly important if future mistakes are to be avoided and effective problem-solving approaches utilized.

Successful problem solving is rarely easy. It usually requires perceptive anticipation, careful analysis, thorough planning, and the involvement of people who can offer useful information, ideas, and constructive assistance. There is no shortcut or easy way to successful problem solving.

Problem solving can be thought of as a separate process or, perhaps more appropriately, as the effective utilization of most if not all of the administrative processes previously described. Whether or not an administrator employs all of these administrative processes will depend in most circumstances on the nature of the problem. But certainly it is likely that before most problems can be solved, the administrator will need to take the steps of identifying and diagnosing the problem, setting goals and making decisions; and he will also need to plan, organize, initiate, communicate, and coordinate the action. Additionally, in many situations the administrator will need to delegate responsibilities before a problem can be resolved, and frequently his problem solving will involve him with groups. Finally, before he can know whether the problem has been successfully resolved, he will have to evaluate.

So in a real sense, problem solving is not a separate or unique process but a synthesis of many different but related steps or subprocesses. When problems are not solved, the difficulty can frequently be traced back to a failure to engage in or enact effectively one or more of the subprocesses.

EVALUATING

Evaluating represents one of the most important processes that a school administrator can employ, but one which, unfortunately, seems to be among the least frequently utilized. Evaluation can be defined as the process of examining as carefully, thoroughly, and objectively as possible an individual, group, product, or program in order to ascertain strengths and weaknesses. [25] The school administrator should engage in the evaluative process in relation to the following three areas: (1) evaluation of others, e.g., teacher evaluation, (2) evaluation of a school product, process, or program, and (3) evaluation of self.

Observation would suggest that school administrators spend the greatest proportion of their evaluation time focusing on assessment of staff, and the least amount of time on self-evaluation. While it appears that in response to pressures for greater school and administrator accountability the administrator is spending more of his time on product, process, and program evaluation, most of these efforts could be characterized as unplanned, superficial, and sporatic. (It is true that there are notable exceptions to this criticism.) In most schools there is virtually no carefully planned, in-depth attempt to evaluate the various programmatic aspects of the school on a regular basis. And the same criticism could be made about administrators' attempts to engage in self-evaluation.

Although a lack of evaluation skills may act as a deterrent, perhaps the main barrier to more extensive evaluating is that it is potentially threatening to the administrator. Despite this obstacle, the administrator needs to recognize that in the absence of a carefully planned, in-depth evaluation in the three areas previously identified, little significant improvement is possible. For this reason then, the need for evaluation and specific ideas for engaging in evaluation will be stressed throughout the book.

A FINAL NOTE

By now it should be clear to the reader that the job of the school administrator is a multifaceted one composed of many tasks and processes. While some tasks or processes may be more important than others, depending on the nature of a situation, an administrator should attempt to master all of them so that when the need arises, he can respond competently. If an administrator can effectively perform the tasks and processes identified in this chapter, he should be in a good position to meet the problems and challenges which may confront a school.

Review

1. Identify the main administrative task areas.
2. Why is it so important for an administrator to be competent in the processes of problem identification and problem diagnosis? Explain the specific steps of each process.
3. Describe the functions of and recommended steps for each of the following processes: decision making, planning, organizing, and coördinating.
4. Why might an administrator be reluctant to delegate some of his duties to someone else? Under what circumstances *should* an administrator delegate a task to someone else?
5. In communicating with others and in working with groups, what factors does an administrator need to be knowledgeable about when he tries to initiate action on the part of others?
6. What principles should an administrator utilize when attempting to solve problems?

Notes

1. A major source of ideas for the development of figure 3.1 was Robert S. Fisk, "The Task of Educational Administration," in *Administrative Behavior in Education,* ed. Roald F. Campbell and Russell T. Gregg (New York: Harper & Row, 1957), chap. 6.

2. For an important and still relevant discussion of these processes, see Russell T. Gregg, "The Administrative Process," in *Administrative Behavior in Education,* ed. Roald F. Campbell and Russell T. Gregg (New York: Harper & Row, 1957), chap. 8.

3. John K. Hemphill, "Administration as Problem-Solving," in *Administration as Decision-Making,* ed. A. W. Halpin (Chicago: Midwest Administration Center, 1957), p. 96.

4. G. A. Koester, "The Study of the Diagnostic Process," *Educational and Psychological Measurement* 14 (Autumn 1954):437-86.

5. Samuel Goldman, *The School Principal* (New York: The Center for Applied Research in Education, 1966), pp. 43-44.

6. Daniel E. Griffith, "Administration as Decision-Making," in *Administrative Theory in Education,* ed. A. W. Halpin (Chicago: Midwest Administration Center, University of Chicago, 1958), p. 122.

7. For a more extensive discussion of the process of decision making and the importance of involving others, see Richard A. Gorton, *Conflict, Controversy and Crisis in School Administration and Supervision* (Dubuque, Iowa: Wm. C. Brown Company Publishers, 1972), chap. 8.

8. William H. Curtis, *Educational Resources Management System* (Chicago: Research Corporation of the Association of School Business Officials, 1971), chap. 3.

9. William B. Castetter and Helen R. Burchell, *Educational Administration and the Improvement of Instruction* (Danville, Ill.: Interstate Printers and Publishers, 1967), pp. 10-11.

10. These questions are similar to those which an administrator would ask in applying the technique of PERT, i.e., Program Evaluation Review Technique. See John McManama, *Systems Analysis for Effective School Administration* (West Nyack, N.Y.: Parker Publishing Co., 1971), pp. 54-59.

11. C. S. Bumbarger, "The Administrator as Coordinator," in *The Principal as Administrator,* ed. D. A. Mckay. An ERIC Report: Ed-044-803, 1969, pp. 35-40.

12. Carl Heyel, *Organizing Your Job in Management* (New York: American Management Association, 1960), pp. 126-35.

13. F. Enns, "Influencing an Element in the Administrative Process," in *The Principal as Administrator,* ed. D. A. Mckay. An ERIC Report: Ed-044-803, 1969, pp. 47-52.

14. For an excellent description of a principal engaging in the process of initiating, see William W. Wayson, "A New Kind of Principal," *National Elementary Principal* 50, no. 4 (February 1971), pp. 9-19.

15. For an extensive discussion of the role of the administrator as communicator, receiver of communication, and seeker of communication, see Gorton, *Conflict, Controversy and Crisis* chap. 9.

16. Walter D. St John, *A Guide to Effective Communication.* An ERIC Report: Ed-057-464, 1970, p. 6.

17. On formal characteristics, see W. W. Charters, Jr., "An Approach to the Formal Organization of the School," in *Behavioral Science and Educational Administration,* ed. Daniel F. Griffiths (Chicago: University of Chicago Press, 1964), pp. 243-44. For informal characteristics, see Lawrence Iannaconne in the same source, pp. 233-42.

18. For additional discussion of the informal characteristics of a group and the effects of these characteristics upon the operation of the school, see Gorton, *Conflict, Controversy and Crisis* chap. 13.

19. Kurt Lewin et al., "Patterns of Aggressive Behavior in Experimentally Created Social Climates," *Journal of Social Psychology* 10 (1939):271-99.

20. Adapted from material developed by Russell D. Robinson, Professor of Educational Leadership, University of Wisconsin—Milwaukee.

21. Gorton, *Conflict, Controversy and Crisis,* p. x.

22. Adapted from a list of leadership behavior performed by supervisors in a group setting. See *Group Processes in Supervision* (Washington, D.C.: Association for Supervision and Curriculum Development, 1958), p. 128.

23. Ray Cross, "A Description of Decision-Making Patterns of School Principals" (Paper presented at A.E.R.A. Annual Meeting, New York, February 1971).

24. Gorton, *Conflict, Controversy and Crisis,* chap. 10. Also see Jacob W. Getzels et al., *Educational Administration as a Social Process* (New York: Harper & Row, Publishers, 1968), pp. 145-50.

25. For an earlier but still relevant discussion of the role of the administrator in evaluation at the building level, see Hart K. Douglas, *Modern Administration of Secondary Schools* (Boston: Ginn & Co., 1963), chap. 25. For a more recent treatment of evaluation, see Larry Benedict, *A Practical Guide for Evaluation* (Washington, D.C.: Bureau of Elementary and Secondary Education, 1973).

4

The School Administrator:
Roles, Expectations, Social Factors

The role of the school administrator is in a state of flux. Often referred to as the "man in the middle," the occupant of the position frequently wanders about like Moses in search of the Promised Land.[1] The "Promised Land" which the school administrator seeks is represented by a clear role definition of what he is supposed to do, the authority to carry out his responsibilities, and the respect which he feels he deserves for handling a job which has become one of the most difficult and complex in American education.[2]

There are many reasons why the job of the school administrator has become so difficult—reasons which will be identified and discussed later in the chapter. However, it is evident that if the school administrator is to respond effectively to the challenge of his position, he will need to become more aware of different role options, more knowledgeable about the role that important others expect him to adopt, and have a better understanding of the various social forces that affect his role. The following sections will discuss each of these three important aspects of the job of the school administrator.*

MAJOR ROLES OF THE SCHOOL ADMINISTRATOR

There is no shortage of opinions, proposals, or conceptualizations regarding the role of the school administrator.[3] A review of the literature on the subject reveals that, at one time or another, six major roles have been proposed: (1) manager, (2) instructional leader, (3) disciplinarian, (4) human relations facilitator, (5) change agent, and (6) conflict mediator. While it is unlikely that an administrator will be required to enact all six of these roles simultaneously, he should attempt to become competent in each role so that he can perform it effectively when and if the situation requires.

The following summary descriptions are intended to provide the administrator with a brief introduction to each of the six roles; other chapters of the book will present related discussions of these roles, and references are listed at the end of this chapter for further study.

---

*Most of the discussion in this chapter relates more to the principalship than to other positions at the middle management level. The other positions will be discussed in the next chapter.

MANAGER

In the eyes of many people, the school administrator is first and foremost a manager. It was based on this general concept that the position originated in the 1800s, [4] and though other roles have since been proposed, the concept of the administrator as manager has persisted.

As manager, the school administrator is expected to procure, organize, and coordinate both physical and human resources so that the goals of the organization can be attained effectively. His main role is to develop or implement policies and procedures which will result in the efficient operation of the school. In fact, the popularized notion of a manager is, "one who keeps things running smoothly."

It should be noted that the term "manager" conveys a negative connotation for certain individuals. [5] Many administrators, in particular, don't like to think of themselves as managers; the term "leader," which will be discussed later, is perceived by them as a more attractive appellation. However, a school administrator should recognize that when different people and resources are brought together in one location (in this case, a school building), there is a need for someone to organize, schedule, and coordinate the entire operation. That "someone" at the building level has typically been the school administrator.

Consequently, rather than resisting the role of manager, the school administrator should accept and implement the role in such a way that the school is efficiently managed, yet he is in a position to be available for other role options. By successfully performing the role of manager, an administrator can help others to accomplish tasks and goals, and in the process can generate a more positive attitude toward his contribution to the school.

INSTRUCTIONAL LEADER

The role of the school administrator as an instructional leader has had a long history. [6] Although the school administrator was at first more a manager than a leader, it wasn't long before the instructional leadership dimensions of the position began to be emphasized in the educational literature and at various professional meetings which administrators attended. [7] It is probably safe to say that leadership, often referred to as "educational leadership," or "instructional leadership," has been widely accepted by administrators as the raison d'être for the continued existence of their position at the building level.

But one of the problems in connection with the proposed role of the school administrator as instructional leader is that people define the role in different ways and with varying degrees of precision, thereby creating confusion for the administrator who is expected to carry out the role. [8] For example, to some, the principalship is a leadership position, and *any* activities in which the principal engages in order to improve instruction are leadership activities. To others, there are *certain* types of activities or actions, such as classroom observation, in which the principal is expected to participate if he is to function as an instructional leader. Compounding the problem is the fact that the principal is frequently encouraged to be an instructional leader and yet may not be perceived by teachers as possessing the subject matter expertise necessary for helping them to improve.[9] This problem and other aspects of the role of the administrator as an instructional leader will be explored in chapter 11.

DISCIPLINARIAN

The importance of the disciplinary role of the school administrator has been revealed by several studies. For example, when teachers and parents are asked to comment on the role which they expect the school administrator to play in the school, disciplinarian is usually cited as his major—perhaps even his *most* important role.[10] Students also tend to see the school administrator as a disciplinarian (although there is some doubt as to whether they approve of this role.)[11]

On the other hand, principals tend to reject the idea that being a disciplinarian is their major role, and frequently assign this responsibility to the assistant principal. However, research has shown that an increasing number of assistant and vice-principals also seem reluctant to accept the disciplining of students as the primary responsibility of their position.[12]

Generally, school administrators resist or reject the role of disciplinarian because of the negative connotation of the term and because the duties associated with the role are frequently frustrating, irritating, and unpleasant to perform. The term, "disciplinarian," traditionally has implied one who *punishes* someone else: in this case, usually a student.

Punishing students can be a very vexing and frustrating job, as anyone knows who has had to assume this responsibility. Although modern concepts of discipline emphasize more positive approaches to improving student conduct, the fact remains that working with student misbehavior problems represents a difficult assignment with few rewards, which may explain administrators' negative reactions to the role. Nevertheless, it should be pointed out that student conduct still constitutes a major problem in many schools, and important reference groups who are associated with the school will probably continue to expect the principal and/or an assistant to play the role of disciplinarian.

FACILITATOR OF HUMAN RELATIONS

The human relations role of the school administrator originated in the early 1920s and was given initial impetus by the publication of a book by Mary

Parker Follett [13] entitled *Creative Experience.* In this book and in her other writings, Follett emphasized the importance of an administrator's concentrating as much on meeting the personal needs of employees and developing cooperative and harmonious relationships among them, as on achieving the productivity goals of the organization. Later studies by Elton Mayo provided empirical support for Follett's approach, [14] and books by Griffiths and others attempted to incorporate concepts of human relations into the theory of school administration. [15]

The school administrator should, of course, practice good human relations in all aspects of his job, and in relationships with people generally. However, the two areas in which this becomes particularly important are in the developing of high staff morale, and a humanistic school environment. The specific human relations skills involved in achieving these two goals will be identified in later chapters.

CHANGE AGENT

The role of the school administrator as change agent is of relatively recent origin. [16] Although the administrator has always been expected to some extent to introduce change, it wasn't until the 1950s that this role assumed major importance. Since then the role of change agent has received a great deal of emphasis in the educational literature and at professional meetings. School administrators have been exhorted to introduce all kinds of changes, ranging from individualized instruction to open classrooms. The basic rationale advanced for the role of the school administrator as a change agent is that the educational program of the school should be changed to meet the needs of students to a greater degree; and no one is in better position to help bring about these changes than the school administrator. [17]

The role of the administrator as a change agent is a complex one, involving many aspects. However, the main characteristics of the role include the following: (1) diagnosing the need for change, (2) developing or selecting an innovation, (3) orienting the target group to the proposed change, (4) anticipating problems and resistance to the proposed change, (5) developing and implementing a plan which will introduce the innovation and which will overcome obstacles and resistance to change, and (6) evaluating the implemented innovation and making needed refinements in it.

Of course, whether or not a school administrator can be an effective change agent depends largely on the extent of his vision of educational changes which need to be brought about in the school, and the degree to which he possesses the abilities and commitment necessary to introduce those changes successfully. [18] Also it should be emphasized that change for change's sake is not a valid or constructive goal for the administrator to adopt. The proposed change should have the potential for improving the educational program of the school before it can be considered desirable.

CONFLICT MEDIATOR

The role of the school administrator as conflict mediator is of even more recent origin than that of change agent. [19] Although administrators have always been faced with the need to adjust differences, it wasn't until the mid-sixties that the need to mediate conflict became a major aspect of the school administrator's role. Since that time he has been confronted with, among others, conflicts associated with student activism, teacher militancy, and parental and community demands for greater involvement in school decision making.

At the present time, conflict resolution comprises a major part of the administrator's job. [20] In the role of conflict resolver, the school administrator acts basically as a mediator. [21] He attempts to secure all of the facts in a situation, as well as the perceptions each party to the dispute has of one another and of the issues in conflict. Generally, the administrator's major goal is for each side to recognize some validity in the other party's position, so that compromise can take place and the conflict can be resolved. As the administrator works with all parties to a dispute, whether they be students, teachers, parents, or others, he needs to develop an understanding on their part that neither side is totally right, and that some "give and take" will be necessary before the conflict can be resolved.

When one views the turmoil surrounding education today, it is clear that the role of conflict mediator is an essential one for the school administrator. [22]

REFERENCE GROUPS' EXPECTATIONS FOR THE SCHOOL ADMINISTRATOR'S ROLE

No administrator can simultaneously perform all of the roles previously described, and generally different situations call for different roles. If a school administrator is to make a wise decision about the role he should adopt in a particular situation, he will need to be knowledgeable about the expectations held by various reference groups. These groups include students, teachers, parents, and others who may be associated with the school. Figure 4.1 identifies a number of groups who hold expectations for the role of the school administrator.

While it may be impossible for a school administrator to become knowledgeable about the expectations for his role held by *all* the different groups who are associated with the school, it would appear essential that he

At the Building Level

1. Teachers and other members of the faculty
2. Other administrative personnel in the school
3. Students
4. Clerical and maintenance staff

At the District Level

1. The superintendent
2. Central office administrative/supervisory staff
3. The school board
4. Administrators in other schools

Local and State Groups

1. Parents
2. Parents' organizations
3. Social, labor, and business organizations

4. State department of public instruction
5. Professional organizations
6. Accreditation agencies

Figure 4.1. Reference Groups Who Hold Expectations for the Role of the School Administrator.

become so in the case of four of the groups with whom he has direct contact: students, teachers, parents, and the school administrator's superiors. Although the specific expectations of any of these groups may vary according to the nature of the group, and the local situation, research studies have provided information which should be useful in helping the administrator to develop an understanding of the general orientation of these groups.*

STUDENTS' EXPECTATIONS FOR THE SCHOOL ADMINISTRATOR'S ROLE

Many students have probably never even thought about the role of the school administrator, while others may possess well-conceived ideas about what he should be doing in the school.

A review of the research on students' expectations for the role of the school administrator shows that this area of inquiry has not attracted much interest from researchers. An investigation by Pederson, however, suggests the kinds of behavior which students might perceive to be effective principal behavior and the kinds of behavior which they might perceive to be ineffective. [23] Pederson's study of a random sample of students was conducted in

---

*The following sections are presented in order that an administrator may better *understand* the expectations of certain reference groups; no inference should be drawn that an administrator must conform to these expectations or that all the people in a specific reference group will hold the same expectation.

twenty-five schools. In essence, he asked 1,645 students to describe behavior or actions of their principal which were (1) effective or worthy of praise, and (2) ineffective or deserving of criticism.

The behavior or actions of the principal which students mentioned most frequently as effective were concerned with the principal's *personal* relationships with them. These actions took place in situations in which the principal expressed friendship, courtesy, sincerity, consideration, praise, encouragement, interest toward students, and support of pupils, faculty, and all phases of the school program. Such personal relationship behavior was mentioned by students four times as frequently as any other behavior (of those perceived by the students as effective) on the part of the principal, and therefore strongly indicates the main nature of their expectations for the role of the principal.

Reinforcing the importance of personal relationships between the principal and students were the data on students' perceptions of *ineffective* behavior by the principal. The behavior mentioned most frequently by students as ineffective was also concerned with the principal's personal relationship with students. It involved situations in which the principal had acted in an unfriendly, humorless, discourteous, affected, phony, insincere, inconsiderate, critical, disinterested, or opposed manner towards pupils, faculty, and all phases of the school program.

Although there is little doubt that the principal's personal relationship with students is the most important aspect of students' expectations for his role, Pederson's study produced additional findings [24] which suggest that students also expect the principal to

1. Organize advisory groups which represent the viewpoints of all persons interested in the school. Actions by the principal which treat groups partially would be perceived as ineffective by students.
2. Seek and utilize the recommendations of individuals and all advisory groups in the study and solution of school problems. Failure by the principal to seek or utilize the recommendations of individuals and all types of advisory groups in the study and solution of school problems would be perceived by students as ineffective. Also perceived as ineffective would be neglect by the principal in taking action or following up on proposals or recommendations of official groups or committees.
3. Act immediately to stop the misbehavior of individuals or groups. Excessive delay and inappropriate attempts to correct misbehavior of pupils would be perceived as ineffective action by the principal.
4. Reprimand individuals or groups in a calm, mature, and friendly fashion without harshness or threats. Reprimanding individuals or groups in an unfriendly fashion with harshness or threats, or

exercising judgment without all of the facts and without listening to the other side of the story would be perceived by students as ineffective behavior.

5. Explain school policies, practices, procedures, regulations, and facts regarding rumors for the entire student body. Failure by the principal to adequately explain and consistently apply school policies, practices, procedures, and regulations would be perceived by students as ineffective behavior.

6. Refrain from censoring student publications, assemblies, discussions, books, and films.

7. Assist pupils directly with individual and group learning projects.

8. Intercede with higher authority on behalf of pupils.

9. Write or speak to the entire student body, stimulating their best efforts.

10. Provide time, equipment, and facilities for the educational program.

11. Safeguard the health and welfare of pupils and school personnel.

Perhaps the most dramatic finding of Pederson's study was that approximately one-half of the students rarely observed the principal working on the job. [25] This finding may suggest many implications, but one thing is certain: the school administrator needs to become more visible to students if he is to be perceived by them as performing an important role in the school.

TEACHERS' EXPECTATIONS FOR THE SCHOOL ADMINISTRATOR'S ROLE

Perhaps more than any other reference group, teachers have the opportunity for interaction with the school administrator and are therefore in a better position to develop expectations for his role. As a consequence, research studies on teachers' expectations for the role of the school administrator have been numerous. These studies in general indicate three major expectations which an administrator may anticipate that teachers will hold for his role:

(1) **The school administrator should support his teachers on issues and problems of student discipline.**

Several studies have documented this particular expectation of teachers. Becker, for example, found that teachers wanted the school administrator to support them in discipline cases *no matter who was at fault.*[26] In a similar vein, Willower discovered that the strongest teacher expectation was to the effect that the school administrator always back them in matters involving discipline; [27] and Bridges reported that the administrator's support of teachers in regard to their problems with pupils was valued by teachers more than anything else he could do. [28]

It would appear from studies on teachers' expectations that teachers believe it is less crucial that the school administrator be a strong disciplinarian (although this may be important) than that he back or support the teachers regardless of the nature of their approach to discipline.

(2) **The school administrator should treat teachers as professional colleagues with different but equal roles, rather than as subordinates in a bureaucratic relationship.**

Teachers have improved their educational and professional status in recent years, and research studies point to the fact that many of them no longer recognize the traditional superior-subordinate relationship between the administrator and teachers that existed in the past.

Scully, for example, found that teachers wanted the school administrator to cooperate with them and to regard them as fellow workers, rather than as subordinates. [29] Bidwell's study discovered that teachers expected the school administrator to set clear and fair standards for teachers' behavior. [30] Chase's research revealed that teachers expected the school administrator to show understanding and respect for their competency and work, [31] and Sharpe noted that teachers expected the school administrator to communicate with them frequently and to refrain from curtailing their individual initiative or freedom. [32]

In summary, the main implication of these studies is that teachers expect to be recognized as professionals and to be treated accordingly.

(3) **The school administrator should provide a meaningful opportunity for teachers to participate in school decision making and should include a significant role for teachers in the making of final decisions about those activities directly affecting them.**

All of the studies on teacher expectations that were reviewed point to the desire of teachers for a significant role in school decision making. Chase, for instance, found that teachers expected the school administrator to provide opportunities for their active participation in curriculum development, determination of grouping and promotion, and control of pupils. [33] In addition, teachers emphasized that if they were to serve on a committee, the committee must have the power to make decisions rather than mere recommendations on questions already decided by the principal. Sharma discovered in his study that teachers wanted shared responsibility in all areas of the school program except instructional activities, wherein they wanted total responsibility. [34] The literature continues to show a strong expectation by teachers that the school administrator take an active role in involving them in those decisions which affect the teacher in some professional way. [35]

Whether or not the school administrator should meet all or any of the three main expectations by teachers for his role depends, of course, on many factors. Obviously, it will not always be possible and may not even be desirable for the administrator to meet all of the teachers' expectations. However, he needs to be aware that important consequences are associated with the extent to which he meets teachers' expectations.

Horalick, for example, found that in regard to teachers' evaluation of the principal as a leader, it was more important for him to adhere to certain faculty norms and role expectations than to follow a particular leadership style in interacting with the faculty. [36] Expectations which the faculty held for the principal included the following:

1. He should "back up" teachers in front of parents, even when he considers the teachers to be wrong. If the principal criticizes a teacher, it should be done privately.
2. He should "back up" teachers in front of pupils. If the principal believes that a student is right, the teacher should be told so privately and should never be criticized in the presence of a pupil.
3. The principal should be a good disciplinarian.
4. He should exhibit democratic behavior.

Adherence by the principal to the above expectations was associated with high faculty evaluation of the principal as a leader; a lack of adherence was associated with low faculty evaluation of the principal as a leader.

A major implication of Horalick's research is that the school administrator may not be able to gain acceptance or exert effective leadership with teachers until he meets *or* changes their expectations in regard to his role in the school.

PARENTAL EXPECTATIONS FOR THE SCHOOL ADMINISTRATOR'S ROLE

Parents constitute an important third group that holds expectations for the role of the school administrator. Perhaps more than any of the other groups discussed thus far, parents are heterogeneous in their expectations. Therefore, it is more difficult to generalize about the expectations of any single parents' group, to say nothing of parents' groups in different communities. In addition, there has been surprisingly little research on the expectations of parents for the role of the school administrator. Still, some useful findings can be gleaned from the few studies that have focused on parents' expectations for the school administrator's role.

Buffington, for example, found in his study of parental expectations for the role of the principal that parents expected the principal to engage in the kinds of behavior identified in the following. [37]

Parents' Expectations for the Role of the Principal

I. Develop relationships with parents' groups and the community
   A. Organize parents' groups
   B. Work with parents' groups
   C. Interpret the school to the community

II. Know and help individual parents
   A. Meet parents' complaints
   B. Establish friendly relations with parents
   C. Report to parents on progress of children
III. Work with and care for children
   A. Maintain discipline
   B. Show personal interest in children
   C. Protect health and safety of children
   D. Work with atypical children

As one can see from an examination of the expectations revealed by Buffington's study, they fall into three categories: (1) working with parents' groups, (2) interacting with parents on an individual basis, and (3) working with and showing concern for children. While most administrators would probably feel that the kinds of behavior listed under each of these categories are desirable, there are indications that many parents are not satisfied with the extent to which their expectations have been met by administrators. Although this problem is discussed more fully in the chapters on school-community relations, it seems that administrators—with few exceptions—need to become more aware of the expectations by parents for the role of the administrator, as well as more knowledgeable about the extent to which parents feel that administrators are not meeting their expectations.

SUPERIORS' EXPECTATIONS FOR THE SCHOOL ADMINISTRATOR'S ROLE

Probably many school administrators consider the most important expectations for their behavior to be those held by their superiors.* They are the individuals who had an important role in hiring the school administrator, and they will play a major role in determining his salary, retention, and status in the district, as well as other matters. For these reasons alone, the school administrator will have a tendency to weigh heavily the expectations of his superiors.

In addition, in a bureaucratic organization such as the school, which is operated according to principles of line and staff, the administrator is responsible to and accountable to his superiors. Therefore, it is only natural for him to give a higher priority to the expectations of his superiors than to the expectations of other reference groups. (But a problem for the school administrator arises when his expectations conflict with those of his superiors.

---

*Evidence supporting this point was collected in a study by Gorton. See Richard A. Gorton, "Factors Which Are Associated with the Principal's Behavior in Encouraging Teacher Participation in School Decision-Making." *Journal of Educational Research* 64 no. 7 (March 1971):325-27.

The nature of these conflicts and possible resolutions are discussed elsewhere, and the reader is encouraged to pursue these readings. [38])

Perhaps the best study of superiors' expectations for the role of the school administrator was conducted by Moser. [39] His research showed that superintendents expected their principals to engage in the following kinds of behavior: (1) lead forcefully, (2) initiate action, (3) accomplish organizational goals, and (4) emulate the nomothetic behavior of their superiors.

Nomothetic behavior can be defined as actions which seek to meet the expectations of the institution in which an individual works. As applied to the school administrator-superior relationship, nomothetic expectations mean that the administrator's superiors expect him to pay greater attention to the expectations of the organization for which he works than to his own personal needs or the personal needs of others with whom he may be associated at the building level.

Whether a school administrator will always be able to meet the expectations of his superiors will depend on many factors, including the extent to which the expectations are realistic. Certainly he should attempt to change the expectations of his superiors if he feels that they are not in his best interest or in the best interest of the school. His success in this endeavor will depend as much on his own skill and perseverance as on the receptivity of his superiors for change. In any event, it would be to the advantage of the school administrator to make sure that he accurately understands the expectations of his superiors and considers carefully the consequences of not meeting those expectations.

AGREEMENT AMONG REFERENCE GROUPS

Although there is considerable evidence that the expectations of others for the role of the school administrator frequently conflict with each other, a study by Clifford Campbell suggests some common ground. [40] In Campbell's investigation of the expectations of teachers, parents, PTA presidents, nurses, custodians, and secretaries for the role of the school administrator, all of these groups agreed that the following behavioral characteristics were important for the administrator: (1) show interest in work, offer assistance; (2) praise personnel; (3) back up personnel; (4) assume authority, stand by convictions; (5) allow self-direction in work; (6) make clear his feelings; (7) allow participation in decisions; (8) be a good disciplinarian; be considerate of work load; (9) possess good personal characteristics, and (10) be well organized.

While some of the above-mentioned expectations seem contradictory, and the school administrator cannot realistically expect that reference groups' expectations will always be in agreement, Campbell's research suggests that compatability is achievable to a large extent. The most important step the administrator can take to reach this goal is to make sure that he understands accurately the expectations of reference groups. For, as Roald Campbell has perceptively pointed out,

> An understanding of these expectations, often conflicting in nature, may appear most frustrating. Only by such understanding, however, can the administrator anticipate the reception of specified behavior on his part. Such anticipation seems necessary if the area of acceptance is to be extended and the area of disagreement minimized. Moreover, such understandings are necessary if a program of modifying expectations is to be started. [41]

SOCIAL FACTORS AFFECTING THE SCHOOL ADMINISTRATOR'S ROLE*

The job of the school administrator, has, of course, seldom been without problems. But in the last two decades several social factors have emerged which have made the administrator's job one of the most difficult and challenging in education today. [42] While observers may differ on the nature of the impact, there appears to be fairly general agreement that five factors in particular have affected the role of the school administrator: (1) collective bargaining, (2) student and parent activism, (3) increased involvement of the courts and legislatures in school affairs, (4) societal expectations that the school should solve social problems, and (5) increased size and complexity of schools and school districts.

Collective Bargaining

There seems to be little doubt that collective bargaining has changed the role of the school administrator, at least as regards his relationship to teachers. [43] Prior to collective bargaining the school administrator's relationship with teachers was frequently a paternalistic one. In most situations, he had a choice as to whether or not he should consider teachers' grievances, consult with them about work assignments or involve them in school decision making, and all too often—at least according to teachers' perceptions—he chose not to do so.

The introduction of collective bargaining, however, has meant that in most cases the administrator must consider teacher grievances and must consult with the teachers in regard to work conditions and other matters affecting their welfare. The principal is still the head of the school, but now he must administer with the assistance of faculty input and consultation. Because of collective bargaining, his role has become less authoritarian and more consultative. He can no longer act unilaterally in situations which will

*Most of the social factors discussed in this section are discussed more extensively in other chapters, and therefore will only be touched on briefly here.

affect faculty welfare. While some people may feel that these changes have made the role of the school administrator more difficult, others believe that the changes have also afforded the administrator a greater opportunity to exercise leadership.

Student and Parent Activism

A second major social force which has affected the role of the school administrator has been student and parent activism. [44] Beginning in the middle 1960s students and parents began to challenge the authority of the school administrator and to demand greater involvement in school decision making. This trend, though somewhat abated, has continued. In many schools, student and parent activism has led to more influential student councils and parent organizations, the promulgation of codes of students' and parents' rights, and more active involvement by both students and parents in numerous aspects of school affairs.

Although student activism and, to some extent, parent activism seem to have declined recently, it appears clear that such activism has caused significant changes in the role of the school administrator. No longer can he simply take for granted students' and parents' acceptance of administrative decisions. In many instances the administrator must consult with parents and students on decisions about aspects of the school's operation which affect them. This is not to say that there had been no school administrators in the past who consulted with students and parents prior to making decisions. However, because of student and parent activism, consultation now is a necessity in many situations, unless the administrator wishes to run the very real risk of student and parent alienation or disruption.

While the need for student and parent consultation has made the role of the school administrator more difficult and at times more frustrating, the value of consultation in terms of greater cooperation and potentially improved decision making strongly supports the desirability of this type of role change.

Influence of the Federal and State Government

A third major social force which has affected the role of the school administrator has been the intervention by the federal and state government in educational affairs.* This intervention has taken several forms and has posed new problems for school administrators.

For example, in the past the courts have not often attempted to substitute their judgment for that of school officials in the administration of the schools unless, of course, a serious offense was committed. [45] Recently,

---

*Two excellent books on this topic are David L. Kirp and Mark G. Yudof, *Educational Policy and the Law,* and Harry L. Summerfield, *Power and Process: The Foundation and Limits of Federal Educational Policy,* both published by McCutchan Publishing Co., Berkeley, Calif. 1974.

however, acting in response to challenges to school authority and decision making by students, teachers, and parents, the courts have laid down a number of rulings which have altered the role of the administrator. These rulings have covered a wide range of areas, including student dress and grooming regulations, due process rights, and racial and sex discrimination. [46]

These court decisions have had important effects on the role of the school administrator. The administrator's authority has been reduced, and he is now required to demonstrate that the school has acted fairly and prudently in its relations with others. Although there appear to be many administrators who feel that the courts have "interfered" in school affairs and have made the administrator's job more difficult, the overall result in many situations has been to make the school and the relationships within the school less authoritarian and more humanistic. The extent to which the latter result has been achieved, however, has depended as much on the manner and spirit in which the school administrator has implemented the court decisions as on any other factor.

State and federal legislatures have also passed laws which have tended to increase the difficulty of the administrator's job and alter his role.

For example, state legislation on accountability and evaluation, and the 1974 Education Amendments to the Elementary and Secondary Education Act, Title I, have posed new challenges for the school administrator. The federal legislation requires *every* Title I school to have its own parent advisory council to help plan and evaluate Title I programs. While this type of legislation may be desirable, it does affect the role of the school administrator by requiring him to involve one more group in planning and evaluating certain educational activities.

Whether state and federal laws and regulations on education constitute "interference" in local school affairs can be debated. However, what administrators need to recognize is that state and federal governments do not usually pass legislation affecting a local school situation unless there is evidence that local initiative is not being exercised to correct a serious problem. Perhaps the best alternative for school administrators is to move more quickly to identify and resolve problems on the local level so that state and federal legislative action won't be necessary.

Expectations of Society

Perhaps the social force which has most increased the difficulty of the school administrator's job has been the expectation that the school attempt to play a larger role in resolving many of society's social problems. [47] While some people have always argued that the school should play a more active role in reforming society, this expectation has been spreading in recent years. [48] Now it is not unusual for many people to expect the school to deal with such social problems as poverty, unemployment, crime and vandalism, racial segregation, and illegal drug usage.

Certainly a case can be made that the school should play an active role in trying to resolve social problems, if for no other reasons than because the school is a part of society; and if society needs to change, then the change might best begin with young people, who spend more of their waking moments at school than in any other place away from home. However, it also needs to be recognized that, in attempting to respond to such expectations, the school has added enormously to its mission and to its own problems.

As a consequence, there has been a significant increase in the scope of the school administrator's role and the tensions and frustrations associated with that role. The job of an administrator may be managerial in nature if he is to administer a school with a traditional program in a stable situation. A much more demanding and creative role is required of the school administrator who is trying to deal with social problems in a rapidly changing situation. [49] And more and more school administrators are being confronted with the latter set of circumstances.

Increased Size

Compounding the problems of the administrator is a fifth factor which has affected his role, namely, the increase in size of many schools and school districts. This change has been a trend for some time now, though its future impact may be modified by a decline in the nation's birth rate.

At the individual school level there has been an increase in the size of the student enrollment, which has usually required a larger school plant, an increase in faculty size, more educational programs, and an increase in the use of specialists. All of this has added considerably to the complexity and difficulty of the school administrator's role. [50] Although in many situations the increase in size has also resulted in the addition of assistants to the school's administrative staff, and the introduction of different methods of organization, such as the "school within a school" plan, these additions and changes by and large have not occurred to a sufficient degree to significantly reduce the pressures of size on the role of the school administrator.

The growth in size of many school districts, typically brought about through consolidations and reorganizations, has also affected the role of the school administrator. [51] In a small school district there are often fewer central office administrators and supervisors to whom the building administrator must be responsible, and there is greater flexibility in administering a school without having to worry about how some other school in the district might be affected. A large school district, however, usually has a sizeable central office staff, and with a greater number of schools in the district, there are frequently problems of coordination which affect the role of the school administrator. [52] While some large school districts have attempted to deal with the problem through administrative decentralization, the role of the school administrator in a large school district, remains more managerial in nature, and less autonomous than in a small district.

An increase in school size, when accompanied by an increase in the size of the school district, has posed serious problems for many school administrators. On one hand, they have more responsibility because of the increase in the size of the student body, the school plant, educational programs, the faculty, and the specialist staff. But, on the other hand, the authority for them to act may be severely restricted by the number of central office administrators from whom they must secure approval, and the number of other schools with which they must coordinate their educational programs. This situation has limited the leadership aspects of the role of the school administrator and has caused many of them grave concern. [53]

A CONCLUDING NOTE

The job of the school administrator is a complex and demanding one which is not likely to become less difficult. However, if an individual possesses or can acquire the capabilities and personal qualities referred to in this book, he should be able to respond successfully to the challenges associated with the position. While the six roles identified earlier in this chapter are and will continue to be important in the resolution of school problems and the achievement of school objectives, the school administrator should not feel that he must perform all of these roles himself, if assistance is available. To the extent desirable and feasible the administrator should delegate or share some of these roles with the administrative team or with other appropriate school personnel. The important point is not *who* performs the roles, but that they be performed effectively.

Review

1. Identify the main function and assess the importance of each of the six administrative roles identified in this chapter.
2. What are the major expectations of students, teachers, parents, and superiors for the role of the administrator?
3. To what extent should an administrator meet the expectations of students, teachers, parents, and superiors for his role? What are the advantages and disadvantages of meeting or not meeting the expectations of these groups?
4. Explain how the following social factors have affected the role of the school administrator: collective bargaining, student and parent activism, increased involvement of the courts and legislatures in school affairs, societal expectations that the school solve social problems, and increased size and complexity of schools and school districts.
5. How should the administrator react to parents' demand for a greater role in the school, and accountability on the part of the school?

Notes

1.   Bernard Bard, "On the Razor's Edge," *Saturday Review* 53 (January 1970):58-59. See also Gerald Becker et al., *Elementary School Principals and Their Schools* (Eugene, Oreg.: Center for the Advanced Study of Educational Administration, 1971), pp. 4-7.

2.   Paul B. Jacobson et al., *The Principalship: New Perspectives* (Englewood Cliffs, N.J.: Prentice-Hall, 1973), pp. 1-27.

3.   For example, see George E. Melton and John Stanavage, *The Principalship: Job Specifications and Salary Considerations for the 70s* (Washington, D.C.: National Association of Secondary School Principals, 1970). Also see Hoyt F. Watson, "A Study of Conflicting Concepts Concerning the Future Secondary School Principalship" (Ph.D. diss., Florida State University, 1970); and Terry Barraclough, "The Role of the Elementary School Principal." An ERIC Report: Ed-077-127, 1972.

4.   Paul R. Pierce, *The Origin and Development of the Public School Principalship* (Chicago: University of Chicago Press, 1935), p. 12.

5.   "Administration Is More Than Management," in *Educational Administration*, ed. Robert E. Wilson (Columbus, Ohio: Charles E. Merrill Publishing Co., 1966), pp. 45-46.

6.   See Ellwood P. Cubberley, *The Principal and His School* (Boston: Houghton-Mifflin Co., 1923).

7.   Ibid., p. 43.

8.   For an elaboration of the different definitions of the role, see Lester W. Anderson and Laurence A. Van Dyke, *Secondary School Administration* (Boston: Houghton-Mifflin Co., 1972), pp. 28-29.

9.   Richard A. Gorton, "The Importance of Expertise in Instructional Leadership" (Paper delivered at the convention of the American Educational Research Association, 1971).

10.   Clifford Campbell, "The Elementary Principal as Viewed by His Staff and Parent-Teacher Association Presidents" (Ph.D. diss., University of California, 1964), p. 67.

11.   John D. McAulay, "Principal: What Do Your Children Think of You?" *National Elementary Principal* 47 (January 1968):58-60.

12.   David B. Austin and Harry L. Brown, Jr., *Report of the Assistant Principal* (Washington, D.C.: National Association of Secondary School Principals, 1970), p. 68.

13.   Mary Parker Follett, *Creative Experience* (New York: Longmans, Green, 1924).

14.   Elton Mayo, *The Human Problems of an Industrial Civilization* (Boston: Graduate School of Business Administration, Harvard University, 1946).

15.   Daniel Griffiths, *Human Relations in School Administration* (New York: Appleton-Century-Crofts, 1956).

16.   Edwin M. Bridges, "The Principal and the Teachers: The Problem of Organizational Change," in *Perspectives on the Changing Role of the Principal*, ed. Richard W. Saxe (Springfield, Ill.: Charles C Thomas, Publisher, 1968), pp. 61-78.)

17.   Mark Chesler et al., "The Principal's Role in Facilitating Innovations," *Theory into Practice* 2 no. 5 (December 1963):269-77.

18.   See also Ken A. Tye, "Principal as Change Agent," *National Elementary Principal* 49 (February 1970):41-51.

19.   Roy E. Harkin, "The Principal as Mediator," *High School Journal* 53 (March 1970):334-43.

20.   See Philip K. Piele, "Conflict Management in Education," *ERIC/Com* Research Review (Fall 1971).

21.   For a detailed description of the process of mediating conflict, see Richard A. Gorton, *Conflict, Controversy and Crisis in School Administration and Supervision.* (Dubuque, Iowa: Wm. C. Brown Company Publishers, 1972), chap. 12.

22.   Stephen K. Bailey, "Preparing Educational Administrators for Conflict Resolution." An ERIC Report: Ed-048-646, 1971.

23.   Monroe E. Pederson, "Pupil Expectations of the High School Principal" (Ph.D. diss., University of Southern California, 1970).

24.   Ibid.

25.   For an example of similar findings at the elementary level, see John D. McAulay, "Principal: What Do Your Children Think?" pp. 58-60. In McAulay's study over 60 percent of the students could identify no clear function for the elementary principal.

26. H. S. Becker, "Role and Career Problems of the Chicago Public School Teachers" (Ph.D. diss., University of Chicago, 1951).

27. Donald J. Willower, "The Teacher Subculture." An ERIC Report: Ed-020-588, 1968.

28. Edwin M. Bridges, "Teacher Participation in Decision-Making," *Administrator's Notebook* 12 (May 1964):1-4.

29. E. M. Scully, "Personnel Administration in Public Education: A Study in Human Relationship" (Ph.D. diss., University of Wisconsin, 1945).

30. Charles E. Bidwell, "Some Causes of Conflict and Tensions among Teachers," *Administrator's Notebook* 4 (March 1956).

31. Francis L. Chase, "The Teacher and Policy Making," *Administrator's Notebook 1* (May 1952).

32. Russell T. Sharpe, "Differences between Perceived Administrative Behavior and Role Norms as Factors in Leadership and Group Morale" (Ph.D. diss., Stanford University, 1955), p. 159.

33. Chase, "Teacher and Policy Making."

34. G. L. Sharma, "Who Should Make What Decisions?" *Administrators' Notebook* 3 (April 1955).

35. See recent issues of *Today's Education,* a publication of the National Education Association.

36. J. A. Horalick, "Teacher Acceptance of Administrative Action," *Journal of Experimental Education* 37 (Winter 1968):39-47.

37. Reed L. Buffington, "The Job of the Elementary School Principal as Viewed by Parents" (Ed.D. diss., Stanford University, 1954), p. 943.

38. Discussed more fully in Gorton, *Conflict, Controversy and Crisis in School Administration,* pp. 323-38.

39. Robert P. Moser, "A Study of the Effects of Superintendent-Principal Interaction and Principal-Teacher Interaction in Selected Middle-sized School Systems" (Ph.D. diss., University of Chicago, 1957).

40. Clifford Campbell, "The Elementary Principal," p. 67.

41. Roald F. Campbell, "Situational Factors in Educational Administration," in *Administrative Behavior in Education,* ed. Roald F. Campbell and Russell T. Gregg (New York: Harper & Row, Publishers, 1957), p. 264.

42. "The School Principalship: A Crisis in Middle Management." A collection of ERIC Resources: Ed-044-771, 1970.

43. Ivan Templeton, "Principal's Role in Collective Negotiations." An ERIC Report: Ed-062-688, 1972.

44. For in-depth analysis of student and parent activism, see Gorton, *Crisis, Conflict, and Controversy in School Administration,* chaps. 2, 4.

45. John C. Hogan, *The Schools, the Courts, and the Public Interest* (Lexington, Mass.: Lexington Books, 1974), chap. 2.

46. Ibid., chaps. 3-5.

47. Muriel Crosby, "Impact on Today's Schools," *Educational Leadership* 26 (October 1968):7-8.

48. LuVern L. Cunningham. "Educational Reform and the Principalship." ERIC Report: Ed-052-534, 1971.

49. Norman Goble, "Implications of Social Change for the Administrator." An ERIC Report: Ed-067-742, 1971.

50. William Reiss, *Organizational Complexity, The Relationship between Size of the Administrative Component and School System Size* (Eugene, Oreg.: Center for the Advanced Study of Educational Administration, 1970).

51. Carol Mullins, "School District Consolidation: Odds Are 2 to 1 It'll Get You," *American School Board Journal* 160 (November 1973):23-27.

52. For an excellent discussion of this problem and other selected problems, see James G. Anderson, *Bureaucracy in Education* (Baltimore: Johns Hopkins Press, 1968), pp. 1-37.

53. P. Coleman, "Perils of Bigness: The Case Against Large School Districts," *Educational Administration Quarterly* 8 (Spring 1972):54-62.

5

The Administrative Team

The concept of "team" suggests a group of people working together cooperatively, rather than unilaterally, to achieve a common goal. The main goals of an administrative team should be to develop school policies and procedures, solve common problems, and, in general, to improve education in the schools by utilizing the collective talents and interests of the individual members of the team.[1] The concept is based on the assumption that administrative decision making should be a joint effort rather than the sole responsibility or province of one individual, such as the principal or the superintendent.[2]

While it may not be possible to establish an administrative team in every school or school district, the potential advantages of cooperatively pooling human resources to achieve school and district objectives strongly support the need to organize an administrative team, where feasible. The following sections will discuss, first at the building level and then at the district level, the various aspects of organizing and operating an administrative team.

THE ADMINISTRATIVE TEAM AT THE BUILDING LEVEL

COMPOSITION OF THE TEAM

With few exceptions, the principal should be the one to make the final decision on the composition of the administrative team at the building level. He is the one who is administratively in charge of the school and should, consequently, determine the membership of the team. In determining the composition of the team he should keep in mind that its basic functions are administrative and supervisory in nature. It would appear, therefore, that those individuals in the school who are performing administrative functions or who have supervisory responsibilities should be members of the team. This would include, in most situations, the people occupying the positions identified in figure 5.1.

Figure 5.1 shows the proposed composition of the administrative team and its main characteristics. It indicates that the composition of the administrative team at the building level consists of the principal, the assistant and/or vice-principal, the department heads or unit leaders, program direc-

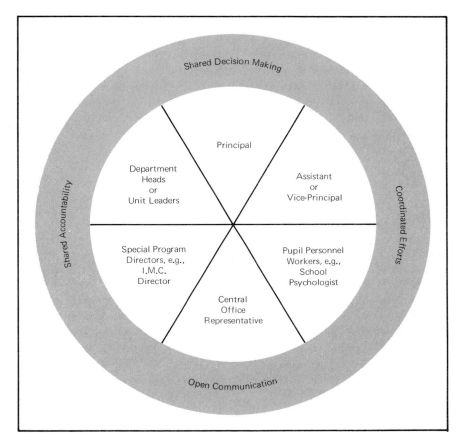

Figure 5.1. Proposed Composition and Characteristics of the Administrative Team at the School Level.

tors, pupil personnel workers, and a central office representative. The latter might be the individual in charge of secondary or elementary school education in the district, or someone else who could represent the central administration's point of view.

Note the recommendation that the pupil personnel workers (such as the school psychologist) and the program directors (such as the director of the instructional materials center) should be members of the administrative team.[3] These persons may not be actually administrators or supervisors in the strictest sense of those terms. But at least some of their responsibilities are administrative or supervisory in nature; more importantly, because of their contacts with students, teachers, and parents, they offer a potentially rich source of insights and perceptions that would be useful to the other members of the team. While it may not be possible or even necessary to include these specialists in all of the team meetings, it seems clear that each of them can make a valuable contribution and consequently should be included as members and attend meetings as appropriate.

STRUCTURE OF THE TEAM

Once the composition of an administrative team has been determined, then its structure should be defined, i.e., how each component of the team should function individually and in relationship to the other components. If the principal has not already assigned responsibilities to each member of the team, this should be the team's first priority. [4]

The next objective should be to define the interrelationships which should exist between the various members of the team. If the administrative team is to operate effectively, each member must know about the responsibilities and roles of the other members, and how all team members can help each other and work together cooperatively. In essence, assisting one another and working cooperatively are the keys to a successful team. The type of structure which is initiated must arrive at these outcomes, or the concept of "team" degenerates into a group of individuals merely trying to promote and protect their own selfish interests or those of the people they represent, rather than the common good of the school. [5]

When establishing the structure of an administrative team the issue of the authority relationships within the team should be faced squarely. An initial question which needs to be answered is, who should head the team? Although various arguments could be made in response to this question, it would appear that in most situations the head of the team will be—and should be—the principal. He is the one who has the overall responsibility for administering the school, and it is he who is held primarily accountable for what goes on in the school.

This does not mean, however, that the principal should play a domineering or controlling role on the administrative team, nor does it mean that he should exercise all of the leadership on the team. [6] On the contrary—the principal's main role should be that of facilitator and resource person for the other team members.* He should try to stimulate their involvement and leadership, and he should attempt to emphasize and encourage cooperation among all members of the team. [7] Although the principal may retain the authority to assign responsibility and then evaluate the performance of the team members, this should be done cooperatively as much as possible.

*Refer to "group leadership behavior" in chapter 3 for further discussion of this point.

ADMINISTRATIVE TEAM PROCESSES

An administrative team is functioning successfully if each member is carrying out his responsibilities effectively, and the various members of the team are working cooperatively with each other. Although many of the activities of the team members will take place outside of their formal meetings, it is during the team meetings that most of the important discussions and decisions will take place, and it is during the meetings that members have their greatest opportunity to interact. [8]

Probably the most important step a principal can take to utilize productively the contributions that members offer during a meeting, and to help the group to function as a unit, is to try to set up an atmosphere conducive to a spirit of cooperation and mutual respect, with an absence of tension or nervousness. In such an atmosphere each member of the team should feel free to contribute ideas and to question other members of the team, including the principal.

The atmosphere at the meetings will depend primarily on what the principal says and does. An organizational structure for the team may have been defined which ostensibly permits a great deal of give and take in discussions. But if the principal dominates and controls discussion during the meetings, it is unlikely that the atmosphere will be conducive to a free exchange of ideas and thoughts by the other members of the team. [9]

While the principal will undoubtedly need to exercise his authority in certain situations, this should be done selectively; his main contribution should be to promote and facilitate interaction and the involvement of everyone on the team.

In addition to helping to set up an atmosphere conducive to openness and freedom of expression, the principal should establish certain processes which are important to the effective functioning of a group, such as those identified in figure 5.2 (p. 88).

The processes recommended are designed to facilitate input from the various members of the team in the development of the agenda, and to provide organization and continuity to the meetings. While one can overemphasize the need for planning and the follow-through after a meeting, a certain degree of preparation and organization is necessary in order to avoid an aimless discussion and few concrete results. It is primarily the principal's responsibility to make sure that these outcomes do not occur.

SELECTED MEMBERS OF THE TEAM AT BUILDING LEVEL

For the administrative team to operate successfully, it is essential that the school administrator have a better understanding of the role and problems of

A.	B.	C.	D.	E.
Soliciting input from team members for the development of the agenda	Preparing background material on agenda items and disseminating these materials and the agenda several days prior to the meeting	Maintaining a written record of important ideas and decisions made during the meeting	Disseminating written minutes to all appropriate parties after the meeting	Following through on decisions or actions taken during meetings

Figure 5.2. Recommended Processes for Team Meetings.

each of its members. Since some of these roles will be presented in other chapters, this section will concentrate on the role and problems of the assistant principal, the department chairman, and the unit leader.

THE ASSISTANT PRINCIPALSHIP [10]

Until recently, the assistant principalship had not received the attention it deserves in most textbooks on administration and supervision, and in the educational literature.[11] To correct this situation, the National Association of Secondary School Principals and the National Association of Elementary School Principals each published a study of the assistant principal.

The elementary school study was conducted among 1,442 assistant principals. The main findings were (1) that assistant principals were found more often in large than in small elementary schools; (2) most assistant principals emerged directly from the elementary school classroom to enter their present position; (3) there were substantially more men than women assistant principals; and (4) most assistant principals had chosen the position because they looked upon it as preparation for the principalship.[12]

Perhaps the least surprising finding of the study was that the primary responsibility of most assistant principals was pupil personnel work, e.g., discipline. Although most assistant principals indicated that they preferred supervision as a major responsibility, only one-fourth of all assistant principals had been assigned supervisory responsibility. This finding suggests that most elementary assistant principals are not obtaining the types of experiences in the assistant principal's position that are comprehensive enough to constitute desirable preparation for a future career as a principal. As we shall see, this state of affairs is not unique to elementary schools.

The second study of the assistant principal, conducted by the National Association of Secondary School Principals, focused in greater detail on the nature of the job of the assistant principal.[13] For example, a diary kept by an assistant principal who participated in the study showed that in a single day he became involved in a wide range of activities, as identified in figure 5.3.

---

1. Scheduled detention of a student
2. Discussed with a boy his failure to get a haircut
3. Saw a parent about a car incident involving a student
4. Talked with a boy who had been late for detention
5. Questioned a boy who had no "permission to ride" sticker on his motorbike
6. Inspected the school grounds
7. Supervised the lunchroom
8. Reviewed a recently published student paper
9. Supervised detention hall
10. "Handled" a student fight
11. Distributed memos to some faculty members
12. Checked the rest rooms
13. Checked a locker for stolen materials
14. Supervised students passing in the hall
15. Discussed with the nurse the matter of a boy's broken nose incurred in a fight
16. Notified parents of a student suspension
17. Reviewed the daily bulletin
18. Suspended a boy for taking part in a theft
19. Interviewed a boy who had "sprung" his locker
20. Questioned a girl about tearing pages from a book

From *The Assistant Principalship.* Used with the permission of the National Association of Secondary School Principals.

Figure 5.3. A Day in the Life of an Assistant Principal.[14]

An examination of the various activities reported by the assistant principal reveals that student control and discipline are his basic responsibilities. This is not surprising since traditionally, and perhaps typically, the main duties of the assistant principal have been in these areas. In schools having an assistant principal, he is the individual to whom students who are discipline problems are referred. He is also the one who has the responsibility of checking on and working with students who are attendance problems. Although student discipline and attendance duties may be shared with the principal, the assistant principal usually shoulders the major responsibility for these two areas.

It would be misleading, however, to think that supervising student discipline and attendance are the only functions of an assistant principal. [15] While it is true that his duties depend in reality on what the principal assigns to him, most assistant principals are given other kinds of responsibilities in addition to student discipline and attendance. Table 5.1 lists those responsibilities identified in the NASSP study of the assistant principal.

The table indicates that assistant principals become involved in a wide variety of activities which span the entire administrative spectrum. Still, it is worth noting that student attendance was identified by the highest percentage of assistant principals as their full responsibility, with student discipline a close second. And, although the study did not investigate this possibility, experience and observation would further suggest that it is these two responsibilities which consume the vast majority of the assistant principal's time.

The responsibilities of working on problems of student discipline and attendance are important ones, and the assistant principal can make a valuable contribution to the school program by carrying out these responsibilities effectively. Nevertheless, it needs to be recognized that frequently these are onerous and frustrating tasks for him, particularly if he is the person primarily responsible. There are many days when an assistant principal may not even be able to leave his office during an entire morning or afternoon because he is seeing students or teachers in regard to student discipline or attendance problems. These typically are not pleasant experiences for an assistant principal, even though he may derive some measure of satisfaction from the feeling that he is trying to help others.

That the role definition of the assistant principal, as conceived in many schools, does not appear to be a satisfying one is underscored by further findings of the NASSP study, presented in table 5.2.

An examination of the data presented in table 5.2 shows that, with the exception of two categories—salary and amount of help received from immediate superior—a smaller percentage of assistant principals (and in most cases, a much smaller percentage) reported that they were "very satisfied" in their current positions in comparison with their previous positions as teachers. Certainly, these data do not provide much support for those educators who would like to view the assistant principalship as a career position, rather than as a stepping stone to the principalship.

Assistant principals who are not as satisfied with their current positions as they were when they were teachers are not apt to remain in their present situations if they receive an opportunity to advance. Nor is it likely that these same individuals can operate at their maximum effectiveness in their present job if that job is not giving them the professional and personal satisfaction which they expect and need.

The findings from the studies have raised questions about whether the assistant principalship as it has been set up in many schools is meeting the needs of the individual occupying the position *or* the needs of the school. Consequently, efforts have been made to improve the position. [17]

Table 5.1. Activities for which
Assistant Principals Share or Have Full
Responsibility in Half or More of the
Schools in the Study. [16]

Item	As Reported by Assistant Principals		
School Management	*Shared*	*Full*	*Total*
School calendars	44	14	58
School daily bulletins	47	14	61
Special arrangements at start and close of school year	80	9	89
Clerical services	52	4	56
School-related building use	43	11	54
Emergency arrangements	57	22	79
Staff Personnel			
School policies	75	1	76
Orientation program for new teachers	67	6	73
Substitute teachers	36	17	53
Teacher "duty" rosters	46	25	71
Faculty meetings	57	22	79
Community Relations			
School public relations program	69	2	71
Administrative representative at school community functions	60	2	62
Informing public of school achievements	51	3	54
Liaison with youth-serving agencies in community	48	8	56
Student Activities			
Assemblies	42	21	63
Student Council	29	19	48
School club program	43	15	58
School dances	53	18	71
Curricular and Instructional			
Evaluation of teachers	52	3	55
Providing instructional materials	41	9	50
Curriculum development	51	5	56
Innovations, experiments, and research	49	4	53
School master schedule	44	17	61
School-wide examinations	39	8	47
Articulation with feeder schools	51	8	59
Pupil Personnel			
Pupil discipline	52	38	90
Orientation program for new students	51	12	63
School guidance program	47	10	57
Pupil attendance	33	49	82

From *The Assistant Principalship.* Used with the permission of The National Association of Secondary School Principals.

Table 5.2. Job Satisfaction of the
Assistant Principal.[18]

	Percent Reporting	
	"Very Satisfied" as Teachers	*"Very Satisfied" as Assistant Principals*
How satisfied were you with this position when you consider the expectations you had when you originally took the job?	70%	48%
How satisfied were you with the amount of time which you devoted to the job?	42%	28%
How satisfied were you with the results that you achieved?	52%	35%
How satisfied were you with the amount of personal satisfaction the job gave you?	66%	40%
How satisfied were you with the amount of recognition the job gave you?	31%	30%
How satisfied were you with the physical working conditions?	32%	30%
How satisfied were you with the amount of assistance you received from your immediate superior(s)?	40%	46%
How satisfied were you with the rapport that you established with the student body?	77%	57%
How satisfied were you with your salary?	8%	24%

From *The Assistant Principalship.* Used with the permission of The National Association of Secondary School Principals.

One approach to making the job of the assistant principal more satisfying and effective has been to divide the responsibilities for student discipline and attendance among two or more assistant or vice-principals, rather than assigning all student discipline and attendance problems to one individual. [19] In this kind of a situation, other tasks such as classroom supervision, curriculum implementation, and administration of student activities are shared by two or more assistant principals, thereby providing each with some variety in his job while utilizing their individual special talents.

One example of this approach may be found in schools, particularly those with large enrollments, where an assistant principal may be assigned the responsibility for a single grade level, such as tenth grade, or, in the case of the elementary school, three grade levels. Included in this assignment are, typically, the maintenance of student discipline and attendance, and/or classroom supervision, curriculum development and implementation, and administration of student activities. Each assistant principal is responsible for the total program at his grade level(s), and the principal provides the overall coordination and leadership for the school.

Whether it is possible for a school to have an assistant principal for each grade level or set of grade levels depends, of course, on the size of a school and the financial circumstances of the school district. However, it seems apparent that apportioning the responsibilities of student discipline and attendance, as well as some of the other administrative and supervisory tasks, among the administrators of the school is a desirable step toward improving the position of the assistant principal, and is consistent with the team concept described earlier.

In the final analysis, though, it is the principal who holds the key to the professional improvement, as well as the morale and satisfaction, of the person who occupies the position of assistant principal. [20] It is generally the principal who delegates to the assistant principal the latter's responsibilities, and it is the principal who provides whatever supervisory help, support, and recognition the assistant principal receives.

While in too many instances the principal still delegates to the assistant principal only those activities and responsibilities that he himself finds less desirable, most principals now seem to recognize that the assistant principalship must become more than just a "dumping ground" for those tasks that the principal doesn't want to handle. If an assistant principal is to become a truly viable member of the administrative team of a school, the principal must provide the kinds of responsibility, support, and recognition which will give the assistant principal an opportunity to make his maximal contribution and meet his professional and personal needs as well.

THE DEPARTMENT CHAIRMAN

A second important member of the administrative team of a school, more typically found at the secondary school level, is the department chairman, often referred to as the department head.

Like the position of assistant principal, the department chairmanship was created in response to increases in the managerial and supervisory functions of the school, but was also a result of the growth of departmentalization in the secondary schools. [21] Once secondary schools became departmentalized, the next logical step was the appointment of an individual to administer the department, and the position of the department chairman came into existence. Although the position is more prevalent in large schools and in departments such as English, social studies, math, and science, there are many schools in which there is a department head for every department in the school. Despite periodic predictions of its demise, the position continues to exist in the vast majority of secondary schools in the country.

Similar to the role and responsibilities of the assistant principal, those of the department head are no more or less than the principal defines them to be. Though often proposed by various educational authorities as a position of instructional leadership, [22] the department chairmanship in practice has frequently been grounded in the quicksand of administrative trivia, and handicapped by inadequate released time to carry out instructional improvement activities.

In many schools it is not uncommon for a department head to be provided with only one period of released time, and to be saddled with various kinds of administrative minutiae ranging from inventorying equipment and furniture, to administering a department's supplies and requisition procedures. This is unfortunate since a department chairman potentially can make a major contribution to the improvement of a school's instructional and curricular program because of the subject matter and methodological expertise of the individual occupying that position. However, before that potential can be realized, a school must define the nature of the position and sufficient released time must be provided so that the department head can more reasonably carry out his leadership responsibilities.

Developing a Job Description

The first step toward improving the position of department head in a school is to develop a comprehensive job description. [23] Sample job descriptions for the department chairman which appear to be comprehensive may be found in an excellent book by Callahan, *The Effective School Department Head.* [24]

To be functional, a job description should be developed cooperatively by those who will be working in the position and those who will be supervising and evaluating its occupants. In the case of the department chairmanship, this means that the department heads themselves should be directly involved with the principal in any process which leads to the revision of a job description already in use or the introduction of a new one. If the individuals who occupy the position of department chairman are to accept fully their responsibilities, then it is essential to obtain their involvement in defining those responsibilities.

Released Time and In-Service

While a department chairman's job description should meet the criterion of comprehensiveness, it cannot be considered a realistic role description unless he is provided with both sufficient time to carry out his responsibilities and in-service training to help him to acquire the knowledge and skills necessary to function as the educational leader of a department. [25] How much released time* should be provided for the department head is not an easy question to answer, but certainly one period is insufficient (except in very small departments) if the school really expects the chairman to function as the leader of a department.

It would appear that the chairman of a small department should be given at least one period of released time to carry out leadership responsibilities. In departments with more than six to eight teachers, two or three periods of released time should be provided, depending on the relative size of the department. [26] It is recognized that the administration of a school or school district must consider financial factors in deciding about released time. However, unless the department chairman is given adequate time, it is unrealistic to assume or expect that he can truly function as the educational leader of the department.

It should also be emphasized that providing sufficient released time will not, of itself, ensure that the chairmen will use the time wisely and productively. Most department heads are good teachers, and some of them are masters of the art. The vast majority of them, however, do not possess the background nor have they received the training necessary to function as educational leaders. [27] They may possess expertise in the methodology and content of their discipline, but they typically lack knowledge and skill in such areas as leadership, classroom supervision, human relations, and curriculum development and implementation. [28]

Before department chairmen will make a maximum contribution to the improvement of the school's educational programs, they will need to be involved in some type of in-service training in the areas just mentioned. Whether this training is conducted by the school district with university assistance or wholly by the school district is not important. What *is* important is that the school or school district provide department heads with *developmental* in-service programs that will help them to acquire the knowledge and skills they need to function as educational leaders. As with released time, the provision of an in-service program has financial implications. But until the department heads are given appropriate training for their responsibilities, they are unlikely to perform them effectively.

Problems

Poorly defined role descriptions, insufficient released time, small salary increment for increased responsibilities, and little or no in-service training

---

*Released time in this context is time beyond that given to the department chairman for class preparation.

for the position represent the major problems that many department heads experience. [29] However, an additional difficulty that is barely mentioned in the educational literature is the problem of role conflict. Role conflict is created when a person has incompatible expectations placed on him by two or more individuals or groups. In the case of the department head, he has expectations placed on him in regard to his behavior by both the principal and the teachers in the department. These expectations may be—and frequently are—incompatible, thereby creating role conflict for the department head.

For example, the teachers in a department typically regard the department chairman as their representative and expect him to be loyal to them and to promote their interests. The principal, on the other hand, is usually the one who has appointed or selected the chairman and consequently generally regards him as the administration's representative to the department, and expects that the chairman will be loyal and promote the administration's interests.

The problem for the department head arises, of course, when either the teachers or the principal wants something to which the other party is opposed. This kind of a situation occurs periodically in a school, particularly in the areas of teacher evaluation and budgeting for departmental needs. While the resolution of the problem can take several forms, depending on the circumstances and the personalities of the participants, there is research evidence to suggest that the loyalties of many chairmen lie first with the teachers of the department.

Cognetta found, for example, in his study of department heads, that a stronger relationship existed between the role expectations of the department head toward his responsibilities and his perception of the expectations of his departmental colleagues than between his role orientation and his perception of the expectations of the administration for his role. [30] In essence, this finding means that department heads may be more influenced by their perception of what the teachers expect them to do than by what the administration appears to want.

Although the study did not focus directly on the behavioral outcomes of a conflict in expectations for the department head between the teachers and the principal, the research data suggest that such a conflict would be resolved in favor of the teachers. This is most likely to occur under conditions in which the conflict in expectations is not highly visible to the administration, or the administrator lacks the authority or power to back up his own expectations for the role of the department head. In any event, it would appear that role conflict is a major and perhaps inescapable part of the job of the department chairman, and one about which the administrator needs to be more sensitive.

THE UNIT LEADER

In elementary schools which have been organized along multi-unit lines, the unit leaders in the building should be included on the school's administrative team.[31]

Each unit in a multi-unit elementary school is headed by a unit leader who is also a member of the instructional improvement committee of the school. Although the Wisconsin Research and Development Center, which originated the position, has stated that, " . . . the responsibility of the unit leader is instructional, not administrative or supervisory," they have gone on to say that "He serves as a liaison between the unit staff and the principal and consultants, and he coordinates the efficient utilization of the unit staff members, materials, and resources."[32] Since all of the latter tasks are administrative in nature, it is recommended that the unit leader be included in the administrative team at the elementary level.*

THE ADMINISTRATIVE TEAM AT THE DISTRICT LEVEL

Although our focus thus far has been on the concept of the administrative team at the building level, the idea originated at the district level, primarily in response to problems created by teacher militancy.[33]

Beginning in the late 1960s, administrators began to find themselves being squeezed out of teachers' organizations. At the same time, more and more pressure was being placed on administrators by both school boards and superintendents to decide whether they were management or "something else." This was not an easy decision for many administrators, who were concerned that the lines of difference between management and teachers were being drawn too rigidly. However, for most school administrators there was little choice: the teacher groups appeared to want them only on terms that were perceived as unfavorable by most administrators, and superintendents and school boards moved quickly to introduce the concept of the administrative team, which seemed to offer a logical or useful home base in the district.

OBJECTIVES OF THE DISTRICT ADMINISTRATIVE TEAM

The district administrative team appears to have two main objectives: (1) to develop and present a unified front in collective bargaining with teachers and in the implementation of the master contract, and (2) to utilize collectively

---

*For further information on the responsibilities of the unit leader, write the Wisconsin Research and Development Center, Madison, Wis. [34]

the talents and interests of individual administrators and supervisors to solve problems and improve education within the district. While writings on the concept of the district administrative team no longer emphasize the first objective, there is little doubt that it remains an important goal of most district teams.

However, the most important objective of an administrative team should be the second one. The full sense of what the achievement of this goal implies, at least to building administrators, was best stated in *Management Crisis: A Solution,* a booklet published by one of the national principals' associations: [35]

> An administrative team represents a means of establishing smooth lines of organization and communication, common agreements, and definite patterns of mutuality among administrators and the Board of Education as they unite to provide effective educational programs for the community. There are two primary parties involved in the leadership of a school district, namely, the board of education whose responsibility is policy-making, and the administrative team (including all administrators) whose major responsibilities include first advising the board in establishing district policies and then guaranteeing their effective implementation. A close, harmonious working relationship between these two parties is obviously vital to the successful operation of a school district.
>
> It should also be clear that an effective administrative team has, in addition to its assigned legalistic and primary role of policy implementation, a vital leadership function to perform. Never before has more interest and concern been raised about the need for strong and united educational leadership. An effective administrative team provides a collective means of strengthening school district leadership, giving individual administrators needed assistance, opportunities, and job satisfaction. [36]

COMPOSITION AND STRUCTURE OF THE DISTRICT ADMINISTRATIVE TEAM

A *district* administrative team should be composed of all of the principals and assistant principals in a district and all of the central office supervisors and administrators. [37] Department heads are not usually included in a district administrative team, nor are other individuals identified in a school's administrative team except as specifically mentioned in this section.

The district team is, of course, headed by the superintendent. While it is difficult to generalize, it seems clear that the other members of the team in many school districts are not of equal status, regardless of what the promotional literature about the team may suggest. Central office administrators, such as assistant superintendents and directors, seem to have greater status on the district administrative team than do principals, and principals seem to be accorded greater status on the team than supervisors. The hierarchical nature of a district administrative team does not mean, however, that the team cannot work together cooperatively and effectively *if* the status differences between the various members of the team do not inhibit or restrict input from the members of the team, and if each person on the team is given a role in which he can make useful contributions and from which he can derive adequate satisfaction.

PROBLEMS OF THE DISTRICT ADMINISTRATIVE TEAM

A building administrator has much to gain from and a great deal to contribute to the district administrative team. However, the team concept at the district level is not without its problems, according to the reports of principals. As implemented in some school districts, the administrative team has stifled creativity and initiative at the school building level, and has provided individual school administrators with little or no involvement in developing, as contrasted with implementing, school policies and procedures.

For example, the objective of some district administrative teams seems to be to promote uniformity in school curriculum, teaching, and rules and regulations among all of the schools of the district. Individual differences are frowned upon. School administrators who attempt to develop a different kind of curriculum for their students or who try to operate their schools in a somewhat different way than the other schools in the district are informed that they are not performing as team members should and that individuality is not desirable or possible under the team concept.

Of course, it should be noted that the issue of centralization and uniformity versus individualization and diversity is not a new problem in education. There has always been some tension, and sometimes a great deal, between the central administration and its desire to achieve district objectives with articulation and correlation among various schools, and the individual school administrator who seeks the autonomy to develop the best educational program possible for "his kids," even if that program differs from the educational program in the other schools of the district. However, the team concept, as it has been implemented in some school districts, has tended to accentuate this tension and has caused significant problems for some building administrators.

A different kind of problem, but an equally important one, which has confronted some school administrators who have tried to work cooperatively on the district administrative team, is their limited role.[38] Building administrators may be regarded by other members of the administrative team as only the implementers of school board policies and procedures. Frequently they are not given an adequate opportunity to participate fully in the development of recommended policies and procedures, and too often their involvement can be characterized as "too little, too late." It should be emphasized that this situation has been improving, and the limited involvement of principals on the district administrative team is certainly not characteristic of all districts. [39] But the establishing of an important role for themselves on the district administrative team continues to represent a significant problem for many building administrators.

Inadequate involvement has caused building administrators in a number of school districts, particularly larger ones, to organize themselves into collective bargaining units.[40] These units, composed primarily of middle management personnel, attempt to bargain with school boards and superintendents in regard to salaries and working conditions, trying in general to advance the professional and leadership role of middle management.

Since an administrators' collective bargaining unit in a school district tends to place the building administrators in a potential adversary relationship with the superintendent and the school board, the district administrative team has been advocated by many educators as a more constructive means of meeting the needs of building administrators for involvement in district decision making. [41] However, as McNally has perceptively observed, " . . . An administrative team's success depends above all on the existence of an atmosphere of mutual trust, cooperation, and open communication among team members." [42] Unless the superintendent and the school board can create and maintain this type of an atmosphere, it seems likely that building administrators will choose to organize a separate bargaining unit, rather than to become members of a district's administrative team.*

CRITERIA FOR EVALUATING THE DISTRICT ADMINISTRATIVE TEAM

While there are a number of important principles which should be followed in setting up and operating a district administrative team, the criteria presented in question form in figure 5.4 are offered to building administrators who are interested in evaluating the usefulness of a district team in terms of their own participation. The same criteria can be adapted for use in evaluating the administrative team at the building level.

*For description of an administrative team at the district level which seems to be working successfully see, Nolan Estes, "How Can We Make the Administrative Team Concept Come Alive?" An ERIC Report: Ed-077-097, 1973.

1. Are the roles and responsibilities of each member of the team, and of the team as a whole, clearly defined?
2. Does the team provide adequate involvement for all members in the development and evaluation of school and district objectives, policies, and procedures?
3. Does the team work on the problems that individual schools are experiencing, as well as on districtwide problems?
4. Does the team provide assistance and help, when needed, to the various members?
5. Do the team philosophy and objectives permit diversity and individual initiative when, in the eyes of the building administrator, such efforts would improve education in an individual school?
6. Is there periodic evaluation of team effectiveness?
7. Is there truly a spirit of good will and cooperation on the part of the various members of the team?

Figure 5.4. Criteria for Evaluating the District Administrative Team.

A FINAL NOTE

There is little doubt that the administrative team approach is potentially a valuable mechanism for facilitating cooperation among administrators, and for better utilizing their individual interests and talents. Whether that potential is realized or not, however, will depend in large part on the extent to which the concept is fully implemented in practice, and on the degree to which all members of the team strive to work together cooperatively in a spirit of mutual trust and confidence.

Review

1. Describe the purposes and functions of an administrative team.
2. Identify the factors that an administrator should consider in defining the composition and structure of an administrative team.
3. How can the administrator increase the effectiveness of team meetings?
4. Discuss the main duties and problems of the assistant principal. How can the problems perhaps be ameliorated?
5. What are the purposes, composition, and problems of the district administrative team? How can the problems be best solved?
6. How can an administrator determine the extent to which a district administrative team is making effective use of his potential contributions?

Notes

1. For a review of the origins of team management, see J. S. Swift, "Origins of Team Management," *National Elementary Principal* 50 (February 1971):26-35.

2. Kenneth A. Erickson and Robert L. Rose, *Management Teams in Educational Administration: Ideal? Practical? or Both?* (Eugene, Oreg.: Oregon School Study Council, 1973), p. 1.

3. For alternative approaches to defining the composition of the team, see Eddy J. Van Meter, "Alternative Team Approaches to Promote Educational Leadership." An ERIC Report: Ed-056-001, 1971.

4. For example, see William H. Jackson and Eugene E. Snyder, "Team Administration at Santa Barbara High School (California)," *Journal of Secondary Education* 46 (March 1971):127-30.

5. David A. Singer, Jr., "Staff Leadership Teams: Listen to Me! (Dammit!)" *Journal of Secondary Education* 46 (February 1971):79-82.

6. For a good description of the reasons for this approach, see Remsis Likert, *The Human Organization* (New York: McGraw-Hill Co., 1967).

7. For evidence of the merits of this approach, see Donald J. Weiss, "A Study of the Relationship of Participation in Decision-Making, Selected Personality Variables, and Job Satisfaction of the Educational Research and Development Council Elementary School Principals" (Ph.D. diss., University of Minnesota, 1968).

8. For an excellent discussion of the various administrative processes that are involved in operating a team outside of meetings, as well as during meetings, see Richard Wynn, *Theory and Practice of the Administrative Team* (Washington, D.C.: National Association of Elementary School Principals, National Association of Secondary School Principals, National Association of School Administrators, and National School Public Relations Association, 1973), pp. 23-35.

9. Although focused on the informal leader, an article by Bradford is well worth reading, as the topic of "hidden agenda" might apply to the principal and team meetings. See Leland P. Bradford, "The Case of Hidden Agenda," *National Elementary School Principal* 37 (October 1957):23-28.

10. Although some may associate the position of assistant principal primarily with the secondary school, it has long existed at the elementary level as well. For example, see Esther L. Schroeder, "The Status of the Assistant Principal in the Elementary School," in *The Elementary School Principalship: The Instructional and Administrative Aspects,* Fourth Yearbook of the Department of Elementary School Principals, ed. Arthur J. Gist (Washington, D.C.: National Education Association, 1925), pp. 389-400.

11. See R. Kindavatter and D. J. Tosi, "Assistant Principal: A Job in Limbo," *The Clearing House* 45 (April 1971), pp. 456-64. However, there are exceptions. An early noteworthy one is by George C. Kayte, *The Principal at Work* (Boston: Ginn & Co., 1941), pp. 369-78.

12. *The Assistant Principalship in Public Elementary Schools* (Washington, D.C.: National Association of Elementary School Principals, 1970).

13. David Austin, *The Assistant Principalship* (Washington, D.C.: National Association of Secondary School Principals, 1970), pp. 10-65.

14. Ibid., p. 5. (A more recent report suggests that the job of the assistant principal hasn't changed much. See, "What Does an Assistant Principal Do?" *Bulletin of the National Association of Secondary School Principals* 57 (October 1973):88-92.)

15. See Sheldon Winston, "Vice Principal: More than a Disciplinarian," *The Clearing House* 46 (September 1971):78-81.

16. Austin, *The Assistant Principalship,* p. 35.

17. The National Association of Secondary School Principals has conducted a number of conferences for assistant principals and is trying to upgrade the position.

18. Ibid., p. 72.

19. Jackson and Snyder, "Team Administration."

20. Frederick A. Bergmann, "The Relationship between Perceptions of Certain Administrators and Teachers of the Leadership Style of the Assistant Principal and Job

Satisfaction, Effectiveness and Confidence in Leadership" (Ph.D. diss., New York University, 1969).

21. An early report of this process can be found in Preston W. Search, "The Larger High Schools," *School Review* 8 (April 1900):225-27. For an early study of the position of department chairman, see Harlan C. Koch, "Some Aspects of the Department Headship in Secondary Schools," *School Review* 38 (April 1930):263-75.

22. For example, see Paul High, "The Supervisory Role of the Department Head," *The Clearing House* 40 (December 1965):213-15.

23. Robert L. Buser and William Humm, "The Department Head Revisited," *Journal of Secondary Education* 40 (October 1970):281-84.

24. Michael G. Callahan, *The Effective School Department Head* (West Nyack, N.Y.: Parker Publishing Co., 1971).

25. For an early recognition of this need, see Harl R. Douglass, *Modern Administration of Secondary Schools* (Boston: Ginn & Co., 1963), p. 14.

26. For evidence on the importance of adequate released time so that the department chairman can perform effectively as an instructional leader, see James A. Hoeh, "The Effectiveness of Department Chairman in the Improvement of Instruction" (Ph.D. diss., University of Michigan, 1969).

27. John J. McNelis, "An Investigation of the Function and Role and Characteristics of Department Chairmen in Selected School Systems throughout the United States as Perceived by Secondary School Principals" (Ed.D. diss., George Washington University, 1969).

28. See Hans G. Stern, "The Role of the Secondary School Department Head in the Improvement of Instruction" (Ed.D. diss., University of California—Los Angeles, 1966).

29. See Lewis M. Ciminillo, "The Department Heads' Perception of the Functions and Characteristics of Their Position" (Ed.D. diss., Indiana University, 1966).

30. Randall A. Cognetta, "The Relationship of Selected Organizational and Personal Variables to the Behavior of High School Department Heads" (Ed.D. diss., Stanford University, 1967).

31. The Multi-unit School was pioneered by the Research and Development Center at the University of Wisconsin, and its operation is now rather widespread. For more information about the multi-unit school, see Herbert J. Klausmeier, "The Multi-Unit Elementary School and Individually Guided Education," *Phi Delta Kappan* 53 (November 1971):181-84.

32. Herbert J. Klausmeier et al., *Individually Guided Education and the Multi-unit Elementary School* (Madison, Wis.: Wisconsin Research & Development Center, 1971), p. 31.

33. *The Administrative Team* (Washington, D.C.: American Association of School Administrators, National Association of Elementary School Principals, National Association of Secondary School Principals, and Association of School Business Officials, 1971).

34. Ibid., pp. 32-34.

35. *Management Crisis: A Solution* (Washington, D.C.: National Association of Secondary School Principals, 1971.)

36. Ibid., pp. 3-4.

37. For an earlier concept of the administrative team, which excluded building administrators, see *Profiles of the Administrative Team* (Washington, D.C.: American Association of School Administrators, 1971).

38. Paul B. Salmon, "Are the Administrative Team and Collective Bargaining Compatible?" *Compact* 6 (June 1972):3-5.

39. See, for example, B. Robert Anderson, "Administrative Team in Motion," *School Management* 17 (March 1973):19-20.

40. Daniel J. McGinley, "It's Working in Philadelphia," *National Elementary Principal* 53 (November/December 1973):26. See also Robert Yeager, "Administrators' Twin Teamster," *Nations Schools* 93 (February 1974):18-19.

41. George Redfern, "School Management: Administrator Union or Management Team?" An ERIC Report: Ed-061-611, 1972.

42. Harold J. McNally, "A Matter of Trust," *National Elementary Principal* 53 (November/December, 1973):23.

6

Organizing the School

Textbooks on school administration frequently include a description of proposed organizational patterns for the elementary and/or secondary school. However, typically lacking in such presentations is a discussion and analysis of the principles and problems associated with the actual organizing or reorganizing of a school. While it is desirable that an administrator familiarize himself with alternative organizational designs,* there are three reasons why it is essential that he become knowledgeable about the principles and problems involved in the organizing of a school: (1) the administrator may be called upon to develop an organizational plan in a new situation for which no organizational pattern has yet been designed, e.g., a new school; (2) he may want to evaluate or revise the organizational plan currently in operation in the school; and (3) he may want or be asked to evaluate and/or make recommendations regarding a proposed *new* plan or design.

Although it is true that few administrators will find themselves appointed to a new school, most administrators will encounter situations in which they are expected to evaluate their current organizational plan or a proposed one. Therefore, an understanding of the principles and problems of organizing a school would seem essential for every administrator.

PURPOSE, PROCESS, AND STRUCTURE

PURPOSE AND PROCESS

Schools are organized in order to facilitate the accomplishment of the objectives of efficient and effective teaching and learning. [1] The organizational plan or design of the school, then, is a means to an end: to achieve the school's objectives. As Urwick noted, ". . . The organization should only exist in order to carry out some specific purposes implicit in the forecast and

*For an overview of different organizational designs at the elementary school level, see Albert H. Schuster and Don Steward, *The Principal and the Autonomous Elementary School* (Columbus, Ohio: Charles E. Merrill Publishing Co., 1973), pp. 66-97. At the secondary school level, see Lester W. Anderson and Lauren A. Van Dyke, *Secondary School Administration* (Boston: Houghton Mifflin, 1972), pp. 75-102.

the plan. Every piece of it should make a definite and authorized contribution to that purpose." [2]

The administrator's responsibility is to organize people, tasks, and services in a way that will facilitate or best accomplish the objectives of the school. In carrying out this responsibility the administrator will be involved in organizing a number of programs within the school. Figure 6.1 identifies the major programs which may generally be found in most schools, and raises the basic organizational question for each program.

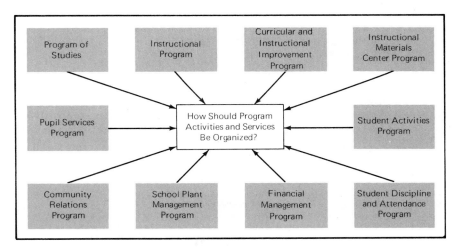

Figure 6.1. Major School Programs.

Although the nature of the programs in figure 6.1 may differ, the process of organizing them is essentially the same. It is one in which the administrator (with the assistance of relevant others) establishes formal structures of responsibility, authority, supervision, communication, and coordination for the people who staff the program so that certain tasks can be accomplished and particular school objectives can be achieved. [3] Figure 6.2 outlines sequentially the basic steps that an administrator should follow in organizing or reorganizing any program or activity.

An examination of figure 6.2 shows that the process of organizing involves the definition of tasks, resources, responsibilities, and relationships. The process also consists of the establishment and application of criteria for evaluating how well the organization of a program (i.e., the outcome of the process of organizing) functions relative to school goals. The organization of a program or activity, like any other facet of education, needs to be evaluated periodically if it is to improve.

1. Task Definition
2. Definition of Resource Needs and Time Parameters
3. Definition of Positions and Associated Responsibilities
4. Selection of Personnel and Assignment of Responsibilities
5. Specification of Authority Relationships
6. Specification of Supervisory Relationships
7. Specification of Communications Relationships
8. Identification of Coordination Needs
9. Establishment and Application of Evaluative Criteria

Figure 6.2. The Process of Organizing.

STRUCTURE

The final product of the process of organizing the programs listed in figure 6.1 is the creation of an overall *administrative design* for the school. The specific elements of the design may vary, depending on local conditions, but in many schools they will include the types of positions and committees identified in figure 6.3.

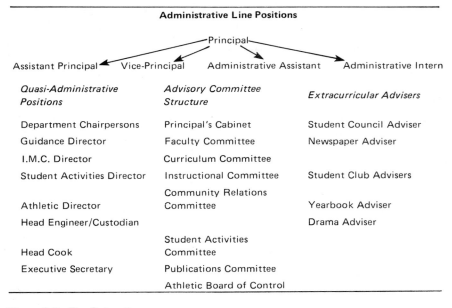

Administrative Line Positions

Principal

Assistant Principal — Vice-Principal — Administrative Assistant — Administrative Intern

Quasi-Administrative Positions	*Advisory Committee Structure*	*Extracurricular Advisers*
Department Chairpersons	Principal's Cabinet	Student Council Adviser
Guidance Director	Faculty Committee	Newspaper Adviser
I.M.C. Director	Curriculum Committee	
Student Activities Director	Instructional Committee	Student Club Advisers
Athletic Director	Community Relations Committee	Yearbook Adviser
Head Engineer/Custodian		Drama Adviser
Head Cook	Student Activities Committee	
Executive Secretary	Publications Committee	
	Athletic Board of Control	

Figure 6.3. The School's Administrative Design: Positions and Committees. [4]

Each of the positions and committees identified in figure 6.3 is usually established in order to organize more efficiently and effectively one or more of the various programs or services which the school provides. For that reason, then, the positions and committees represented in figure 6.3 constitute important components of the administrative design.

However, a school's administrative design does not merely identify various positions and committees. The total design includes the relationships between and among the positions and committees; these relationships are generally specified and depicted in an organizational chart. Figure 6.4 presents an example of an organizational chart at the elementary school

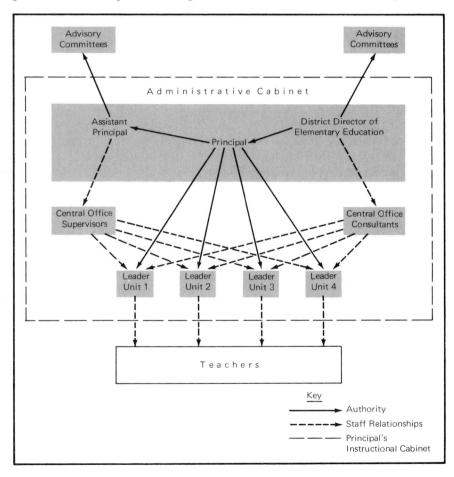

Figure 6.4. Elementary School's Organizational Chart.

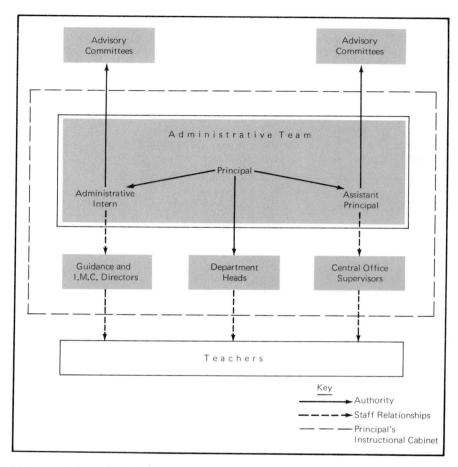

Figure 6.5. Secondary School's
Organizational Chart.

level; a secondary school's organization is charted in figure 6.5. Both examples are composites developed from a study of many different types of organizational charts and are intended to serve as illustrations rather than as prototypes.

It should be noted that an organizational chart may not identify all the administrative positions, committees, and interrelationships within a school.* However, in pictorializing the administrative design, the ad-

*An organizational chart may depict the formal organization of a school but will seldom reflect the school's *informal* organization. For a discussion of the informal organization and its relationship to the formal organization, see Richard A. Gorton, *Conflict, Controversy and Crisis in School Administration and Supervision.* (Dubuque, Iowa: Wm. C. Brown Company Publishers, 1972), chap. 13.

ministrator should address himself to two basic questions: (1) Does the organizational chart include the *important* aspects of the administrative design? and (2) Does the chart accurately reflect what is really happening in the school? The answers to these two questions will not be easy to validate, but they will determine the primary usefulness of any administrative chart. [5]

THE HUMAN ASPECTS OF ORGANIZING

Organizing the school involves (or, at least, *should* involve) more than identifying positions and defining relationships on an organizational chart. The most important factor that an administrator should consider in organizing a school are the *people* associated with it. Since they are the ones who will be occupying the various positions in the organizational design, it isn't likely to function very well unless it is sufficiently compatible with their needs.

INSTITUTIONAL EXPECTATIONS AND PERSONAL NEEDS

The goal of the administrator should be to formulate an organizational plan that will meet the expectations of the institution, i.e., the school, and also the needs of the people who are associated with the institution, e.g., teachers. Presented in figure 6.6 is a model which identifies the crucial variables that an administrator should consider, and their potential relationships.

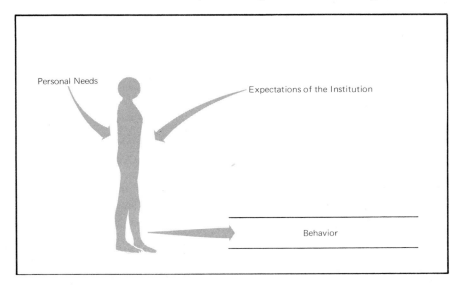

Figure 6.6. Two Major Factors which Influence An Individual's Behavior. [6]

As figure 6.6 indicates, the behavior of an individual (and by implication, that of a group) is influenced by two variables: institutional expectations and personal needs. *Institutional expectations* are those policies and responsibilities, defined by the school board and administration, which relate to an individual's role in the school. *Personal needs* are the inner feelings that an individual develops about a situation or about another person, which can affect the former's behavior. The model presented in figure 6.6 suggests that, if the expectations of an institution and the personal needs of an individual are in agreement, problems are not likely to occur; if these two variables are not compatible, conflict may arise.

Actually, in most school situations the expectations of the institution and the personal needs of an individual are seldom either in complete agreement or in total conflict. The goal of the administrator, however, should be to try to bring the two factors into as much congruence as possible. This means that in developing or revising an organizational design, the administrator should attempt to become aware of the personal needs of the people who will be occupying the different positions, and to utilize this information in defining roles and relationships.

Before attempting to become more aware of the needs of the people who will play a role in the administrative design of the school, the administrator should examine his preconception of those needs. McGregor believes that administrators hold one of two conceptions of employees, which he refers to as "Theory X" and "Theory Y." [7] School administrators who hold Theory X about employees perceive teachers as disliking responsibility and preferring to be led. Such administrators therefore develop an organizational design which takes those characteristics into consideration. Theory Y administrators, on the other hand, believe that most people possess the potential for responsibility and independence, and it is the job of management to develop an administrative design which will realize that potential.

Probably few administrators are purely one type or another. However, it seems likely that most administrators possess some type of preconception about the needs of their employees. Rather than relying on that preconception, an administrator should also take into consideration research on the needs of people.

For example, Trusty and Sergiovanni, utilizing an adapted model of Maslow's needs theory, discovered in a study of teachers that esteem, autonomy, and self-actualization were the greatest needs the teachers felt. [8] This finding is consistent with data collected by Corwin, who found that teachers tended to desire autonomy, professional esteem, and self-actualization opportunities and resisted organizational expectations which emphasized standardization of work, job specialization, and centralized decision making. [9] (The latter characteristics, however, may be intrinsic to any institution, such as the school, which is organized along bureaucratic lines.) [10] Further research on the needs of teachers is reported in chapter 9, Administrator Staff Relations.

It should be pointed out that some observers, such as Argyris, have advanced the thesis that the expectations of the institution appear to be inherently in conflict with the personal needs of the individual. [11] Whether or not this is true, however, would seem to depend on the extent to which an administrator takes into consideration the personal needs of people when he develops or revises the school's organizational design. The goal in this regard should be to provide an organizational structure which will humanize the school by accommodating as much as possible the personal needs of the people who are associated with it. [12]

While the administrator is not the only one who should be striving to humanize the school, he certainly is a key figure. As Barnes noted in reporting on a study conducted by the University of Texas Research and Development Center, "More than anyone else the principal created the climate in which [the teachers] taught; he set the limits, handed out rewards and punishments, and most important, constructed the invisible value and power structures of the school." [13] The administrator can make a major contribution to the humanizing of the school by taking into consideration the personal needs of those who are associated with it.

The key questions which the administrator must ask, according to Erickson, are,

> Am I willing to risk being authentic and honest? Am I willing to receive criticism without getting defensive? Am I willing to really listen to the ideas of others around me? Am I threatened if a staff member displays more insight into a problem than I? Do I need to feel superior to other individuals around me? Do I realize that any or all others may see the world differently than I? Am I really willing to work together with others to solve different management problems? [14]

Until the administrator answers these questions satisfactorily, he is not likely to take into consideration sufficiently the needs of others in the development of the administrative design and a humane school.

INFORMAL ORGANIZATION

There is evidence suggesting that, if the administrator fails to consider personal needs sufficiently in developing the formal organization of the school, the people who are associated with the school (students, teachers, and others) will develop their own *informal* organization in order to meet those needs. Several writers, including Griffiths, [15] Iannacconne, [16] and Gorton, [17] have described the informal organization of the school and have discussed its effects on school personnel. Essentially, the informal organization usually consists of a network of interpersonal associations which grow out of the social contacts and interactions of those members of the formal organization who share common responsibilities, problems, interests, or other personal characteristics. Examples of the informal organization are the small group of teachers who always eat lunch together and discuss school problems, or the school secretary and the librarian who belong to the same bowling team and exchange gossip about "what is going on in school."

The impact of the informal organization can be harmless and even therapeutic, or it can be negative and pernicious. [18] If it provides people with an opportunity for needed socializing, communication, or problem solving that the formal organization doesn't facilitate, then the informal organization can make a positive contribution. On the other hand, if the informal organization thwarts the implementation of administrative policy, restricts the productivity of individuals or groups, or generates dissatisfaction, it can exert a decidedly negative effect. It would appear from various studies reviewed by the writers mentioned above, that the informal organization has potential for both positive and negative influence. Therefore, the task of the administrator is to become more aware of the operation of the informal organization in the school, and to try to capitalize on its positive aspects, while minimizing its negative effects.*

PROPOSED CRITERIA FOR EVALUATING AN ORGANIZATIONAL DESIGN

There is no shortage of ideas for organizing or reorganizing the different aspects of the elementary or secondary school. Organizational plans such as The Administrative Team, Differentiated Staffing, Team Teaching, The Curriculum Associate Structure, The Unitized School, and others have been proposed in recent years and now, almost yearly, one or more new proposals for reorganizing some aspect of the school program is offered. [19] Although many textbooks on administration describe and, in some cases, recommend several of these major approaches to organizing the school, the intent of this section is to identify and discuss briefly some specific criteria by which the administrator can evaluate current or proposed plans for organizing the school. Armed with these criteria, the administrator should be better able to diagnose strengths and shortcomings in an organizational plan, and should be able to determine whether the current design of the school needs revision.

In examining either the school's current organizational plan or a proposal for reorganizing the school, the administrator should attempt to seek answers to the following questions:

*For help in this regard, see Richard A. Gorton, *Conflict, Controversy and Crisis in School Administration.* (Dubuque, Iowa: Wm. C. Brown Company Publishers, 1972), pp. 342-48.

1. **What are the objectives of the current or proposed organizational plan? What is it trying to achieve? Will the plan improve learning and teaching in the school?**

   The most important question an administrator can ask about any organizational plan, current or proposed, is, "What is it trying to achieve?" Organizational plans are usually justified on the grounds of being more efficient or representing a better utilization of people than alternative approaches. These are not unimportant considerations. However, an administrator should also attempt to ascertain the specific ways in which an organization plan will improve teaching and/or student learning.

   Teaching and the resultant learning are the main responsibilities of the school, and any organization plan should ultimately justify its worth on the basis of the degree to which it improves or facilitates these two functions. In addition, it would be well for the administrator to ask how the organizational plan is or will be affecting the attitudes of those who are associated with the school. An organizational plan which is not acceptable to the majority of the students or the professional personnel in a school will probably not operate successfully over a long period of time, even though it may seem like a good organizational plan in other respects.

2. **To what extent are the responsibilities of each position and committee in the organizational plan clearly, accurately, and fully described and understood by all concerned?**

   Positions or committees, once identified in an organizational plan, should be defined in terms of the responsibilities or tasks which need to be performed. For example, the terms "team leader," and "director of the instructional materials center," are not self-explanatory regarding the duties of the holders of the positions. Although an individual appointed to one of these positions may already have a *general* idea of what he is to do, based on the title of the position and tradition or practice, the specific responsibilities of the position should be explicitly and completely defined for all concerned.

   The specification of the responsibilities of each position and committee is particularly crucial in the case of proposed new approaches to organizing a school. Frequently, it is only from examining the specific responsibilities associated with each position or committee that an administrator can ascertain how a proposed organizational plan is supposed to operate. In addition, if the occupant of a new position is to make a desired contribution to achieving the objectives of the organizational plan, he must understand fully the responsibilities which are associated with the position.

Also, evaluation of a person occupying a new position becomes very difficult if the responsibilities of the position are poorly defined or communicated.

3. **Are the authority and supervisory relationships between positions or individuals clearly, accurately, and fully described and understood by all concerned?**

Most organizations operate on the basis of line and staff relationships.* Although the concepts of line and staff can be complex, they essentially involve the important questions of who is over whom, and who supervises whom in an organizational plan.

For example, people who are involved in an organizational design need to know the nature and scope of their own authority over others, and those subordinate to that authority also need to know and understand its nature and scope. In most schools' organizational plans, however, the question of authority is frequently not clearly defined. [20] The authority of an individual occupying a certain position may be implied by his location on an organizational chart, but the nature and scope of that authority is seldom explicated. As a consequence, authority is sometimes exercised when the basis for it is nonexistent or misunderstood, or there may be a failure to exercise authority when it *should* be employed.

A similar problem can occur in connection with a lack of specification of the staff supervisory relationships between people. The administrator needs to ask himself, "Do the people who are supervising and those who are to be supervised understand adequately the nature and scope of the responsibilities of the former?" It is particularly important that the supervisory responsibilities be specified in the case of new positions or in situations where supervision has not traditionally been associated with the position, e.g., unit leaders, department heads. Unless the nature and scope of the supervisory responsibilities of all positions in an organizational plan are made explicit to both those who are to supervise and those who are to be supervised, effective supervision will be hampered.

4. **Are the lines of communication between and among positions and committees clearly, accurately, and fully described and understood by all concerned?**

In assessing an organizational plan the administrator needs to ascertain whether the plan specifies who is supposed to communicate with whom. [21]

---

*For an excellent discussion of the theory and the criticisms of line and staff organizations, see Daniel E. Griffiths et al., *Organizing Schools for Effective Education* (Danville, Ill.: Interstate Printers, 1962), pp. 23-28.

Communication should be vertical, horizontal, and reciprocal in an organizational design. It should be vertical, in that the plan should designate desired communication lines between an individual (such as the vice-principal) and the people who are subordinate to him. The communication should be horizontal in that the organizational plan should specify desired lines of communication among individuals occupying the same level of position, e.g., among department heads or unit leaders.

And in the case of either vertical or horizontal communication, it should be reciprocal, that is, it should be made clear that communication can be initiated by any of the individuals who are linked to each other in a communication network, rather than by only one person. This is especially important in a hierarchical organization such as the school, where there is always a potential danger that communication will be only one way: from superior to subordinate.

Whether or not any of these kinds of communication lines function as intended will depend, at least in part, on whether they have been specified in the organizational plan and are understood and accepted. [22] For example, if the organizational chart fails to indicate desired communication among department heads or unit leaders in regard to common problems and approaches to situations, it may occur only sporadically at best. It is true that there may be some informal conversation between these persons in any case, and the mere specification of communication lines will not guarantee that the desired communication will actually occur. But the place to begin, in trying to promote and facilitate communication among individuals is in the organizational plan, where channels of communication should be clearly identified.

5. **Is there adequate coordination between people, and among tasks and programs?**

Coordination has already been discussed as an important administrative process. The administrator should in his examination of a current or proposed organizational plan, attempt to identify any potential or actual, unnecessary overlap or omission in positions, duties, and program services. Perhaps two or more individuals occupying the same position are performing a function which should be carried out by only one of them. Or, two individuals, e.g., guidance counselor and school psychologist, may be offering similar services to the same party, the student, and their efforts may need to be interrelated so that they complement and supplement each other rather than conflict or duplicate. Essentially, what the administrator should be trying to do in providing adequate coordination in the organizational plan is to connect or relate people, tasks, and services so that they strengthen one another and avoid unnecessary duplication or omission. [23]

6. **To what extent are the physical facilities, secretarial help, supplies, and time adequate to perform the responsibilities identified in the organizational plan?**

The administrator will probably find that the vast majority of organizational plans do not address themselves sufficiently to this question. Most organizational plans are long on supporting rationale, but tend to ignore or pass over lightly some of the conditions necessary to implement the plan successfully. For example, if a school is to have learning coordinators as part of an instructional improvement plan, the plan should specify the type of office space the coordinators will receive, the degree of secretarial help to which they will have access, the amount of supplies that will be provided for them, and the extent of released time that will be assigned for carrying out their responsibilities. Any organizational plan that does not identify and define these conditions for each of its positions or committees is deficient.

Although current as well as proposed organizational plans should identify the resources needed for implementation, this identification is particularly important for the latter. Unless a proposed plan clearly identifies the extent to which physical facilities, secretarial help, supplies, and released time will be provided for the people occupying positions or serving on committees, it will be difficult if not impossible to determine in advance whether or not the new plan will work. A proposed plan may be sound in theory and rationale, but unless it provides for certain conditions related to its implementation, the plan may not be successful in its operation.

7. **To what degree does the organizational plan take into consideration the personal needs of the individuals who are a part of the plan?**

The importance of this question was discussed earlier in the chapter. In the final analysis, the success of any organizational plan will depend largely on the abilities and personalities of those who are responsible for implementing it. An organizational design may look good on paper. But if it has not taken into consideration the personal needs of those people who will be carrying out the plan, it will be critically deficient. An important aspect of the assessment of any organizational plan, then, is the determining of the degree to which the personal needs of the individuals associated with the plan have been accommodated.*

*An instrument which could help in the assessment is *The School Organizational Development Questionnaire,* designed by David J. Mullen and Thomas M. Goolsby, Jr., and described in an Eric Report: Ed-089-431, 1974.

8. **To what degree does the organizational plan provide for the in-service training of new people appointed to an established position, or the appointment of current staff members to a new position?**

Individuals usually must receive training before they can competently carry out their assigned responsibilities. People new to a position, such as department heads, may have already received some training for their responsibilities while in college, but in many instances this training will not be sufficient, and further work will be needed.

The provision of training for people who are to occupy positions in a *proposed* organizational plan is also important. Typically the individuals who will staff these new positions, such as team leaders or unit leaders, will not have been trained for their responsibilities in college or elsewhere. If they are to perform their new responsibilities successfully, they will need in-service training. Therefore, the administrator should examine any proposed new plan to ascertain the degree to which it provides adequate in-service training for those individuals who are to carry out new responsibilities.

9. **Does the organizational plan provide some means by which the achievement of or progress toward its objectives can be evaluated?**

Every administrator should be concerned about whether the current organizational plan is working or whether a proposed one would work better. But he will be unable to arrive at that determination unless the objectives of the current or proposed plan are defined in such a way that evaluation is possible.

Even if this task has been accomplished, however, evaluation may not occur unless the organizational plan specifies some means by which assessment of effectiveness or success can take place. Student achievement testing, teacher observation and rating, interviews, questionnaires, and systematic observations are all examples of possible techniques for measuring the effectiveness of an organizational plan. [24] The evaluation procedure which should be used will depend, of course (among other things), on its availability and the nature of the organizational design. But the important thing is for the administrator to recognize that any organizational plan should provide a method by which its effectiveness can be measured periodically.

Most of the emphasis in discussing criteria for evaluating an organizational plan has focused on assessing the merits of a *proposed* plan. Needless to say, those same criteria can and should be applied to the assessment of the present organizational plan in operation in the school. Too frequently new proposals are subjected to a more rigorous evaluation than that accorded the traditional design. Both should be examined by the administrator to ascertain the extent to which they meet the criteria discussed in this section.

SYMPTOMS OF A POORLY FUNCTIONING ORGANIZATIONAL PLAN

At this point the reader may well inquire, "But aren't there any shortcuts to applying the recommended criteria? Are there any symptoms, for example, that might indicate that the current organizational plan isn't functioning as well as it should be?"

Actually, there are certain symptoms or indications which suggest deficiencies in a school's *current* organizational plan. These are presented in figure 6.7.

Symptoms	Possible Deficiencies
1. People don't seem to know what the program or the committee or their position is supposed to achieve ultimately.	No clearly defined objectives.
2. People are uncertain as to what they are supposed to do.	Lack of specification as to position or committee function and responsibilities.
3. People are uncertain about to whom they should turn for help or for a specific decision.	Inadequately defined supervisory relationships.
4. There is interpositional or departmental conflict about who is subordinate to whom.	Inadequately defined authority relationships.
5. There is little or no communication between people occupying different positions or serving on different committees.	Malfunctioning or nonexistent horizontal, vertical, and reciprocal lines of communication.
6. People do not know what others are doing; there is duplication of efforts on some tasks, while other tasks are neglected.	Lack of coordination between positions, committees, or departments, with respect to responsibilities and services.
7. Responsibilities and tasks are not fully carried out.	Inadequate released time, secretarial help, physical facilities, supplies, or in-service training.
8. No one seems to have a very good idea about whether or not the organizational plan is working effectively.	Absence of or failure to implement a means by which the effectiveness of the plan can be evaluated.

Figure 6.7. Diagnosing a Poorly Functioning Organizational Plan. [26]

It should be pointed out that these symptoms of poor organization may not be easily visible to the administrator. No administrator likes to think that the school's organizational plan is deficient in some respect, and therefore he may not be looking for weaknesses. But since the people who are involved in the organization may not believe that it is in their best interest to inform the administrator about their dissatisfaction, he will need to take the initiative in probing for the kinds of symptoms presented in figure 6.7, if he is to pinpoint inadequacies in the current organizational plan. [25]

IMPROVING AN ORGANIZATIONAL PLAN

In the two foregoing sections criteria for evaluating an organizational plan were discussed, and symptoms were presented which suggest possible deficiencies in a plan. Armed with this kind of knowledge, the administrator should be at a point where he is prepared to take specific action to improve some aspect of the school's organizational design. What that action should be will depend, of course, on the particular deficiencies that the administrator discovers in the organizational plan of the school when he applies the criteria previously discussed. However, typically the administrator, with the help of relevant others, will be involved in one or more of the following actions in improving a school's organizational plan:

1. Rethinking and revising the objectives of the school's organizational plan, so that they are directly related to the improvement of teaching and learning, and are stated in such a way as to make evaluation of the achievement of the objectives more feasible.
2. Making sure that the objectives of the organizational plan are adequately understood by the people who function as a part of the plan or who are affected by it.
3. Defining more completely and specifically the responsibilities and function of the different positions and committees included in the organizational plan.
4. Rethinking and further specifying the authority, supervisory, and coordination relationships between and among positions, committees, and programs.
5. Defining more explicitly and completely the communication lines among positions and committees in the organizational plan.
6. Reexamining the need for additional or improved in-service training, physical facilities, secretarial help, supplies, and released time for those people participating in the organizational plan, and making whatever provisions seem appropriate and possible.
7. Instituting some means by which the effectiveness of the organizational plan can be evaluated on a systematic and regular basis.

A FINAL NOTE

Initiation of the actions previously recommended should result in a more effective organizational plan. However, improving the plan will not be an easy task. It is unlikely to occur unless the administrator can work cooperatively with important others in the school (such as the faculty) and constructively utilize their insights to improve the plan. It is also unlikely to result unless the administrator and those with whom he works are willing to devote considerable time, effort, and thought to the various steps that have been recommended in this chapter. And finally, improvement of the plan will probably not occur unless the administrator himself takes the initiative to begin examining and involving other people in an evaluation of the school's organizational plan. The administrator is the one who must lead the way, and no organizational plan is likely to be improved significantly unless he assumes this important responsibility.

Review

1. Why should an administrator be knowledgeable about principles and problems of organizing a school?
2. Define the purpose and process of organizing.
3. Discuss the factors an administrator should consider in regard to the "human aspects" of organizing.
4. What are the symptoms of a poorly functioning organizational plan? How can an administrator improve an organizational plan?

Notes

1. Charles E. Bidwell, "The School as a Formal Organization," in *Handbook of Organizations*, ed. James March (Chicago: Rand McNally & Co., 1965).

2. L. Urwick, *The Elements of Administration* (New York: Harper & Brothers, 1943), p. 42.

3. This definition of organizing is an extension of one proposed by Luther Gulick, "Notes on the Theory of Organization," in *Papers on the Science of Administration*, ed. Luther Gulick and L. Urwick (New York: Institute of Public Administration, 1937), p. 13.

4. For a description of a rather comprehensive administrative structure, see Catherine Hopper and William Hansen, "A Changing School," *Bulletin of the National Association of Secondary School Principals* 56 (February 1972):48-49. An interesting discussion of a rather innovative administrative design at the elementary level is presented by Arthur Blumberg et al., "The Elementary School Cabinet: Report of an Experience in Participative Decision-Making," *Educational Administration Quarterly* 5 (Autumn 1969):39-52.

5. A penetrating criticism of the accuracy and completeness of organizational charts may be found in Stephen Knezevich, *Administration of Public Education* (New York: Harper & Row, Publishers, 1975), pp. 52-54.

6. Figure 6.6 is adapted from Jacob W. Getzels and Egon G. Guba, "Social Behavior in the Administrative Process," *School Review* 65 (Winter 1957):423-41.

7. Douglas McGregor, *The Human Side of Enterprise* (New York: McGraw-Hill, 1958), pp. 16-90.

8. Francis M. Trusty and Thomas J. Sergiovanni, "Perceived Need Deficiencies of Teachers and Administrators," *Educational Administration Quarterly* 2 (1966):168-80.

9. Ronald Corwin, "Professional Persons in Public Organizations," *Educational Administration Quarterly* 1 (Autumn 1965):1-22.

10. Lloyd Bishop and Julius George, "Organizational Structure: A Factor Analysis of Structural Characteristics of Public Elementary and Secondary Schools," *Educational Administration Quarterly* 9 (Autumn 1973):66-80.

11. Chris Argyris, "Individual Actualization in Complex Organizations," *Mental Hygiene* 44 (April 1960):226-37.

12. Ralph H. Ojemann, "Humanizing the School," *National Elementary Principal* 50 (April 1971):62-65. Also see *Bulletin of the National Association of Secondary School Principals* 56 (February 1972).

13. Melvin W. Barnes, "Administrator's Role in Humanizing the School," *National Elementary Principal* 49 (February 1970):38.

14. Kenneth A. Erickson, *Humaneness . . . Essential for Successful Management* (Eugene, Oreg.: Oregon Study Council, 1974), pp. 1-2.

15. Daniel E. Griffiths, *Human Relations in School Administration* (New York: Appleton-Century-Crofts, 1956), pp. 317-25.

16. Lawrence Iannaccone, "An Approach to the Informal Organization of the School," in *Behavioral Science and Educational Administration,* ed. Daniel E. Griffiths (Chicago: University of Chicago Press, 1964), pp. 233-42.

17. Richard A. Gorton, "The School as an Informal Organization," in *Conflict, Controversy and Crisis in School Administration and Supervision* (Dubuque, Iowa: Wm. C. Brown Company Publishers, 1972), chap. 13.

18. Ibid., pp. 341-47.

19. See ERIC Clearing House on Educational Administration, "Alternative Organizational Forms: Analysis of Literature and Selected Bibliography," An ERIC Report: Ed-043-111 (1970).

20. For an excellent discussion of the problems that this can create, see Amitai Etzioni, *Modern Organizations* (Englewood Cliffs, N.J.: Prentice-Hall, 1964).

21. A good example of a method for establishing whether or not this has been accomplished can be found in a report by Howard H. Greenbaum, "The Appraisal of Organizational Communication Systems." An ERIC Report: Ed-067-708 (1972).

22. For an excellent analysis and discussion of communication patterns within a school, see W. W. Charters, Jr., "Stability and Change in the Communication Structure of School Faculties," *Educational Administration Quarterly* 5 (Autumn 1969):15-38.

23. For additional discussion of the principles and problems of coordination in a formal organization, see W. W. Charters, Jr., "An Approach to the Formal Organization of the School," in *Behavioral Science and Educational Administration,* ed. Daniel E. Griffiths (Chicago: University of Chicago Press, 1964), chap. 11.

24. A good source of ideas and techniques for evaluating the effectiveness of a school's organizational design is Richard A. Schmuck's *Handbook of Organization Development in Schools* (Eugene, Oreg.: University of Oreg. Center for the Advanced Study of Educational Administration, 1972).

25. See J. L. Hurwitz et al., "Some Effects of Power on the Relations between Group

Members," in *Group Dynamics in Research and Theory,* ed. Darwin Cartwright and Alvin Zander (New York: Harper & Row, Publishers, 1960), pp. 800-809.

26. For an excellent elaboration of some of these inadequacies, see Willard R. Lane et al., *Foundations of Educational Administration: A Behavioral Analysis* (New York: Macmillan Publishing Co., 1967), chaps. 8-9.

7
Budget and
Plant Management

In most discussions concerning the role of the school administrator primary emphasis is placed on the educational leadership aspects of the position. Budget and facilities management, if mentioned at all, frequently receive only cursory attention. Yet, efficient and effective administration of the school budget and plant can often mean the difference between leadership envisioned and leadership realized. Although an administrator may possess worthwhile ideas for improving the school's educational program, little will be accomplished without an understanding of budget and facilities management.

BUDGET MANAGEMENT

A short but useful definition of the budget is ". . . the blueprint of what the educational program will be and what it will cost."[1] The school administrator's role in relation to the budget consists of three tasks: (1) developing the budget, (2) administering the budget, and (3) evaluating the efficiency and effectiveness of the services and products funded by the budget. A discussion of the concepts, practices, and problems associated with each of these tasks will follow.

DEVELOPING THE BUDGET

The school administrator's role in developing a budget may be a limited or an important one, depending on the degree to which the budget process in the school district is centralized.[2] In a centralized budget process the school administrator's responsibility is typically restricted to reporting to the district office data relative to the number of students and teachers who will be assigned to the school for the following year, and the extent to which capital improvements are needed for the building. The central office of the district then develops the budget for each school based on preëstablished formulae which determine the allocations for the various budget categories.[3] For example, the district budget formula for library books may be $1.50 for each student enrolled in a school. Thereby, a school of 750 students would receive a budget allocation of $1,125 for the purchase of library books, whereas a school of 1,000 would receive $1,500.

Under a centralized budget building process, the role of the school administrator is a very limited one. However, the advantages of this approach are that the allocation criteria are applied objectively and evenly, and the development of the budget proceeds efficiently.

In a *decentralized* budget process the administrator is assigned responsibility for developing the budget for the school, based on the unique characteristics of the students and/or the educational program in the building.[4] In this budget approach, the administrator is encouraged to involve teachers, parents, and even students in developing the budget for the school.* Each of these groups may be requested to identify and define their needs relative to the replacement and/or addition of products and services. Throughout the process there is emphasis on involving a wide variety of people and developing a budget which will reflect the unique needs of a particular school.

Although a budget developed under a decentralized process is seldom accepted without some changes by the district administration, proponents of this budgeting process generally feel that it is more likely to reflect the needs of each school than is a centralized approach. It is also argued that the greater involvement of teachers, parents, and students which is encouraged under a decentralized method capitalizes on their insights and helps them to understand the problems and parameters of budget building. The disadvantage of a decentralized budget process, according to Candoli and associates, is that it may result in a situation in which, "Each school becomes a small kingdom within itself and cooperative efforts among and between schools can become difficult."[5]

Of course, the budget-building process in many schools is neither totally decentralized nor centralized, but a combination of the two. For example, one pattern is for the central office to determine the initial budget allocations for each school, based on preëstablished formulae, but give each administrator an opportunity to present a case for *raising* the budget allocation to accommodate any specific category for the school. The salient advantage of this budget system is that it establishes a degree of equity among schools in terms of budget allocations, while providing for additional financial support for any school which can demonstrate that due to certain conditions or circumstances it merits a higher budget allocation than the district standard formula allows. The disadvantages of this method are that (1) the budget is still formulated largely on the basis of central office's assumptions about the needs of each school rather than on an assessment by the people at the building level, and (2) there is a tendency for building administrators to accept the district office's determination of their budgets, in order to avoid the

---

*For a good example of this type of an approach, see Nolan Estes, "Operation 'Citizen Involvement' Spells Help for School Challenges" *Educational Leadership* 31 (January 1974): 365-68.

arguments and "hassles" which may be required to secure a higher budget allocation for their schools.

It should be noted that any budget process will have disadvantages as well as advantages, and the only purpose of this analysis is to explore several alternatives.

PPBS

A relatively new approach to budget building about which the school administrator should be knowledgeable is PPBS: Planning, Programming, Budgeting System.[6] This budgetary concept, borrowed from the U.S. Department of Defense and private industry, promises to revolutionize school budgeting. Simply defined, PPBS is ". . . a management tool that can be used to plan and arrange a district's activities and resources."[7] While traditional approaches to budgeting also emphasize planning and programming, these budgeting processes are not organized to the same degree around programs and program objectives as are those in PPBS.* Nor is evaluation emphasized to the same extent.

Perhaps the best way for the school administrator to understand PPBS is to compare this budget process with the traditional approach and to see an example of how the budget is organized under each. Figure 7.1 presents an outline of the process of PPBS along with the traditional approach.

PPBS	**The Traditional Approach**
Stages:	Stages:
1. Assess educational needs.	1. Ascertain teacher needs in the areas of supplies, books, etc.
2. Define educational objectives and the criteria and methods to be used in evaluating the objectives.	2. Determine the merits of teachers' budget requests on the basis of perceived need.
3. Determine programs and priorities to achieve objectives.	3. Estimate the cost of teacher requests.
4. Ascertain and cost-estimate the resources needed to carry out programs	4. Organize the budget around categories of needs, e.g., instructional supplies, books, etc.
5. Organize the budget around program areas and objectives.	

Figure 7.1. PPBS vs. the Traditional Approach: The Process[10]

*Recently the new budget process has been referred to as PPBS, PPBES (Planning, Programming, Budgeting, Evaluating System), and ERMS (Educational Resources Management System). The latter term and concept (ERMS) are used most typically by school business managers. An important book prepared by the research staff of the Association of School Business Officials entitled, *Educational Resources Management System,* is recommended reading for all school administrators. (It is published by the Research Corporation of the Association of School Business Officials, Chicago, 1971.)

As one can see by comparing the two approaches shown in figure 7.1, PPBS places a much greater emphasis on defining and evaluating program objectives and on relating the funds which the school purportedly needs to the achievement of those objectives, rather than to the nature of the items being funded. For an example of how the budget is organized and presented under the two approaches, see figures 7.2 and 7.3.

Although PPBS appears to represent a more logical and effective method of budget building, it is not without its limitations. Experience has shown that the process can be extremely time-consuming. Also, it places an emphasis on relating budget allocations to definable objectives and defining certain educational objectives has proved to be a difficult and frustrating task.[8] Still, when one considers both the advantages and disadvantages, it would seem that PPBS offers the school administrator a very good conceptual tool for the budget building process.[9]

School _____ Date _____

Current Enrollment _____ Anticipated Enrollment _____

Resources Needed

	Account No.	Current Costs	Projected Costs
Personnel Certified	_____	_____	_____
Personnel Noncertified	_____	_____	_____
Instructional Supplies	_____	_____	_____
Noninstructional Supplies	_____	_____	_____
Capital Equipment	_____	_____	_____
Maintenance	_____	_____	_____
Food Services	_____	_____	_____
Transportation	_____	_____	_____

Figure 7.2. Traditional Budget Format: An Example. [11]

Program Title _____ Program Level _____ Program No. _____

For period beginning _____ and ending _____

Program objective(s) _____ (The space on this form is less than _____

_____ would be needed in actual practice) _____

Program Description _____

_____

Program Criteria and Evaluation Methods _____

_____

_____

Anticipated Enrollment _____ Personnel Assigned _____

_____

_____

Resource Requirements	Current Year	Next Year	Following Year	Following Year
Salary and Teacher Fringe Benefits	_____	_____	_____	_____
Supporting Staff	_____	_____	_____	_____
Textbooks	_____	_____	_____	_____
Supplies	_____	_____	_____	_____
A.V.	_____	_____	_____	_____
Maintenance	_____	_____	_____	_____
Capital	_____	_____	_____	_____
Other	_____	_____	_____	_____

Figure 7.3. Example of a PPBS Format.[12]

PROBLEMS OF BUDGET BUILDING*

Since the school administrator's responsibility in the budget-building process is greater when a decentralized approach is utilized, it would be advisable for him to be aware of problems he might encounter in implementing this method. These problems are not necessarily inherent in the decentralized approach to budget building, nor do they occur in all schools, but they may arise if the administrator fails to take certain safeguards. These problems, and recommended precautionary measures, fall into several areas.

Budget Requests Based on Acquisitiveness or Lack of Knowledge

The school administrator who involves teachers and others in the budget-building process will sometimes receive budget requests from people who don't actually need what they are requesting, or who don't know very much about the item that they are requesting or how they are going to use it. For example, the administrator may receive a request from a grade-level chairman who would like an additional typewriter which would be used by six teachers who already have access to two other typewriters. Or, the administrator may receive a request from the math teachers to include in the next year's budget a computer terminal which would be installed in one of the mathematics classrooms. In this case the math teachers may be convinced about the educational value of a computer terminal but may lack the knowledge or skills for effectively utilizing the computer terminal in the math program.

One of the best safeguards for preventing problems of acquisitiveness or lack of knowledge from affecting the budget process is to require those individuals who submit budget requests to state in writing the rationale for proposing each item, how it will be used, and the extent to which those who will be using the item possess or will need to acquire additional knowledge and/or skill for effective utilization. The school administrator should also require any person making a budget request to indicate in the rationale whether the proposed item is desirable or essential. A "desirable" item might be defined as one that would improve a situation, but that failure to purchase would not be detrimental to the educational process; an "essential" item could be defined as something that is necessary in order to prevent a deterioration of a situation, or to implement a particular program successfully. A suggested format for securing this kind of information will be included in the discussion of the next problem in budget building.

*For some reason, the role of the school administrator and the problems he encounters in developing the budget are given limited attention in the educational literature. Therefore, the ideas presented in this section are based primarily on the experiences of a number of principals who have been interviewed.

Lack of Specificity on How the Proposed Budgeted Item Will Increase Student Learning

Budget requests may be for replacement or additional items.* Proposed additional items may reflect increased enrollment, or they may represent projected improvements in the program of the school. A problem is created when the school administrator receives budget requests that are unrelated to increased enrollment or do not clearly specify either how the proposed item will improve student learning or how such an improvement in student learning would be assessed. The individuals or groups who propose improvement items which are additions to the budget may believe that the items are necessary for a better school program, but unless that belief can be translated into a statement of how the improvement will come about and how it will be assessed, the administrator will be in a poor position to make a judgment on the validity of such budget requests. Questions for which the administrator must obtain answers from the proponents of new budget improvement items are, "How will the new item(s) help the students, and how will we determine whether or not the improvement has been achieved?"

A budget proposal form which the school administrator might consider using to ameliorate the problems discussed in the previous two areas is presented in figure 7.4 (p. 130).

Although the budget request form recommended in figure 7.4 may seem complicated and imposing, it asks only for the type of information that an administrator needs in order to evaluate a budget request properly. If a person making a budget request has carefully and thoroughly considered all of the various implications of the request, he should have little difficulty in completing the form. The advantage of this kind of a budget proposal form is that it increases the probability that there will be adequate investigation and consideration supporting each budget request.

Lack of Expertise in Evaluating Budget Requests

The typical school administrator is a generalist working with a group of teachers who are subject matter specialists. The administrator may have specialized in some aspect of the school program such as social studies or mathematics when he was an undergraduate. But it is unlikely that the administrator possesses a very thorough understanding of all of the subject disciplines which comprise the educational program. Consequently, during the budget-building process the administrator will receive requests to include in the proposed budget certain items about which he may know very little.

For example, an administrator may receive from the science teachers a request to order a number of lab kits. The administrator may have taken only

---

*Budget requests may also represent a reduction in products or services; such requests are not typical, although they should be encouraged when appropriate.

Name _____   Subject _____   Date _____

Budget Classification No. _____   (Check appropriate spaces)

_____ Replacement   _____ Desirable

_____ Enrollment   _____ Essential
          addition

_____ Improvement addition

Description of Item _____

_____

_____ Unit Price: _____

Justification: _____

_____

_____

(Include in your justification the reasons why the item is needed, why it is desirable or essential, how it will improve learning opportunities, and how the improvement can be assessed before the next budget year.)

Figure 7.4. Budget Proposal Form.

one or two college courses in science and may have no idea whether these particular kits are essential or even desirable. He may be able to ask the science teachers a few general questions about the lab kits, but unless the administrator is personally knowledgeable about the subject, he will probably be unable to ask the penetrating, probing questions which need to be raised in evaluating the request. [13]

In this kind of a situation an administrator has three main alternatives. Since the teachers are in a better position to know what they need than he is, he can accept the science teachers' recommendation that they need the lab kits, although this procedure can result in the administrator's becoming a rubber stamp for budget requests rather than an evaluator of them.

Another alternative for the administrator is to try to become more knowledgeable in the area for which the budget request is being made. But while this approach is feasible to a limited extent and should be utilized as much as possible, it is not a complete answer to the problem, in light of all of the other responsibilities that an administrator must perform.

A third alternative for the administrator is to utilize consultant help from a department chairman, a subject-matter supervisor in the district office, or perhaps even someone at the university or state department level to help with evaluating budget requests of a specialized nature. Assuming that such consultant help is available (a condition not always existent), the administrator should be careful in selecting the consultant to make sure that the latter will be objective in making assessments. The contribution of the consultant will be of inverse value if he has a vested interest in "building an empire" in the subject area.

Requests for a Specific Brand of an Item vs. Centralized Bidding

Many individuals who request a budget item don't want just any make of the item, but desire a particular brand or model. For example, the teacher who feels that a 3-M model of the overhead projector is superior does not want any other brand. Or the orchestra instructor may request a musical instrument manufactured by a certain company. The problem is that the desire to specify a particular brand of an item is antithetical to the purchasing procedures of many school districts which believe in, and may be required to solicit bids on budget items, and then select the company submitting the lowest bids. Therefore, teachers are seldom encouraged to specify the particular make of the item that they request.

School districts are, of course, obligated to obtain the best price possible in purchasing products and services. However, the primary factor determining whether a particular product or service should be purchased should be the extent to which the item will be effectively utilized. Durability and cost are other important factors. Still, it makes little sense for a school district to purchase low-priced items if teachers or students will not utilize them effectively. Also, as one budget expert observed, "It is a principle of good management, as well as of good human relations, that the people who are to use equipment and facilities be given some voice in suggesting the materials they believe would be most effective to carry out the job."[14]

On the other hand, there is a certain amount of teacher turnover which makes the policy of always budgeting and purchasing the exact brand of an item that a teacher requests a risky one. Perhaps the best resolution of this overall problem is for a school district to involve teachers and students—the users and consumers of the products and services—to a greater extent in establishing the *criteria* for budgeting and purchasing items. This procedure would increase the possibility that factors in addition to cost and durability would be given consideration in the budgeting and purchasing of products and services, and should result in greater utilization of these items.

Inadequate Consultation Between the District Office and Individual Schools

Because the budget-building process is a complex operation, it requires a great deal of consultation. Consultation is, of course, important in all aspects of administration, but is of extreme importance in the budget-building process. If the district's central office and the individual schools do not consult sufficiently and coordinate their efforts effectively, the process of developing the budget may become disjointed and frustrating for many of those involved. Unfortunately, in all too many cases the latter consequences are prevalent.

A lack of consultation between the district's central office and the individual schools can occur at two main points during the budget process: (1) at the beginning and (2) after the school budget is delivered to the central administration. At the beginning of the budget process the school administrator needs to know certain basic facts about the budget situation in the district. For example, he needs to know of any financial parameters under which the district and/or school must operate for the coming year. He needs to know the program priorities of the district and the expectations of the district's central office for program development in the school. He needs to know the extent to which he is free to involve teachers, students, and parents in the budgeting process for the school, and whether there are any budget limits under which they must work. The problem is that, in many districts, the school administrator is not consulted at all in regard to this kind of information, or the consultation is such that the information given to him by the district is vague or inaccurate in light of what eventually happens when the proposed budget is sent to the district's central office.

It is after the budget is sent from the individual school to the district office for review and final approval that the second type of inadequate consultation may occur between district administrators and school level administrators. At this point, in too many instances, the proposed school budget is modified and changed by the district administrators without anything more than *pro forma* consultation with the school administrator. Proposed items are cut and substitutions are made, but the school administrator may not discover that these changes have been made until the approved budget is returned later in the year. The inadequate consultation, if acknowledged at all by the district office, is typically justified on the basis of insufficient time and "no other choice."

It would be unfair to indict district administrators totally for the problem of inadequate consultation between them and the school level administrators. The school administrators themselves have not always taken the initiative to consult with the district administration, or taken advantage of the opportunity to consult. For example, it is particularly important for the school administrator to confer with the district business manager on all aspects of the budget.

Also, in regard to inadequate consultation, it needs to be recognized that district administrators are not free agents in making budget decisions; they are subject to many pressures from the school board and other groups.

It is additionally true that consultation with school administrators is difficult to achieve in districts with a large number of schools. However, despite these obstacles, greater effort should be made by all concerned to increase the extent of consultation between the central office and the individual school in all phases of the budget-building process. Through better consultation, the ambiguities and frustrations of the budget-building process could be considerably reduced, thereby contributing to a more constructive and acceptable budget.

ADMINISTERING THE SCHOOL BUDGET

RESPONSIBILITIES AND PROBLEMS

Once the proposed budget is finally approved by the school board, the administrator's main responsibilities relate to purchasing and accounting procedures. Typically, these procedures are predetermined by the district office and implemented by the schools. [15]

The school administrator is usually given the responsibility of making sure that the school operates within its allocated budget and does not overspend in any of the budget categories. To carry out this responsibility effectively, the administrator needs to obtain periodic (at least monthly) budget status reports. These reports should provide information on how much money has been spent up to a certain date, how much money has been encumbered (designated for purchase of products or services but not actually spent), and how much is left in each budget account.

In most medium and large school districts a budget status report is provided periodically to each school administrator. In those districts which don't provide that kind of a service for the administrator, he will need to instruct the school secretary or bookkeeper to prepare budget status reports. Without such reports, the school administrator cannot effectively monitor the spending of funds. It should be noted that even in those districts which provide budget status reports to the school administrators, the reports are usually a month behind the expenditures. This means that it may be necessary, toward the end of the budget year, for the school administrator to keep some type of internal accounting of the money spent, so that the allocated budget will not be exceeded.

As a school administrator manages the budget during the year, he may encounter problems which have occurred in many school districts. First of all, certain people in the school, perhaps even the administrator, may want to purchase an item which has not been included in the budget. Or individuals or departments may want to borrow from one budget account (e.g., capital expenditures) to supplement another budget account (e.g., instructional supplies) which was inadequately budgeted.

Generally, district accounting and purchasing philosophies and procedures tend to discourage, if not actually prohibit, budget transfers from one account to another. The rationale usually given to the school administrator is that he should have budgeted for the item desired, and if permission is given for one school to engage in this practice, other schools may want to do the same thing, and budget planning would become meaningless. There may also be city or state governmental regulations which make budget transfers impermissible. [16]

Despite the need to exercise control over the expenditure of funds previously approved by the school board, it would nevertheless appear that insofar as possible there should be flexibility in the spending of those funds. The school administrator should not be permitted to exceed the total amount budgeted for the school, but he should be allowed to adjust the funding in budget categories to meet new situations. The sums of money in the various budget accounts should not be perceived as limits, but as guidelines which can be changed if the situation warrants revision, so long as the administrator does not exceed the total amount in the budget.

This solution would also resolve another problem which has frustrated many school administrators. The difficulty occurs when funds left unspent by a school during one budget year must revert back to the agency that authorized the funds, i.e., the school board or city hall, instead of being credited to the school for the ensuing year. If school administrators were given greater flexibility in adjusting budget accounts, the money which was not used during the year for one budget account could be applied in areas where the need is greater than anticipated, and the unused funds would not be "lost," as far as an individual school is concerned. Of course, such flexibility could be misused, in that administrators might not plan their budgets carefully enough, knowing that they could adjust budget accounts later. However, this is not an inevitable disadvantage and could be avoided with appropriate inservice education and close monitoring.

ADMINISTERING THE STUDENT ACTIVITIES ACCOUNT

The student activities account is one aspect of the budget which deserves special attention, since it is a potential trouble spot. This account usually is not a part of the educational budget previously discussed and is administered primarily at the school level with district supervision. The account involves the funds collected and disbursed for various extracurricular and student activities. Included are monies derived from fees charged for athletic events, plays, concerts, the student newspaper and the annual, extra-class activities, and special fund-raising projects.

The total sum of money in the activities account in any one year can be large, and there have been criticisms of the way the money has at times been spent and the way the account has been administered. While the activities account is usually audited by an independent agency, the principal of a school is relatively free to authorize the expenditure of funds for purposes he thinks important. This practice has led in some instances to the expenditure of money for items which would not have been approved if submitted in the educational budget. In other situations it has resulted in some very large activities funds, the monies of which were put into savings accounts, thereby earning interest. Although seldom has there been anything illegal about the principal's action in relation to the student activities account, administration of the account has frequently been sloppy; therefore better guidelines and supervision would appear to be needed.

First of all, the school administrator needs to recognize that the monies collected and disbursed are *public* funds, and the courts have ruled that "the proceeds of those activities belong to the board of school directors and must be accounted for in the same manner that the other funds of the school district are accounted for."[17] The school board may delegate to the school administrator the responsibilities of collecting and disbursing the funds, and if so, he is accountable for the manner in which he carries out these responsibilities.

Secondly, the school administrator needs to design and implement a responsible system for collecting, disbursing and monitoring the spending of student activities monies. Such a system should include the following characteristics:[18]

1. School board authorization for the collection of student activities fees.
2. The involvement of students and teachers in determining the establishment and size of student activities fees and in decisions about how monies are to be spent.
3. The maintenance of school records of monies collected and disbursed, showing that the procedures enumerated below are being followed:
   a. a receipt is issued to the individual from whom money is received,
   b. a deposit receipt is obtained from the bank, indicating that all monies have been deposited upon being received,
   c. the amount which is deposited is recorded in a student activities account under the appropriate fund,
   d. a requisition form, requiring the signature of the activity sponsor, is used to initiate purchases, with purchases involving large sums of money requiring the approval of the principal additionally,
   e. school checks are used to expend monies and to pay student activities bills,

    f. all expenditures are recorded in the student activities ledger, under the appropriate fund.

4. The provision of a budget-status report for each activity sponsor and for the school administrator, on a monthly basis.

5. A yearly audit and review of the purposes for which student activity monies have been spent, conducted by the district office with the involvement of the school administrator and activities' sponsors.

As one might suspect, administering the student activities account can be very time-consuming, and this responsibility might be delegated to the school's business manager or another member of the staff. However, even if the responsibility is delegated, the final accountability is still that of the school administrator. The administrator is the one who is ultimately responsible, so he must be sufficiently knowledgeable and involved to explain the transactions that occur.

EVALUATING BUDGET UTILIZATION: EFFECTIVENESS, EFFICIENCY

A third function of the school administrator in relation to the budget is to evaluate its effectiveness and efficiency.[19] Budget effectiveness is determined by evaluating the extent to which the funds allocated for each of the programs in the school are achieving their objectives. Budget efficiency is determined by evaluating the extent to which the products and services purchased with budget funds are purchased at the lowest price consistent with the items' usability, durability, and reliability. It also involves the monitoring of products and services utilization. Budget effectiveness and efficiency should both be important concerns of the school administrator, particularly in a time of limited funds.

Until recently it was difficult, if not impossible, to talk meaningfully about evaluating budget effectiveness and efficiency.[20] Budgets were organized according to account categories which, in most cases, bore little if any relationship to school programs or objectives. However, with the advent of PPBS (Planning, Programming, Budgeting System), it is now possible for the administrator to evaluate more accurately the effectiveness and efficiency of the budget. Under PPBS the budget is organized according to educational programs whose objectives have been defined, and for which criteria and methods of evaluation have been identified.

Under this system, if the administrator wants to find out whether or not the funds for a particular program are being utilized effectively, he can evaluate the extent to which the objectives are being achieved, and then make a judgment about whether or not that achievement is sufficient, considering the funds allocated. It should be emphasized that part of the basis for that judgment must relate to whether or not increased funding of the same program or funding of a different program to reach the same objectives would result in *greater* achievement of those objectives. A program should not be judged as effective or ineffective by itself, but only in comparison to what the alternative may cost and achieve.

For an example of how PPBS can be used to evaluate budget and program effectiveness, see figure 7.5.

Program Alternatives for Teaching Remedial Reading to a Class of 9th Grade Students

	Class Size	Personnel	Equipment	Total Estimated Costs	Per Student Cost	Predicted Results
Program Option No. 1	10	1 teacher	None	$ 9,500.00	$950	Increase one grade level
Program Option No. 2	20	1 teacher	Overhead Projector	$ 9,800.00	$490	Increase 1/2 grade level
Program Option No. 3	35	1 teacher, 1 aide	None	$14,000.00	$400	Increase 1/4 grade level

Figure 7.5. Cost Effectiveness Analysis.[21]

Once the budget has been approved by the school board, the school administrator's role in evaluating budget efficiency is generally limited to monitoring and preventing wasteful use of funds.[22] Any product or service which is inefficiently utilized, either because of wastefulness or underutilization, merits the administrator's attention. He especially needs to watch for excessive use of supplies, underutilization of equipment, and inefficient use of time and personnel. Evaluating the efficiency of the expenditure of funds is never a popular task. But in situations of limited financial support for education, a school administrator cannot abdicate this important responsibility.

SCHOOL PLANT MANAGEMENT

Winston Churchill is reported to have said, "We shape our dwellings and then our dwellings shape us." The physical environment in which we work can and does influence what we do and how we feel. For example, it can affect our flexibility in teaching, our communication patterns, the amount of noise and extent of discipline problems in the school, and many other facets of the total educational enterprise. A well-maintained, bright, sparkling, flexible, physical facility suggests a school that people care about. Such a school does something positive for the spirit of the individuals who occupy the building.

On the other hand, a school which is poorly maintained, institutional-looking, and inflexible in its structure suggests a school in which people have lost interest and lack pride. That type of school tends to dull the spirit of the people who must spend their work days, weeks, and months there. Although the importance of the school plant's appearance and flexibility can be overemphasized, there is little doubt that they do affect the feelings and behavior of the people who occupy the building. Since the school administrator will ultimately be held accountable for the management of the school plant, a discussion of the nature of his responsibilities is appropriate. Those responsibilities fall into three general areas: (1) maintaining the school plant, (2) scheduling facilities, and (3) school plant planning.

MAINTENANCE OF THE SCHOOL PLANT

The administrator is not, of course, responsible for personally maintaining the school plant. The school district has hired custodians and related workers to perform the actual tasks of keeping the school clean, bright, and in good repair. [23] However, the school administrator cannot assume that these tasks will be carried out effectively without some supervision on his part. The administrator, or someone to whom this responsibility is delegated, will need to supervise the custodians and monitor their work as it relates to the general appearance and condition of the building and grounds. If the school administrator is fortunate enough to have a conscientious head custodian, the supervisory responsibility of the administrator will be greatly reduced. But it should be noted that such custodians are not always available, and in many schools some supervision and monitoring by the school administrator will probably be required. [24]

While the nature and extent of the administrator's responsibilities for supervising the custodians and monitoring the maintenance of the school plant and grounds will vary, depending on local conditions, the following general responsibilities are proposed: [25]

1. *Keeping informed about the work schedule and specific respon-sibilities of each member of the custodial staff.* The school administrator should know the work schedule of each person on the custodial staff and should be knowledgeable about who does what.

2. *Touring the school building and grounds regularly for the purpose of observing the extent to which they are being kept clean, neat, and in good repair.* Admittedly, the administrator may have other higher priorities, leaving limited time for this kind of activity. But if he cares enough about the appearance of the school building and grounds, he will try to schedule such tours every week or two. They can be veritable "eye openers."

3. *Designing some method or procedure for students, teachers, or others to bring to the attention of head custodian and/or the school administrator any problems in plant and grounds maintenance or appearance.* A form could be developed for this purpose, or perhaps the administrator could simply point out to students and teachers the procedure to follow when a maintenance problem occurs. (It should be noted that there will be students and teachers who will be reluctant or won't take time to report a problem directly to the custodians.) There may also be value in the practice of the administrator's receiving the reports, or at least a copy of the reports, so that he can become better informed about the maintenance problems in the building.

4. *Developing a good working relationship with all of the custodial staff, particularly the head custodian.* The custodial staff should be treated with the same respect and human relations approach as any other group of employees in the school. They perform an important job and, if dissatisfied, can make things difficult for the school administrator and teachers.

The appearance of the school plant and grounds should, of course, be the concern of everyone, including students and teachers. However, the administrator must assume the overall responsibility for making sure that the school plant and grounds are kept clean, neat, and in good repair. [26] This responsibility is one which the administrator should not avoid and for which he should rightly be held accountable.

SCHOOL PLANT SCHEDULING

Facilities scheduling is a second major component of plant management. Someone must be responsible for scheduling facilities in a way that will promote appropriate and maximum usage. That person is frequently the school administrator, although the responsibility may be delegated to someone else in certain situations.

School facilities must be scheduled to accommodate (1) the regular educational program of the school, (2) the school's student activities program, and (3) requests of people who would like to use the building at night, on weekends, or during the summer for recreational or adult programs.

There are many different approaches to scheduling the regular educational program of a school, and references are provided for the reader who wishes to explore this subject in depth.[27] However, relatively little attention has been paid in the educational literature to facility scheduling for the extracurricular program or for the recreational and adult programs at night and on weekends.[28] If the administrator finds that there is considerable demand for the use of the school facilities after the end of the school day, he will probably need to assign to a staff member the responsibility for setting up and administering a system for handling requests and scheduling facilities. This system should be coordinated with the custodians' work load and schedule, if problems are to be avoided. In a small school, the individual who has overall responsibility for facilities scheduling may well have to be the principal himself. In a larger school, the principal can delegate this responsibility to an assistant principal, or it may be assigned to the head custodian.

Facility scheduling is usually not regarded as a particularly interesting or rewarding aspect of school administration. Nevertheless, it is a task requiring effective performance, though it need not become a time-consuming or frustrating experience if approached in an organized manner.

SCHOOL PLANT PLANNING

The administrator's major responsibilities for school plant planning are twofold: (1) planning for changes in the existing structure, such as remodeling or additions, and (2) planning for a new facility.[29]

In a time of educational change, many school plants simply do not provide sufficient flexibility or comprehensiveness to accommodate the various proposals for improving the educational program of the school, and modernization of old buildings is a constant need.[30] Not all communities can afford to build a new school, so an administrator may need to consider ways in which his present facility can be remodeled or expanded.* Since form should follow function, the administrator should first determine, in cooperation with relevant others, the kind of educational program to be implemented in the school, and then consider needed changes in the physical plant.

Having ascertained the type of educational program which the school should implement, the administrator can logically move to the next step—analyzing the physical facilities required by that program and then identifying the need for remodeling or expanding the present school plant.[31] In tak-

---

*For those administrators in a district or school with a declining enrollment the report, *Fewer Pupils/Surplus Space* provides helpful suggestions on how to make good use of surplus space. The report is published by the Educational Facilities Laboratories, 477 Madison Ave., N.Y. 10022.

ing this step the school administrator will want to consult with appropriate facilities specialists in the district office, at the university, and at the state department of public instruction. Assistance in estimating the cost of making changes in the physical plant should also be secured. As a result of conferring with various experts the school administrator should be in a position to submit to the school board for its consideration (1) a document which describes the type of educational program that will be possible with the modification of facilities; (2) preliminary sketches showing the proposed change; and (3) the estimated cost to the district. [32]

School plant planning for remodeling or expanding takes time and preparation. However, there is little doubt that many of our school plants need remodeling or expansion if they are to accommodate needed improvements in the educational program. [33]

While most school administrators are more likely to participate in planning for facility remodeling or expansion, some administrators will be fortunate enough to become involved in planning for an entirely new school building. This is a task which will challenge the creativity, patience, and endurance of any administrator. At the same time, it can be a very exciting and rewarding activity.

Instead of a discussion of the innumerable details of planning for a new building, some general principles which should be followed are presented below. [34]

1. *Define the educational objectives which are to be achieved in the new school and the programs and activities which will be implemented in order to achieve those objectives.* This effort should result in a document formally referred to as "the educational specifications" of the school. [35] These educational specifications should be as detailed and precise as needed to enable both the administrator and the architect to understand the type of educational program which the new building is to house.

2. *Involve in the planning of the new facility as many of those people who will occupy the new building as possible, e.g., students, teachers.* It may be more convenient and efficient for an administrator to exclude these people, but this will increase the risk that the new facility will not be functional for their needs. The administrator may choose to establish committees, solicit recommendations from individuals, or attempt some other alternative in securing input.

   Regardless of the approach chosen by the administrator, however, a determination should be made in advance that the ideas and recommendations which are generated from the involvement of teachers, students and others will be carefully considered and will not be rejected simply because they might be more expensive than other ideas. Obviously, there are financial parameters within which the school board and the administrator must operate. However, if the participants in the planning process, particularly teachers, gather the impression that cost is going to be the main criterion in assessing the worth of a recommendation, they are unlikely to contribute their time and effort. A school district does not need to involve many people in the planning of a new facility if the basic objective is simply to build the least expensive plant possible.

3. *Study the educational literature on school plant planning.* It makes no sense to "reinvent the wheel," and many mistakes can be avoided by reviewing the recommendations and experiences of others. [36]

4. *Define the nature and scope of the responsibilities of the architect for the project.* In too many situations the architect's responsibilities, particularly as they pertain to making decisions about the educational program to be housed in the school and the type of physical facilities needed, are not clearly delineated. As a result, the architect may end up making decisions about the nature of the new building which are, in reality, educational decisions.

5. *Devise a master plan and time schedule which will program within a specified timetable the planning and implementation activities that need to be accomplished by a certain date.* Unless an overall plan identifies and sequences the various steps to be carried out within a specific time frame, it is unlikely that the new facility will be completed on schedule. An excellent tool which the administrator should utilize in developing and implementing the master plan is PERT-CPM, i.e., Program Evaluation and Review Technique and Critical Path Method.*

6. *Develop criteria and procedures for evaluating the new facility after it is in operation.* Any new structure, regardless of how well conceived and planned, will have defects or deficiencies which may need to be corrected and which should be avoided in the planning of the next facility. In evaluating a new facility, strong consideration should be given to involving the people who are most affected by it: students and teachers.

A FINAL NOTE ON BUDGET AND PLANT MANAGEMENT

The school budget and plant represent important vehicles for improving educational opportunities for students. Whether the full potential of these

---

*For a good explanation of PERT-CPM, see Robert L. Granger, *Educational Leadership* (San Francisco: Intext Educational Publishers, 1971), pp. 117-38.

means is realized will depend in large part on the school administrator. He will undoubtedly face problems and will need to work within certain financial and physical constraints. However, in the final analysis, the administrator's success in providing the best possible budget and physical facilities for the school will depend for the most part on his *knowledge, resourcefulness,* and *persistence.*

Review

1. What are the steps involved in and the advantages and disadvantages of the centralized budget process? The decentralized budget process?
2. Describe the main elements of the Planning, Programming, Budgeting System (PPBS). What are its advantages and disadvantages?
3. Discuss the major problems associated with the process of developing the school budget.
4. Identify those factors that characterize the effective administration of the student activities budget.
5. Describe the major responsibilities of the administrator in maintaining the school plant, scheduling facilities, and school plant planning.

Notes

1. Leo M. Casey, *School Business Administration* (New York: Center for Applied Research in Education, 1964), p. 13.

2. New York State University, *School Business Management Handbook: Budget* (Albany: State Educational Department, 1956), pp. 65-67.

3. See D. Lloyd Nelson and William M. Purdy, *School Business Administration* (Lexington, Mass.: Heath Lexington Books, 1971), pp. 94-95.

4. I. Carl Candoli et al., *School Business Administration: A Planning Approach* (Boston: Allyn & Bacon, 1971), p. 173.

5. Ibid., p. 174.

6. Three excellent books for an in-depth study of PPBS are S. A. Haggart et al., *Program Budgeting for School Planning* (Englewood Cliffs N.J.: Educational Technology Publications, 1971); Robert F. Alioto and J. D. Jungherr, *Operational PPBS for Education* (New York: Harper & Row, Publishers, 1971); Stephen J. Knezevich, *Program Budgeting* (PPBS) Berkeley, Calif.: McCutchan Publishing Co., 1973).

7. Thomas F. Koerner, *PPBS and the School: New System Promotes Efficiency, Accountability* (Washington, D.C.: National School Public Relations Association, 1972), p. 6.

8. For additional information on problems associated with PPBS, see William A. Jenkins and Greg O. Lehman, "Nine Pitfalls of PPBS," *School Management* 16 (January 1972):1-6.

9. For a very good review of the literature on PPBS, see Philip K. Piele, "Planning, Programming-Budgeting Systems." An ERIC Report: Ed-058-622, 1972.

10. PPBS process adapted from Alioto and Jungherr, *Operational PPBS*, p. 52.

11. Adapted from "How to Do It Yourself," *School Management* 8 (January 1964): 163-64.

12. Adapted from the following sources: Dale H. Scott, "How PPBS is Being Used in California," *School Management*, 15 (February 1971): 13; and Rosalyn S. Heyman, "Firsthand Experience with PPBS at the Classroom Level," *Bulletin of the National Association of*

Secondary School Principals 56 (October, 1972):46. The entire October issue of *The NASSP Bulletin* contains many good ideas about PPBS. Also, for an excellent example of how PPBS can be applied to the elementary school, see Darrel S. Willey and H. Wesley Hander, "Program Budgeting—A Kindergarten Approach," *School Business Affairs*, June 1970, pp. 143-45.

13. For help in regard to this problem, see R. Louis Bright, "Should Educators Generate Specifications for the Purchase of Equipment?" An ERIC Report: Ed-039-736, 1970.

14. New York State University, *School Business Management*, p. 41.

15. Oscar T. Jarvis et al., *Public School Business Administration and Finance* (West Nyack, N.Y.: Parker Publishing Co., 1967), p. 129.

16. Candoli et al., *School Business Administration*, p. 218.

17. See re German Township School Directors, 465 and C. 562 (1942).

18. For further help in setting up such a system, see E. V. Samuelson et. al., *Financial Accounting for School Activities* (Washington, D.C.: U.S. Department of Health, Education, and Welfare, 1959).

19. For an earlier but still relevant discussion of this concept and its procedures, see Leon Onsiew and William B. Castetter, *Budgeting for Better Schools* (Englewood Cliffs, N.J.: Prentice-Hall, 1960), chap. 5.

20. For an interesting description of an innovative approach in this area, see Clark C. Abt, "Design for Education System Cost Effectiveness Model," in *Efficiency in Resource Utilization in Education* (Paris: Organization for Economic Cooperation and Development, 1969), pp. 65-91.

21. For further elaboration and discussion of the concepts leading up to figure 7.5, see *Educational Resources Management System* (Chicago: Research Corporation of the Association of School Business Officials, 1971), pp. 241-65.

22. An excellent discussion of problems and procedures is presented in Philip H. Coomp and Jacques Hallak, *Managing Educational Costs* (New York: Oxford University Press, 1972), pt. 3.

23. Joseph J. Baker and Jon S. Peters, *School Maintenance and Operation* (Danville, Ill.: Interstate Printers and Publishers, 1963), p. 14.

24. Richard Tonigan, "Do-It-Yourself Ideas for Principals Facing Plant Management Problems," *School Management* 16 (June 1972):35.

25. For an excellent study of administrative policies and procedures in this area, see Joseph R. Frola, "Administrative Policies and Practices for the Selection, Training and Supervision of School Custodians and Their Relationships to the Quality of Custodial Services in Selected School Districts" (Ph.D. diss., University of Pittsburgh, 1971).

26. For a very good review of the literature on this topic, see Philip K. Piele, "Building Maintenance." An ERIC Report: Ed-003-928, 1972.

27. See Anthony Saville, *Instructional Programming* (Columbus, Ohio: Charles E. Merrill Publishing Co., 1973).

28. One important exception to this would be a valuable study completed by the U.S. Department of Health, Education, and Welfare. See R. N. Finchum, *Extended Use of School Facilities* (Washington, D.C.: U.S. Department of Health, Education, and Welfare, 1967). This is a very useful report for any administrator regarding the topic of facility scheduling for recreational and adult education activities.

29. Donald J. Leu, *Planning Educational Facilities* (New York: Center for Applied Research in Education, 1965).

30. For needs criteria and ideas for remodeling older buildings, see Earl J. Shobe, "Criteria for Deciding to Remodel the Existing School." An ERIC Report: Ed-018 -079, 1967.

31. For ideas on how to renovate older buildings to allow for changing educational practices, see John D. L'Hote, "Major Considerations in School Modernization." An ERIC Report: Ed-018-951, 1967.

32. For some good ideas in this regard, see McLeod, Ferrara, and Ensign, *School Renewal* (New York: Educational Facilities Laboratories, n.d.).

33. For a good review of the literature on this topic, see Alan M. Baan, *Building Renovation and Modernization.* An ERIC Report: Ed-004-022, 1972.

34. Useful literature on new school plant planning includes Nickolaus L. Engelhardt, *Complete Guide for Planning New Schools* (West Nyack, N.Y.: Parker Publishing Co., 1970); and James J. Morisseau, *Design and Planning: The New Schools* (New York: Van Nostrand Reinhold Co., 1972). Another important source of literature on the topic of school plant planning, with which every administrator should maintain contact is The Educational Facilities Laboratories, 477 Madison Avenue, New York, N.Y. 10022.

35. For a comprehensive review of the literature on this topic, with sources on ideas for developing educational specifications for the elementary, middle, junior high, and high schools, see Philip K. Piele, "Educational Specifications." An ERIC Report: Ed-058-620, 1971.

36. The ERIC Clearing House on Educational Management at Eugene, Oregon, is a good source for reviewing the literature on school facilities and school plant planning.

Part 3

Staff Personnel and Instructional/ Curricular Leadership

8

Staff Recruitment, Selection, and Induction

Griffiths has observed, "It is axiomatic that a school system is only as good as the people who make it." [1] Therefore, every school administrator should be interested in improving the quality of the professional staff. Three important processes by which an administrator can take a major step toward the achievement of this goal are personnel recruitment, selection, and induction. Although the availability and turnover of personnel will tend to influence the priority given to these three processes, they still represent significant means by which an administrator can improve the quality of the staff.

STAFF RECRUITMENT

Staff recruitment may be defined as the active pursuit of potential candidates for the purpose of influencing them to apply for positions in the school district. The goal of a school's or district's staff recruitment program should be to attract applications from the best people available, both beginning and experienced. [2] Although a surplus of candidates for a position may decrease the difficulty of finding a qualified candidate for a vacancy, the objective of a district's recruiting should be to attract the *most* qualified and outstanding individuals. Since most staff recruiting programs are centralized at the district level, either in a personnel office or under the jurisdiction of a central office administrator, the focus in this section will be on ways in which a school administrator can most effectively work with the central office in the recruitment of staff.

ASSESSING NEEDS

The first important way in which a school administrator can help the district administration in the recruitment of staff is by providing them with data on personnel needs for the school. There are at least three major categories of staff personnel needs for which a school administrator should provide data to the central office: [3]

1. Increased or decreased enrollment which creates a need for more staff or a reduction in staff.
2. Changes in the educational program which necessitate additional or differently trained staff.

3. Staff resignations or transfers which may create a need for new personnel.

For recruitment to be effective, the district office must receive data about all three categories of staff needs, at the earliest possible date during the school year. By studying the enrollment figures for his own school and its feeder schools, and by estimating from census figures and the previous years' student turnover, an administrator should be able to project to the central office by January any staff needs related to potential increases or decreases in the student enrollment in the school for the following year. [4]

Estimating the need for new staff due to changes in the educational program will not be easy. But if the school administrator approaches the change process systematically, target dates can be established which will permit the administrator to indicate to the district office by early spring the existence of vacancies for additional or specially trained staff. Although it may be difficult for the administrator to meet these target dates, it should be recognized that the later personnel needs are reported to the district office for the purpose of recruiting, the harder it will be to find highly qualified staff still available.

The administrator may also encounter considerable difficulty in estimating staff needs which may be created by resignations or transfers. Some districts require that staff transfers from one school to another within the district take place by a certain date, but resignations can and frequently do occur late in the spring, and even into late summer. Some administrators try to survey their staffs in March or April to ascertain who may be leaving but the data obtained is not always valid or reliable. Teachers who will eventually resign may not want the administrator to know that they are even thinking about resigning, until they have actually secured another job. The best the school administrator can do in these circumstances is to "keep his ear to the ground," and report staff needs to the district office as soon as he can.

THE ADMINISTRATOR'S ROLE IN RECRUITING

The actual recruitment of staff, as mentioned earlier, is typically organized by a personnel office in larger school districts or by a district administrator, such as the superintendent or an assistant, in smaller school districts. Two methods are generally used by school districts to recruit personnel: (1) the dissemination to university, state, and private placement bureaus of brochures describing the district and its employment opportunities, and (2) visitations by district recruiting teams to personnel placement offices. [5]

It would appear that the school administrator could make a useful contribution to both of these recruiting approaches. Certainly the administrator should, at the minimum, be involved in reacting to the strengths and weaknesses of the district's current brochures, or in helping to develop proposed brochures which will be sent to teacher placement bureaus and to candidates who inquire about the district. For most potential candidates, the district's brochures are the first tangible information they receive about a school system, and the likelihood that they might be interested in exploring staffing opportunities at a particular school will be influenced by the quality of the brochures.

The school administrator should also be involved in orienting the district's recruiting team to the school's particular staffing needs.[6] In the past, building administrators were often included on districts' recruiting teams, but currently this practice is less typical. Although the school system's team is recruiting for the entire district (not just for one administrator's school), if the team is to be maximally effective it will need to be aware of and give attention to the specific staffing needs of individual schools. To accomplish the latter objective, the recruiting team will need to receive orientation about the school in which the vacancy has occurred from the administrator, and to the extent possible from the faculty of the school. If the district's philosophy or procedures do not provide an opportunity for such orientation, the school administrator should take the initiative to bring about changes in this regard. A perspective must be developed to the effect that the district should be recruiting teachers to meet the needs of *individual* school programs, staffs, and clienteles, rather than just hiring teachers "at large," or as interchangeable components.

Perhaps the best way a building administrator can develop this perspective is to work closely with the district recruiting team in the development of position descriptions pertaining specifically to the vacancies in the school, which can then be disseminated to all interested candidates, and subsequently used in the interviewing process. A position description usually contains the title of the vacant position, its primary function, major responsibilities, qualifications, special assignments, and the organizational relationships of the position.[7] There need not necessarily be a separate position description for each vacancy in an administrator's school. However, to the extent to which a vacant position is unique, a position description should be developed. A sample position description is shown in figure 8.1.

THE ADMINISTRATOR'S MAJOR CONTRIBUTION

It should be pointed out that probably the most important contribution which a school administrator can make to the effective recruitment of staff is to help the school develop an excellent educational program and good working conditions. Obviously, potential candidates may also weigh other fac-

Title: Diagnostic Teacher (Certificated)
Suggested Position Level: Teacher Basis
Days Per Year of Employment: 200 (Full-time)
Reports to: Model Cities Project Director, Educational Resource Team, and the Principal
Supervises: Project Teacher and Aides (Functionally)
Major Duties and Responsibilities:

1. Diagnoses children referred for learning problems.
2. Assists in diagnosis of children referred for behavior problems.
3. Assesses the needs of children referred for learning problems.
4. Trains project teachers in the use and interpretation of individual standard and nonstandard tests.
5. Trains project teachers and preprofessionals in individual analysis of student needs.
6. Correlates educational activities of cooperating school teachers with those of project teachers relative to referred children.
7. Works with individual children referred with the intention of confirming diagnoses.
8. Works with the language curriculum specialist in developing recommendations of specific educational programs and techniques.
9. Provides relevant information based on observation and evaluation to the behavioral counselor, to facilitate planning of behavioral approaches.
10. Attends all staffings on referred children both in cooperating school and project setting.
11. Maintains written records on all referred children.
12. Conducts, together with the language/curriculum specialist, in-service sessions.
13. Assists with functional responsibilities in the absence of the project director.
14. Assists in maintaining ongoing internal program continuity and acts as liaison between cooperating school and project director.
15. Assists project director in planning and developing orientation and program structure of proposed implementation of P.E.R.T.

Figure 8.1. A Sample Position Description. [8]

tors in deciding whether to pursue a staff vacancy, such as the size of the school and community, and cultural opportunities. But a school or district which becomes recognized in the state as a leader in education and a good place to work (or known to be *striving* toward these goals) will thereby do more to improve its success in staff recruiting than perhaps anything else it could do. [9]

On the other hand, a school or district with a fair, poor, or possibly even no image or reputation for being a good place to work and for offering a quality educational program will probably be hampered in its recruiting efforts. Therefore, the most important steps that a school administrator can take in helping the district office to recruit staff, is to concentrate initially and continuously on the improvement of the educational program and on working conditions within the school. While to many this may seem obvious, it needs to be emphasized, since regardless of what else a school administrator or school district might do by way of recruitment, there must be a solid basis in working conditions and in educational accomplishments before recruitment of quality candidates will show significant success. [10]

STAFF SELECTION*

Although the school administrator is generally involved to only a limited extent in staff recruitment, he should play a major role in staff selection.

However, it should be noted that in some school districts, usually those in large cities, the school administrator's role in staff selection can be described as peripheral. In these situations the personnel department of the district selects new staff for the schools, and the building administrator may not find out who will be joining the staff until just before school opens. While it is true that in many of these circumstances the school administrator has been given an opportunity to specify to the personnel department the kinds of new staff needed, it is the personnel department rather than the school administrator who ascertains and decides whether or not candidates for a particular vacancy meet the appropriate prerequisites.

In spite of what may seem to be advantages in efficiency when a personnel department (or, for that matter, other central office administrators) selects the staff, it would appear that as long as the building administrator is held accountable for the performance of the staff, he should be directly involved in the staff selection processes. As Corbally and his colleagues have emphasized,

> He [the principal] is in the best position to know his personnel needs, and no one else is better able to provide an analysis of the responsibilities to be taken over by the new person. . . . And because the principal is most directly connected with future orientation and development of the person, by participating in the selection he automatically assumes some of the responsibility for assuring the success of the teacher. [11]

It would seem that there is sound rationale for the proposition that the building administrator should be given an opportunity to interview and recommend candidates for employment and assignment at the school. [12] The administrator should also be able to appeal (to the superintendent) a directive from the district office to assign to the school an individual not wanted on the staff by the administrator. It is recognized that these

---

*For a good review of research on teacher selection, see Donald Gerwin, *The Employment of Teachers,* part 1. (Berkeley, Calif.: McCutchan Publishing Corp., 1974).

recommendations define a major role for the school administrator in staff selection and, by implication, a lesser role for the personnel department. However, the contributions of both are important, and the building administrator should attempt to capitalize on the expertise of the personnel department whenever possible.

STAFF SELECTION PROCESS AND TEAM

Staff selection can be conceptualized as a process consisting of a series of sequentially interdependent steps, as depicted in figure 8.2.

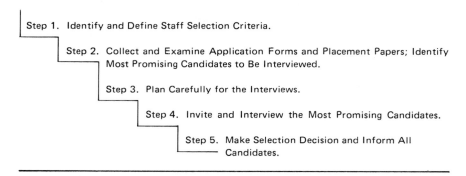

Step 1. Identify and Define Staff Selection Criteria.

Step 2. Collect and Examine Application Forms and Placement Papers; Identify Most Promising Candidates to Be Interviewed.

Step 3. Plan Carefully for the Interviews.

Step 4. Invite and Interview the Most Promising Candidates.

Step 5. Make Selection Decision and Inform All Candidates.

Figure 8.2. The Staff Selection Process.

    The first step in the staff selection process is to define the characteristics of new staff members the school seeks to employ. Many schools or districts complete this first step by simply identifying the grade level or subject which the teacher will be assigned, e.g., third grade, science. They may have other criteria in mind when they identify the vacancy, and they frequently apply additional criteria in making the final selection decision, but initially there appears to be a lack of specificity. However, it would seem to make good sense to identify and define, at the very beginning of the selection process, the kinds of characteristics and qualifications which the school or school district expects the candidates to possess.

    To help him identify and define the selection criteria, the administrator may want to organize a *staff selection team,* and involve such people as a department head, a team leader, and an assistant principal on the team. [13] Selection of those for whom involvement on the team would be relevant will depend on the nature of the vacancy, but for certain openings, guidance counselors, students, and even parents could make a valuable contribution to defining the selection criteria, interviewing candidates, and even making staff selection recommendations. [14] It should be recognized that the school board has the authority to make final decisions on staff selection, and the building administrator may want to reserve the final determination on who to recommend to the superintendent and, ultimately, the school board. But this should present no real barrier to the nonadministrative members of the staff selection team as long as they understand their role and that of the building administrator.

In defining staff selection criteria, the school administrator and the selection team should give consideration to the following questions:

1. Is it important that the candidate believe in a particular kind of educational philosophy? If so, what are the specifics of that philosophy?
2. What kinds of teaching techniques should the candidate be qualified to use, e.g., inquiry method, discussion leader?
3. What should be the candidate's approach to student discipline and control?
4. How important is it that the candidate be able to work effectively with others, e.g., colleagues, students?
5. What kinds of personal characteristics do we want the candidate to possess, e.g., type of personality, appearance?
6. What kinds of educational background and training do we expect the candidate to possess, e.g., degree, teaching experience?
7. What evidence is available that would provide significant support to any of the staff selection team's answers to the first six questions?

The final question will undoubtedly be the most difficult and frustrating one for the school administrator and staff selection team to answer, but it is an extremely important question and should be raised at each point at which responses to the other questions are being considered. It seems likely that most schools or districts define their staff selection criteria on the basis of personal preference and experience rather than on a systematic investigation of research on teacher effectiveness.* While the former factors are not unimportant, the staff selection criteria should, so far as possible, be based on factors which research has demonstrated to be related to teaching effectiveness. [15]

ANALYZING PLACEMENT PAPERS

After the selection criteria have been defined, then the staff selection team needs to identify and employ procedures for collecting and examining candidates' data which pertain to the criteria. The two procedures most typically

*These research findings will be discussed in the chapters on staff evaluation and instructional supervision.

utilized by schools or districts are an examination of applicants' placement papers and a personal interview with candidates. Although these procedures possess certain advantages, each also has certain weaknesses of which the school administrator needs to be more aware.

An examination of placement papers has as its main purpose the screening of applicants so as to determine which ones should be invited for personal interviews. A candidate's placement papers may contain a great deal of useful information, depending on how the forms are designed. But the person or team who examines this information needs to keep in mind that the primary objective of the individual who completes a written application and submits placement papers is to project a favorable image. For example, it is unlikely that an applicant will list someone as a reference or ask someone to write a recommendation for him unless the candidate is reasonably sure that a favorable recommendation will be sent. It is also unlikely that a candidate will knowingly reveal in a statement of philosophy anything which might impair the possibility of securing a job. Certain information requested is factual, of course, such as the number of years taught, or the age of an individual, but most of the content of an application form or placement papers is subjective and therefore should not be accepted at face value.

It is useful to keep in mind while examining recommendations or ratings of candidates that the frame of reference of the person writing the statement or making the recommendation is generally unknown and consequently, one can seldom be absolutely sure what the ratings or recommendations mean. Also, a rater or person writing a letter of recommendation for an employee may not convey his true feelings for fear of losing the employee (or for fear of *not* losing him!) For these reasons, then, the administrator should carefully scrutinize the data contained on application forms and placement papers, and should exhibit considerable caution in drawing firm conclusions about candidates, based only on such data. [16] Perhaps the best use of placement credentials is to develop hypotheses and questions about candidates, which can later be explored during a personal interview.*

PLANNING AND CONDUCTING THE INTERVIEW

After application forms and placement papers have been examined by the staff selection team, a decision should be made to invite for interviews those individuals who seem to meet the selection criteria to the greatest extent. The team may interview each candidate, the administrator may decide to conduct

*This recommendation is buttressed by evidence from a study which found that, for the most part, candidates' placement papers did not differentiate between effective and ineffective teachers. See Paul Arend, "Teacher Selection: The Relationship Between Selected Factors and the Rated Effectiveness of Second Year Teachers." An ERIC Report: Ed-087-102, 1973.

the interview unilaterally, or another type of interviewing arrangement may be implemented. Regardless of who is conducting the interview, however, careful planning is a key to its success.

The importance of planning for the interview is underscored in a study by Clower, who found that (1) most interviews were not effective in revealing a candidate's ability to teach, his philosophy of education, or his basic preparation for teaching, and (2) applicants were leaving the interviews with only a hazy idea regarding possible employment.[17] Apparently, more thorough planning for the staff selection interview is needed if it is to accomplish its intended purpose. Planning for a staff selection interview should include consideration of the questions identified in figure 8.3.

---

1. What are the objectives of the interview? What do we hope to accomplish?
2. How can we best establish rapport with the candidate at the beginning of the interview, to facilitate communication and candor?
3. What kinds of questions should be asked during the interview to ascertain what we want to know or confirm about the candidate? How should these questions be sequenced?
4. What are likely to be the objectives of the candidate during the interview? What does he/she hope to achieve?
5. What kinds of questions is the candidate likely to ask?
6. What kinds of information or knowledge do we want to be sure that the candidate has been given before leaving the interview?

Figure 8.3. Key Questions in Planning for an Interview.

During the interviews, the staff selection team should attempt to convey an atmosphere of friendliness and warmth, but team members should recognize that their primary objective is to determine candidates' suitability for a particular staff vacancy. This means that the selection team will need to ask penetrating questions of each candidate to reveal individual strengths *and* weaknesses, since many if not most candidates will attempt to project their best image and will seldom volunteer information or be very open about their limitations.

In asking questions the administrator should try to avoid six common errors in interviewing: (1) posing questions that can be answered by "yes," or "no," thereby eliciting little information from the candidate, (2) asking unimaginative questions for which the astute applicant already has prepared answers, (3) asking leading questions which suggest the "correct answers," (4) asking questions which reveal the interviewer's attitude on the questions, (5) asking questions which are unrelated to the task, and (6) asking questions which were already answered on the candidate's application form or resume. [18] Instead, the administrator and the staff selection team should concentrate on asking questions which require candidates to discuss in depth their background, qualifications, and interest in the vacancy.

After an interview the members of the staff selection team should discuss their impressions, and then attempt to rate the candidate on the extent to which he met the previously defined selection criteria. Perhaps at this point a decision will be made to hire or reject a particular candidate, although there is value to interviewing all candidates scheduled for conferences before a final decision is made. It is important that the selection team should be sure to maintain a *written* record summarizing impressions of the rating given to each candidate. Such a record will he helpful later, when a final decision on hiring must be reached, or in the eventuality that any question may be raised about the selection process.

When all of the candidates scheduled for conferences have been interviewed and evaluated, the selection team should be ready to make a final decision on the individual whom they will recommend for employment. At this stage the administrator and the selection team should be aware of the degree to which their own personal biases may potentially influence their decisions.

For example, a study by Merritt disclosed that principals are more attracted to candidates with attitudes about education that are similar to their own, than to candidates with dissimilar attitudes. [19] This finding would not appear to possess any special significance unless one also knows that the principals in the study preferred candidates with attitudes similar to their own *regardless* of whether the candidates had high or low qualifications. Highly qualified candidates were selected by the principal only when they possessed attitudes about education similar to his own, and candidates with low qualifications were selected over more highly qualified candidates when the former possessed attitudes about education which were similar to those of the principal.

A major implication of Merritt's study is that an interviewer's attitude can exert an important influence on the evaluation of a candidate—an influence which could result in the rejection of a highly qualified individual in favor of one who may be less qualified. Awareness of this possibility by the administrator and the selection team, and a conscious attempt toward greater objectivity should help a great deal to avoid this pitfall. While it is certainly important that there be a reasonable degree of attitude similarity between new staff and the administrator in regard to how they view education, improving educational opportunities for students will hardly be achieved by rejecting highly qualified candidates in favor of those with lower qualifications but with attitudes more similar to those of the administrator. In selecting staff, a certain amount of diversity in thinking is desirable and perhaps should even be deliberately sought by a school administrator.

STAFF INDUCTION

After the new members of a staff have been hired, the process of induction or orientation should begin immediately. Staff induction is a process by which recently employed individuals are helped to become oriented to a new environment, which includes the community, the school system, the teaching position, and the people with whom they will be working.[20] The importance of the process is underlined by the observations of McCleary and Hencley:

> Orientation requires sensitive planning and careful execution. It is during the orientation period that new staff members gather their first impressions concerning the school's policies, objectives, leadership, and method of operation. Moreover, it is at this time that initial acquaintance is made with colleagues and with the community inhabitants, characteristics, agencies, and services. Since first impressions are often lasting, every effort should be expended during orientation to assure that new staff members gain correct understanding of the many facets of school and community life.[21]

PROBLEMS OF NEW STAFF

To plan an effective orientation program for new staff, the administrator will need to be knowledgeable about the problems they may encounter. An analysis of research on the problems of beginning teachers in adjusting to their new environment suggests that they frequently experience difficulties in the following major areas during their first year of teaching: (1) knowing what is expected of them, (2) planning and organizing for teaching, (3) motivating and evaluating students, (4) controlling and disciplining students, (5) establishing friendly and cooperative relationships with other members of the school or district, (6) communicating with parents and the community, and (7) achieving personal and professional self-confidence.[22]

Whether the problems experienced by new teachers during their first year result from their own deficiencies or from a poor induction program, or both, is not certain. However, there is some evidence to indicate that many school and district induction programs can be characterized as "too little, too late."[23] Most school districts seem to give considerable emphasis, before school starts, to orienting new staff members to the school district itself; but orientation to the community (particularly the community adjacent to the school), and to teaching in the assigned school, seems lacking. There also appears to be little or no follow-through during the year, once initial orientation activities have been concluded.[24] As a result, many new teachers continue to develop questions and feelings similar to those reported in a survey of beginning teachers after the third week of school, and identified in figure 8.4.[25]

1. "Why don't I have any permanent classroom or office of my own?"
2. "How can the school expect me to teach in my minor area?"
3. "What, exactly, is my total assignment in this school?"
4. "What do I do to motivate the kids to learn what I am teaching? And how do I evaluate and grade these kids?"
5. "What do I do about the kids who can't learn? How do I handle the troublemakers in my classes?"
6. "How do I handle this angry parent who keeps calling me to complain about the way I'm treating her child?"
7. "How does one get accepted in this school by the older teachers?"
8. "I am unsure. Do the students and the other teachers really like me, accept me, and think I am a good teacher?"

Figure 8.4. Questions of New Teachers During the First Semester.

Questions like the ones presented in figure 8.4 support the need for a *continuous* induction program. As the National Education Association has pointed out, "The orientation of teachers is something that cannot be done in a single day or single week or in a matter of weeks." [26]

A RECOMMENDED INDUCTION PROGRAM

The induction process should actually begin when the new staff member is employed and should continue through the first year until the individual has adjusted successfully to the school environment. The process should include the following steps and provisions: [27]

Phase I. *Before the Beginning of the School Year*
   A. A letter should be sent by the principal to all new staff members, welcoming them to the school and offering to help with any questions or problems they may be facing. The letter should also extend an invitation to come to the school to confer about questions or problems. If possible, the new staff member should be informed in the letter about his specific teaching assignment and schedule, and told how to secure a copy of text material to use in class.
   B. The new staff member should be sent any material which would help orient him to the school or community prior to the preschool workshop, e.g., teacher handbook.
   C. An experienced staff member should be identified and assigned to help the new member of the staff become orientated to the

school, and to aid the beginner with any special problems that may arise during the school year, either in or out of the classroom. If feasible, the experienced staff member should be given released time to carry out this responsibility of helping a beginning teacher, and new staff should be given a reduced teaching load until they get "their feet on the ground."[28]

Phase II. *Initial School Workshop and New Staff Orientation*
   A. New staff members should be introduced to the entire faculty at the first meeting.
   B. Separate meetings for new staff members during the initial school workshop should be scheduled which focus on the following topics:
      1. nature of the student body and the surrounding community
      2. school philosophy and objectives
      3. overall school operating policies and procedures
      4. the role of supporting personnel in the school or district, e.g., guidance counselor, and apporopriate referral procedures
      5. discipline policies and procedures
      6. attendance policies and procedures
      7. requisitioning procedures and the use of supplies.

   During these separate meetings, new staff members should be encouraged to ask questions, and time should be provided at later meetings, if necessary, for questions to be raised which may not have been answered in exploring the above topics.* The goals of the initial workshop in regard to inducting new staff members should be to help them begin to function effectively in a new setting and to become known and accepted by the total school faculty.

Phase III. *Follow-Up Induction Activities*
   As indicated earlier, staff induction should not be a "one-shot affair" during the initial school workshop, but should be a continuous process during the entire first year of the new staff member's employment. Although certain new faculty members may need less orientation and in-service help than others, the following activities should be beneficial to most of the new staff during the first year:

---

*The administrator might consider showing a filmstrip, entitled, "Thank God It's Friday," which depicts the problems of a beginning teacher during the first year. This 25-minute sound filmstrip could be used to stimulate questions on the part of new teachers in the school, and may be ordered through the National Association of Secondary School Principals.

A. Monthly "rap sessions" with the principal and other appropriate individuals for the purpose of discussing the questions, problems, and experiences encountered by new staff members.

B. Individual conferences, as needed, with the principal and the assigned "buddy" teacher. The availability of these conferences will need to be made explicit and their use periodically encouraged before they will be utilized by new staff members to the degree desired.

C. Interclass and interschool visitations to observe the demonstration of various teaching techniques.

D. Specific supervisory assistance early in the year with attendance, discipline, and grading. These three areas seem to give the greatest problems to new staff members, and they will appreciate concrete suggestions from the administrators of the school.

Phase IV. *Evaluation of the Induction Program*

The induction program is no different than any other program, in that it must be evaluated if it is to be improved. An important source of assistance in evaluating a program is its users, which in this case are the new staff members. Therefore, the school administrator should attempt during the year (particularly toward the end of the year) to obtain evaluative feedback from the new members of the staff about the strengths and weaknesses of various components of the induction program, with recommendations for improvement. By securing such feedback, the administrator will not only convey the fact that he cares about the feelings and perceptions of new staff members, but he will also be in a much better position to improve the school induction program for the following year.

A FINAL NOTE

In many school systems, the building administrator's involvement in staff recruitment, selection, and induction is limited. This is regrettable, since there is a long and continuing tradition of holding the administrator accountable for the performance of the professional staff in the school. It would appear reasonable that if the building administrator is to be held accountable, he should play a significant role in the recruitment, selection, and induction of the professional staff. Certainly no other administrator is in a better position to know the needs of the school. Therefore, an important prerequisite for any effective staff recruitment, selection, and induction program is the major involvement of the building administrator.

Review

1. What is the main purpose of the district's recruiting program? Describe the ways in which an administrator can make an important contribution to that program.
2. Why is it important for the building administrator to be involved directly in the process of staff selection?
3. Identify the steps involved in the staff selection process. How might the use of a staff selection team help with the process?
4. Describe the factors an administrator should consider in determining staff selection *criteria* and in analyzing placement papers.
5. Discuss the factors an administrator should consider in planning for and conducting the staff selection *interview*.
6. What is the main purpose of a staff induction program? What types of problems do many beginning teachers encounter, and what kinds of steps should a school take to prevent and/or ameliorate these types of problems?

Notes

1. Daniel E. Griffiths et al., *Organizing Schools for Effective Education* (Danville, Ill.: Interstate Printers and Publishers, 1963), p. 165.

2. Bernard H. McKenna, *Staffing the Schools* (New York: Teachers College, Columbia University, 1965), p. 1.

3. Dale L. Bolton, *Selection and Evaluation of Teachers* (Berkeley, Calif.: McCutchan Publishing Corp., 1973), pp. 50-54.

4. William B. Castetter, *Administering the School Personnel Program* (New York: Macmillan Co., 1962), p. 174.

5. Dale L. Bolton, "Teacher Recruitment and Selection." An ERIC Report: Ed-043-797 (1971), pp. 2-3.

6. Samuel Goldman, *The School Principal* (New York: Center for Applied Research in Education, 1966), p. 52.

7. Bolton, *Selection and Evaluation of Teachers*.

8. Adapted from a Position Guide of Milwaukee Public Schools, Milwaukee, Wis.

9. Robert J. Babcock, "How to Hook Those First-Year Teachers," *School Management* 12 (March 1968):60-63.

10. Paul Fitzgerald, "Recruitment of Teachers—A Need for Re-evaluation," *Personnel Journal* 2 (April 1970):312-14.

11. J. E. Corbally et al., *Educational Administration: The Secondary School* (Boston: Allyn & Bacon, 1961), pp. 149-50.

12. This principle has long been supported by the American Association of School Administrators, which has stated that "Since principals have a big stake in the outcome, they should have a voice in the selection of candidates." American Association of School Administrators, *Staff Relations in School Administration* (Washington, D.C., 1955), p. 35.

13. Bolton, *Selection and Evaluation of Teachers*.

14. Vincent C. DiPasquale, "Teacher Selection as an Imperative for the Improvement of Our Schools." An ERIC Report: Ed-049-164 (1970), p. 23.

15. See Ned A. Flanders and Anita Simon, "Teacher Effectiveness," in *Encyclopedia of Educational Research,* ed. Robert L. Ebel (New York: Macmillan Co., 1969), pp. 1423-37. For an up-dated review of research on the topic, see chap. 10.

16. Also see Henry C. Gozarth, "A Study of the Validity of Letters of Recommendation for Screening Candidates for Foundations of Educational Administration at the University of Texas." (Master's thesis, University of Texas, 1956.)

17. Helen L. Clower, "The Use of the Personal Interview in the Selection of Teachers." (Ed.D. diss., University of Southern California, 1963).

18. Richard H. Magee, "The Employment Interview—Techniques of Questioning," *Personnel Journal* (May 1962):241-45.

19. Daniel L. Merritt, "Attitude Congruency and Selection of Teacher Candidates," *Administrator's Notebook* 19 (February 1971).

20. William Vanderlip, "Teacher Orientation—A Program with a Purpose," *The Clearing House* 42 (May 1968):526.

21. Lloyd E. McCleary and Stephen P. Hencley, *Secondary School Administration: Theoretical Bases for Professional Practice* (New York: Dodd, Mead and Co., 1965), p. 287.

22. See George W. Bond and George S. Smith, "The First Year of Teaching," *National Elementary Principal* 47 (September 1967):8. Also see Richard Wisniewski, *New Teachers in Urban Schools: An Inside View* (New York: Random House, 1968); and Kevin Ryan, *Survival Is Not Enough: Overcoming Problems of Beginning Teachers* (Washington, D.C.: American Federation of Teachers, 1974).

23. Sol Taylor, "Orientation and In-Service Education Programs for Beginning Secondary School Teachers." (Ed.D. diss., University of Southern California, 1971.)

24. Ibid.

25. Richard A. Gorton, "Questions of New Teachers after the Third Week of School" (unpublished study, 1969).

26. "Editorial: Welcome to the New Teacher," *National Education Association Journal* 52 (October 1963):10.

27. Adapted from *Guidelines for Principals: Project on the Induction of Beginning Teachers* (Washington, D.C.: National Association of Secondary School Principals, 1969).

28. For ideas on how to structure this relationship properly, see Patricia Swanson, "A Time to Teach—and a Time to Learn," *Bulletin of the National Association of Secondary School Principals* 52 (October, 1968):74-84.

9
Administrator-Staff Relations

The school administrator works with a variety of people, including students, teachers, and parents. Although no single individual or group should be considered by the administrator to be more important than another, there is little doubt that his relationship with the staff will significantly influence his effectiveness as a leader. While a positive relationship won't guarantee effective administrative leadership, it is difficult to conceive how an administrator could continue to function successfully as a leader if his relationship with the staff were a negative one.

In the sections which follow, two aspects of administrator-staff relationships are explored: (1) staff satisfaction and morale, and (2) collective bargaining.

STAFF SATISFACTION AND MORALE

DEFINITION AND PURPOSE

Most administrators recognize the importance of developing and maintaining high staff satisfaction and morale, even if they are not sure how to achieve these goals.

Satisfaction and morale are attitudinal variables which reflect positive or negative feelings about a particular situation or person(s). The two concepts are often used synonymously in the educational literature, and it is easy to understand why. The state of one's morale reflects the extent of his satisfaction with a situation or person. Satisfaction can also refer to one's feelings about himself or the situation in which he finds himself, although most studies of the concept have concentrated on the latter. Both terms can refer to the attitudinal characteristics of either a group or an individual.

Many attempts have been made to define the terms "satisfaction" and "morale." The term *satisfaction,* as it applies to the work context of teaching, seems to refer to the degree to which an individual can meet his personal and professional needs in the performance of his role as a teacher. [1] *Morale*, on the other hand, as defined in the educational literature seems to hold a broader meaning. Gross, for example, in his study of staff leadership in the schools, identified the following six indices of teacher morale:

1. Displays a sense of pride in the school
2. Enjoys working in the school

3. Displays a sense of loyalty to the school
4. Works cooperatively with fellow teachers
5. Accepts the educational philosophy underlying the curriculum of the school
6. Respects the judgment of the school administrators. [2]

High staff satisfaction and morale can be considered either as ends in themselves or as necessary conditions for achieving the educational objectives of a school. If the two are considered as ends in themselves, then the administrator is assuming that high staff satisfaction and morale are intrinsically valuable. Although, high satisfaction and morale are certainly desirable, it may be necessary in *some* circumstances for an administrator to actually create some teacher dissatisfaction in order to improve a stagnant situation. Such action must be taken thoughtfully and carefully, with the realization that important and needed changes generally will not occur as long as people are satisfied with the status quo.

The writer's position is that high staff satisfaction and morale may be desirable as ends in themselves, but their primary value is in helping to achieve other kinds of worthwhile goals. These goals would include staff stability, cohesiveness, and increased effectiveness. Although research on the consequences of high or low staff satisfaction and morale is not conclusive, it would appear that the extent of staff satisfaction and morale can influence the degree to which the goals previously mentioned can be achieved. [3] For these reasons then, the administrator needs to understand better the factors which contribute to low or high staff satisfaction and morale, and based on that understanding he should develop conditions which will build and maintain the latter.

FACTORS WHICH AFFECT STAFF SATISFACTION

Most of the major conceptual and empirical work on employee satisfaction had, until recently, been performed in the business sector. [4] Perhaps the most valuable contribution was that of Frederick Herzberg. Herzberg theorized that the factors which satisfy employees and the factors which dissatisfy employees are mutually exclusive and are not aligned along a continuum. [5] He found, for example, in his study of accountants and engineers that the factors presented in figure 9.1 contributed to satisfaction *or* dissatisfaction, but not to both.

Herzberg found that the existence of the five factors listed in figure 9.1 under "Satisfaction" tended to affect the employees' attitudes in a positive direction. However, interestingly, a reduction of these same factors did *not* result in job *dissatisfaction*. On the other hand, an improvement in one or more of the eleven factors listed under "Dissatisfaction" in figure 9.1 tended

Satisfaction	Dissatisfaction
1. Achievement	1. Salary
2. Recognition	2. Possibility of growth
3. Work itself	3. Interpersonal relations (subordinates)
4. Responsibility	4. Status
5. Advancement	5. Interpersonal relations (superiors)
	6. Interpersonal relations (peers)
	7. Supervision—technical
	8. Company policy and administration
	9. Working conditions
	10. Personal life
	11. Job security

Figure 9.1. Herzberg's Satisfaction/Dissatisfaction Factors

to reduce employee dissatisfaction, but this change did not ensure employee satisfaction.

A major implication of Herzberg's research would appear to be that the administrator cannot assume that modification of a factor creating dissatisfaction will automatically result in job satisfaction, nor can it be assumed that failure to maintain a satisfactory condition will inevitably result in staff dissatisfaction. Different factors seem to be involved in creating satisfaction or dissatisfaction on the part of employees.

Following Herzberg's work several studies in education have been initiated in an attempt to verify his findings. Sergiovanni, for example, conducted a study of 3,382 teachers and discovered that achievement, recognition, and responsibility contributed predominantly to staff satisfaction.[6] Advancement was not a factor which was associated with satisfaction of teachers, or, for that matter, with dissatisfaction. The work itself was a potential source of either satisfaction or dissatisfaction.

As revealed in Sergiovanni's investigation, those factors which seemed to contribute primarily to teacher dissatisfaction were poor relations with peers and students, unfair or incompetent administrative and supervisory policies and practices, and outside personal problems. The remaining factors associated with dissatisfaction in Herzberg's study (see fig. 9.1) turned out to be potentially significant for creating either satisfaction or dissatisfaction. It should be noted that the conditions affecting satisfaction or dissatisfaction, or both, as reflected in Sergiovanni's study, did not vary with the sex, teaching level, or tenure status of the teacher. (Related studies by Johnson[7] and Adair[8] have supported, in essence, the findings of Sergiovanni regarding the validity of the Herzberg model for education.[9])

It would appear then, that by and large the same factors do not hold equal potential for creating staff satisfaction or dissatisfaction: the conditions which create staff satisfaction seem to be associated with the work itself, while the conditions which contribute to dissatisfaction seem to be associated with the environment of work, particularly the interpersonal relations aspect of that environment. These findings are consistent with Maslow's theory that individuals have a hierarchy of needs and that lower level needs such as security must be met before the higher level needs such as achievement or responsibility become important. [10]

FACTORS WHICH AFFECT STAFF MORALE

While much of the research on staff satisfaction and morale has been based on the Herzberg model, findings from other studies also merit consideration by the administrator. Strickland, for example, identified a number of factors (presented in figure 9.2) which were perceived by teachers to contribute to the raising or the lowering of their morale.

(In descending order of importance)

Raises Teacher Morale	*Lowers Teacher Morale*
1. Cooperative and helpful coworkers who share ideas and materials	1. Lack of relief from pupil contact during the school day
2. A helpful and cooperative principal	2. Clerical duties
3. Appreciative and cooperative parents	3. Lack of cooperation and support from principal
4. Adequate supplies and equipment	4. Inadequate school plant
5. Freedom in classroom teaching	5. Lack of staff cooperation
6. Respectful pupils	6. Excessive teaching load
7. An adequate school plant	7. Low salary
8. Pupils interested in school work	8. Lack of parental cooperation and interest
9. A helpful supervisor	9. Poor pupil discipline
10. A well-organized school with formulated policies	10. Lack of proper equipment and supplies

Figure 9.2. Factors Which Raise or Lower Teacher Morale. [11]

In another study, involving 5,000 teachers in twenty-four school systems Redefer discovered that the two factors most significantly related to the morale of the faculty were the evaluation given by the administrator to the teachers and the quality of education in the individual schools. [12] A major implication of his findings is that if an administrator wants to build and maintain good faculty morale, one of the more important things he can do is to attempt to develop the best possible educational program. If teachers feel that they are associated with a good education program, then possibly some of the other factors which may contribute to low or high morale will not seem so important.

The research results reported thus far on staff satisfaction and morale have implied, if not stated explicitly, the importance of the administrator's behavior. A study by Lambert further documents this importance. [13]

Lambert studied the relationship between faculty morale and school principals' leadership behavior in twenty-one schools. The research instruments used to collect data from the teachers were Halpin's *Leader Behavior Description Questionnaire* and the *Purdue Teacher Opinionnaire.* An analysis of the data showed that high "leader behavior" scores were associated with high morale scores, and that the "consideration" component of the *Leader Behavior Description Questionnaire* was more closely correlated with teacher morale than was the "initiating" component. [14] (The consideration factor reflects the extent of mutual trust, respect, and warmth between a leader and the group with whom he is working; the initiating factor is concerned with a leader's establishing for a group the necessary procedures, channels of communication, and ways of getting a job done.) Lambert found, in addition, that when the teachers in the study perceived their morale as low, they also perceived the total educational environment as low.

Concluding this section on teacher morale is a study by Napier identifying twelve factors which were associated with *high* teacher morale: [15]

1. The administrator's understanding and appreciation of the teacher as an individual
2. The confidence the teacher has in the administrator's professional competence
3. The support the teacher receives from the administration regarding discipline problems
4. Teacher participation in the formulation of policies that affect them
5. Adequate facilities and equipment; adequate teaching supplies
6. Teaching assignments which are commensurate with training
7. Fair and equitable distribution of extracurricular assignments
8. Professional training provided through an in-service program
9. Job security
10. An adequate policy for leave of absence
11. A fair and equitable distribution of the teaching load
12. Salaries that are comparable with professions requiring equal training.

The results of Napier's research again underscore the importance of the administrator's exhibiting educational leadership, consideration for others, and the development of a good educational program, as essential conditions for building and maintaining high staff morale.

RECOMMENDATIONS

Research studies on staff satisfaction and morale can be instructive. However, unless the findings are translated into recommeded courses of action, they will represent little more than interesting reading. Therefore, based primarily on the findings presented in the previous sections, the following guidelines are offered to the administrator who wishes to develop and maintain high staff satisfaction and morale in the school.

1. **Attempt on a regular basis to obtain systematic feedback from the staff as individuals and as a group, on their perceptions of the problems, concerns, and issues which they feel affect them personally or the school generally.**

    The administrator cannot hope to develop and maintain high satisfaction and morale on the part of the staff unless he knows what is on their minds; and he cannot realistically hope to arrive at this knowledge without actually asking the staff periodically for this information. Two procedures for achieving this goal would be the administering of anonymous questionnaires each semester, asking the staff to identify what they see as the main problems and issues affecting the school, and a principal-teacher "rap period" scheduled at least biweekly for teachers who want to discuss problems and issues on an individual basis.

2. **Exert a major effort toward improving the satisfaction which teachers derive from classroom teaching.**

    The research on teacher satisfaction and morale indicates that when teachers feel a sense of accomplishment from teaching and receive due recognition for their efforts and performance, teacher satisfaction and morale are high.*

    Improving the conditions under which teachers teach—size of class, type of facilities, quantity and quality of teaching materials, problem nature of the class, the quality of administrative and supervisory supporting services, and increasing opportunities for initiative, responsibility and achievement—are administrative contributions which should increase the likelihood that teachers can obtain a sense of accomplishment from their endeavors. [16] Recognition for their accomplishments could take the form of a personal tribute at a faculty or PTA meeting, an individual letter

---

*For an interesting report of a study on this point, see Roland B. Kimball, "A Study of Rewards and Incentives for Teachers," *Phi Delta Kappan* 55 (May 1974):637-38.

with a copy for the teacher's personnel file, or a recommendation for advancement on the salary scale.

3. **Strive to improve the operation of the school and the overall quality of the educational program of the school.**

People feel pleased and proud to work in a school that is efficiently administered and that offers a quality educational program. [17]

A poorly organized school with a limited or mediocre educational program is bound to affect adversely the morale and satisfaction of its teachers. According to Redefer, one of the major factors associated with faculty morale is the quality of the school's educational program. Consequently, the administrator who improves the quality of a school's educational program will concurrently be improving the morale of the faculty.

4. **Try to be sensitive to problems of an interpersonal nature between and among teachers, students, and parents, and try to mediate these problems when appropriate.**

Problems of interpersonal relations seem to be one of the main factors which contribute to low teacher satisfaction and morale, according to research. The administrator will probably experience difficulty in ascertaining these kinds of problems, however, because in many instances the people involved may be reluctant to talk to him about them. He can partially overcome this handicap by becoming more aware of what is going on in the school and by showing understanding and compassion when such problems are brought to his attention. The administrator himself may not always be in the best possible position to mediate these kinds of problems, but he certainly will need to take steps to see that they are resolved, if he wants to avoid a decline in faculty morale.

5. **Provide meaningful participation for teachers in the decision-making processes of the school.**

There is considerable evidence that teachers desire a more active and meaningful role in school decision making. [18] Research evidence also suggests that increased teacher involvement can result in higher faculty morale. Leiman, for example, concluded in his study that teachers who participated in school administration manifested: [19]

   a. Higher morale than teachers who did not participate
   b. More positive attitudes toward their principals, their colleagues, and their pupils, and
   c. Higher regard for themselves and for the teaching profession.

6. **Practice good human relations in your own interactions with the faculty as a whole and with individual faculty members.**

The type of relationship between the faculty and the school administrator is probably one of the most important factors affecting faculty morale. [20] If that relationship is perceived as a good one, faculty morale is likely to be high; if it is perceived as a poor one, faculty morale is likely to be low.

A major factor influencing the type of relationship that exists between a faculty and the administrator will be the kind of human relations that he practices. Although obviously many different ingredients contribute to good human relations, the following seem essential for any administrator:

a. Be sensitive to the needs of others.
b. Attempt to explain the reasons for your actions.
c. Try to involve others in decisions about the school.
d. Be open to criticism; try not to be defensive.
e. Be willing to admit mistakes and to make changes.
f. Be honest and fair in your interactions with others.

A critical review of twenty-five years of research on morale concluded that whether or not teachers were satisfied depended primarily on the quality of the administrative relationships in which teachers were involved and the quality of the leadership they received. [21] And a study of education in an urban setting found that significant improvement in reading skills was related to high teacher morale which was associated with principal leadership behavior. [22] Therefore, a major key to high faculty morale and satisfaction seems to be the leadership behavior of the school administrator.

COLLECTIVE BARGAINING AND THE SCHOOL ADMINISTRATOR

Beginning in the 1960s a new element entered into the relationship between the faculty and the school administrator: collective bargaining. [23] Although previously many school boards and administrators, on their own initiative, had informally consulted with teachers about conditions of employment, and the operation of the school, introduction of the concept of collective bargaining meant that the school board and administrators were required to consult and negotiate with the teachers about these matters. [24] As a result, school boards and administrators were no longer free to make unilateral decisions affecting the faculty's welfare, but had to share decision-making authority with the teachers. Since most, if not all of the decision-making authority which teachers wanted to share had traditionally been considered management's prerogatives, teachers' attempts to gain and expand their rights under collective bargaining were certain to affect the role of school administrators, particularly the school principal.[25]

For the building administrator, collective bargaining has raised four basic questions: (1) What should be the role of the school principal in collective bargaining? (2) What should be his role in contract administration? (3) What should be his role in grievance procedures? and (4) What should be his role in a teachers' strike? Although the principals' role in these four areas is in a state of transition, the following sections will discuss recommendations and problems associated with each of the four roles.

THE PRINCIPAL'S ROLE IN COLLECTIVE BARGAINING

At the outset of collective bargaining between school boards and teacher groups, most principals seemed uncertain as to whether or not they should participate.[26] Early opinions among principals ranged from a desire to remain detached from collective bargaining for fear of jeopardizing their relationship with teachers, to a preference and concern that building administrators be involved in all aspects of collective bargaining lest they lose significant decision-making authority to the faculty. Eventually, the latter conception of the role of the building administrator in collective bargaining prevailed, as evidenced by a statement by Benjamin Epstein in an official document of The National Association of Secondary School Principals:

> The members of NASSP feel very strongly that principals and other administrators must be included in every phase of collective decision making whenever their fate and that of the schools for which they are responsible are to be determined.[27]

Statements published by The National Elementary Principals Association during the 1960s showed that it, too, supported the concept of involving the principal in all aspects of collective bargaining that affect his role.[28]

While the official position of the principals' associations and the eventual opinion of most principals was that the principal should be involved in all aspects of collective bargaining between school boards and teachers that affect his role, this concept was not immediately accepted by either of the latter two groups.

In the early years of collective bargaining, many teachers and school boards seemed to feel that the building administrator should be excluded from the process of collective bargaining; surprisingly, most superintendents seemed to concur.[29] It was not until later that district administrators and school boards began to recognize the desirability of involving principals in the process of collective bargaining. Not only could principals contribute useful ideas and perceptions to the formulation of a district's bargaining proposal, but their reactions to the teachers' bargaining demands were essential for the development of an educationally sound and enforceable master contract. [30]

Although not all building administrators participate to the same extent in the collective bargaining process, it would appear that the following guidelines are appropriate to the effective utilization of a building administrator's talents:

1. Building administrators should be involved in the *formulation* of the school board's bargaining position. Specifically, *all* building administrators should be asked (prior to the development of the board's bargaining proposal to teachers) to submit suggested items which relate to education at the school building level for consideration during the bargaining process.

2. Building administrators should be represented on the negotiation team for the school board or on an advisory committee which gives counsel to the negotiation team during the bargaining process. The most appropriate way of involving the building administrators in the bargaining process is not easy to determine, and will depend to a large extent on school board and administrative philosophies, along with conditions within the local district. Obviously, not all building administrators can be involved equally, and different forms of participation may be appropriate. However, the key factor is that regardless of the form of involvement, it is essential that the building administrators' point of view be presented and adequately considered during the bargaining process.

3. Building administrators should, as a group or through their representative, be given an opportunity to evaluate the implications of any item considered during collective bargaining which may affect the operation of the school, their role in the school, or their relationship with others associated with the school. Building administrators are usually the ones who are primarily responsible for interpreting and enforcing the provisions of the master contract. Many of the items which are negotiated affect them and the operation of the school. They should therefore be given an opportunity to evaluate the effect of these factors on the school and its administration.

Building administrators can and should play an important role in the formulation of the school board's bargaining position and during the bargaining process itself. [31] If a school board and a superintendent choose to ignore the building administrators' abilities and perceptions, they run the risk not only of alienating an important component of their management team, but also of failing to capitalize on a valuable source of ideas and insights.

THE PRINCIPAL'S ROLE IN CONTRACT ADMINISTRATION

The final product of the bargaining process is a master contract between the school board and the teachers' group. The master contract contains in essence the various agreements which were reached during collective bargaining, to which management and employees alike are expected to adhere.

The school principal is usually viewed by the school board and the district administration as their main agent in administering the master contract, since the vast majority of the teachers are located at the school building level. The principal is the chief administrator at this level, so he is the one who is expected to interpret and enforce the master contract for management. He may be able to secure assistance from the district office when significant questions or problems arise, but he typically has the main responsibility at the building level for administering the master contract.

Contract administration at the building level usually consists of two major tasks: (1) interpreting the language and intent of the provisions of the contract, and, (2) enforcing the terms of the contract.* A third task, implementing the grievance procedures, can be considered a part of contract administration but is sufficiently important to warrant separate treatment in the next section.

Interpreting

The role of the principal in interpreting the language and intent of provisions of the master contract can be a difficult or easy one, depending on the precision with which the contract was written and the degree to which he received adequate orientation about the contract before he was expected to begin administering it. [32]

Master contracts which contain such phrases as, "if at all possible," "when feasible," and "every effort will be made," may provide the school board and/or teachers with desired flexibility but also place a large interpretative responsibility on the school principal. It is true that he may, if in doubt, be able to seek guidance from the district administration. However, the guidance which he receives from this source, although usually helpful, may not arrive in time, may *not* be useful, or may not agree with the teachers'

---

*For a very good discussion of contract administration by the school principal, see Gilbert R. Weldy, *Administering a Negotiated Contract* (Washington, D.C.: National Association of Secondary School Principals, 1973).

interpretation of the contract. As a result, in too many situations the school principal is forced to make his own interpretation of the language of the contract or else he finds himself in the middle between the district office's interpretation of the contract and the teachers' interpretation of the master contract.

A related problem which many principals have encountered in administering the master contract arises from the fact that they received inadequate orientation to the provisions and intent of the contract *prior* to its implementation. They were given a copy of the master contract, sometimes even *after* the teachers in the building received their copies, and were then instructed to administer it to the best of their ability. There have been occasions when the principal did not even receive a copy of the master contract until after the opening of school in the fall, although the master contract had been finalized earlier.

If the principal is to administer the master contract effectively, he should be provided with a comprehensive orientation to the contract *prior* to its implementation, and he should have an opportunity to ask questions about any of its features.[33] An orientation of this nature would minimize incorrect interpretations of the contract and should result in more uniform and consistent applications of its provisions. Certainly, such an orientation program would make it easier for the principal to effectively administer the master contract in the school.

Enforcing

Interpreting the master contract is one aspect of contract administration. Enforcing the provisions of the contract, particularly in regard to teachers, is a second important responsibility of the school principal. While some may assume that there is only one way to enforce the rules of a contract, a research study of rule enforcement by principals revealed three approaches, each with its consequences for administrator-faculty relations.[34]

Utilizing the Gouldner model of bureaucratic administration, Lutz and Evans investigated the effects of three types of rule administration by principals: "mock," "representative," and "punishment-centered." *Mock* administration was defined as nonenforcement of the rules when teachers failed to observe them. *Representative* administration was defined as the cooperative acceptance of the rules by principal and teachers, accompanied by enforcement by the principal and obedience by the teachers. *Punishment-centered* rule administration was characterized by the principal's use of threat or punishment in order to achieve rule adherence by teachers. It should be noted, however, that no school was run solely through the use of one type of rule administration.

After spending a considerable length of time making observations, conducting interviews with the personnel, and collecting questionnaire data in six schools, the researchers succeeded in documenting the effects of each type of rule enforcement.

Positive feelings between the principal and the teachers seemed to be associated in most instances with mock administration of the rules. Nonenforcement was usually associated with such rules as board policy on smoking, the use of school telephones, teacher time cards, and the use of sick leave. In most of the situations when the principal ignored a rule, he felt that extenuating circumstances surrounded its violation by a teacher.* Nevertheless, it appeared in some cases that the administrator was concerned about the lack of rule enforcement.

In those instances when the principal engaged in representative rule administration, tension between teachers and the principal developed initially but subsided over time. With few exceptions, warmth and friendliness were observed in the relationship between the principal and staff, and a high rating of principal leadership was given by teachers whose principal exhibited representative rule administration as his dominant style. The researchers further discovered that when the principal engaged in representative rule enforcement, he initiated considerable informal, as well as formal, contact with teachers. As a result, complaints and problems frequently were resolved informally before they ever reached the grievance stage.

The key to effective representative rule enforcement seemed to be *intensive and extensive communication,* that is, explaining the rule and the reasons for it, and working with teachers on interpretation of the rule. Regular meetings between the principal and the teachers' building representative also appeared to be particularly helpful in reducing initial tensions and avoiding problems.

Data from the study indicated that punishment-centered administration was likely to produce negative consequences. Principals who tended to adhere to every rule and who used or threatened punishment in order to enforce the rules were regarded as "running a tight ship" but were usually given low leadership ratings by their teachers. More important, perhaps, was the fact that the tension and hostility which developed as a result of punishment-centered rule enforcement persisted beyond the original disagreement, thereby creating an atmosphere for potential future conflict between the administrator and the teachers.

Although the results of any study cannot be generalized for situations which are different, a school principal should realize that the quality of the

---

*In one research study, "mock" rule administration by principals was associated with superintendents who behaved in an authoritarian manner, e.g., high control methods. See William Caldwell and James Easton, "The Relationship Between the Superintendents' Management Behavior and Teachers' Perceptions of the Principal's Rule Administration Behavior." (Paper presented at American Educational Research Association Annual Meeting, 1974.)

relationship between himself and the staff will be affected by the approach he takes in enforcing the provisions of the master contract. Whether or not he should enforce every rule may, of course, depend in many instances on factors beyond his control. But the available research suggests that representative rule administration, as defined earlier, results in the most positive consequences in principal-staff relations.

THE PRINCIPAL'S ROLE IN GRIEVANCE PROCEDURES

A major objective of collective bargaining by teacher groups has been to secure the inclusion of grievance procedures in the master contract of the district. Although prior to collective bargaining, many school districts had informally mediated teacher grievances, these procedures did not, in the eyes of the teachers, sufficiently safeguard or guarantee their rights to a fair hearing and appeal.[35] Therefore, teacher associations and unions have concentrated on gaining formal grievance procedures in the master contract and, at the present time, most master contracts contain some type of formal grievance procedure for teachers.

A grievance procedure is, essentially, a method or process which requires the parties to a dispute to discuss and try to resolve the dispute, with an opportunity for appeal to a higher authority by either of the parties in disagreement with the initial resolution of the matter.[36] The two main purposes of such a procedure are to prevent either party to a dispute from acting unilaterally to resolve the matter, and to guarantee the right of appeal. If a master contract contains a grievance procedure, the administrator must respond to a teacher grievance by attempting to work out a cooperative solution.

Although there can be considerable disagreement over what constitutes a grievance under a master contract, grievances typically arise under the following conditions:[37]

1. a misinterpretation or incorrect application of the provisions of the master contract
2. an intentional violation of the provisions of the master contract
3. a practice contrary to school board policy
4. unfair or discriminatory behavior which may not be prohibited by the contract or school board policy, but which causes someone to feel that he has been wronged.

The latter condition listed above is, in many contracts, defined as a complaint rather than a grievance, and it may be handled informally by the administrator rather than by going through formal procedures and appeal.

Whether a teacher actually files a grievance with the administration will depend on many factors. First of all, one of the four conditions previously identified will need to be alleged. Second, the teacher will have to feel strongly enough about his grievance to lodge a formal protest to the administration. At this point the role of the building representative for the teachers' group will become very important.* The teacher with a grievance will normally go to the building representative before registering his protest to the principal. If the building representative is supportive, then the teacher is likely to file the grievance. If, on the other hand, the building representative indicates to the teacher that he doesn't have a legitimate grievance, or if the building representative attempts to persuade the teacher to resolve the matter informally rather than going through formal procedures, the teacher may never initiate the grievance with the administration. The role of the building representative can be crucial in determining whether or not a grievance should be or will be filed with the administration.

In examining research on the role of the building representative, it would appear that whether or not a building representative will encourage a teacher to file a grievance will depend to a large extent on the building representative's relationship with the administration of the school.[38] A study of this relationship showed that building representatives who felt that the administration had not communicated with them sufficiently and had not consulted with them frequently enough in school decision making tended to file more teacher grievances than those building representatives who were satisfied with the communication and participation provided by the administration. A negative attitude by the building representative toward the administration was also likely to increase the number of teacher grievances filed. The main implication of this research is that the school principal would be well advised to develop a good working relationship with the building representative for teachers. A positive relationship may not prevent *all* grievances, but it should do much to reduce unnecessary ones.

If a teacher and the building representative decide to file a grievance, they should follow the procedures specified in the master contract, which usually include the following steps:[39]

1. The teacher submits his grievance directly to the principal, within five days[†] after the teacher knows about or experiences the conditions giving rise to the grievance.

---

*Sometimes referred to as "chapter chairman," a building representative is an individual at the building level who represents the teachers in matters involving the master contract.

†The time limitations specified in the contract may vary slightly from one district to another.

2. If the grievance is not resolved to the satisfaction of the teacher within five days, the teacher can appeal the principal's decision to the superintendent or his representative.

3. Within five days of receipt of the written appeal, the superintendent or his representative, the teacher, and all other relevant parties, e.g., principal, building representative, meet in an attempt to resolve the matter. The administration must give its position on the grievance within five days after the meeting.

4. If the administration's response is not satisfactory to the teacher, he can appeal the matter to the school board. The school board or a subcommittee of the board then meets and must render a written decision within twenty days of the hearing.

Finally, arbitration by an outside agency may be part of the grievance procedure if the school board and the teachers have agreed to this previously, or if it is required by law. [40]

The principal's role during grievance procedures, particularly in the initial stages, is crucial. Many, if not most grievances can be resolved at the building level without going through additional steps of appeal—*if* the school principal performs his role effectively. While his role will vary somewhat, depending on the specific circumstances, the principal should carry out the following steps in relation to grievance procedures. [41]

1. **Study all the provisions of the master contract in order to understand them completely and accurately.** Resolving a teacher grievance will require that a principal possess a good understanding of the master contract. If he is not knowledgeable about the master contract, he may give the teacher an incorrect interpretation, or, worse yet, challenge a teacher's correct interpretation of the contract. During a grievance procedure the principal must be able to interpret the master contract correctly, and to do this, he must be knowledgeable about all aspects of that contract.

2. **If possible, attempt to resolve teacher concerns prior to their reaching the stage of formal grievances.** Many grievances can be resolved before they are formally filed with the principal of a school. A principal should try to be aware of teacher complaints and attempt to resolve them before they develop into formal grievances.

He should also attempt to be sensitive to the concerns of the teachers and make every feasible effort to improve working conditions and education in general in the building. These actions will not only help to reduce the number of grievances filed in a building but will also create a more positive attitude on the part of the teachers and the teachers' representative toward the principal if a situation ever reaches the formal grievance stage.

3. **The administrator should maintain his poise upon receiving a teacher grievance and no one should assume that the filing of a grievance constitutes a personal attack on the administrator of the school.** If the principal views the grievance in personal terms, he is less likely to be objective in his response to it, and his emotions may adversely affect the possibility of successfully resolving the grievance.

Neither should the district administration and school board use the number of grievances filed in a school during the year as a major basis for evaluating a building administrator's effectiveness. A large number of grievances in a building may indicate something about a principal's effectiveness, but it may only reflect a very militant faculty in that particular building. Grievances are filed for many reasons, and more investigation and study will be needed before a fair conclusion can be reached about their relationship to administrator effectiveness.

It also needs to be recognized by administrators that grievances are not necessarily "bad." They can represent positive opportunities to correct misunderstandings and to improve school conditions.

4. **If a teacher's concern reaches the grievance stage, try to understand the grievance from the teacher's point of view.** This does not mean that a principal should necessarily agree with a teacher or forget that he is representing management during a grievance proceeding. However, if the principal is to avoid any invalid assumptions or interpretations about the teacher's grievance, he must do everything possible to understand how the teacher views the situation which caused the grievance. While this type of understanding may not in itself resolve the grievance, it will reduce unnecessary conflict and appeals of the principal's proposed resolution of the grievance and it should result in a more positive attitude on the part of the teacher toward the principal.

5. **Consult with the district administration if there is doubt about how to proceed before and during the grievance conference.** Usually someone in the district administration has the responsibility of helping principals when grievances arise. This individual can be a source of considerable assistance to the principal who is unsure about some aspect of the master contract or about what course of action he should take in trying to deal with a teacher's grievance. Consultation between the principal and the district administration when a grievance arises is usually desirable and sometimes essential for appropriate resolution of the grievance.

6. **Set a conducive atmosphere for communication during the grievance conference, and provide and seek information which will help both parties to decide on the best course of action to take.** The principal should try to provide a quiet, private setting for the grievance conference, and during that conference he should try to facilitate communication as much as possible. He

should avoid interrupting the teacher or responding defensively. If appropriate, he should consider letting the teacher and the teacher's representative tell their view of the grievance first.

Under no circumstances should the principal attempt to negotiate with the teacher or make any precipitous decisions during the conference. The principal should offer whatever remedy is available under the master contract, but should not go beyond that. His basic task should be to provide and seek information that will enable him to make a proper decision on the disposition of the grievance, and that will give the teacher and the teacher's representative an adequate basis upon which to reach a decision about how they will proceed with the grievance.

7. **Give a response in writing to the teacher, concerning the disposition of the grievance after the conference(s).** The principal should not attempt to communicate to the teacher any final decision about the disposition of a grievance until there has been time after the grievance conference to think about the situation and, perhaps, to consult with the central administration. Then, when he has reached a final decision, it should be communicated in writing to the teacher, in order to minimize any inadvertent or intentional misinterpretations of the principal's decision. A written record of the principal's disposition of a grievance could become very important should the teacher decide to appeal the principal's decision.

8. **Make every effort to maintain a positive relationship with the teacher and the building representative, even if the grievance is appealed by the teacher to the principal's supervisor.** Obviously, this recommendation will frequently be difficult to implement. No one likes to have his decision challenged and appealed, and it would be perfectly normal for the principal to experience some negative feelings toward the teacher and the building representative if they should appeal his decision. However, the principal should remember that he will probably still be working with both of them long after the grievance is finally settled. For this reason, he should attempt to maintain as positive a relationship with the teacher and the building representative as possible during the appeal process, regardless of behavior on their part which may be upsetting to him at the time.

9. **Make sure that the solution is implemented fully, no matter what the final resolution of the teacher's grievance may be.** Regardless of whether the final resolution of the teacher's grievance supports or rejects the original decision by the principal, it is his responsibility to see that the solution is implemented promptly and fully. Lack of follow-through, particularly if the grievance is decided in favor of the teacher, can negatively affect relationships between the principal and other teachers and may result in future unnecessary grievances.

THE ADMINISTRATOR'S ROLE
IN A TEACHERS' STRIKE

Not all teacher grievances and collective bargaining can be resolved to the satisfaction of the teachers, and in some cases they may use the strike as their ultimate strategy for achieving their objectives.

Teachers' strikes usually put a severe strain on the relationship between the school administrator and the faculty. Unfortunately, the building administrator will in most cases be placed in an adversary relationship with teachers in the school. Although the building administrator may not be without sympathy for the teachers' cause, he will be expected by the school board and the district administration to represent management during the strike.[42] Their main expectation for the principal will be that he carry out all the school board's directives, even if their implementation may impair his current or even future relationships with the staff.

While the specific role of a school administrator in a teachers' strike will vary, depending on particular circumstances, it would appear that in most situations he will need the ability to anticipate problems accurately, to plan thoroughly, to be resourceful, and to maintain a sense of humor and perspective.

Obviously, the various problems that may occur during a teacher's strike cannot always be accurately anticipated in advance. However, to the extent to which the administrator can accurately anticipate problems and plan thoroughly for avoiding or ameliorating problems, the strike is less likely to be a disruptive force. If unanticipated problems do occur during a teachers' strike, the administrator will be dependent on his ability to respond quickly to rapidly-moving events. Certainly, he should not act impetuously. But failure by the administrator to move quickly and imaginatively during a teachers' strike could put him on the defensive and limit his options. In many situations the administrator will need a high degree of resourcefulness if he is to avoid being overcome by events which he did not adequately anticipate.

Finally, the administrator will need to possess a good sense of humor and a long-range perspective, if he is to come through a strike successfully. Many events during the strike will be frustrating and irritating to him. Teachers' motives may seem questionable, and it may be difficult not to perceive the teachers and anybody who agrees with them as "the enemy." Nevertheless, the administrator should avoid taking himself too seriously or questioning the motives of others.

He should, of course, do whatever he thinks is right in a strike situation, but before he acts, he should remember that he will still need to work with many of those same teachers long after the strike has been terminated. While he may be forced during the strike to take steps that will temporarily impair his relationship with them, he should refrain as much as possible from taking action which will permanently make it difficult to work successfully with the faculty after the strike.

A FINAL PERSPECTIVE

With the advent of collective bargaining and grievance procedures, the relationship between the school administrator and the staff has changed. The relationship is now frequently a frustrating and uneasy one in which both the administrator and the staff are unsure of each other's intentions and reliability. As a result, polarization and conflict between the administrator and the staff have increased in many schools.

Despite the frustration and irritating aspects of some staff actions, the administrator should not forget that the staff may represent the most important resource in the school for helping to educate students, and without its support and commitment there is very little the administrator will be able to accomplish in regard to bringing about educational improvement. Therefore, the administrator needs to work to build and maintain high staff satisfaction and morale without becoming disillusioned or bitter when members of the staff behave in ways which the administrator feels are undesirable. This obviously will not always be easy but will be necessary for a cooperative, productive relationship.

Review
1. Define "staff satisfaction" and "morale." What is the main purpose or function of each?
2. What are the factors that affect staff satisfaction? What factors affecting staff morale are common to the studies reported in this chapter?
3. Discuss the steps an administrator can take to develop and maintain high staff satisfaction and morale in a school.
4. What should be the role of the building administrator in administering the master contract? What problems might he encounter and how should he approach these problems?
6. Discuss those factors that may influence a teacher with regard to whether or not he files a grievance. What should be the role of the administrator in responding to a grievance?
7. Identify those characteristics an administrator should possess before, during, and after a strike.

Notes

1. Eldon D. Johnson, "An Analysis of Factors Related to Teacher Satisfaction-Dissatisfaction" (diss., Auburn University, 1967), chap. 2.

2. Neal Gross and Robert E. Herriott, *Staff Leadership in Public Schools: A Sociological Inquiry* (New York: John Wiley & Sons, 1965), p. 35.

3. For example, see Lester W. Anderson, "Teacher Morale and Student Achievement," *Journal of Educational Research* 45 (May 1953):393-96. Also see Hussein S. Koura, "An Experimental Study of Students' Achievement in Relation to the Morale of Selected Secondary School Teachers" (Ph.D. diss., University of Michigan, 1963).

4. An important exception would be a study by Robert Hoppock, *Job Satisfaction* (New York: Harper & Row, Publishers, 1935).

5. Frederick Herzberg et al., *The Motivation to Work* (New York: John Wiley & Sons, 1959), p. 114.

6. Thomas Sergiovanni, "Factors Which Affect Satisfaction and Dissatisfaction of Teachers," *Journal of Educational Administration* 5 (May 1967): 66-82.

7. Eldon D. Johnson, "An Analysis of Factors."

8. John W. Adair, "A Study of Job Factors That Affect Teacher Morale" (Ed.D. diss., Cornell University, 1967).

9. It should be noted that there is some evidence that does not uphold Herzberg's theory. For a review of this evidence, see John M. Maas, "A Study of the Relationship Between Specified Characteristics of Teachers and Their Perceptions of Job Satisfaction and Job Dissatisfaction Factors" (Ph. D. diss., University of Minnesota), 1968.

10. Abraham Maslow, *Motivation and Personality* (New York: Harper & Row, Publishers, 1954.)

11. Figure developed on the basis of data collected by Benjamin F. Strickland, "A Study of Factors Affecting Teachers' Morale in Selected Administrative Units of North Carolina" (Ed.D. diss., University of North Carolina, 1962). Also see Thomas T. Smith, "The Relationship between Selected Professional Concerns of Experienced Elementary Teachers and Teacher Morale" (Ph.D diss., University of Michigan, 1973).

12. Frederick L. Redefer, "Factors That Affect Teacher Morale," *Nation's Schools* 63 (February 1959):59-62.

13. Donald B. Lambert, "A Study of the Relationship between Teacher Morale and the School Principal's Leader Behavior" (Ed.D. diss., Auburn University, 1968).

14. For additional supporting evidence on this point, see Martin P. Murphy, "An Investigation of the Relationship between Teacher Morale and Organizational Climate in Selected High Schools" (Ed.D. diss., University of Massachusetts, 1974). Also see Joseph Grant, Jr., "A Comparison of Teacher Morale in Selected Open and Closed Climate Elementary Schools" (Ph.D. diss., University of Maryland, 1973).

15. Thomas G. Napier, "Teacher Morale" (Ed.D. diss., University of Nebraska, 1966).

16. For evidence on teachers' perceptions of the importance of these factors, see "Teacher Opinion Poll: Teacher Morale," in the NEA Research Department, *National Education Association Journal* 55, no. 9 (December 1966):p. 55. For more recent evidence, see the same source, 49 no. 4 (December 1971):102-8.

17. See Norman L. Sommers, "Factors Influencing Teacher Morale in Selected Secondary Schools" (Ph.D. diss., Kent State University, 1969).

18. For a review of this evidence, see Richard A. Gorton, *Conflict, Controversy and Crisis in School Administration and Supervision* (Dubuque, Iowa: Wm. C. Brown Company Publishers, 1972), chap. 3.

19. Harold Leiman, "A Study of Teacher Attitudes and Morale as Related to Participation in Administration" (Ph.D. diss., New York University, 1961). For recent research on this point, see Charles E. Godshall, "A Diagnosis of the Management Styles of High School Principals" (Ed.D. diss., University of Southern California, 1974).

20. Varon L. Howell, "Staff Morale in Elementary Schools: Influenced by Principal Initiated Common Behavioral Incidents" (Ed.D. diss., Brigham Young University, 1974).

21. C. E. Blocker and R. C. Richardson, "Twenty-five Years of Morale Research—A Critical Review," *Journal of Educational Sociology* 36 (January 1963): 200-210. For more recent research on this point, see Bruce Q. Buerkens, "The Relationship between Job Satisfaction of School Teachers and Their Perceived Conflicts with School Officials, Principals, Other Teachers, and Parents" (Ed.D. diss. University of Missouri, 1973).

22. First National City Bank, *Public Education in New York City* (New York: First National City Bank, 1969).

23. M. Chester Nolte, "Status and Scope of Collective Bargaining in Public Education." An ERIC Report: Ed-043-100 (1970), p. 11.

24. Ibid., pp. 12-14.

25. "Special Feature on Professional Negotiations," *Today's Education* 54 (February 1970): 33-38.

26. C. Taylor Whittier, "Intervention between Administrators and Teachers," *Educational Leadership* 27 (October 1969): 44-47.

27. Benjamin Epstein, *The Principal's Role in Collective Negotiations between Teachers and School Boards* (Washington, D.C.: The National Association of Secondary School Principals, 1965), p. 6.

28. See, for example, Department of Elementary School Principals, *Professional Negotiations and the Principalship* (Washington, D.C.: Department of Elementary School Principals, 1969), p. 126. See also, "Proposed 1970 Resolutions," *National Elementary Principal* 66 (February 1970):64-65.

29. See John A. Thompson, "The Principal's Role in Collective Negotiations between Teachers and School Boards" (Ph.D. diss., University of Wisconsin, 1968). For a somewhat more positive but generally similar perception of the role of the principal in collective negotiations, see Stephen Milton Poort, "Attitudes of Selected Kansas Superintendents, Principals and Teachers toward the Involvement of Principals in a Collective Negotiations Environment" (Ed.D. diss. University of Kansas, 1968).

30. Clifford H. Edwards and Keith R. Burnett, "The Principal's Role in Negotiations," *Contemporary Education* (May 1970):311-13.

31. One individual who has given considerable thought to the role of the principal in collective bargaining is Terrance E. Hatch. His ideas were instrumental in the development of the three guidelines presented. See Hatch, "The Principal's Role in Negotiations," in *Upsurge and Upheaval in School Law* (Topeka, Kans.: The National Organization on Legal Problems of Education, 1969), pp. 6-21. See also Adam G. Geyer, "A Role Model for Principals in Collective Negotiations between Teachers' Organizations and Boards of Education" (Ph.D. diss., Fordham University, 1973).

32. Thomas P. Gilroy et al., *Educator's Guide to Collective Bargaining* (Columbus, Ohio: Charles E. Merrill Publishing Co., 1969), pp. 47-49.

33. Myron Lieberman, "Administering Your Contract with Teachers," *School Management* 13 (October 1969):12-15.

34. For the total report of this study, see Frank W. Lutz and Seymour Evans, "The Union and Principal Leadership in New York City Schools." An ERIC Report: Ed-029-400 (1968). For later studies on the topic, see John A. McDannel, "The Effects of the Elementary Principal's Rule Administration Behavior on Staff Militancy and Leadership Perception" (Ph.D. diss. Pennsylvania University, 1973).

35. National Education Association of the United States, *Addresses and Proceedings of the One Hundred and Fifth Annual Meeting* (Washington, D.C.: National Education Association, 1967), p. 500.

36. Richard G. Neal, *Grievance Procedures and Grievance Arbitration in Public Education* (Washington, D.C.: Educational Services Bureau, 1971), p. 7.

37. Adapted from Robert E. Phay and John C. Lillie, *A Grievance Procedure for Public School Employees* (Chapel Hill: North Carolina University, 1973), p. 3.

38. Allan M. Glassman and James Belasco, "Grievance Procedures in Public Education: An Empirical Case Study." (Research paper presented at the Annual Meeting of the American Education Research Association, 1972.)

39. For an excellent review of the literature on grievance procedures and a proposed model grievance procedure, see Danforth M. White, Jr., "Grievance Procedures Criteria for Certificated Personnel" (Ed.D. diss., University of Southern California, 1971).

40. Richard Neal, *Grievance Procedures,* pp. 34-35. Also see Phay and Lillie, *A Grievance Procedure*, pp. 6-18.

41. Although surprisingly little has been written about the principal's role during grievance procedures, the following sources were helpful in developing the recommendations in this section: Neal, *Grievance Procedures,* pp. 22-24,29; C. Nichols, "Formal Grievance Procedures," *Office Executive* 33 (October 1958):26; Frank W. Lutz et al., *Grievances and Their Resolution* (Danville, Ill.: Interstate Printers, 1967); and Edward D. Kramer, "Grievance Procedures: The Principal's Role Where There Is a Negotiated Contract," *Bulletin of the National Association of Secondary School Principals* 55 (May 1971):159-67.

42. Thomas A. Shannon, "The Principal's Management Role in Collective Negotiations, Grievances, and Strikes," *Journal of Secondary Education* 45 (February 1970):51-56.

10

Staff Evaluation

Staff evaluation and supervision represent two interdependent means for improving the professional resources of a school. Staff evaluation is a process whereby the strengths and limitations of an individual or group are identified and defined. Supervision is a process designed to capitalize on the strengths and correct the weaknesses of an individual or group.

Evaluation and supervision are interdependent, in that one cannot usually achieve maximum effectiveness without the other.[1] Staff evaluation without supervision can lead to anxiety, frustration, and resistance on the part of the recipient of the evaluation. The individual or group may have been informed through evaluation about certain areas which need to be improved but, in the absence of appropriate follow-up supervision, may not be able to remedy the deficiencies. On the other hand, staff supervision without adequate prior evaluation tends to lack focus and is often misdirected. The individual (or group) in such a situation is the recipient of assistance which is not based on an accurate diagnosis of need and, as a result, is not likely to accept or profit from the supervision.

In the sections that follow, various aspects of staff evaluation will be discussed; the next chapter will focus on staff supervision.

THE DISTRICT'S STAFF EVALUATION PROGRAM

There is no uniform program of staff evaluation which operates in all school districts. However, there are some basic program characteristics which most districts share in common.

The staff evaluation program in most districts is formally designed, that is, its purposes, procedures, and schedules are usually officially established, and approved by the school board. The main purposes of the program are to identify needs for staff supervision and to reach a determination on whether staff, particularly new members, should be retained or dismissed.[2] These purposes are realized through a process of evaluating the staff on the extent to which they meet criteria for effectiveness, as previously defined by the district.

The typical evaluation program is usually initiated in the early fall in every building in the district and is conducted by the principal, perhaps with the assistance of another administrator or supervisor. The principal visits the classroom of each staff member who is to be evaluated during the year, and then holds an individual follow-up conference to present and discuss observations and conclusions. During the conference the principal reviews with the staff member the district's rating scale on which the principal has recorded his evaluation of the strengths and weaknesses of the individual. The rating scale, along with comments and recommendations, forms the basis for identifying needs for supervision and for reaching a determination on whether or not a staff member should be retained for the following year.

An example of the type of rating scale used in many school districts is presented in figure 10.1.

Teacher Rating Form

Instructions: Please evaluate the teacher on the following characteristics. The evaluation should take place on the basis of classroom observation and a follow-up conference.

Characteristics (Check appropriate space)

Personal Factors	*Outstanding*	*Satisfactory*	*Unsatisfactory*
Appearance	_____	_____	_____
Cooperation	_____	_____	_____
Sense of humor	_____	_____	_____
Tactfulness	_____	_____	_____
Health	_____	_____	_____
Attendance and punctuality	_____	_____	_____

Comments _____

Professional Factors			
Flexibility	_____	_____	_____
Loyalty to school system	_____	_____	_____
Judgment	_____	_____	_____
Professional ethics	_____	_____	_____
Rapport with staff	_____	_____	_____
Rapport with students	_____	_____	_____
Rapport with parents	_____	_____	_____

Comments _____

Teaching Performance and Classroom Management

Classroom organization and appearance	_____	_____	_____

Figure 10.1. A Sample District Evaluation Instrument.

(continued)

Personal Factors	Outstanding	Satisfactory	Unsatisfactory
Mastery of subject matter	_____	_____	_____
Teaching techniques	_____	_____	_____
Command of English language	_____	_____	_____
Reports and records	_____	_____	_____

Comments _____

_____ Teacher's Signature (Does not indicate approval of evaluation, only that teacher has reviewed the evaluation with the principal.)
_____ Principal's Signature
_____ Date
cc: Personnel File

Figure 10.1. Continued.

A number of questions could be raised about the validity and reliability of the factors included in the sample district evaluation instrument and about the format of the instrument itself.* As Cook and Richards point out, such teacher ratings may". . . reflect the expectations of the evaluator more than the actions of the teacher."[3] However, the purpose of presenting the sample at this stage is only to show the type of rating instrument that is frequently used in staff evaluation. More will be said later about the *desired* composition and format of a staff evaluation instrument.

PROBLEMS AND ISSUES IN STAFF EVALUATION

The school administrator should be aware that the district's staff evaluation program may be perceived by many teachers as a "mixed blessing." Most teachers probably accept evaluation as inevitable and potentially valuable, but many question its usefulness and value in practice.[4]

It should be emphasized that evaluation problems and issues do not exist in all schools, but wherever they are prevalent, they impair the effectiveness of the program. For this reason the major issues and problems associated with the staff evaluation program will be analyzed so that the administrator may become better able to avoid their occurrence in his own school.[5]

---

*It should be noted that the instrument presented in figure 10.1 was developed after an examination of many district teacher evaluation forms and does not represent any one *particular* district.

CROSS-PURPOSES

As indicated earlier, the main purposes of the district evaluation program are (1) to identify needs for supervisory assistance and (2) to reach a determination about whether or not a staff member should be retained or dismissed.

In the eyes of many teachers, these objectives are incompatible and in direct conflict.* To achieve the first objective, the staff member should be open, candid, and cooperative about revealing or confirming his limitations with the administrator. On the other hand, however, if the staff member wants to be retained or promoted, he will naturally want to be seen in the best light, and it may be to his disadvantage to willingly reveal his limitations or confirm the perceptions of the administrator about specific deficiencies.

Several consequences can result from this conflict in the purposes of the district's staff evaluation program. First of all, achieving the objective of identifying needs for supervisory assistance is impaired because of the reluctance of staff members to identify their weaknesses, for fear that they won't be retained or promoted.

Secondly, since staff members feel that there are risks to participating fully in the district's evaluation program, they tend to fall back on informal evaluation by their colleagues. While informal evaluation can be helpful, its effectiveness is limited by its sporadic and isolated nature. The one important advantage of colleague evaluation is that it typically possesses few risks for the staff member being evaluated, and it can give a teacher assistance which he may not be receiving from the district evaluation program.

A third consequence of conflict in the purposes of the district evaluation program is that it has a poor image in the eyes of many teachers. They view the program as threatening, punitive, of little help, and not in their best interests. Consequently, they are often not very receptive to attempts by administrators to evaluate them.

If administrators are to avoid these consequences, they will need to concentrate on resolving the apparent conflict in purposes in many staff evaluation programs. Recommendations to this end will be presented later in the chapter.

LACK OF STAFF INVOLVEMENT

A major complaint of many teachers is that they have not been involved to any significant degree in the development of the district staff evaluation

---

*Some educators, however, do not see these purposes as necessarily incompatible. See Harold McNally, "What Makes a Good Evaluation Program?" *National Elementary Principal* 52 (February 1973):24.

program, particularly as it relates to criteria and process of evaluation.* As a result the evaluative criteria and procedures designed by the administrators in such a district do not reflect teachers' ideas. This means that the professional staff members are being evaluated by criteria and a process on which they had little to say and about which they may disagree.

The consequences of a lack of staff involvement in developing criteria and procedures for evaluation can be deleterious to efforts by a school administrator to suggest improvements to the faculty. If the staff has not participated in the development of the evaluation criteria and process, the likelihood is increased that they won't accept or be receptive to either one.

LOW PRIORITY GIVEN TO SELF-ASSESSMENT

The primary emphasis in many school districts' evaluation programs appears to be on external evaluation. With few exceptions, little attention is given in the evaluation plan to the need for teachers to engage in *self*-evaluation (as well as external evaluation) for professional growth. The implicit assumption seems to be that teachers are either unwilling or unable to participate in a program of self-evaluation. It is also possible that administrators in these districts feel that the perceptions of teachers about their strengths and limitations are not important.

The potential advantages resulting from self-evaluation as a parallel activity to external evaluation are (1) a more analytical look by teachers at their strengths and weaknesses, (2) a lessening of defensiveness on their part regarding external evaluation by the administrator. However, whether teachers would be willing and able to engage in a program of self-evaluation for professional growth would appear to depend on their degree of trust and confidence in the administration, and the extent to which the administration has provided in-service training for the teachers to help them become more competent and objective in analyzing their own behavior. If these conditions can be met, then self-evaluation by teachers can and should be a valuable activity for teachers and administrators alike.

CRITERIA BASED ON PERSONAL PREFERENCE

The selection of criteria to be used for staff evaluation is undoubtedly one of the most important decisions in designing an evaluation program. The criteria are standards against which the teachers are to be evaluated and can

---

*The administrator should be forewarned, however, that many teachers are no longer willing to accept their lack of involvement. See "NEA Report," *National Education Association* 10 (April 1971):pp. 4-6.

usually be found in the district's rating form for evaluating members of the staff.

The question that many teachers raise about the district's rating form is, to what extent are the criteria presented based on personal preference, and to what degree are they based on research which supports their importance in working with students? Although the answer to this question may vary, depending on the school district, it would appear from an examination of numerous evaluation forms that the selection of criteria is based more on personal preference than on any research evidence or theoretical foundation. [6]

Part of the problem is that administrators who select the staff evaluation criteria frequently have not adequately investigated the research on teacher effectiveness.* However, another equally important aspect is the likelihood that uniform criteria penalize teachers with different personalities who can teach effectively with different classes, using different methods and/or materials, under different classroom conditions. [7] If true, then there should either be different evaluation criteria for different teachers and situations, or the criteria should emphasize the outcomes of teaching more than the personality of the teacher or the process of teaching. [8]

In any regard, the administrator needs to realize that, to a large extent, the criteria used in the district evaluation program are probably based more on personal preference than on research or theory. The disadvantages of this subjective approach to teacher evaluation were pointed out by Medley who found in his studies that, "teachers who looked most effective to supervisors were not actually the most effective in helping pupils learn." [9]

POOR COMMUNICATION

In many schools the purposes, criteria, and process of staff evaluation are not adequately communicated to the staff. [10] It is not unusual in those schools for the staff, particularly new members, to be uninformed about the criteria and process of the district evaluation program until they actually encounter them. Although most staff members are aware that the process of evaluation involves observation by an evaluator and a follow-up conference to discuss the results of the evaluation, questions about the nature, time, and frequency of observations and conferences are often not resolved. And in many cases, teachers are observed for the purpose of evaluation without their possessing first hand knowledge of the criteria on which they are to be evaluated.

Poor communication about the evaluation process can result in uncertainty and anxiety on the part of staff members. They don't know exactly

---

*Two basic sources which the administrator should consult are (1) Barak Rosenshine, *Teaching Behavior and Student Achievement* (London: National Foundation for Educational Research in England and Wales, 1971), and (2) Robert Travers, ed., *The Second Handbook of Research on Teaching* (Chicago: Rand McNally & Co., 1973).

what to expect from the evaluation, and therefore, they may not participate cooperatively in the process or accept the administrator's findings. The administrator who wishes to avoid these consequences will make every attempt to inform the staff in advance about the purposes, criteria, and procedures of evaluation.

PROBLEM OF INADEQUATE EXPERTISE

In recent years teachers have become better prepared and more specialized in their subject matter and teaching methodology. Many teachers now question whether the administrator, who has, typically, been out of the classroom for several years, and who may have specialized in only one aspect of the curriculum as an undergraduate, has the expertise to evaluate them. [11] As a result, administrators have sometimes experienced difficulty in evaluating teachers and, in particular, in getting them to accept administrative judgments about their strengths and weaknesses. [12]

It would make little sense to minimize the importance of expertise in evaluating a professional staff. If the administrator is to do a competent job of evaluating teachers and obtaining their acceptance of his findings, he will need to be knowledgeable and expert in the various areas of curriculum, teaching methods, learning theory, and other facets of the educational program. It will also be in his interest to capitalize on and utilize as much as possible the expertise possessed by department heads, unit leaders, and other sources of assistance within the school and school district.

Staff evaluation today can no longer depend on the expertise of one individual, such as the principal. All appropriate sources of assistance within the school need to be organized by the administrator for staff evaluation.

ABSENCE OF DUE PROCESS

There are two types of due process: procedural and substantive. [13] In staff evaluation, *procedural* due process means, at the minimum, that before any adverse action is taken against a staff member (such as dismissal or denial of salary increase), the individual is given written notification and documentation of the reasons for the action and is provided an opportunity to present evidence that might reduce the severity of the action or eliminate its need entirely. [14] It also usually means that before adverse action is taken, the individual must be given sufficient opportunity to remedy his weakness, and his supervisor must make every reasonable effort to help the person accomplish this goal.

Substantive due process in staff evaluation means that the criteria used in evaluating an individual are not arbitrary and are directly related to the job. [15]

Although there is no complete record on the extent to which schools follow standards of due process, it is worth noting that when teacher dismissal cases reach the courts, the court more often rules against the school if it has failed to follow standards of due process than for any other reason. [16] While schools are legally required to provide due process to tenured teachers, the law regarding nontenured teachers has not been conclusively established. [17] Be that as it may, it seems clear that due process is consistent with professional standards, even if it is not legally required, and should be considered by the school administrator in the case of nontenured teachers as well as tenured ones.

The main purpose of due process is to ensure that an individual has received a fair and just decision. In staff evaluation this means that the criteria must be legitimate, the individual must be informed of his shortcomings, he must be given sufficient opportunity to correct them, and he must be provided with adequate supervision to do so. These four conditions (legitimate criteria, notification of weakness, sufficient time to correct weakness, and adequate supervision) represent practices which are professionally sound—regardless of whether or not they are legally required. Neglect by the administrator of any of these aspects may not be prohibited by law in the case of nontenured teachers, but it is surely a professional inadequacy. The administrator who insists that due process be followed in *all* staff evaluation will not only avoid possible legal entanglements at a later date, but will also be meeting high professional standard in regard to staff evaluation.

INADEQUATE FOLLOW-UP AFTER EVALUATION

As supervision without adequate prior evaluation tends to be misdirected, evaluation without immediate and constructive follow-up supervisory assistance can lead to anxiety, frustration, and resistance on the part of its recipients. And judging from the reports of many teachers, there is too frequently a lack of immediate and constructive supervisory assistance following the evaluation process. In such situations teachers are informed of their weaknesses or limitations but are given no specific help in improving. Informing a teacher that he needs "better class control" or " greater student participation" may identify a shortcoming, but unless the individual is given supervisory assistance in achieving better class control or greater student participation, he may be unable to improve. Worse yet, informing an individual of a weakness without giving him adequate help in correcting it may harm the person's self-concept and lead to a negative attitude toward evaluation on his part.

The solution to this problem should be obvious: evaluation must be followed with immediate and constructive supervisory assistance, of the nature described in the next chapter.

LIMITED ASSESSMENT OF THE PROGRAM

The staff evaluation program, like any other program, needs to be assessed regularly if it is to improve and meet the needs of the people involved. Regrettably, assessment of the strengths and weaknesses of the staff evaluation program is frequently haphazard and sporadic. Whatever assessment does occur tends to rely on the random impressions of administrators and usually includes limited or no feedback from the staff members themselves.

Perhaps the greatest need for improvement in a school's staff evaluation program is for periodic and systematic examination of the strengths and weaknesses of the program. The school administrator, with the help of the faculty, should play a major role in achieving this objectives.

RECOMMENDED PROGRAM OF STAFF EVALUATION

There are undoubtedly educators who would advocate complete elimination of any program of administrator evaluation of staff, in light of its many problems. [18] Realistically, however, administrators in most, if not all, districts, will probably continue to be assigned the responsibility for evaluating staff. Consequently, it would appear that the only viable resolution of the problems of teacher evaluation lies in the *improvement* of the program, not in attempts to eliminate it. Staff evaluation *can*, under the right conditions, lead to significant professional growth. [19]

The objectives of the recommended staff evaluation principles [20] presented below are to strengthen the evaluation program and avoid the problems previously identified. The procedures and difficulties in implementing each principle will also be discussed.

Principle 1. **The two main purposes of the staff evaluation program should be separated to the extent possible.**

The primary problem associated with the purposes of staff evaluation is that the use of evaluation as a basis for personnel decisions, such as dismissal or promotion, is viewed by many teachers as antithetical to the objective of using evaluation as a means for improving an individual's performance. Compounding the problem is the fact that in most schools the administrator is placed in the position of conducting both kinds of evaluation.

One solution is to separate the two main purposes of staff evaluation as much as possible. An example of this approach is the teacher evaluation program at Newport-Mesa, a unified school district in southern California. [21] In this district the principal, aided by representatives from the staff, evaluates the teacher in regard to the degree to which he has achieved predetermined student learning objectives, and this evaluation becomes the basis for personnel decisions such as teacher retention or promotion. Evaluation for the purpose of staff improvement, however, is separated entirely from the purpose and process just described, and is carried out by a team of colleagues who observe the teacher and work with him on self-improvement activities. The principal is not involved at all in evaluating for improvement; the perceptions and judgments made by the team of teachers are not communicated to him nor are they used for decisions related to retention or salary increase.

A disadvantage of this approach is that it appears to exclude the school administrator and his insights from the process of evaluation for staff improvement. However, it is possible that an administrator cannot reasonably expect the staff to respond openly and candidly if he attempts to evaluate them in order to identify areas for self-improvement *and* as a basis for making crucial personnel decisions. One feasible solution seems to be the separation of those two purposes and the designation of different people to accomplish each.

Principle 2. **The staff evaluation program needs to emphasize self-evaluation as much as external evaluation by the administrator.**

Each teacher to be evaluated by the administrator should be given the opportunity to evaluate himself on the criteria used by the district. If the other principles recommended in this chapter are implemented, then the administration should have the trust and confidence of the teachers, necessary prerequisites for any program of self-evaluation. In-service training to help the teachers become more competent and objective in analyzing their behavior may also be necessary.

Ideally, teachers will be engaged continuously in self-evaluation, but formal efforts in this regard should begin at and proceed through the same time period during which the administrator is conducting evaluations of the teachers. At the end of the self-evaluation process, a teacher's evaluative perceptions should be shared with the administrator who, in turn, should discuss his perceptions with the teacher. As a result of this sharing of evaluative data, the principal or the teacher, or both, may decide to revise the original perceptions and conclusions or engage in further investigation and analysis.

Self-evaluation by the teacher can be a useful activity for a teacher's professional growth. It can also provide an administrator with valuable information which should lead to a more accurate and fairer evaluation of the teacher.

Principle 3.   **Staff members need to be involved in the formulation, assessment, and appropriate revision of the total district evaluation program, including the definition of evaluative purposes, criteria, and procedures.**

To facilitate acceptance of the district's evaluation program, the staff members themselves need to be involved by the school administrator in developing, assessing, and revising the program.* To implement this principle, the administrator should establish a standing committee of the faculty to examine the present evaluation program and to suggest revisions. The committee should be composed of nontenured as well as tenured teachers, and the administrator should chair the committee. Its recommendations would probably be only advisory to the central office, but if its members did their homework, the committee could be a powerful force for changing and improving the staff evaluation program in the district. Part of its function should be to secure periodic and systematic feedback from the entire staff on the perceived strengths and weaknesses of the evaluation program, with recommendations for improvement.

Principle 4.   **The staff evaluation criteria and evaluation instrument should be based primarily on research on teacher effectiveness rather than on personal preference.**

To implement this principle, the school administrator with appropriate staff involvement will need to investigate the research on teacher effectiveness and then propose to the central office a revision in staff evaluation criteria that will be based more on research and less on personal preference. This does not mean that the criteria cannot reflect some philosophical orientation, but it is recommended that the majority of the criteria should not rest on that subjective foundation.

It is recognized that research has not been very productive in identifying characteristics of effective teaching. As, Rosenshine and Furst have noted,

---

*The American School Boards Association seems to favor this principle. It states, " . . . evaluation is not something done to teachers; it is done with teachers. It is a cooperative undertaking, carried on with mutual respect." "School Board Policies on Teacher Evaluation: Educational Policies Development Kit." An ERIC Report, Ed-058-657, 1971, p. 5.

"We know very little about the relationship between [teachers'] classroom behavior and student gains."[22] Nevertheless, insofar as possible, staff evaluation should reflect the best evidence and theory available about teaching effectiveness.

For example, Rosenshine and Furst reviewed fifty studies of teacher effectiveness and identified a number of effectiveness categories which should be considered in developing staff evaluation criteria.[23] These categories include (1) variability of materials, techniques, and tasks , (2) clarity of presentation, including organization, (3) enthusiasm, (4) task orientation reflected in the businesslike and achievement orientation of the teacher, (5) student opportunity to learn, (6) teacher use of student ideas, (7) - teacher use of concepts which provide direction for students, and (8) types of questions used, including, "what?" "where?" "why?" and "how?" questions, as well as those believed associated with convergent and divergent behavior.

Some of these factors, such as enthusiasm, are high inference variables while others, such as types of questions used, are low inference variables. Low inference behaviors require little or no inference by the observer regarding whether or not the particular teaching behavior has occurred; high inference variables require considerable inference by the observer as to whether or not the behavior has occurred.[24] Although the criteria for evaluating teaching should contain as few high inference behaviors as possible (because of the resulting problem that observations of the same teacher behavior may lead to different inferences), high inference variables can be useful in staff evaluation if they are further analyzed into more precise measures.

The work of Rosenshine and Furst has been extremely valuable in identifying possible criteria for evaluating teaching effectiveness, but there are other studies of teacher effectiveness which should also be considered by the administrator. For example, research by Gage found that using questions to elicit different kinds of thought processes and behavior, establishing appropriate frames of reference prior to the introduction of material, and achieving closure or summarizing major points at various times during and at the end of the lesson were important teaching skills.[25]

Jenkins and Bausell discovered in their study of *teacher* beliefs about the behaviors of an effective teacher that a teacher's rapport with the class and his willingness to be flexible as the situation required were the two most important factors.[26] Sabine found in his investigation of how *students* rate their teachers that the two most important characteristics of a teacher (as perceived by students) were (1) that the teacher was "demanding," and (2) that the teacher "cared."[27] Apparently, most students want a teacher who will not only challenge them and make them work, but who will also be interested in them as people and not just as students.

Although the research on teaching effectiveness is not conclusive, the administrator is encouraged to base staff evaluation criteria more on appropriate findings and theory than on personal preferences. There is little doubt that the relevance and validity of the criteria will influence greatly their acceptance by the staff.

In addition to the importance of the relevance and validity of the criteria for staff evaluation, the instrument or rating scale which is used to apply the criteria to teacher performance should possess the following characteristics: [28] (1) It should be reliable, that is responses to it should be consistent; (2) it should be reasonable in cost; (3) it should be efficient to use and easy to understand; and (4) it should be diagnostic in nature, i.e., provide information which helps the teacher to improve rather than information which is confined to identifying weaknesses.* The last factor is exceedingly important because a teacher's receptivity and perception of the evaluation's value are likely to be limited if the evaluation instrument only makes judgments about his performance without helping the teacher to understand how he can improve. [29]

The school administrator needs to realize that bringing about changes in the staff evaluation criteria and the evaluation instrument will not be an easy task, particularly if the selection of criteria and instrument is viewed by the central office administrators and supervisors as their responsibility, and if they have considerable emotional investment in the use of existing criteria and instrument. Nevertheless, teachers deserve to be evaluated by criteria and an instrument which are directly related to their effectiveness in the classroom, and the school administrator should exert his leadership toward the achievement of that objective. [30]

Principle 5.   **The purposes, criteria, and procedures of staff evaluation need to be clearly communicated periodically to all staff members.**

The administrator should not assume that staff members are familiar with or will remember from year to year the evaluation purposes, criteria, and procedures. At the very least, *new* members of the staff should be informed of these elements before evaluation proceeds.

The most desirable approach would be for the administrator to schedule a meeting, after the first few weeks of school, with all staff members who are to be evaluated during the year and to review with them the purposes, criteria, and procedures to be used in the evaluation program. At that meeting certain points can be emphasized or clarified, and questions can be

*For a review of a broad range of possible evaluation instruments, see Pamela Rosen, *Assessment of Teachers* (Princeton, N.J.: Educational Testing Service, 1973), and *Evaluation Systems for Education: Descriptive Abstracts* (Washington, D.C.: National Education Association, 1973).

answered. The objectives of such a meeting would be to develop understanding and acceptance of the evaluation program, and to relieve anxiety and apprehension, particularly on the part of new staff members.

Once the administrator is ready to begin the evaluation process, he should schedule a conference with each individual to be evaluated and attempt to reach agreement with him on objectives and the proposed means for reaching those objectives. [31] This agreement should then be the focus of the classroom observations and other techniques which the administrator employs in making his evaluation, as well as the main topic of the follow-up conference during which the administrator discusses with the staff member the evaluative judgments made. The primary advantage of this approach is that administrator and teacher agree in advance on those aspects that will be examined during the evaluation process.

Principle 6. **The evaluation process should include an examination of all major relevant school factors which may be affecting the staff member's performance.**

The primary basis for reaching evaluative conclusions about the performance of a faculty member is usually the classroom visitation, during which most if not all of the attention is typically given to the teacher's behavior. However, many factors can influence a teacher's performance and student learning in a school.* These include the instructional materials, the curriculum, the school schedule, the physical conditions in the classroom, the size of the class, and the types of students in the classroom. These factors, and any others that seem relevant should be examined and considered by the administrator in evaluating a member of the staff.

Principle 7. **The school administrator needs to utilize to the maximum extent possible the expertise of others in evaluating staff members.**

The principal can no longer assume, if he ever could, that he possesses all of the expertise necessary for competently evaluating staff. Evaluation, as we have learned over the years, is a very complicated process and its effectiveness depends on an understanding of learning theory, human relations, supervision theory, the teacher's subject area, and teaching methodology. It is recognized that some people may feel that the school administrator possess all of the expertise he needs in order to evaluate teachers. However, the position taken by the author is that the school administrator cannot conduct evaluation effectively by himself, and that the staff evaluation program will be improved if he capitalizes on the expertise of others in the school or school district.

*Evidence on this point is presented in the next chapter.

The specific approach recommended is that the principal organize a staff evaluation team, [32] composed of himself, the central office subject supervisor, and the appropriate department head or unit leader. The latter two individuals normally possess specialized expertise in the curriculum and teaching method of a particular subject area and should complement the administrator, who is a generalist and whose in-depth knowledge of those aspects is likely to be limited. The administrator has, however, much to contribute to the evaluation process, particularly in the areas of class management and total-school perspective, and of course, he is responsible for making the final evaluation decisions at the building level.

While the team approach to evaluation has much to recommend it, problems may arise, depending on the purposes for which the administrator uses the team. If he wants the team to evaluate teachers for personnel decisions, as well as for staff improvement he is likely to experience difficulty in securing the cooperation of the department head (or unit leader) and the central office supervisor. Both will probably be interested in the objective of staff evaluation for improvement, but they may not want to participate in the other kind of evaluation for fear of losing the confidence of the teachers with whom they work. Paradoxically, if the administrator uses the team only for the staff improvement objective, he loses their expertise for the other purpose of staff evaluation. There is no easy answer to the problem, and its final resolution will depend on the administrator's assessment of conditions in his own school and school district. However, it seems likely that there will be difficulties in utilizing the same personnel and approach for both objectives of staff evaluation.

Principle 8.   **Following the evaluation, the school administrator and others working with him need to provide staff members with specific and constructive suggestions and supervisory assistance to help them improve.**

A staff evaluation program which only points out strengths and weaknesses of an individual without helping him to correct his limitations or to capitalize on his strengths is professionally inadequate. In order to improve, a person will usually need to receive *specific* and *constructive* assistance and support, and he will also need appropriate time in which to make the necessary changes. Whether the evaluation program is perceived by the staff in a positive light will probably depend as much on the adequacy of follow-up supervisory activities as on the perceived fairness and validity of the evaluation itself. Therefore, the various supervisory alternatives discussed in the next chapter should be utilized by the administrator whenever feasible.

Principle 9.   **Due process should be followed in the evaluation of all staff, nontenured as well as tenured, whenever it appears that the**

evaluation may result in an adverse personnel decision for an individual.*

Some readers may regard this recommendation as controversial, particularly as it applies to nontenured teachers. Many administrators may feel that due process is awkward, time-consuming, and very inefficient, and that they should provide no more due process than required by law. However, the right to due process in the case of a decision perceived as unfair or invalid is basic to our democratic heritage and should cause the administrator no overwhelming concern if his personnel decisions are based on solid evaluation practices.

It is conceded that due process may be awkward, time-consuming, and inefficient; and it is agreed that it may not be legally required in all situations. However, the basic intent of the administrator should be to act fairly. Due process is designed to minimize the possiblity of unfairness. It should also help the administrator to do a more *professional* and *competent* job of evaluating staff.

The specific due process procedures recommended for *all* staff evaluations are the following: [33]

    a. Written identification of strengths and diagnosis of weaknesses with specific recommendations on how to improve. The diagnosis and recommendation for improvement should be given to the staff member in sufficient time *before* any final personnel ratings or decisions are made for the year so that the individual has adequate opportunity to correct or ameliorate his weaknesses.

    b. Intensive follow-up supervisory assistance by the administrator and others who are working with the administrator, to help the staff member improve. The administrator should maintain written documentation on all efforts made to improve the staff member and the latter's response to those efforts. Both kinds of information will be needed if, at a later date, the staff member should challenge a decision of the school district in the case of dismissal or salary consideration.

    c. Advance notice in writing to the staff member, in circumstances involving an adverse personnel decision, of the reasons for the decision, and notification of an opportunity to have a hearing with the administrator in order to review the decision and the reasons for it.

---

*The administrator who wishes to examine a description of what appears to be a good program for removing the ineffective teacher should see Roger Place, "Removing the Incompetent Practitioner." An ERIC Report, Ed-089-237, 1974.

  d. A hearing with the administrator to review an adverse personnel decision, if requested, and the opportunity to appeal the administrator's decision to his immediate superior and, if necessary, to the school board and to the courts.

  e. Publication to all staff members of the previous four procedures. A major principle of due process is that those who are to be affected by an adverse decision should be informed of their right to these procedures. Although an administrator may be willing to adopt these procedures if *requested,* due process will not become a reality in an evaluation program unless the administrator takes the initiative to explain these procedures to all staff members and emphasize their availability.

Principle 10. **The staff evaluation program should be assessed systematically every year or two for the purpose of identifying areas for improvement.**

  This principle, hopefully, requires no additional explanation of its rationale. The way in which the assessment is to be accomplished may take a number of different forms, but one condition is essential: those who are being evaluated should be surveyed on their perceptions of the program's strengths and weaknesses and their ideas on how it could be made more effective.

A FINAL PERSPECTIVE

The staff evaluation program has had a checkered past and continues to be perceived by many as a necessary evil. However, it *can* be an important means not only of improving the staff, but also for reaching specific personnel decisions—but only under certain conditions. Since it is likely that staff evaluation will continue to be one of the school administrator's major responsibilities, it is essential that he work to improve the program. The discussion and recommendations presented in this chapter have been designed to help him achieve that goal.[34]

Review
1. Define the terms *staff evaluation* and *staff supervision.* What is the relationship between the two?
2. Identify the main characteristics of the typical staff evaluation program.
3. What are the major problems and issues that are associated with the staff evaluation program?

4. Distinguish between "substantive" and "procedural" due process. What are the steps in procedural due process?
5. How can the staff evaluation program be improved?
6. Discuss several research studies of which the administrator should be aware in determining teacher effectiveness.

Notes

1. Bernard H. McKenna, "A Context for Teacher Evaluation," *National Elementary Principal* 52 (February 1973):23.

2. These can be referred to as instructional and administrative purposes. See Harold McNally, "Teacher Evaluation That Makes a Difference," *Educational Leadership* 29 (January 1972):353.

3. Martha A. Cook and Herbert C. Richards, "Dimensions of Principal and Superior Ratings of Teacher Behavior," *Journal of Experimental Education* 41 (Winter 1972):13.

4. See Harold M. Klonecky, "The Relationship of Teacher and Administrator Views of the Component Parts of Teacher Evaluation" (Ph.D. diss., University of Southern California, 1972).

5. One of the main sources for identification of the problems and issues associated with teacher evaluation was a research study by Richard B. Boege, "A Study of the Procedures for Evaluating Classroom Teachers in Certain School Districts in the State of Washington" (Ed.D. diss., Washington State University, 1970). Also see Olaf P. Rostad, "Teachers' Perceptions of Important Issues in the Evaluation of Teachers: An Exploratory Study" (Ed.D. diss., University of Oregon, 1973).

6. A good source for examining teacher evaluation forms is the report of the periodic survey by Educational Research Service, Washington, D.C.

7. This hypothesis is based on research by William G. Cunningham, "Teachability Grouping Revisited" *Phi Delta Kappen* 59 (February 1975):428-29.

8. For a description of the latter approach, see W. James Popham, "Found: A Practical Procedure to Appraise Teacher Achievement in the Classroom," *Nation's Schools* 89 (May 1972):59-60.

9. Donald Medley, "Indicators and Measures of Teacher Effectiveness: A Review of Research." An ERIC Report: Ed-088-844 (1971), p. 6.

10. For a good discussion of this point, see Everette J. DeVaughn, "Policies and Procedures and Instruments in Evaluation of Teacher and Administrator Performance." An ERIC Report: Ed-061-607 (1971).

11. For an elaboration of the position by a teacher, see Phyllis Johnston, "A Teacher's Thoughts on Evaluation," *NASSP Spotlight* 20 (February 1973).

12. C. R. Ingils, "Let's Do Away with Teacher Evaluation," *The Clearing House* 49 (1968):601-6.

13. Everette DeVaughn, "Teacher Employment, Legal Aspects: Separation and Demotion," *The Encyclopedia of Education* (New York: Macmillan Co., 1971), 9:21.

14. David Rubin, *The Rights of Teachers* (New York: American Civil Liberties Union, published in cooperation with Avon Books, 1972), pp. 139-45.

15. Ibid., pp. 144-45.

16. Lee O. Garber and Reynolds C. Seitz, *The Yearbook of School Law* (Danville, Ill.: Interstate Printers, 1973).

17. For a description of the crucial factors in his situation (from the teacher's point of view), see "U.S. Supreme Court Supports Teachers' Due Process Rights," *Today's Education* 61 (September 1972):38-39.

18. See, for example, David E. Dail, "Self Appraisal: A New Approach to Evaluation, *School and Community* 66 (February 1970):p. 22.

19. There is not much evidence on this point, but see "NEA Report," *National Education Association* 10 (April 1971):4-6.

20. Most if not all of these principles have been recommended in the past by one author or another. For a particularly good review of the literature on the topic, and related recommendations, see Stephen Stuart, "Criteria for Programs of Appraising Teacher Performance and Their Applications to Current Practices in Ohio" (Ph.D. diss., Ohio State University, 1971).

21. For a full description of the program, see Fred Niedermeyer and Stephen Klein, "An Empirical Evaluation of a District Teacher's Accountability Program," *Phi Delta Kappan* 53 (October 1972):100-103.

22. Barak Rosenshine and Norma Furst, "Research on Teacher Performance Criteria," in *Research in Teacher Education,* ed. B. Othanel Smith (Englewood Cliffs, N.J.: Prentice-Hall, 1971), p. 37.

23. Ibid., pp. 44-54.

24. Barak Rosenshine, "Enthusiastic Teaching: A Research Review," *School Review* 78 (August 1970):500.

25. Nate L. Gage, "An Analytical Approach to Research on Instructional Methods," *Phi Delta Kappan* 49 (June 1968):602-03.

26. Joseph R. Jenkins and Barker R. Bausell, "How Teachers View the Effective Teacher." An ERIC Report: Ed-075-364 (n.d.).

27. Gordon A. Sabine, "How Students Rate Their Schools and Teachers." An ERIC Report: Ed-052-533 (1971). Also see James Kenny et al., "How Students See Teachers." An ERIC Report: Ed-077-921 (1972).

28. John E. Bolen, "The Dilemma in Evaluating Instruction," *National Elementary Principal* 52 (February 1973):72-75.

29. For examples of several diagnostic instruments which are currently being used in teacher evaluation, see Suzanne Stemock, "Evaluating Teacher Performance." An ERIC Report: Ed-059-166 (1972), pp. 21-32.

30. For help in this area, see American School Boards Association, "School Board Policies on Teacher Evaluation: Educational Policies Development Kit." An ERIC Report: Ed-058-657 (1971).

31. For a good description of the approach, see George B. Redfern, "Evaluating Secondary School Teachers," *American Secondary Education* 2 (September 1972):7-12.

32. The NEA appears to favor the team approach to evaluation. See Larry Wicks, "Teacher Evaluation," *Today's Education* 62 (March 1973):43.

33. These recommendations for due process are based in large part on a study by Robert Norman, "Implications of the Constitutional Guarantee of Due Process for the Teacher Evaluation Function as Experienced by the Principal" (Ed.D. diss., University of Virginia, 1972).

34. An excellent short booklet containing many useful ideas for improving teacher evaluation is The National Center for Educational Communications' *Teacher Evaluation Prep, 21* (Washington, D.C.: United States Office of Education, 1971).

11

Supervision of Instruction

Supervision may be defined as those activities, engaged in by one or more individuals, which have as their main purpose the improvement of a person, group, or program. [1]

At the building level the administrator is involved in a variety of situations which call for supervision. Three major areas over which an administrator exercises supervision are student activities, attendance and discipline, and the curriculum. But probably the most important area for which an administrator has supervisory responsibilities is the instructional program. [2]

The instructional program comprises all of the factors and conditions within a school that influence student learning. Though there may be some who would view supervision of staff as identical with supervision of instruction, the latter concept, as we shall see, is really much broader. The teacher is perhaps the most important instructional variable affecting student learning, but not the only factor. Others include the size of the class, the type of physical structure and arrangement of the room, and the educational and socioeconomic characteristics of the students. [3] Therefore, while supervision of staff will be emphasized in this chapter, the administrator will also be encouraged to examine and utilize other significant instructional variables which influence student learning.

ADMINISTRATIVE CONSIDERATIONS

CAN THE ADMINISTRATOR FUNCTION AS A SUPERVISOR?

The role of the school administrator as an instructional leader has frequently been proposed. However, there is increasing indication, supported by accumulating research, that teachers—the main recipients of an administrator's instructional leadership—do not recognize him as the instructional leader of the school.*

Campbell, for example, asserts that, "The educational administrator is working with professionals who feel, often rightly, that they know more

*For an excellent analysis of this problem, see Arthur Blumberg, *Supervisors and Teachers: A Private Cold War* (Berkeley, Calif.: McCutchan Publishing Corp., 1974).

about teaching and learning than he does."[4] Erikson states that, "With the influx of additional personnel, there is a tendency to look beyond the principal for help with classroom problems to persons such as colleagues, subject matter specialists, supervisors, and professors."[5] Goldman maintains that, "Those who are now principals and those who aspire to the principalship in the future had best become accustomed to the fact that there is no longer any possibility of their serving as instructional leaders, a role declared by every principal to be his goal, and which so few have ever attained."[6]

Several studies on the role of the administrator as an instructional leader would appear to support the point of view described above. For instance, Clear asked social studies teachers whom they would normally approach first for assistance when they encountered an instructional problem. No teacher listed the administrator. Most identified a colleague as the individual whom they would approach first if they encountered an instructional problem; next in frequency was listed the department head.[7]

In another study, Marquit found that teachers saw principals as significantly less effective in improving instruction than principals saw themselves. The principals tended to perceive themselves as effective instructional leaders, but their teachers did not concur.[8] Studies by Corwin[9] and Sharma[10] indicated a lack of teacher acceptance of the administrator's role as an instructional leader.

Apparently the main problem the school administrator faces in this regard is that his instructional leadership is no longer based on an expertise differential.[11] Most teachers are as well, if not better prepared in subject matter and teaching methodology than the administrator. As Ball suggests,

> They [the teachers] know their subject matter, they know how to teach, they know a great deal about pupil behavior and motivation, and are in the best sense of the term, professionals. Many teachers today know a good deal more about their own jobs than even the best principal can, and it's been a long time coming for principals to recognize this fact.[12]

As a result of their increased expertise, teachers have become more militant in their expectations for professional autonomy and less receptive to attempts by the administrator to exercise instructional leadership.[13] Their attitude is characteristic of the problems with which any administrator must cope if he tries to exercise leadership over professionals without expertise as a source of his leadership.[14]

In spite of questions raised about the viability of the concept of the administrator as an instructional leader, the fact remains that in many school situations he is the one to whom major supervisory responsibilities at the building level are assigned.[15] Therefore, he frequently must assume these responsibilities, whether or not others feel that he can perform them competently. On the other hand, it seems clear that if the administrator is to exercise instructional leadership *effectively,* he must become more knowledgeable and proficient in supervision.* He will also need to utilize to a far greater degree those other resources of instructional expertise which exist within a school and school district.

THE INSTRUCTIONAL IMPROVEMENT TEAM

An important objective of any administrator who is trying to improve instruction should be to organize and utilize effectively all appropriate and available sources of expertise. Personnel in a school or district who may (or should) be assigned supervisory responsibilities for improving instruction include the assistant principal, the department head or unit leader, and the central office subject matter supervisor. The degree to which all of these individuals are assigned supervisory responsibilities may vary somewhat from one district to another. However, each of these persons generally possesses special knowledge, skill, or insight which an administrator should attempt to utilize in improving instruction. The administrator can capitalize on the talents of these individuals in two ways: (1) by making explicit to them (and to the people with whom they associate) the nature and extent of their supervisory responsibilities, and (2) by organizing them into an instructional improvement team.

The instructional improvement team is a relatively recent concept in education and it has not been implemented in many schools. [16] Its basic purpose is to improve instruction by mobilizing and organizing the various kinds of expertise which exist in a school. The team usually includes the principal and the department heads (or unit leaders) but can—and perhaps should—also include central office supervisors if the latter are available.

The main activities of the team should be to evaluate the effectiveness of the instructional program and to study, develop, and implement ways in which it can be improved. The team should not, however, become directly involved in the evaluation of staff for the purpose of making personnel decisions. That function should be left to the staff evaluation team, which was discussed in the previous chapter.

An example of the kinds of activities in which an instructional improvement team may become involved is shown by a team agenda, presented in figure 11.1.

The agenda for meetings of the instructional improvement team should be developed on the basis of members' input and should be distributed

*There is evidence that those administrators who are perceived by teachers to possess instructional expertise will be sought out by teachers if they have an instructional problem. See Richard A. Gorton, "The Importance of Administrative Expertise in Instructional Leadership" (Research paper presented at a meeting of the American Research Association, 1971).

1. Presentation of the Iowa Test results.
2. Discussion of how the test results relate to the achievement of the educational objectives of the school or organizational units within the school.
3. Identification of needed improvements.

Figure 11.1. Instructional Improvement Team Meeting Agenda.

several days before the meeting in order to give participants an opportunity to consider it and prepare for the meeting.

The instructional improvement team should be involved in all aspects of the supervisory process. Supervision no longer should be the sole province of one person, the principal. While the principal may be held ultimately responsible for supervision and the improvement of instruction in a school, he cannot accomplish the job alone. The team approach which has been emphasized in other chapters of this book also seems to offer the greatest possibility for instructional improvement in the school.*

A PROPOSED PROCESS OF INSTRUCTIONAL SUPERVISION

The ultimate goal of instructional supervision should be to improve student learning, but its more immediate objective is to improve the instructional program. To achieve the latter purpose, the administrator in his role as supervisor should engage in a number of activities. If these activities are interrelated and sequential rather than random, they constitute a process. The process of supervision is really the administrator's design to accomplish the objective of improving the instructional program.

The process of instructional supervision which will be recommended in this chapter is the problem-solving approach. This approach is not new, of course, but its utilization as the main process of instructional supervision has been limited, at least insofar as discussion in the educational literature is concerned. [17] The main steps in the process are presented in figure 11.2.

In order to help the administrator better understand and utilize the problem-solving approach to instructional supervision as outlined in figure 11.2, the major aspects of the process will be discussed in some detail.

*Since it may not be feasible for every administrator to establish an instructional improvement team, the following sections will concentrate on his own role as a supervisor. However, if an instructional improvement team can be organized, the recommended principles and practices should be implemented on a team basis.

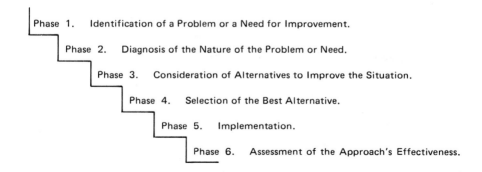

Figure 11.2. A Problem-Solving
Approach to Instructional Supervision.

IDENTIFICATION OF A PROBLEM OR A NEED FOR IMPROVEMENT

The administrator's objective in his role as supervisor is to improve instruction.* However, in order to accomplish that objective he must first determine which elements of the instructional program need to be improved. To arrive at that determination the administrator should consider at least three major sources of assistance in the identification of problems or needs of the instructional program: (1) people who are associated with the school, (2) professional standards and/or recommendations, and (3) local research.

People Who Are Associated with the School

Students, teachers, parents, and the central administration all represent potentially excellent sources of assistance for identifying instructional program needs and problems. Since most of these groups are closely involved with the instructional program, they are in a good position to suggest areas needing improvement. Although some of these people may, on their own initiative, recommend instructional improvement needs to the administrator, he should not depend on or limit his feedback to only those few individuals.

If an administrator is really interested in securing input from students, teachers, parents, and the central office, he should survey these groups *regularly* to ascertain their perceptions and ideas on which aspects of the instructional program need to be improved. Such a survey would not have to

---

*The term "administrator" in this context includes the principal, assistant principal, and department head or unit leader, but the concepts discussed could apply to any type of supervisor.

be long and complicated, and it could provide useful information if it only included several questions. An example is presented in figure 11.3.

---

1. What are the three *most* important classroom problems which you believe impair your effectiveness as a teacher?
2. What are three ways in which *each* of the problems listed above could be ameliorated?
3. Would you be willing to work on a committee to help resolve these problems?

Figure 11.3. A Teacher Survey to Identify Instructional Problems.

Using a type of survey similar to the one shown in figure 11.3, the National Education Association found from a national sampling of teachers that the problems which had the most effect on the teacher's work were: (1) the wide range of student achievement, (2) working with too many students in each class, (3) too many noninstructional duties, and (4) too many students indifferent to school. [18]

An administrator may feel that the results of a national survey are not valid for his school. If so, then he should conduct a local survey. However, whether or not an administrator agrees with the perceptions of teachers on which aspects of the instructional program need to be improved, feedback can help him to have a better understanding of their attitudes. And if a majority of teachers see too many noninstructional duties, for example, as a major impediment to teaching, it would probably be to the administrator's advantage to investigate the validity of their perception.

Professional Standards and Recommendations

A second important source for helping to identify instructional improvement needs is the body of recommendations and standards proposed by professional organizations and educational authorities. For example, regional accrediting associations such as the North Central Association publish standards which member schools are expected to meet, and which can be used by an administrator to identify areas for instructional improvement. [19] The National Association of Secondary School Principals, The National Association of Elementary School Principals, and The Association for Supervision and Curriculum Development also publish recommendations for improving instruction in the schools. In addition, articles and books are written each year by educational authorities who advocate various improvements in the instructional program.

For example, one article which should be useful to administrators who want to improve instruction is, "What Psychology Can We Feel Sure

About?" by Goodwin Watson. [20] He has identified fifty different psychological principles on how students learn, established by research. Four of these are listed below:

1. Behaviors which are rewarded (reinforced) are more likely to recur.
2. Reward (reinforcement) must follow almost immediately after the desired behavior and be clearly connected with that behavior in the mind of the learner in order for the reward to be most effective.
3. Sheer repetition without indication of improvement or any kind of reinforcement (reward) is a poor way to attempt to learn.
4. Threat and punishment have variable and uncertain effects upon learning; they may make the punished response either more or less likely to recur; they may set up avoidance tendencies which prevent further learning. [21]

These and the other forty-six psychological principles described in Watson's article represent valuable criteria which an administrator could use to identify aspects of instruction which need to be improved. By observing the extent to which a teacher bases his instruction on sound psychological principles, the administrator can identify ineffective or counterproductive teaching styles and take appropriate supervisory action.

Another publication that contains helpful ideas for improving instruction is *Microteaching* by Allen and Ryan. [22] Their discussion of component skills of teaching is based on considerable work at Stanford University and offers the administrator a basis for analyzing and improving the teaching process. Although fourteen skills are identified in the book, nine seem particularly noteworthy: (1) establishing set, a skill designed to capture students' attention and interest in a topic at the beginning of its introduction, (2) utilizing rewards and punishment to influence student behavior, (3) asking questions, (4) establishing relevant frames of reference, a skill designed to help the student understand a topic better by looking at it from several points of view, (5) recognizing nonverbal cues, (6) varying the stimulus field, e.g., changing tone or pitch of teacher's voice, (7) completeness of communication, (8) lecturing, and (9) bringing closure, the skill of concluding a lesson by showing students the connection between what they knew at the beginning of class and what was presented during the lesson. [23]

Since an entire book has been written that describes, explains, and illustrates the use of these component teaching skills, no attempt will be made to discuss them further. However, the administrator's attention is directed to this publication as an example of a source of ideas which could be helpful in the improvement of instruction. [24]

Local Research

A third source of assistance for identifying instructional improvement needs is local research, initiated or coordinated by the building administrator. The purpose of this type of research is to ascertain the effectiveness of the instructional program and the various conditions which influence its effectiveness. Although some administrators may shudder at the term "research," it can legitimately include a variety of activities which most administrators should be able to conduct with appropriate assistance.

Three suggestions for local research are

1. Follow-up study of graduates; follow-up study of dropouts. Both studies can yield useful information about the effectiveness of the instructional program and the conditions affecting it. These kinds of studies should be initiated on a regular basis and can be conducted through the use of questionnaires and in-depth interviews.

2. A study of how much time is spent in the classroom on student participation and involvement as contrasted with teacher presentation. Effective student learning generally requires active participation by the learner. A research question which the administrator could explore through classroom observation is, "How much student *participation* in the learning process is taking place in the school?" The answer to this question could identify a major need for instructional improvement.

3. An analysis of test data to ascertain progress toward or the achievement of the educational objectives of the school. Although an evaluation of the extent of achievement of educational objectives should not be *limited* to an examination of test data, these data can be helpful in suggesting possible areas in need of instructional improvement. The administrator should, of course, be cautious in drawing firm conclusions about the instructional program based solely on test data, and it probably would be well to secure consultant assistance in interpreting the relationship between the test results and the achievement of educational objectives.

These are only several examples of local research which would be appropriate. By organizing such research efforts an administrator can begin to pinpoint weaknesses in the instructional program so that corrective action can be taken. In the absence of this kind of research activity, the administrator will frequently lack the data necessary to ascertain the effectiveness of the instructional program.

In concluding this section on the identification of needs for improving instruction, it should be emphasized that the improvement of instruction depends on ideas of what instruction *should* be and data on what it *is*. If the administrator does not possess or seek both kinds of information, he is dependent on his own subjective preferences for improving instruction, surely a weak basis for an administrator who should exercise *professional* judgment.

DIAGNOSIS OF THE NEED
FOR IMPROVEMENT

Identification of a need for improving instruction should be followed by diagnosis of that need. Diagnosing a need simply means determining its nature and the reasons for its existence.

For example, suppose the administrator observes that several teachers talk too much during their classes and don't provide students with enough opportunity to participate in class discussion. The initial question he should ask in attempting to diagnose the situation is, why are the teachers behaving this way? To obtain the answer to this question the administrator may need to explore several alternative explanations and questions:

1. The subject matter or skill being taught doesn't lend itself to class discussion and requires considerable teacher presentation. (Is this really true? Why?)
2. The teacher has developed the habit of talking or explaining too much. (Why has this happened? What special needs of the teacher are being met by so much talking?)
3. The teacher lacks skills for developing class discussion; all or many of the students lack discussion skills. (Is this true? What specific skills are missing?)
4. There are few or no rewards or incentives for either the teacher or the students to participate in class discussion.

In examining a problem situation the administrator may find that a single factor explains the undesired behavior or condition. Frequently, however, there will be more than one reason. Therefore, in the initial stages of diagnosis, the administrator should concentrate on identifying a broad range of possible explanations for a problem, and then attempt to focus on the more important and relevant factors that best explain why the problem exists. Once a problem has been completely and accurately diagnosed, the administrator will be in a position to consider possible solutions.

Accurate diagnosis of a problem is an important prerequisite for successful problem solving, since a proposed solution to a problem is likely to be based on its diagnosis. Inaccurate diagnosis is frequently the reason why an instructional problem is not satisfactorily resolved. Usually in such a situation the wrong solution has resulted from failure to properly diagnose the problem. Until instructional problems are properly diagnosed, the administrator cannot expect to improve instruction.

IMPROVING INSTRUCTION: MAJOR ALTERNATIVES

After an instructional problem has been accurately diagnosed, the administrator is in a position to consider possible solutions for improving the situation. In the following sections, rather than examining alternatives for a *particular* problem, a wide range of supervisory techniques, procedures, and programs available to the administrator will be described in order to develop greater awareness and understanding of his main options for improving instruction.* Discussion of supervisory alternatives will be divided into two parts: (1) working with an individual and (2) working with a group.

IMPROVING INSTRUCTION: WORKING WITH AN INDIVIDUAL

CLASSROOM VISITATION AND THE CONFERENCES

Perhaps the supervisory technique used most frequently by administrators is the classroom visitation, with preconference and follow-up conference. Although they can be treated as separate supervisory techniques, they are usually employed in conjunction with each other; seldom will a visitation have much value for a teacher without the preconference and the follow-up conference. [25] The three components, conceptionalized as a cycle, are depicted in figure 11.4.

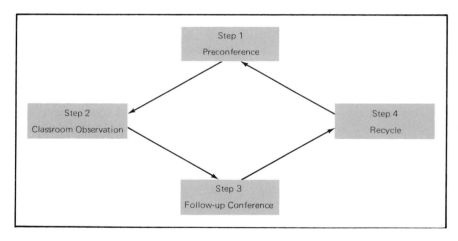

Figure 11.4. The Process of Classroom Observation.

*Since one chapter cannot possibly do justice to the topic, the reader is encouraged to consult the following source for additional depth: James R. Marks et al., *Handbook of Educational Supervision: A Guide for the Practitioner* (Boston: Allyn & Bacon, 1971).

The preconference, which involves the administrator and the teacher who is to be observed, is very important to the effectiveness of the classroom observation. [26] The objectives and activities of the preconference include:

1. Developing rapport between the administrator and the teacher who is to be observed.
2. Establishing the purposes and function of the classroom observation.
3. Identifying the aspects of the instructional program that are to be observed.
4. Developing procedures which will be used during the observation.
5. Identifying the roles that the administrator and the teacher will perform during the observation.
6. Indicating the purposes and nature of the follow-up conference to be held after the classroom observation.
7. Answering the teacher's questions about the classroom observation and the follow-up conference.

It should be emphasized that numbers 2 through 6 should be agreed upon cooperatively rather than imposed by the administrator. At the end of the preconference the teacher should feel that he has been meaningfully involved in the supervisory process and that the administrator has the teacher's best interests at heart. The interpersonal relationship that develops between the administrator and the teacher will in most cases significantly influence the effectiveness of the supervision, perhaps more than any other factor. [27]

Following the preconference the administrator should initiate the classroom observation(s). The classroom observation or visitation should be used to identify and diagnose strengths and areas in need of improvement. Through classroom visitation the administrator can identify teacher and classroom improvement needs and can observe conditions which may be impairing student learning. The administrator should also find the classroom visitation useful in identifying effective teaching and for gaining a more complete and accurate picture of the total instructional program in the school. (Several sources that describe observational systems or instruments which should be of help to the administrator in conducting classroom observations are listed at the end of this chapter. [28])

The administrator will need to recognize, however, that classroom observations may not be viewed by many teachers as a positive and constructive contribution to their effectiveness. [29] Poor planning by the administrator for the classroom visitation, little or no follow-up on the observation, and a lack of constructive suggestions to the teacher on how to improve have all cast considerable doubt for many teachers on the value of the classroom visitation. Added to these factors is the anxiety created by the classroom observation when it is conducted for the purpose of teacher evaluation.

Since most of these negative factors associated with the classroom observation can be corrected by the administrator, he should not reject the classroom visitation as one of his supervisory alternatives, despite possible teacher opposition. It would be to his advantage, though, to be aware of the attitude of many teachers about classroom visitations and to take appropriate steps to make sure that visitations are positive experiences.

After the administrator has completed his classroom observations and has identified and diagnosed a teaching problem, which is impairing the effectiveness of the instructional program, a follow-up conference with the teacher will probably be needed in order to improve the situation.*

The follow-up conference can be a useful supervisory technique for accomplishing the following objectives:

1. Developing a better understanding on the part of each participant in the conference of the way in which each person sees the classroom situation, and the reasons for those perceptions.
2. Exploring possible solutions to an instructional problem.
3. Designing and agreeing upon a plan of action to improve the classroom situation.
4. Reviewing progress made by the teacher in attempting to improve the classroom situation.

Whether any particular follow-up conference between an administrator and a teacher should include all four of these objectives will depend on the conditions which brought about the conference. However, accomplishing all four purposes will obviously, in most cases, take more than a single meeting.

It should be pointed out that the success of a conference will depend in large part on the amount of planning invested by the administrator in preparation for the meeting. Factors such as the time and location of the conference, the seating arrangement, establishing and maintaining rapport during the conference, the objectives of the meeting, identifying and sequencing questions to be asked, anticipating questions the teacher may raise, and deciding how to close the conference—all will need to be considered by the administrator.† Successful conferences cannot take place without adequate planning, and there is evidence that many supervisory conferences are not successful. [30]

---

*A follow-up conference can be useful for discussing a teacher's strengths and should not be limited to discussing only the teacher's weaknesses.

† For an earlier but still relevant discussion of these points see George C. Kyte, *The Principal at Work* (New York: Ginn & Co., 1952), pp. 274-76. For more recent work in the area see Ray Hull and John Hansen, *Classroom Supervision and Informal Analysis of Behavior* (Eugene, Oreg.: Oregon School Study Council, 1972), pp. 6-10.

The value of the supervisory conference is not restricted to its use in conjunction with the classroom visitation. An individual conference can be used by the administrator to discuss with the teacher a variety of items which may be impairing instruction: class scheduling, the homework policy, grading, or nature of the text material, for example. However, since the classroom observation and the preconference and follow-up conference are generally linked in people's minds, as well as in practice, the discussion has focused for the most part on the purpose and planning for those types of conferences. [31]

VIDEOTAPE ANALYSIS AND MICROTEACHING

A problem in trying to improve the instructional program that is encountered by most administrators at one time or another is created by the difference in the way that the teacher and the administrator perceive what has occurred in the classroom. An approach to this difficulty is for the administrator to utilize, in cooperation with the teacher, a videotape recorder to help both of them analyze the classroom situation. [32] This equipment can capture on tape for both teacher and administrator the actual dynamics of what has happened in the classroom, thereby enabling them to review and study the tape, and to analyze it for the identification of strengths and areas needing improvement in the instructional program. [33]

In addition to helping an administrator and teacher develop a better understanding of and agreement on the specific aspects of the instructional program needing improvement, the videotape machine can also be used by a teacher to examine videotapes of colleagues or outside experts demonstrating effective employment of instructional techniques and procedures.* Through this kind of study a teacher can observe a model of how a particular teaching technique should be employed and learn how he might use the same technique in his classroom. While undoubtedly many teachers could benefit from studying the videotapes without supervisory assistance, it is recommended that, at least in the beginning, the administrator work with the teacher in analyzing the tapes.

Although studying videotapes should prove to be of value to a teacher who is trying to improve his methods and skills, an administrator or a teacher may feel that there is a need to *practice* a teaching skill before it is incorporated in classroom procedures. Again, the videotape equipment can play an important role in increasing the effectiveness of the teacher's practice sessions. Prior to use of the video equipment, the major problem an individual faced in deriving significant benefit from practice was that he normally could not observe how well he was accomplishing a task while it was

*For further information on materials and procedures, write The Far West Regional Laboratory, 1 Garden Circle, Hotel Claremont, Berkeley, Calif. 94705, or write Macmillan Co., Front and Brown Streets, Riverdale, N.J. 08075.

being performed. Once the event had occurred, it was too late to observe it; therefore, he was dependent on the perceptions of others who described it to him. However, by utilizing a video machine a teacher can now tape his practice session with students and then view the tape to see how well he performed a particular skill and how he might improve in the next practice session. This process is referred to as "microteaching." [34]

The video recorder's essential function in supervision is to capture the reality of a situation for later study, analysis, and evaluation. It can be used by the administrator and teacher to identify strengths and limitations in the instructional program, to analyze model teaching to gain ideas for self-improvement, and to provide feedback on progress that is being made in developing a particular teaching skill. [35] It is without question a very useful supervisory tool for improving the instructional program, and any school lacking access to a videotape machine should investigate the possibility of obtaining one.

INTERCLASS AND INTERSCHOOL VISITATION

Too many administrators attempt to improve instruction by *telling* the teacher what needs to be changed in the classroom situation. While the technique of telling may work in some cases, a much more successful supervisory approach is to *show* the teachers a more effective way of conducting instruction. In some cases the administrator himself might demonstrate the change he is advocating. It may be more realistic and likely, however, for him to identify individuals in (or outside) the school who can most appropriately and effectively demonstrate a new technique or procedure.

For example, one teacher in the school may be particularly skillful in leading a class discussion; another person might be good in the area of establishing student self-discipline, and another in evaluation techniques. The administrator should attempt to capitalize on the talents of these people and others by organizing a program of interclass and interschool visitation for teachers who would like to improve their skills in a particular area. The interclass visitations might take place during a teacher's released period, or another type of accommodation could be made by the administrator. Interschool visitations could take place during an in-service day or, if necessary, a substitute teacher might be hired in order for a member of the staff to view a class in another school.

Organizing a program of interclass and interschool visitations will not be an easy task for the school administrator. It can be accomplished, but it requires effort and resourcefulness. There will be scheduling problems to be resolved, and the cooperation of those who are to be visited must be secured. However, interclass and interschool visitations are two excellent means by which teachers can actually see a technique or procedure demonstrated, instead of listening to an administrator talk about it. For this reason, then, both kinds of visitations are recommended as desirable components of a good supervisory program.

USE OF THE PROFESSIONAL LIBRARY

Most schools have some type of professional library. The primary purpose of the professional library is to provide an opportunity for staff members to improve themselves through reading or viewing various kinds of print and nonprint materials.

Undoubtedly some members of the staff use the professional library on their own initiative and derive great benefit from it. However, observation and experience would suggest that many members of the faculty of a school seldom, if ever, use the professional library except in completing a university course or for other special reasons. [36] It would appear that in most schools the professional library plays a minimal role in the improvement of instruction.

Whether the professional library can play an important role in improving instruction in a school will depend on many factors. However, two factors appear to be critical. First of all, the faculty should be involved by the librarian in selecting materials and in deciding on the location of the professional library. [37] Secondly, the administrator must show that he perceives the professional library as an important part of the school. If he tends to ignore the library in his own reading or is unfamiliar with the collection, he will not only fail to provide a good model for the faculty but will also be in a poor position to utilize the library's resources in working with the staff.

The materials in a professional library can, if properly selected, be useful in helping a teacher to improve himself. But before they receive much use, the administrator must show that he is interested in the professional library's resources, and he must become sufficiently familiar with the resources to recommend them appropriately to others.

IMPROVING INSTRUCTION: WORKING WITH GROUPS

Most supervisory procedures that involve working with groups come under the rubric of in-service education. Although in-service education is frequently advanced by educators as a corrective to many problems, [38] like so many other aspects of education it has come under attack in recent years.

Perhaps the strongest indictment was made by Davies who asserted that, "In-service teacher training is the slum of American Education—disadvantaged, poverty-stricken, neglected, psychologically isolated, whittled with exploitation and broken promises, and conflict." [39] Periodic surveys would tend to support the conclusion that in-service programs are not perceived by teachers as very effective in meeting their needs. [40]

How can in-service education be improved? Based on an analysis of various critiques of in-service programs, [41] it would appear that the following conditions must be met:

1. The administrators of the school must be committed to the importance of in-service education and must plan carefully for the development, implementation, and evaluation of in-service activities.
2. Teachers need to be involved in the establishing of the *need* for in-service and in the development, implementation, and evaluation of the program.*
3. The in-service program must be viewed by teachers as contributing to *their* professional growth rather than meeting administrative needs.
4. Time and funds must be provided by the administration to plan, carry out and evaluate in-service activities.

While the presence of these four conditions may not *guarantee* a successful in-service program, their absence would seem to limit its chances of success. Additional factors that the administrator will need to take into consideration in planning and implementing specific in-service activities are discussed in the following sections.

DEPARTMENTAL OR UNIT MEETINGS

Most schools hold departmental or unit meetings periodically during the year. These meetings offer an important opportunity for an administrator to improve instruction by working with a group of teachers. Unfortunately, such meetings usually take place after a long day of school, and frequently only items of a "housekeeping" nature are discussed. However, the potential for discussing and exploring issues, problems and new approaches to instruction is definitely present at a departmental or unit meeting. The key people for capitalizing on that potential are the school administrator and the department heads or unit leaders.

If the departmental or unit meeting is to become an important means of improving instruction, the school administrator will need to work with the department heads or unit leaders to extend their vision of the purposes and uses of these meetings, and should hold the chairmen or unit leaders accountable for focusing their meetings to a larger extent on instructional im-

*One type of program which seems to meet this criterion is a teaching center. For more information on the relatively new kind of in-service program see *Teaching Centers: Toward the State of the Scene* (Washington, D.C.: American Association for Teacher Education, 1974).

provement purposes. Most department heads and unit leaders, because of a lack of training, do not take the initiative to utilize their meetings for discussion of instructional improvement activities. They need help and encouragement from the school administrator.

There is a wide variety of possible instructional improvement topics which could be explored during department or unit meetings. The following four examples should illustrate the range of possibilities:

1. Examination of departmental or unit objectives to ascertain the degree of understanding and consensus on overall objectives and the objectives for each grade level.
2. Consideration of an assessment program to provide data on the extent to which departmental or unit objectives are being met.
3. Presentation and demonstration of available supplementary resources from the instructional materials center.
4. Development of a uniform grading or homework policy for the department or unit.

These four topics are only suggestive of the kinds of instructional improvement activities which a department or unit could consider during its meetings. [42] This does not mean that the school administrator can realistically expect that *all* departmental or unit meetings can be devoted entirely to instructional improvement topics. There are admittedly legitimate housekeeping tasks, such as requisitioning and budgeting, which a department or unit must accomplish during its meetings. However, one of the primary purposes of these meetings should be to focus on instructional improvement.

FACULTY MEETINGS

The faculty meeting is probably one of the most abused and most often criticized of all group supervisory activities. [43] It is generally scheduled at the end of the school day when teachers are tired, it is frequently informational in nature and dominated by the principal, and it seldom provides for much teacher participation and involvement. Also, since the advent of the master contract for teachers, the time allowed for faculty meetings is frequently of such short duration that little of an instructional nature can be discussed. On the other hand, the faculty meeting represents one of the few vehicles available to the school administrator during the year for bringing the total faculty together to consider instructional concerns. [44] By correcting the abuses of the faculty meeting, it can be used profitably for instructional improvement purposes.

One of the major constraints which an administrator must overcome in order to utilize the faculty meeting effectively is that, with the exception of very small schools, the size of the faculty usually limits the amount of participation which can take place. [45] Recognizing this limitation, it would appear that faculty meetings should be used primarily for problem identification and decision making, and that the actual investigation of a problem and exploration of alternative solutions should be carried out by subcommittees of the faculty, who would report their recommendations to the total faculty and administration for a final decision. This would make possible a more effectively conducted faculty meeting, and yet the administrator (with the faculty, if appropriate) could make the final decision on a matter. The alternative is for 40 to 100 people to attempt to determine the nature of a problem, the reasons for its existence, and possible alternative solutions—under conditions of apathy, fatigue, large group size, and limited time frame.

If a school administrator is to utilize the faculty meeting more productively, he should try to follow rather simple but important principles:

1. **The meeting should be scheduled during school time, if possible, rather than at the end of the day.** Some schools dismiss students early on one afternoon every week or two in order to provide greater time for faculty consideration of a topic.

2. **Faculty input should be sought in developing the agenda.** This may mean establishing a faculty meeting planning committee (required by some master contracts) or simply requesting the faculty to submit items for the agenda. In any regard, faculty members' input is important in the development of the agenda if they are to play more than a passive role at the meetings.

3. **The agenda and all related materials for the faculty meeting should be distributed to the staff at least two days before the date of the meeting.** If faculty members are to react, discuss, and make decisions on agenda items at the meeting, they will need an opportunity to become aware of and think about the topics to be discussed, and to study the related material prior to the meeting. It is conceded that some faculty members—perhaps even a large proportion—won't take or find time to consider the agenda and related materials before the meeting, even if they receive them in advance. However, many teachers *will* find this procedure helpful.

4. **The school administrator should employ as much as possible the group leadership skills identified in chapter 3.** His role during the faculty meetings should be to

   a. Create an atmosphere which is friendly and nonthreatening but task-oriented.

   b. Guide the discussion in such a way that as many people

       as possible who would like to and should participate during
the meeting may have an opportunity to do so.

   c. Clarify questions, comments, or statements so that intentions,
meanings, and implications are not left ambiguous.

   d. Keep the group focused on the topic under consideration,
and limit wandering from the subject.

   e. Summarize periodically where the group appears to be in relation
to the topic, and what remains to be done.

   f. Mediate differences of opinion. [46]

5. **Minutes of the meeting should be maintained that will indicate important points made, questions raised that are yet to be resolved, commitments made, and decisions reached.** The minutes are a useful record of what transpired during the meeting and can be used for self-improvement analysis and for providing continuity from one meeting to another.

6. **Minutes of the meeting should be disseminated to the total faculty and other relevant parties, e.g., the immediate superior in the central office.** Each member of the faculty needs a record of what transpired during the meeting, if understanding of and commitment to decisions reached during the meeting are to be maintained. It is also useful to provide space at the end of the minutes for reactions by faculty members for the purpose of obtaining feedback from individuals who, for one reason or another, did not comment during the meeting itself.

7. **Follow-up activities need to be initiated after the faculty meeting in order to implement decisions which were reached and to investigate questions or problems that were raised.** A fairly common complaint of many teachers about faculty meetings is that there is no follow-through afterwards. If the faculty is to feel that their meetings are worthwhile, the administrator will need to initiate and coordinate appropriate follow-up activities after the meetings.

    Faculty meetings can be a valuable group activity for the improvement of instruction if the previously described principles are followed. New approaches to teaching can be demonstrated, instructional problems can be identified, and/or recommendations from subcommittees on school philosophy, objectives, grading, and grade level articulation, for example, can be considered and decided upon. The value of the faculty meeting is limited mainly by the size of the faculty and the degree of resourcefulness and organizational skills possessed by the administrator.

COMMITTEE WORK

Committee work is an appropriate problem-solving procedure for improving instruction as well as an excellent group activity for staff development. As a result of committee interaction and investigation of an instructional problem, each member of a committee can benefit in terms of increased awareness, understanding, and (possibly) new skills.

An administrator should attempt to utilize committees in the improving of instruction whenever it appears that a situation would be more thoroughly investigated and considered if several people were involved rather than only one individual. The primary rationale for establishing a committee, rather than assigning only one person, should be that the other people whom the administrator might involve possess additional knowledge, skill, or insight which will be helpful in the accomplishment of a task. That task may be investigating a possible instructional problem, identifying alternative solutions, or gaining acceptance from the entire faculty on a recommended course of action.

In working with a committee to improve instruction the administrator will need to apply the concepts and skills discussed in chapter 3. In addition, he will need to be clear about the objectives of the committee, its role, and his own role; and he should communicate this information to the other members of the committee.

If, for example, a committee's role is to be strictly advisory and the administrator plans to reserve for himself the final decision, this fact should be presented to the committee members at the outset. A significant factor which has contributed to the ineffectiveness of the committees and the disillusionment of committee members is the ambivalence or vagueness of the administrator in regard to the objectives and role of the committee, and the role of the administrator in relationship to the committee. A precise understanding of these points on the part of everyone involved will do much to avert serious problems at a later date.

WORKSHOPS AND INSTITUTES

The three main types of school workshops or institutes are:* (1) the preschool workshop for staff before classes formally begin in the fall, (2) the in-service workshop held during the school year on in-service days or Saturdays, and (3) the summer workshop. Since the preschool workshop has already been discussed in conjunction with orientation for new staff, this section will concentrate on the other two types of workshops.

---

*Since there are more similarities than differences between workshops and institutes, the discussion will focus on workshops and refer specifically to institutes only when appropriate.

The primary purpose of in-service workshops that take place during the school year should be to explore a problem, topic, or new approach to instruction in greater depth than would be possible during a faculty or committee meeting. A workshop can include a combination of activities for the total faculty, small groups, or individuals. Figure 11.5 presents a typical format for an in-service workshop scheduled during the year.

Workshop Theme: Improvement of Reading

8:15-8:30	Coffee and socializing in Room 201
8:30-8:45	Welcome and an overview of the Workshop
8:45-9:45	Presentation by Dr. Hiller, "Data on the Effectiveness of the School's Reading Program and Ways to Improve It."
9:45-10:00	Break
10:00-11:45	Small Group Discussions about the implications of Dr. Hiller's presentation
11:45-1:00	Lunch
1:15-4:00	Team and individual teacher planning of instructional techniques and materials that might improve our Reading Program

---

Figure 11.5. Sample Format for In-Service Workshop.

The success of an in-service workshop will depend on the degree of administrative planning, organization, and faculty input which have been invested in the design and implementation of the workshop. The last factor, faculty input, is tremendously important. If the faculty or their representatives have not been involved in choosing the theme and in planning for the workshop, its success will be uncertain. The administrator needs faculty involvement so that in planning the workshop he can capitalize on the thinking and insight of the staff and increase their receptivity to it. In most cases the faculty will not be very receptive to unilateral administrative decision making and planning in regard to an in-service workshop.

It should be noted that workshops, like other kinds of group meetings, suffer from a lack of follow-through. It almost seems that, regardless of the ideas, questions, or discussions explored during a workshop, there is very little indication two days later that it has had any discernible effect on what is taking place in the school. Part of the problem, of course, may be that little was accomplished during the workshop; but another hypothesis is that no one has assumed the responsibility of following through on what was achieved.

Certainly, all school personnel have a professional responsibility for workshop follow-up activities. But the administrator himself must shoulder the major responsibility for initiating, coordinating, monitoring, and evaluating the activities. If he does not assume this responsibility, it is unlikely that anyone else will, and the value of the workshop will be quite minimal.

The points which have been made about in-service workshops held during the year also apply to summer workshops. Recently, participants in summer workshops have been remunerated, and problems of motivation and receptivity to workshop topics and activities have been correspondingly reduced. However, careful planning, systematic organization, considerable faculty input, and adequate follow-through after the workshops are just as important for summer workshops as for those held during the year. [47] Both types offer an excellent mechanism for staff development and for improving instruction if the conditions recommended in this section are present.

A FINAL NOTE

The last step in the recommended approach to instructional supervision is assessment. No program can be significantly improved without assessment, and there is considerable evidence (referred to previously) that the instructional supervision program currently in operation in many schools is badly in need of improvement. Therefore, in addition to implementing the various suggested procedures described in this chapter the administrator should, with the involvement and help of the faculty, periodically assess the effectiveness of the different components of the school's instructional supervision program.

Review

1. How should the terms "supervision" and "the instructional program" be defined?
2. What problems may the administrator face in trying to initiate the role of supervisor or instructional leader? How can these problems be best addressed?
3. Identify the main steps of the process of instructional supervision.
4. How can an administrator identify the need for instructional improvement and define the nature of that need?

5. Define the objectives and main activities of the preconference, the classroom visitation, and the follow-up conference.
6. Describe the essential characteristics of the major options the administrator has available for working with an individual and with a group.
7. How can in-service programs be improved?
8. In what ways can faculty meetings be improved?

Notes

1. For the historical roots of this definition, see Ross Neagley and N. Dean Evans, *Handbook for Effective Supervision of Instruction* (Englewood Cliffs, N.J.: Prentice-Hall, 1970), pp. 1-7.
2. Paul B. Jacobson et al., *The Principalship: New Perspectives* (Englewood Cliffs, N.J.: Prentice-Hall, 1973), p. 135.
3. For an excellent review of research on the impact of these variables, see Bikkar S. Randhawe and Lewis L W. Fu, "Assessment and Effect of Some Classroom Environment Variables," *Review of Educational Research* 43, no. 3 (Summer 1973):303-20.
4. Roald F. Campbell, "What Peculiarities in Educational Administration Make It a Special Case?" in *Administrative Behavior in Education,* ed. Andrew W. Halpin (Chicago: Midwest Administration Center, University of Chicago, 1958), p. 172.
5. Donald Erickson, "Changes in the Principalship," *National Elementary Principal* 44 (April 1965).
6. Harvey Goldman, "The Evolving Role of the School Principal," mimeographed (Milwaukee: University of Wisconsin—Milwaukee, 1969), p. 17.
7. Delbert K. Clear, "Supervision in Educational Organization," *Institute of Staff Relations Journal,* Spring 1971.
8. Lawrence J. Marquit, "Perceptions of the Supervisory Behavior of Secondary School Principals." An ERIC Report: Ed-020-579 (1968).
9. R. G. Corwin, "Teacher Militancy in the United States: Reflections on the Sources and Prospects," *Theory into Practice* 7 (April 1968):96-102.
10. G. L. Sharma, "Who Should Make What Decisions?" *Administrator's Notebook* 3, (April 1955).
11. Norman J. Boyan, "The Emergent Roles of the Teacher and the Authority Structure of the School." An ERIC Report:Ed-011-937 (1966).
12. L. B. Ball, "Principal and Negotiations," *High School Journal* 52 (October 1968):22-29.
13. Corwin, "Teacher Militancy," pp. 96-102.
14. A. Etzioni, "Administrative and Professional Authority," in *Complex Organizations: A Sociological Reader* (New York: Holt, Rinehart & Winston, 1961).
15. For example, see Dayton Benjamin, *How Principals Can Improve Instruction* (Santa Monica, Calif.: A. C. Croft, Inc., 1970).
16. Mary Yager, "Building Successful Administrative-Supervisory Teams in Junior and Middle Schools " (Paper presented at the Annual Convention of the National Association of Secondary School Principals, 1974).
17. A somewhat similar but more complex approach is described by Glen Eye et al., *Supervision of Instruction* (New York: Harper & Row, Publishers 1971), pt. 4.
18. National Education Association, "Finding Out What Teachers Need and Want," *Today's Education* 61 (October 1972):34.
19. North Central Association, 5454 South Shore Drive, Chicago, Ill.
20. Goodwin Watson, "What Psychology Can We Feel Sure About?" *Teachers College Record* 61, no. 5 (February 1960):253-57.

21. Ibid., p. 254.

22. Dwight Allen and Kevin Ryan, "Component Skills Approach," in *Microteaching* (Reading, Mass.: Addison-Wesley, 1969), chap. 2.

23. Ibid.

24. Ibid.

25. Monte S. Norton, "Are Classroom Visits Worthwhile?" *Clearing House* 35 (September 1960):41-43.

26. John D. McNeil, "Supervision of Instruction: The Relationship of Theory and Practice to Accountability." An ERIC Report: Ed-064-803 (1972).

27. George A. Churukian and John R. Cryan, "Interpersonal Perceptions as a Factor in Teacher Perceptions of Supervisory Style." An ERIC Report: Ed-064-233 (1972).

28. One observation system that has been helpful to a number of administrators was developed by Ned Flanders, *Analyzing Teaching Behavior* (Reading, Mass.: Addison-Wesley, 1970). Another source is Francis Griffith, *A Handbook for the Observation of Teaching and Learning* (Midland, Mich.: Fendell Publishing Co., 1973). A third source is Anita Simon et al., *Mirrors for Behavior: An Anthology of Classroom Observation Instruments* (Philadelphia: Research for Better Schools, 1970).

29. For evidence on this point and reasons why the problems exist, see Myre M. Toney, "A Study of Administrator, Supervisor, and Teacher Perceptions of the Classroom Visitation " (Ph.D. diss., University of Wisconsin, 1971).

30. See Arthur Blumberg, "Supervisor-Teacher Relationships: A Look at the Supervisory Conference," *Administrator's Notebook* 19 (September 1970).

31. For additional discussion of classroom observation and conferencing, see Morris L. Cogan, *Clinical Supervision* (Boston: Houghton-Mifflin Co., 1973).

32. For ideas on how this might best be done, see Harry M. Wenner, " An Assessment of Video Tape as a Tool in the Improvement of Teacher Classroom Effectiveness " (Ed.D. diss., University of Minnesota, 1969).

33. The original developmental work on the utilizing of the videotape recorder for the improvement of teaching behavior was done at Stanford University. For a description of this work and the possible use of the videotape recorder, see Allen and Ryan, "Component Skills Approach," pt. 5.

34. For additional information on this concept, write for a copy of *Minicourses Work* (Superintendent of Documents, U.S. Government Printing Office, Washington, D.C. 20402. Ask for circular no. 1780-0863.)

35. An excellent review of research on the use of the videotape recorder was conducted by Frances F. Fuller and Brad A. Manning, "Self-Confrontation Reviewed: A Conceptualization for Video Playback in Teacher Education," *Review of Educational Research* 43, no. 4 (Fall 1973):469-528.

36. In fact, there is evidence that teachers are neither regular readers of professional literature or aware of what is written. See Theodore W. Hipple and Thomas R. Giblin, *The Professional Reading of Teachers of English* (Gainesville, Fla: Florida Educational Research and Development Council, College of Education, University of Florida, 1971).

37. For help in selecting materials for the professional library, see *Standards for School Media Programs* (Chicago: American Library Association, 1969), pp. 33-35.

38. National Society for the Study of Education, *In-Service Education* (Chicago: University of Chicago Press, 1957).

39. Quoted in Louis J. Rubin, ed., *Improving In-Service Education, Proposals and Procedures for Change* (Boston: Allyn & Bacon, 1971), p. 38.

40. For evidence on this point see "Research Report" section and frequent articles in *Today's Education,* published by the National Education Association. Also see Jack L. Brimm and Daniel J. Tollett, "How Do Teachers Feel about In-Service Education?" *Educational Leadership* 21 (March 1974):522-24.

41. Two particularly excellent critiques of in-service education are Rubin, *Improving In-Service Education, Proposals and Procedures for Change*; and Jay Comras and Robert Mosterman, "A Rationale for Comprehensive In-Service Programs," *Clearing House* 46 (March 1972):424-26.

42. For several interesting approaches to making these meetings more interesting and productive, see Ben M. Harris, *Supervisory Behavior in Education* (Englewood Cliffs, N.J.: Prentice-Hall, 1975), pp. 79-83.

43. Kay Winters, "Perk Up Your Faculty Meetings," *NEA Journal* 55 (October 1966):30.

44. Kimball Wiles, *Supervision for Better Schools* (New York: Prentice-Hall, 1967), p. 255.

45. Association for Supervision and Curriculum Development, *Group Process in Supervision* (Washington, D.C.: National Education Association, 1948), p. 49.

46. Wiles, *Supervision for Better Schools*, pp. 189-94.

47. For additional ideas along these lines, see Arnold Finch *Growth In-Service Education Programs That Work* (Englewood Cliffs, N.J.: Prentice-Hall, 1969).

12

Administrator's Role in Curriculum Improvement

An understanding of the administrator's role in curriculum improvement is essential for any administrator who wishes to increase educational opportunities for students. The curriculum of the school has been defined in a variety of ways, but is defined in this chapter as the subject matter content and its organization and objectives in the program of studies offered by the school.[1] Curriculum improvement will refer to any change in the subject matter content or in its organization and objectives which results in increased student learning.[2] The emphasis on curriculum improvement rather than administration of the curriculum reflects the priority given in this book to the leadership dimensions of the administrator's role.[3]

The following sections will focus on the role of the school administrator in bringing about curricular improvement. Three aspects of this role will be analyzed: (1) *assessing* the need for curricular improvement, (2) *planning* for curricular improvement, and (3) *implementing* curricular improvement.

DISTRICT-WIDE VERSUS SCHOOL-BUILDING APPROACH TO CURRICULUM IMPROVEMENT*

THE DISTRICT APPROACH

The district-wide approach to curricular improvement usually involves teacher and administrator representatives from different schools within a district, serving on a committee or curriculum council to investigate and develop ways in which some aspect of the district's curriculum can be improved.[4] As a part of this method, subcommittees are established for each discipline in the curriculum, and members of the superintendent's staff provide direction and supervision for the various committees. Generally, the major intended outcome of the district-wide approach to curriculum improvement is to bring about needed curricular change in all of the schools within the district. A concern for curriculum articulation and correlation among subjects, grades, and schools also characterizes this method.

---

*It is recognized that curriculum improvement efforts can also take place at the county, state, and national levels, but the emphasis in this chapter will be on intradistrict approaches.

The extent to which a school administrator becomes involved in district-wide curriculum improvement efforts will vary with his own vision and capabilities, the size of the district, the district's concept of curriculum improvement, and its perception of the administrator's role. However, in situations wherein an administrator's potential contribution is recognized, a district may expect him to perform a number of responsibilities. These include (1) serving as a member of the district's curriculum council or on one of the district's curriculum subcommittees, (2) keeping informed about major curricular trends and innovations, (3) working on curriculum improvement projects with the curriculum director and/or the director of elementary or secondary education, (4) involving the school's teaching staff in problem identification and curriculum committee work at the district level, and (5) working in a staff relationship with K-12 subject matter area coordinators and with fellow elementary and secondary principals in the exchange of curriculum improvement ideas. [5]

The district-wide approach to curriculum improvement offers several advantages. It tends to result in greater coordination of activities and promotes better curricular articulation and correlation between subjects, grades, and schools. It also provides access to a broader array of resources and expertise than might be possible with another method. And, since the superintendent's staff is usually directly involved in the curriculum council and committees, there is greater likelihood that a proposed curricular change will receive his and the school board's ultimate approval. [6]

On the other hand, the district-wide approach to curriculum improvement has several weaknesses, according to its critics. [7] It can stifle creativity and diversity at the building and classroom levels because of its emphasis on coordination and uniformity of curriculum in all schools. In addition, it can lead to teacher apathy about curriculum improvement at the building level, as a result of limited involvement in the district-wide approach and a feeling that little can be accomplished unless the central office directs the change. In response to these criticisms, the school-building approach has been advanced as an equally valid means of curriculum improvement.

SCHOOL-BUILDING APPROACH

The school-building approach to curriculum improvement differs from the district-wide approach primarily in that the *impetus* for change occurs at the building rather than at the district level. As Caswell and his colleagues have pointed out:

> . . . the 'grass roots' [school building] approach which views the individual school as the operational and planning unit . . . means that problems which are dealt with on a system-wide or partial-system basis

should arise out of work done by individual staffs and feed back into use through these staffs. The channel is from the individual school to the system and back to the individual school, rather than from the top down as under the traditional system-wide approach. [8]

It is generally assumed in the school-building approach that a curricular change which is initiated in one school in a district need not always be implemented in the other schools in that district. The premise is that, to some extent, the schools of a district serve different student clienteles and, for that reason, should be permitted to develop different curricula. This does not mean, however, that each school should be permitted to "go it alone." Underscoring this point, the Association for Supervision and Curriculum Development emphasized in one of its yearbooks:

> Building principals, however, must not assume that the individual schools within a school system are completely autonomous. Some attention must be given to the need for a system-wide program . . . The problem to be solved is how the building units can be stimulated to develop the best program possible for the neighborhoods which they serve, and at the same time, make their appropriate contributions to the total system of which they are parts. [9]

While there can be several advantages to the school-building approach to curriculum improvement, including greater involvement of personnel, more responsiveness to the needs of the local student clientele, and improved opportunities for the proposed curricular change to be implemented in the classroom, the method is not without its limitations. The performance of school-building administrators and staffs in generating and maintaining the impetus for curricular change has been spotty. In addition, sole reliance on the building-level approach to curriculum improvement has in many instances resulted in a patchwork district curriculum with poor articulation and correlation between grades and among schools.

Although these potential disadvantages, like those of the district-wide approach, are not necessarily inherent in the building-level approach, it seems clear that for an administrator to rely on a single method would be a mistake. *Both* the district-wide and the school-building approaches are needed for effective curriculum improvement, and the goal for the administrator should be to capitalize on the strengths of each method while minimizing its disadvantages.

Regardless of which approach to curriculum improvement is utilized, the involvement of the school administrator would appear to be essential. Perhaps Spalding put it best when he said,

The principal has much to contribute to the curriculum program. He is the one person who is concerned with every aspect of the life of his school. His interest in its success provides a strong and direct motivation for his efforts to secure curriculum improvement. He is better able than anyone else to discover the needs of his school. He knows best the contributions that the members of his staff can make . . . His interest in the growth of his teachers requires that he should have responsibility for the best single means for securing that growth—work on the curriculum. [10]

ASSESSING THE NEED FOR CURRICULUM IMPROVEMENT

The school administrator who is interested in curricular improvement should initially concentrate his efforts on assessing the need for improvement. There is little reason to begin changing the curriculum until the nature of the need for improvement has been fully and accurately assessed. All too frequently, proposals for curriculum improvement are advanced and implemented without an accurate assessment of the real need for such improvement. As a result, curricular change occurs but not necessarily improvement. [11] The only valid criterion for ascertaining whether a curricular change results in significant improvement is whether the change better enables the school to achieve previously defined educational objectives. As Caswell has noted, "No matter how elaborate a program may be or how enthusiastic the staff, unless in the end the experiences of pupils are changed so that the educational outcomes are better than before, the work cannot be considered successful." [12]

An administrator can assess the need for improvement in at least two ways: (1) by evaluating a school's current program of studies, utilizing previously defined and accepted criteria, and (2) by studying and evaluating various proposals which are offered for the improvement of the curriculum. In either case, the administrator must develop or utilize a comprehensive set of evaluative criteria for assessing the need for curricular change. Without previously defined criteria, the administrator's assessment of the need for curricular improvement is likely to be unsystematic, idiosyncratic, and superficial. Using well-defined, comprehensive criteria, an administrator will be better able to assess the need for improvement in a current program of studies as well as to evaluate the potential of curriculum improvement proposals advanced by others.

Fortunately, there is no shortage of recommended criteria for assessing the need for curricular improvement. Over the years, a number of educational authorities have proposed criteria for evaluating the school curriculum. [13] A synthesis of their main points has been developed and is presented below in question form, with accompanying discussion.

EVALUATIVE CRITERIA FOR ASSESSING THE NEED FOR CURRICULAR IMPROVEMENT

1. **Has the school established clearly stated, operationally-defined, educational objectives?**

The school curriculum should be based on the educational objectives of the school. If a school lacks clearly stated, operationally-defined educational objectives, its curriculum is more likely to be based on tradition and/or fad than on desired student learning outcomes. Most schools have educational objectives of one kind or another, but these objectives are frequently not stated in a form which facilitates assessment of the need for curricular improvement. Therefore, the administrator should begin his efforts to improve the curriculum by working with others to develop clearly stated, operationally-defined educational objectives for the school.

2. **Are the courses in the curriculum helping to achieve school objectives?**

No course in the curriculum is an end in itself. It should relate in some demonstrable way to the achievement of school objectives. Undoubtedly, some courses exist in a curriculum for reasons other than their contribution to achieving the objectives of the school. The administrator needs to identify these courses and attempt to develop their relationship with overall school goals, or consider the elimination of the courses from the curriculum.

3. **Does the curriculum meet the needs of all students? Is it comprehensive?**

A comprehensive curriculum should meet the needs of the noncollege-bound as well as the collegebound students. It should provide for the needs of low-ability and average students, as well as the academically talented. It should also provide for the needs of students with special handicaps, as well as the needs of other kinds of exceptional students. In addition, the school should recognize that students have immediate as well as long-range needs, and that both should be accommodated through the curriculum. For example, the immediate need of a student to develop a healthy self-concept is as important as his long-range need to gain knowledge and skills for a career. (Perhaps the most useful conception of the needs of students has been advanced by Havighurst who postulates that people have particular tasks which need to be mastered at certain stages in their development.) [14]

A second way of raising the question about the comprehensiveness of the school curriculum is to ask, "To what extent does the curriculum help students to deal successfully with the various social influences which are or will be affecting their lives?" These social influences may include but are not limited to television, racial problems, poverty, war and peace, marriage and divorce, interpersonal relations, and urbanization. For example, in a society in which the typical student spends almost as much time at watching television as at studying in school, the curriculum should help students to utilize more effectively this important medium of information and attitude change. [15]

The essential point is that if the school is to prepare students for a constructive and productive life, the curriculum should reflect the realities of that life. [16] The alternative may be what Noyes and McAndrew have observed: "The student is filled with facts and figures which only accidentally and infrequently have anything to do with the problems and conflicts of modern life or his own inner concerns." [17]

4. **Does the curriculum reflect the needs and expectations of society, as well as the needs of the students?**

The school does not operate in a vacuum. It is an agent of society and therefore its curriculum must reflect to a reasonable degree societal expectations and needs. Although our society is a pluralistic one and is frequently in a state of flux, it is still possible for an administrator to ascertain general expectations in regard to what the school should be teaching. The Gallup survey presented in chapter one is an example of the type of information which an administrator should obtain. [18]

5. **Does the content of the curriculum provide for the development of student attitudes and values, as well as knowledge and skills?**

Whether this question can be answered affirmatively will largely depend on whether or not the educational objectives of the school emphasize the development of student attitudes and values, as well as knowledge and skills. While some authorities seem to feel that the school should limit its role to developing knowledge on the part of its students, others assert with equal conviction that the school can and should help students to develop attitudes and values. [19]

In reality, of course, the school already teaches attitudes and values, directly and indirectly, through its emphasis on punctuality and neatness, its penalties for cheating, and its lack of acceptance of certain styles of dress and grooming. The pertinent question would appear to be *not* whether the school *should* teach attitudes and values but *which* attitudes and values should the school attempt to develop, and how should the school curriculum provide for their development?

6. **Are the curriculum materials appropriate for the interests and abilities of the students?**

The major assumption behind this question is that, for successful learning to occur, the curriculum materials must be at the interest and ability level of the students using them. If materials are too difficult for students to read or understand, learning will be impaired; if the materials are too easy and insufficiently challenging, the teacher will have difficulty in motivating students to learn. Moreover, if the curricular materials fail to take into consideration students' interest levels and attention spans, learning will be adversely affected. [20]

One approach an administrator can take is to utilize the help of a reading consultant to ascertain the reading level of materials used by each grade, and compare those levels with the reading levels of the students. The author once conducted such a study in a school and discovered that in a ninth grade class the reading level of the biology materials was at a 12th grade level. Since in any class there is a range of student reading abilities, there will, in situations like this one, be problems in learning for a number of students as long as only one textbook is used for the entire class.

A possible solution to this kind of problem is the use of multiple texts and nonprint media to accommodate the different interests and abilities of students within a class. A good indicator of the need for curricular improvement in a school is the extent to which a single text approach is being utilized in the classrooms.

7. **Are the educational objectives for each subject in the curriculum clearly stated and operationally defined?**

Earlier, the point was made that the school curriculum should be based on the overall educational goals of the school. However, even though the subjects included in the curriculum should relate directly to overall school objectives, each subject should have specific objectives of its own which represent interpretations of the more general school goals.

The objectives for each subject should be stated clearly and should be operationally defined if they are to provide direction and guidance to both teachers and students in the learning situation, and if the objectives are to be helpful in evaluating the extent to which a subject is achieving preëstablished goals. The achievement of educational objectives, whether they be school or subject objectives, is very difficult to assess if the objectives are stated vaguely, or if, as is the case in some situations, they are nonexistent.

8. **Are the various subjects in the school curriculum achieving their proposed objectives?**

Probably one of the most important efforts that an administrator can make in identifying the need for curricular improvement is to investigate the extent to which each of the subjects in the curriculum is achieving its proposed objectives. While the administrator cannot do this alone, he can initiate the investigation and can organize and coordinate the expertise of others, in an evaluation of the achievement of course objectives. Methods of assessment could include the use of standardized tests, teacher-constructed tests, interviews, and questionnaires. While each of these evaluation methods possesses certain limitations as well as strengths, the most serious deficiency of all would be incurred as the result of an administrator's failure to initiate any assessment merely because an evaluation tool could not be found that will accomplish exactly what he wants.*

9. **Is there subject matter articulation between grade levels, and correlation among the various subjects of the curriculum?**

The curriculum content introduced at each grade level (at each phase in nongraded schools) should be built upon and be articulated with the subject matter introduced in the previous grade. Gaps or omissions in the sequencing of the content of the curriculum tend to cause problems for the learner. In each curricular area the subject matter content should be composed of sequentially-linked building blocks which the learner masters as he proceeds through the school system.

In addition, efforts should be made to correlate wherever possible the subjects offered at a particular grade level. The correlation may take the form of what is referred to as "core curriculum" or it may only represent an effort to relate certain topics within two or more subjects. [21] The school curriculum has often been criticized for its fragmentation, and there is little doubt that there needs to be better correlation between its various subjects.

In concluding this section, it should be pointed out that the administrator should not be the only one who is involved in identifying needs for curricular improvement. Since students, teachers, parents, and central office personnel have contact with the school curriculum in one way or another, their assessments and recommendations for improvement should be solicited regularly, and utilized whenever appropriate and feasible. [22]

THE ADMINISTRATOR'S ROLE IN PLANNING CURRICULUM IMPROVEMENT

In many school situations the school administrator is too busy with other aspects of managing the school to become directly involved in planning curriculum improvement. [23] Also, his major role in relation to curriculum is too often perceived as implementing a proposed curricular change which has been prepared or planned by someone else. Indeed, in recent years more and more planning for curricular improvement has taken place outside of the school building, by district committees, and state or national groups. [24]

Be that as it may, the school administrator can still play an important role in planning for curricular improvement if he possesses educational vision, group leadership skills, and initiative. A twofold role is recommended: (1) working directly with groups or committees who are planning

*For an excellent in-depth treatment of basic concepts of educational evaluation, see W. James Popham, ed., *Evaluation in Education: Current Applications* (Berkeley, Calif.: McCutchan Publishing Co., 1974).

curriculum improvement, and (2) encouraging and evaluating proposals for improving the curriculum.

THE COMMITTEE APPROACH TO PLANNING CURRICULUM IMPROVEMENT

It should be noted that planning for curricular improvement can be accomplished by individuals, and sometimes the best way to *begin* planning for a curricular change is on a limited scale, with one individual. However, most of the planning for curricular improvement will probably be done by committees, so the concepts and issues discussed previously (chap. 3) in conjunction with group leadership skills, should be considered. [25]

In utilizing the committee approach to curricular improvement, the administrator will need to adopt a plan of action to guide the committee's efforts. Although there are undoubtedly several ways to proceed, a proposed process for an administrator and a curriculum improvement committee to follow is presented in figure 12.1.

Step	Committee's Activities
1	*Identify and define the need* for curriculum improvement.
2	*Analyze the advantages, disadvantages, and costs* of different proposals for improving the curriculum. Related changes and steps needed to implement a proposed curricular improvement should also be identified by the committee.
3	*Report* (both verbally and in writing) to all interested parties, e.g., school board. The report should contain the committee's analysis and recommendations.
4	*Secure approval* of the committee's recommendations.
5	*Initiate a pilot project* to test the validity of the proposed curricular improvement and to identify the need for revision before full implementation.
6	*Determine the success* of the pilot project and decide whether to revise curriculum improvement proposal, implement "as is," or reject it.
7	*Implement* the curriculum improvement change on a broader scale, if the pilot project is successful.
8	*Evaluate* the curriculum improvement change periodically after its implementation to ascertain the need for further refinements.

Figure 12.1. A Curriculum Improvement Committee's Process.

The process identified in figure 12.1 intentionally goes beyond *planning* for curricular improvement so that the reader can receive an overview of the total recommended process of curriculum improvement. There may be additional steps that could be added to the process, but an attempt has been made here to focus on the most important components. Although the proposed process emphasizes the group approach, it should be noted that the method proposed can be utilized on an individual basis as well.

The administrator's role in working with a curriculum improvement committee should be that of consultant and facilitator. [27] Generally the administrator will be interacting with committee members who possess greater expertise than he in the particular curricular area under consideration. Therefore, it is unlikely that he will be able to contribute much subject matter knowledge. However, the administrator can assist other people on the committee by helping them to define their function, to follow a process such as the one presented in figure 12.1, and to work together cooperatively and productively as a commitee. He can also facilitate their actions by securing necessary resources, removing obstacles, and helping them to increase their problem-solving capabilities.

Problems

In establishing a committee for curriculum improvement, the administrator should be aware of teacher attitudes toward committee work. While not all teachers can be assumed to possess identical attitudes, studies have revealed that many teachers have had negative experiences while serving on committees. For example, McQuizz found that teachers encountered three basic problems in trying to perform committee work: (1) lack of time, (2) lack of recognition or rewards, and (3) lack of follow-through on the committee's recommendations. [28]

Perhaps the most serious of these problems is lack of time, which is one problem that must be resolved if the committee is to be able to proceed. [29] During the school year, teachers, students, and parents are busy and, for all practical purposes, their only available time is after school or on weekends. Neither of these times is particularly desirable, due to the fatigue factor in late afternoon and evening, or to potential conflicts with other commitments. A partial resolution of the time problem, as it affects teachers and students, is to dismiss school early one day each week in order to permit curricular planning and other kinds of professional activities to take place. A number of schools have adopted this procedure, apparently with good results. Other possibilities include preschool workshops, better use of faculty and departmental meetings, utilization of substitute teachers, and in-service days during the year. [30]

Another partial solution to the problem of inadequate time is to schedule committee meetings during the summer to plan for curricular improvement. This can be an ideal time since school is not in session, and people are more available to work on the curriculum. But the administrator should keep in mind that some of the individuals whom he might select to work on committees may prefer to attend summer school or take vacations. The administrator should also consider the possibility that he may be unable to secure a very high level of participation without remunerating committee members for their summer work for the school. Assuming that these problems can be avoided or resolved with careful advance planning and resourcefulness by the administrator, the summer months may indeed provide an excellent opportunity for a school administrator and a curriculum committee to engage in planning for curricular improvement.

Consultants

In formulating a curricular improvement committee, an administrator should give some attention to the need for outside help. The teachers, students, and parents on the committee and even the administrator may be familiar with the current program and associated problems, but they may not be fully aware of new approaches to the improving of a particular curricular area.* A consultant from the district's central office, a university, the state department of public instruction, or another agency or organization might be able to offer valuable ideas and insights.

If the administrator and the committee decide that a consultant would be useful, they should define as precisely as possible, before employing the individual, the nature of the consultant's contribution and his relationship to the committee. Frequently, when these factors are not adequately defined by the committee or communicated to the consultant, his expertise is not properly utilized or his performance does not meet the expectations of the committee. Consultants can often make an excellent contribution to a committee, but the expectations of the committee and the role of the consultant must be clearly defined in advance.

Approval

The school administrator should recognize that any proposed curricular changes which result from committee work must ultimately be approved by the superintendent and the school board before implementation can proceed. It is important, therefore, to keep the superintendent and school board informed at each stage of the planning process. This might be done through periodic progress reports and/or by actually including a representative from the central office and/or the school board on the committee which is doing the planning for curricular improvement. Regardless of the method used to

---

*One study revealed that school principals relied more on salesmen to learn about curriculum innovations than on any other individual or group. See Thomas V. Ruff and Donald C. Orlich, "How Do Elementary School Principals Learn About Curriculum Innovations?" *Elementary School Journal* 7 (April 1974): 389-92.

keep the superintendent and the school board informed, the importance of effective communication cannot be overemphasized. Many potentially good curricular improvement plans have encountered resistance or have even been rejected because they caught the superintendent or school board by surprise.

ENCOURAGING AND EVALUATING PROPOSALS FOR CURRICULUM IMPROVEMENT

A second major role of the administrator in planning for curriculum improvement should be to encourage and evaluate proposals from various individuals or groups, both inside of and outside of the school system. The administrator can encourage proposals for the improvement of the curriculum from people within the school system by (1) making known his interest in receiving such proposals, (2) trying to secure released time for individuals or small groups to work on curriculum improvement proposals, and (3) by giving recognition to those who develop curricular improvement proposals. To be effective these kinds of encouragement cannot be limited to a single announcement or indication of interest. Instead, the administrator must demonstrate an *active, ongoing, visible* commitment to receiving proposals for curriculum improvement.

In addition to encouraging the generation of curriculum proposals from within the school or district, an administrator needs to become better informed about those proposals that are advanced from the outside, by state and national organizations, agencies, and groups. As mentioned earlier, much curriculum change has originated with national curriculum committees. [31] If the administrator is to capitalize on the ideas and thinking of people outside the school in regard to curricular reform, he will need to make a conscious effort to keep well informed about new proposals for improving the curriculum.

Encouraging others to develop proposals and attempting to become better informed himself about various ideas which are proposed for improving the curriculum, however, are not the only dimensions to the administrator's role in curriculum planning. He also has a responsibility to evaluate curriculum improvement proposals carefully as to their appropriateness and feasibility. A sample work sheet which should be helpful to the administrator in reaching a determination on the merits of curricular improvement proposals is presented in figure 12.2.

Although the suggested work sheet is recommended especially for evaluating the merits of curriculum improvement proposals, it could be used to assess the strengths and weaknesses of various other kinds of proposals, as well. It is primarily designed for helping the administrator and those who are assisting him to focus on a number of important questions that should be addressed by any proposal. By seeking answers to these kinds of questions,

---

Name _____ Date _____

Title of Proposal _____

1. What diagnostic methods or procedures were used to identify and define the problem or need?
2. What are the characteristics of the target population to which the proposal is addressed?
3. To what extent are the understandings, skills, attitudes, or values which the proposed program seeks to improve (the desired outcomes) clearly identified and stated in terms that will make evaluation possible?
4. To what degree does the proposal make clear *how* the recommended program will accomplish the objectives which are set forth?
5. To what degree is there evidence that potential problems (as well as strengths) of the proposed program have been identified, assessed, and possible solutions recommended?
6. To what extent does the proposal recognize the need for and make provision for in-service education for faculty and/or orientation activities for students and parents, to help ensure successful implementation of the proposed program?
7. Have the costs of the different aspects of the proposed program been fully assessed?
8. What procedures have been included in the proposal for ascertaining the progress/effectiveness of the program on a nine-week, semester, or yearly basis?

Summary

Strengths of the Proposal

Limitations of the Proposal

Priority Rating Assigned the Proposal

Figure 12.2. A Proposal Assessment Work Sheet.

the administrator should be better able to assess the strengths and weaknesses of a proposal and make a judgment about its overall worth.*

THE ADMINISTRATOR'S ROLE IN IMPLEMENTING CURRICULAR IMPROVEMENT

It has already been noted that a major obstacle to curriculum improvement, from the teacher's point of view, is the lack of follow-through on committee recommendations. The occurrence of this problem is often a result of the ad-

*If the administrator adopts this work sheet, it would be advisable for him to distribute copies of it, in advance, to those who are thinking about preparing a proposal, so that they may be aware of how their proposal will be evaluated, and so that they may use the work sheet themselves in evaluating their proposal.

ministrator's failure to understand the process of and barriers to implementing a proposed curriculum change.

Implementing curricular improvement usually necessitates a modification in the *attitudes* and *role* of the staff, as well as in subject matter or its organization. For example, a proposed social studies curriculum which emphasizes student analysis and discussion of major problems and issues in American history may require, if the new curriculum is to be successfully implemented, that the teacher change his attitude about how American history is best taught and learned, and his conception of the role of the teacher and the student in the classroom.

The teacher who continues to lecture and limits the students' role to merely responding to questions may implement the proposed curricular change to the extent that he uses different subject matter and materials, but full effectiveness will not be achieved unless the teacher's and students' roles also change. Therefore, in attempting to implement curricular improvement, the administrator must recognize that curricular change also involves *people* change in order to be totally successful.[32] Too often this point has been ignored, or given insufficient consideration, and the implementation of curricular improvement has correspondingly suffered.

POSSIBLE BARRIERS TO CURRICULAR CHANGE

When implementing a proposed curricular improvement the administrator should perform the role of change agent. In this role, the administrator should be trying to bring about a modification both in the curriculum *and* in people's attitudes and roles in regard to the curriculum. People whose attitudes and roles may need to be modified and who may present resistance or obstacles to change include faculty, students, parents, central office staff, and school board members. Of course, different people resist change for different reasons, and it is often rather difficult to ascertain the real reasons for their opposition. However, the major barriers to implementing curricular change (or, for that matter, most kinds of change) that may be inherent in a specific situation and of which the administrator should be aware include the following:[33]

> *Habit.* Habit is the tendency of people to behave in the same way that they have always behaved. Proposed change challenges habit, and the challenge is frequently met with resistance.
>
> *The bureaucratic structure of the school district.* The school district as a bureaucratic institution emphasizes the maintenance of order, rationality, and continuity. Uniformity of educational programs and procedures among the schools of the district seems to be valued, whereas diversity does not. Attempts by individual schools to introduce

new programs or procedures are often viewed with suspicion. Because of these attitudes and the hierarchical structure of the district, proposed change may be diluted before it is finally approved, or it may be rejected because it threatens the stability of the institution.[34]

The lack of incentive. Change can be a difficult and frustrating experience for the individuals or groups involved. Although the administrator may be personally convinced of the benefits which will accrue if a proposed change is adopted, he can seldom guarantee those benefits or offer incentives (monetary or otherwise) to persuade others to adopt the innovation. As a result, he is dependent upon his own ability to influence others to adopt a proposed change for which there may be high personal costs in terms of time and frustration, and no immediate gain.

The nature of the proposed change. Innovations can vary according to complexity, financial cost, compatibility with the other phases of the school's operation, and ease of communicability. Some innovations, because of these factors, are more difficult to introduce into a school system than other proposed changes. Therefore, the characteristics of the innovation itself may constitute a major obstacle or problem in securing its adoption.[35]

Teacher and community norms. Teacher and community norms can act as significant barriers to innovating in the schools. There is evidence that a teacher may receive disapproval from his colleagues for adopting an innovation; and efforts by the administrator to bring about change in a teacher's role or methods may be viewed as a challenge to that teacher's professional autonomy.[36] Research has further revealed that community groups may feel threatened by change because of its implications for upsetting the stability of the power relations within the community.[37] Both sets of norms—teacher and community—can act as a powerful source of resistance to the administrator who is trying to introduce a particular innovation.

Lack of understanding. People may resist a proposed change because they don't possess an adequate or accurate understanding of it. Their deficiency may be caused by a failure on their part to pay close attention at the time that the proposed change was explained, or, on the other hand, information about the change may have been poorly or inaccurately communicated. In any respect, a lack of understanding of a proposed change can act as a significant deterrent to its successful implementation.

A difference of opinion. A proposed change may be resisted because of an honest difference of opinion about whether it is needed, or whether it will accomplish all that its proponents claim. The difference in opinion may be based on conflicting philosophies and values of education in regard to teaching and learning, or it may result from variant assessments of how much improvement would actually occur if the proposed change were implemented. If the difference of opinion centers on the amount of improvement that will take place, resistance may be reduced with the introduction of new evidence of potential success. However, if the difference of opinion is based on conflicting educational philosophies and values, the administrator will probably find it extremely difficult to remove this source of resistance.

A lack of skill. A proposed change may be resisted by any individual or group that will be required to perform new skills and roles. [38] The change from traditional roles and skills to new ones is viewed as an unsettling experience to many people. Therefore, any innovation which will require new skills or roles on the part of the participants should be accompanied by an in-service program that will enable them to develop the new skills or roles.

Resistance to change is a complex phenomenon, and the administrator should spend a considerable amount of time in diagnosing its source(s) before he draws any conclusions about how it might best be reduced. [39] In many situations there will be more than one reason for resistance to change, and the administrator should assess the validity of each of the possible factors identified above. By accurately diagnosing the reasons for resistance, the administrator will be in a better position to ameliorate it and smooth the way for successful implementation of proposed curricular improvement. [40]

THE PILOT PROJECT APPROACH
TO CURRICULAR CHANGE

If an administrator is unable to overcome people's resistance to a proposed curricular change, he might attempt to initiate a pilot project, i.e., a scaled-down version of the originally proposed change. The proposed innovation might be reduced in terms of size, length of operation, or number of participants involved. For example, rather than introducing a new school-wide language arts curriculum, the change could be implemented on a pilot basis at only one grade level. Or, perhaps, rather than implementing a curricular change at one grade level, several units of the curriculum could be introduced by all of the teachers of the school during the first semester of the school year. Other variations of the pilot project approach are also possible.

The pilot project approach to curriculum improvement implementation has several definite advantages. It can be conducted with a fewer number of participants and can involve those who would be more willing to try out new curricular ideas. If the pilot project is successful, its results may favorably influence other people who initially resisted the proposed change.

A pilot project can also be useful in identifying and refining defects or weaknesses in the original curriculum proposal which were not perceived earlier. Most proposed curricular changes, whether emanating from study and planning within a district or from other school situations, require adaptation and refinement before they can be used successfully by an entire grade level, department, or school. And finally, a pilot project may prove useful in demonstrating that a proposed change will *not* work, either because of a defect in the concept of the proposal or because local conditions make it impossible to implement.

The pilot project approach is not the only approach to curriculum implementation, nor is it a panacea for resistance to change. But it does offer important advantages, and it should be considered by the administrator.

KEY FACTORS IN CURRICULUM IMPLEMENTATION

Despite thousands of dollars and untold hours expended each year by districts in the development of curricular improvement plans or guides, the limited evidence available indicates that those plans are poorly implemented. For example, in Krey's study of thirty-six elementary schools, thirteen junior high schools, and five senior high schools, teachers reported very little classroom implementation of district curriculum guides.[41] The modal response of the teachers about the extent of curricular implementation was, "No implementation."

Krey discovered in his investigation that four major factors were directly related to the degree to which curricular plans for improvement were actually implemented in the classroom:

1. The extent to which teachers felt a need for some kind of orientation and in-service activities to help them implement curricular plans
2. The extent to which teachers received an opportunity to participate in the *planning* of orientation and in-service activities to help them implement curricular plans
3. The extent to which teachers received an opportunity to participate in the *evaluation* of those orientation and in-service activities
4. The extent to which teachers felt they had a professional obligation to participate in curriculum implementation.

Krey's study emphasizes the need for orientation and in-service activities to help teachers implement curriculum improvement proposals and plans. It also suggests the importance of faculty *involvement* in the planning and evaluation stages if orientation and in-service activities are to be perceived by teachers as worthwhile.

An important implication of the study is that the school administrator should not assume that a curriculum improvement proposal or plan can be successfully implemented in the classroom without appropriate orientation and in-service activities for the teachers of the school. Such activities might include: (1) workshops to familiarize teachers with all aspects of the curricular plan; (2) clinics to provide teachers with an opportunity to practice using the materials or techniques contained in the curricular plan before implementing them in the classroom; and (3) evaluation sessions for teachers, held after the curricular plan has been implemented in the classroom, for the purpose of identifying strengths and weaknesses of the plan and making appropriate revisions. Although the degree of implementation of proposed curricular improvement would also seem to depend on the merits of the particular proposal or plan (a factor not studied in the research), it would appear from Krey's investigation that little curriculum implementation will occur without adequate orientation and in-service activities for the staff.

In working with teachers on implementing proposed curricular improvements, the administrator should also be aware that their perception of his own attitude toward implementing a particular curricular plan is important. Edwards, for example, found in his study of essentially the same schools examined in Krey's research, that the more the teachers perceived the principal as personally accepting the curriculum improvement plans and *holding teachers responsible* for implementation, the more likely were the teachers to report a higher level of curriculum implementation in their classrooms. [42] The key factor seemed to be the teachers' perceptions of the administrator's attitude, rather than the administrator's *actual* feelings about the importance of curriculum implementation. Teachers who perceived that their principal personally accepted the curriculum improvement plans and intended to hold teachers accountable for implementing the plans, reported a higher implementation level than those teachers who perceived the opposite—regardless of how their principal actually felt about the implementation of the curriculum plans.

It would appear, then, that if the administrator is interested in increasing classroom adoption of proposed curricular improvement plans, it will not be sufficient for him to hold a positive attitude about those plans; he must also accurately communicate to teachers his feelings about the importance of implementing the proposed curriculum improvement.

A FINAL NOTE

The main thrust of this chapter has been on the administrator's role in curricular improvement. Curricular improvement is seldom an easy task, and it will be difficult for the school administrator to resist pressures to concentrate on more manageable activities. However, it needs to be recognized that the school administrator is a pivotal person in any attempt to improve the curriculum. He can either be an initiator and facilitator, or he can be a resister and a rejector. For as McNally and others earlier pointed out,

> . . . changing the curriculum in order to keep it abreast of current demands for education is a difficult undertaking. The success with which the task can be discharged is directly related to the administrative provisions in a school system. Administrative arrangements may either facilitate curriculum change or make it difficult, if not impossible.[43]

Review

1. Define the terms "the school curriculum" and "curriculum improvement."
2. Discuss the main characteristics, and the advantages and disadvantages of the district approach to curriculum improvement. The school-building approach.
3. What criteria can an administrator use to identify the need for curriculum improvement?
4. Describe the administrator's role in working with a group that is trying to improve the curriculum. What problems should the administrator be aware of in trying to involve teachers in curriculum improvement activities? How might these problems be overcome?
5. How can the administrator encourage and evaluate curriculum improvement proposals?
6. Discuss the major barriers and obstacles to introducing curriculum improvement. How might the use of the pilot project approach help ameliorate these problems?
7. What are the key factors that an administrator needs to take into consideration in trying to implement curricular improvement?

Notes

1. This is a narrower definition than is typically advanced for the curriculum. It does not include instructional activities or extracurricular activities because the writer feels that there is value to analyzing these aspects separately from curriculum. The interrelationships between the three are acknowledged, however. For a review of the different ways of defining the curriculum, see Elliott W. Eisner and Elizabeth Vallance, *Conflicting Conceptions of Curriculum* (Berkeley, Calif.: McCutchan Publishing Corp., 1974).

2. Albert Oliver, *Curriculum Improvement* (New York: Dodd, Mead & Co., 1965), pp. 12-15.

3. J. Lloyd Trump and Delmas F. Miller, *Secondary School Curriculum Improvement* (Boston: Allyn & Bacon, 1973), p. 12.

4. For an extended discussion of this approach, see Edward A. Krug et al., *Administering Curriculum Planning* (New York: Harper & Brothers, 1956), chap. 3.

5. L. Neagley Ross and N. Dean Evans, *Handbook for Effective Curriculum Development* (Englewood Cliffs, N.J.: Prentice-Hall, 1967), pp. 136-37.

6. Ronald C. Doll, *Curriculum Improvement: Decision-making and Process* (Boston: Allyn & Bacon, 1964), p. 258.

7. Vernon E. Anderson, *Principles and Procedures of Curriculum Improvement* (New York: Ronald Press, 1965), p. 176.

8. H. L. Caswell et al., *Curriculum Improvement in Public School Systems* (New York: Bureau of Publications, Teachers College, Columbia University, 1950), p. 72.

9. Association for Supervision and Curriculum Development, *Leadership for Improving Instruction, 1960 Yearbook* (Washington, D.C.: Association for Supervision and Curriculum Development, 1960), pp. 62-63.

10. Howard G. Spalding, "What Is the Role of the Principal in Curriculum Work?" *Bulletin of the National Association of Secondary School Principals* 40 (April 1956):388.

11. For an excellent review and analysis of how different curriculum proposals have come into being, see Michael W. Kirst and Decker F. Walker, "An Analysis of Curriculum Policy-Making," *Review of Educational Research* 41 (December 1971):479-509.

12. Caswell, *Curriculum Improvement,* p. 98.

13. For example, see J. Galen Saylor and William M. Alexander, *Curriculum Planning for Modern Schools* (New York: Holt, Rinehart & Winston, 1966), pp. 254-56. Also see pp. 44-45 in their new book, *Curriculum Planning for Schools* (New York: Holt, Rinehart & Winston, 1975.

14. Robert J. Havighurst, *Developmental Tasks and Education,* 3d ed. (New York: David McKay Co., 1972), pp. 43-82.

15. To begin, see Robert Liebert et al., *The Early Window: Effects of Television on Children and Youth* (Elmsford, N.Y.: Pergamon Press, 1973).

16. For a good example of the main elements of such a curriculum, see Neil Postman and Charles Weingartner, "Making Contact toward a Relevant Curriculum," in *Radical School Reform,* ed. Beatrice Gross and Ronald Gross (New York: Simon & Schuster, 1970).

17. Kathryn J. Noyes and Gordon L. McAndrew, "Is This What Schools Are For?" *Saturday Review,* December 21, 1968, p. 65.

18. George H. Gallup, "Fourth Annual Poll of Public Attitudes toward Education," *Phi Delta Kappan* 56 (September 1972), p. 35.

19. For a review of this debate, see the March, 1971, issue of the *Phi Delta Kappan.*

20. An excellent resource which every administrator should utilize to help the school determine the effectiveness of curriculum materials, particularly those that are commercially produced, is the Educational Products Information Exchange Institute, New York City.

21. Hilda Taba, *Curriculum Development: Theory and Practice* (New York: Harcourt, Brace and World, 1962), pp. 407-11.

22. For an interesting example of how students can be involved in assessing the need for curricular improvement, see George L. Stephens, "Student Perceptions of Selected Aspects of the Secondary School Curriculum" (Ed.D. diss., University of Nebraska, 1970).

23. Kathryn V. Feyereisen et al., *Supervision and Curriculum Renewal* (New York: Appleton-Century-Crofts, 1970), p. 103.

24. An excellent review of the origins of this type of curriculum change is presented in John I. Goodlad, *School Curriculum Reform* (New York: Fund for the Advancement of Education, 1964). Also see Robert W. Heath, editor, *New Curricula* (New York: Harper & Row, Publishers, 1964).

25. Also see an older but still relevant work by Kenneth D. Benne and Bozidar Muntyan, *Human Relations in Curriculum Change* (New York: Dryden Press, 1951). This book presents excellent ideas on working with groups in introducing curricular change.

26. The process recommended in figure 12.1 is an adaptation of one presented in Forrest E. Conner and William J. Ellena, eds. *Curricular Handbook for School Administrators* (Washington, D.C.: American Association of School Administrators, 1967), p. 315.

27. Harry L. Walen, "A Principal's Role in Curriculum Development," *Bulletin of the National Association of Secondary School Principals* 51 (November 1967):37.

28. Thomas McQuizz, "Participation in Curriculum Committees by Classroom Teachers in

Selected Colorado School Systems" (Unpublished document, University of Colorado, 1962), p. 180.

29.   F. E. Stratemeyer et al., *Developing a Curriculum for Modern Living* (New York: Bureau of Publications, Teachers College, Columbia University, 1957), p. 669.

30.   See J. Lloyd Trump and Delmas F. Miller, *Secondary School Curriculum* (Boston: Allyn & Bacon, 1968), p. 374.

31.   An excellent source for reviewing such proposals is William J. Ellena, ed. *Curriculum Handbook for School Executives* (Arlington, Va.: American Association of School Administrators, 1973).

32.   G. Sharp, *Curriculum Development as Re-Education of the Teacher* (New York: Bureau of Publications, Teachers College, Columbia University, 1951), p. 2.

33.   Richard A. Gorton, *Conflict, Controversy and Crisis in School Administration and Supervision* (Dubuque, Iowa: Wm. C. Brown Company Publishers, 1972), pp. 154-55.

34.   Max. G. Abbott, "Hierarchical Impediments to Innovation in Educational Organizations," *Change Perspectives in Educational Administration,* eds. Max G. Abbott and John T. Lovell (Auburn, Ala.: Auburn University, School of Education, 1965), pp. 40-53.

35.   Everett M. Rogers, *Diffusion of Innovations* (New York: Free Press of Glencoe, 1962), pp. 12, 124.

36.   Sam Sieber, *Organizational Resistances to Innovative Roles in Education* (New York: Columbia University, Bureau of Applied Social Research, 1967).

37.   Ralph B. Kimbrough, "Community Power Structure and Curriculum Change," in *Strategy for Curriculum Change,* ed. Robert R. Leeper (Washington, D.C.: Association for Supervision and Curriculum Development, 1965), pp. 11-28.

38.   Neal Gross et al., "An Attempt to Implement a Major Educational Innovation, A Sociological Inquiry" (Paper presented at the Center for Research and Development in Educational Differences, Harvard University, 1968).

39.   Richard A. Gorton, *Conflict, Controversy and Crisis,* pp. 151-60.

40.   For a good review of strategies for introducing planned curriculum innovations, see M. R. Lawler, *Strategies for Planned Curricular Innovations* (New York: Teachers College Press, 1970).

41.   Robert D. Krey, "Factors Relating to Teachers' Perception of Curricular Implementation Activities and the Extent of Curricular Implementation." (Ph.D. diss., University of Wisconsin, 1968).

42.   Conan S. Edwards, "The Principal's Relationship to the Implementation of Official Curriculum Plans" (Ph.D. diss., University of Wisconsin, 1968).

43.   Harold McNally et al., *Improving the Quality of Public School Programs* (New York: Bureau of Publications, Teachers College, Columbia University, 1960), p. 28.

Part 4

Student Problems, Services, and Activities

13

Student Discipline Problems

The majority of students in most schools do not misbehave. However, a minority of students (apparently an increasing minority) do misbehave and their behavior is becoming one of the major problems that confront administrators and their professional staffs. Since an examination of a number of books on school administration revealed little or no attention to this topic, an attempt will be made to treat this important subject in some detail.

FACTORS AFFECTING THE PREVENTION AND REDUCTION OF STUDENT MISBEHAVIOR

The prevention and resolution of student discipline problems have long been responsibilities of the school administrator. In the early days of education these were *major* responsibilities.[1] Through the years, other duties—particularly in the area of instructional improvement—have been added to the administrator's job, but maintaining appropriate student discipline has continued to rank as one of his more important responsibilities. Recent surveys of the public and of educators, which have identified student discipline as one of the most significant problems facing the school, suggest that it will continue to occupy much of the administrator's time.[2]

The amount of time that an administrator should spend on discipline problems will depend on many variables, including the nature of the student population.* However, it would appear that two factors which will influence his effectiveness are: (1) his perception of the causes of discipline problems, and (2) the approaches he utilizes to prevent or resolve them. In this chapter, an emphasis will be placed on careful classification and diagnosis of student discipline problems, and organizational considerations for preventing and reducing them. Although the focus of most of the discussion will be on student misbehavior, the administrator and the staff should always keep in mind that their ultimate objective should be to develop *self*-discipline on the part of all students.

---

*References to "student discipline problems" will include student attendance problems inasmuch as they are often of a disciplinary nature.

TYPES OF DISCIPLINE PROBLEMS

All schools do not experience the same kinds of discipline problems, but the differences seem to be mainly a matter of degree rather than type.* For example, at one time, vandalism was thought to be a problem only for large city schools, and of little concern to rural or suburban schools. Recently, however, this particular problem has been encountered in a variety of locales.[3] At present, there are probably few student discipline problems which are unique to only one kind of school or school setting.

Although schools report a wide variety of student discipline problems, they seem to fall into four general categories. These categories are identified in the classification system presented in figure 13.1.

Misbehavior in Class	Misbehavior Outside Class (But in School or on School Grounds)	Truancy	Tardiness
1. Talking back to the teacher	1. Fighting	1. Cutting class	1. Frequently being late to class
2. Not paying attention	2. Vandalism	2. Skipping school	2. Frequently being late to school
3. Distracting others	3. Smoking		
4. Vandalism	4. Using illegal drugs		
5. Profanity	5. Student dress		
6. Cheating	6. Theft		
7. Assault	7. Gambling		
	8. Littering		
	9. Student activism		
	10. Located in unapproved area		

Figure 13.1. Types of Student Discipline Problems.

A difficulty encountered in designing any system of classifying problems is that one's definition of what constitutes a problem will largely determine what is included in the system.[4] In the classification system presented in figure 13.1, the areas included are those which are most typically reported by the schools as student discipline problems.[5] However, it should be noted that

*Those who think that student discipline problems are confined to the secondary school should refer to Ann C. Berlak, "An Interview Study of Ten Elementary Aged Boys' Conception of Authority and Deviant Behavior at School" (Ph.D. diss., Washington University, 1971).

it is possible for an administrator to narrow or broaden the scope of problems included in a classification system (thereby reducing or increasing his responsibilities) merely by changing the definition of what constitutes student misbehavior.

For example, under the category "Misbehavior Outside Class," many schools consider that a student has misbehaved if he goes to certain areas of the school without an approved pass from a teacher or the main office. In such schools, a student who wants to go to a restroom or somewhere else within the building, must secure a pass. If he is found in the hallways or restroom without the pass, he can be sent to the vice-principal's office for a "talking to" or for assignment to detention. In this kind of situation it is not anything *disruptive* the student has done in the hallways or the restroom that has precipitated a problem; rather, his mere physical presence in a given part of the school that has been defined as "off limits" without a pass has been determined to be student misbehavior. The implication is not that there aren't places in the schools where a pass may be necessary for the student's presence (although it would seem to be a little difficult in many school situations to justify such a pass for going to the restroom), but that an administrator can narrow or broaden the scope of his responsibilities for student discipline, depending on his definition of what constitutes a problem.

In considering the types of student misbehavior for which the school should assume responsibility for disciplining, the administrator and staff should try to make a distinction between student misbehavior which is within the appropriate jurisdiction of the school and student misbehavior which is more properly handled by outside agencies. Vandalism and selling illegal drugs, for example, are student behavior which in most schools are subject to disciplinary punishment. However, since these particular student actions are also violations of the law, it is debatable whether the school has a legitimate role in disciplining students, in addition to whatever consequences are imposed upon them by the police or the courts. As the publication *Guidelines for Student Rights and Responsibilities* points out, "Standards of conduct . . . need not prescribe school discipline for offenses committed within the school which are already adequately provided for by criminal law, unless the presence of the student in school would constitute a danger to the student himself, to other members of the school community, or to the continuation of the educative process."[6]

It should be emphasized that the school probably needs to play a role in *referring, counseling,* and *educating* students who break the law. But whether a school should also act as an institution for determining guilt and administering punishment is doubtful. The school that decides to determine guilt and administer punishment for student misbehavior which is *unlawful* will not only add immeasureably to the number and difficulty of the discipline problems with which it must deal, but may also be subjecting the student to double jeopardy. Therefore, in fairness to the student and in the best interest of the school, the administration and faculty should limit themselves to defining and punishing only student behavior that tends to disrupt education, and which would not be handled more appropriately by some outside agency, such as the police or the courts.

DIAGNOSING DISCIPLINE PROBLEMS

After a school has defined the types of behavior which will be considered as representing student discipline problems, the faculty's and administration's initial approach when encountering such behavior should be to diagnose the reasons for it. Admittedly, there will be cases in which diagnosis of a problem must follow punishment for the misbehavior. But if the intent is to prevent that misbehavior from occurring again, punishment alone will probably not prove to be very effective.* All behavior is caused, and until the administration and faculty can better understand and deal with the causes of student misbehavior, it is likely to recur in the future.

In attempting to diagnose the causes of a student's misbehavior, the administrator is really trying to understand the reasons for the student's actions. Such reasons are typically complex and may not be understood even by the student himself. However, it is essential that the administrator and staff conduct a thorough investigation into the causes of the problem if it is to be resolved successfully. The conclusions which the administrator and staff draw about why the student acted as he did will greatly influence their decision on whether or how the student should be punished, and will also determine further steps that should be taken to prevent the problem from happening again.

Possible Causes

To diagnose a discipline problem accurately, the administrator and staff should investigate the validity of several alternative hypotheses or explanations for the student's misbehavior. Although the nature of the hypotheses will vary for different types of discipline and attendance problems, a taxonomy of hypotheses is presented in figure 13.2.

As an examination of figure 13.2 shows, diagnosing the causes of student misbehavior is a complex task. Any or several of the factors listed could contribute to a student's misbehavior in a particular situation. Since the administrator cannot hope to investigate all of the possible hypotheses at the same time, he must make some decisions about how to proceed. In general, it would appear that his first line of approach should be to investigate the first three hypotheses listed under "Personal Factors" and then

---

*A discussion of this point and supporting evidence is presented in the next chapter.

School-Related Factors	Personal Factors	Home and Community Environment
1. Poor teaching	1. Student doesn't understand the rules	1. Poor authority figures and relationships within the home
2. Irrelevant curriculum	2. Student doesn't understand why the rules exist	2. Crime-infested neighborhood
3. Inflexible school schedule		
4. Insufficient adaptation and individualization of school's programs to a student's educational background	3. Poor educational background	3. Student's activities after school, e.g., work, other activities that keep him up late at night
	4. Undesirable peer relationships	
	5. Student is psychologically disturbed	
	6. Personality conflict between student and teacher	

Figure 13.2. Diagnosing Student Misbehavior: Some Alternative Hypotheses.

those under "School-Related Factors." These are factors over which the administrator and staff can exert some influence and, in many cases, take remedial action.

For example, the following school-related factors may account for a student's behavior and should be investigated. [7]

1. The subject matter may be too difficult.
2. The subject matter may be too easy.
3. The subject matter or the class activities may not be relevant to the student's interests or needs.
4. The class assignment may be too heavy, too light, badly planned, poorly explained, or unfairly evaluated.
5. The course content or activities may not be properly sequenced for this student.
6. The seating arrangement for the student may be poor from a learning point of view.
7. There may be a personality conflict between the student and the teachers.

Each or any combination of these conditions may cause considerable frustration, boredom, anxiety, or hostility in a student, which could be expressed in misbehavior. However, if an administrator can ascertain the particular underlying reasons for a student's misbehavior, he will then be in a position to know which approach to take in remedying the problem.

Although one or more of the other hypotheses listed in figure 13.2 under "Personal Factors" (i.e., B-4, B-5, and B-6), and under "Home and Community Environment," may be valid for a given situation, the school frequently has little or no control or influence over these conditions. This is particularly true in respect to the factors associated with "Home and Community Environment." The school seldom has any control over a student's situation in either his home or neighborhood. Both factors may be important in causing a student's misbehavior in school, but school authorities will probably find it extremely difficult to bring about change in these areas.

This is not meant to suggest that school officials should avoid working with parents and community groups.* However, in many instances of student misbehavior the administrator and staff will find that the most productive approach is to concentrate initially on diagnosing those possible causes of a student's misbehavior which may operate *within* the school and for which the school can offer a remedy. As Howard and Jenkins point out, "Many causes of pupil behavior are deeply rooted in the nature of the institution itself. . . . Progress can best be made in improving discipline through changing the nature of the school itself."[8]

Process of Diagnosis

Although diagnosis in situations involving student discipline problems has yet to be fully developed as a concept or skill, it would seem to include the following kinds of behavior on the part of the administrator and staff:[9]

1. Examination of the student's cumulative record for clues suggesting possible learning problems that might be frustrating him and causing his misbehavior. Examples of such clues would be low reading scores, poor grades in the past, underachievement. [10]
2. Conferences with the student to ascertain his attitude toward school and his feelings about those aspects of the school environment which make it difficult for him to perform as he should and as he would like.
3. Examination of the student's program and schedule. Is it an appropriate program and schedule, considering his background, interests, and attitudes?
4. Review of the curriculum and teacher lesson plans in those areas of the student's program where he appears to be experiencing the greatest difficulty, academically and behaviorally.

*Possible approaches for working with parents and community groups are recommended in the next chapter.

5. Conferences with the student's teachers to ascertain their analyses of the problem.

6. Observation of the student and his interactions with others in various school settings, e.g., classroom, cafeteria, extracurricular program.

7. Conferences with the student's parents to ascertain their attitudes and perceptions of the problem and to evaluate the extent to which they may provide assistance.

Engaging in all of these procedures for one student would admittedly represent a major investment of an administrator's effort and time. (He should by all means utilize the help of the school counselor, psychologist, or other pupil personnel workers.) But in many situations it will not be necessary for the administrator to complete all of the steps outlined above in diagnosing the causes of a discipline problem. Sometimes the root of a problem may be uncovered after completing only two or three steps.

However, if the administrator wants to avoid inaccurate diagnosis of problems, he will be as thorough and comprehensive as possible. He should always bear in mind that if he fails to invest sufficient time and effort in diagnosing the causes of a problem, the time and effort that he has "saved" will need to be reinvested as the problem reoccurs time and again. There is no good administrative substitute or shortcut to comprehensive, in-depth diagnosis of a problem.

ORGANIZATIONAL CONSIDERATIONS

Responding to student misbehavior has thus far been viewed from a problem perspective. There is value, however, in examining student discipline from a programmatic point of view. To maintain appropriate order in the school, roles need to be defined, procedures specified, relationships between roles coordinated, and the effectiveness of these various program elements needs to be assessed periodically.

RESPONSIBILITY FOR DISCIPLINARY
POLICIES AND PROCEDURES

Disciplinary policies and procedures tend to be promulgated at both the school board and the building level. Policies and procedures at the school board level are frequently rather general, and may be no more specific than to delegate to the building administrator the authority to make those rules and regulations which will facilitate learning and maintain order and safety in the school. Some school boards, however, are very specific in defining disciplinary policies and procedures, even to the extent of specifying the type of student conduct which will (or will not) be permitted in the school district.[11] Such specificity is usually for the purpose of maintaining a degree of uniformity throughout the district. It also results in lessening the authority of administrator and staff in the defining of rules and regulations which they may feel are appropriate for the school.

If the responsibility for defining specific disciplinary policies and procedures is delegated by the school board to the building administrator, he will have greater flexibility in developing particular policies and procedures which are appropriate for his own student clientele. But he should always keep in mind that policies and procedures at the building level must be logically related to the initial mandate given by the school board at the time of delegation. So, if the school board has delegated to the building administrator the authority to "make those rules and regulations which will facilitate learning and maintain order and safety in the school," the specific policies and procedures defined at the building level should not go beyond this delegation of authority. It is clear that the administrator is not totally free to make whatever rules and regulations he thinks are best for the school; all school rules and regulations must be based on school board policy, and state and federal law.[12]

THE TEACHER AND STUDENT DISCIPLINE

While the administrator is primarily responsible for administering a school's disciplinary program, the classroom teacher performs one of the most important roles in the program. The teacher is the key person to interpret and implement the school's rules and regulations concerning student behavior, and is the one who typically first identifies, defines, and reacts to a particular student behavior as a problem. Also, as Brown has pointed out, the classroom teacher can play a major role in reducing student misbehavior. The better the teacher's preparation, teaching techniques, personality, and other classroom aspects, the less likely are student misbehavior problems to arise.[13]

Probably the most important step that an administrator can take to decrease the number of discipline problems referred to his office by teachers is to work with the staff, particularly new teachers, in regard to their role in student discipline.* In-service work with the faculty should begin with a review of student discipline policies and procedures and the rationale upon which they are based. Such a review at the start of the school year would be

---

*For an excellent description of the various disciplinary techniques which teachers use in the classroom, see Michael Langenbach and George A. Letchworth, "Disciplinary Techniques: Repertoires and Relationships." An ERIC Report: Ed-049-178, 1971. Also, for an earlier but still relevant discussion of disciplinary techniques which teachers might utilize, see George J. Gnagy, *Controlling Classroom Misbehavior: What Research Says to the Teacher* (Washington, D.C.: National Education Association, 1965).

helpful for clearing up any misunderstanding and might even identify the need to revise some of the policies and procedures. Included in the review could be a discussion with the faculty on their expectations for student behavior.

A good approach to stimulating faculty thinking on discipline would be to give out a short questionnaire in order to secure teachers' perceptions of various factors which affect how they react to different kinds of student behavior. The administrator could develop his own questionnaire or use one of several instruments which are available, such as the Pupil Control Ideology instrument.[14] This questionnaire is composed of twenty statements which suggest factors that may be related to student control and discipline problems. Four sample statements from the instrument are:

- Teachers should consider revision of their teaching methods if these are criticized by their pupils.
- Being friendly with pupils often leads them to become too familiar.
- Pupils can be trusted to work together without supervision.
- Pupils often misbehave in order to make the teacher look bad.

Respondents to the Pupil Control Ideology instrument indicate the extent to which they agree or disagree with each statement. The instrument does not take long to administer, but can provide considerable useful information about the attitudes and philosophies of the faculty toward students, and may pinpoint the direction that an in-service program for the faculty should take.

For example, responses to the instrument might show that many of the faculty are either creating discipline problems through their own actions, or that they are overly concerned about certain kinds of student behavior and insufficiently concerned about other kinds of student behavior. (Numerous studies through the years have suggested that teachers tend to overemphasize control problems and give inadequate attention to problems of a more psychological nature.) A major objective of an in-service program for the faculty, then, might be to develop a more positive philosophy and attitude on their part toward student behavior, with emphasis on the role that a teacher needs to play in promoting student *self*-discipline.*

REFERRAL PROCEDURES

A student should not be referred to the administrator for disciplinary action until the teacher has first conferred with the student about his behavior,

---

*An excellent film for such an in-service program is "Glasser on Discipline." William Glasser, a well-known psychiatrist and author (*Schools Without Failure*) sets forth five basic steps to achieving effective discipline in this twenty-eight minute film. It can be ordered from Media 5, Film Distributers, Hollywood, Calif.

unless it is such that class cannot continue as long as the student is in the room (i.e., disruptive behavior). The person who is best able to resolve discipline problems arising in the classroom setting is the teacher, and the administrator should attempt to foster this approach with the faculty.

However, the experienced administrator knows that not all discipline problems can be resolved at the classroom level, and that some student behavior problems will have to be referred to the administrator for appropriate action. It is at this stage that the administrator needs to call on his organizational and administrative abilities to develop procedures which will facilitate careful consideration of the problems, and accurate and full communication to all concerned. Usually some type of a referral and feedback form will be necessary. Although there are many examples of such forms, the one presented in figure 13.3 has much to commend it. [15]

Several provisions of the form presented in figure 13.3 should be included in any referral procedure. First of all, there should be a *written* record of the initial diagnosis of the problem and the action taken by the teacher and the administrator. Written communication, as opposed to verbal, tends to be more thoughtfully prepared and is less subject to misinterpretation and forgetfulness at a later date. Written communication is particularly important as part of the documentation which may be required later, if more severe disciplinary action taken by the school is challenged at a school board hearing or in the courts.

Secondly, the referral procedures should require the teacher to specify in as much detail as possible the nature of the problem and the action that the teacher has taken to remedy the situation. These two requirements are designed to encourage the teacher to give some thought to why the problem has occurred and how it might be resolved at the classroom level, and to provide the administrator with information on these aspects. Unless the administrator has this information when a student is referred, he is likely to waste time or take the wrong approach with the student. Therefore, before the administrator will be in a reasonable position to take disciplinary or remedial action with the student, he must obtain information about the nature of the problem based on the teacher's perception, and on what the teacher has already tried to do about the situation.

The school's referral procedures should also include a mechanism (similar to the one in figure 13.3) by which the administrator can communicate to the teacher the action that has been taken. Most administrators have good intentions in this regard, but for one reason or another, the job frequently doesn't get done, at least according to teacher reports.

Probably the most efficient and certain way for an administrator to communicate back to the referring teacher is to use a procedure similar to the feedback portion of the form in figure 13.3. This kind of a system not only provides feedback to the teacher, but also provides for the maintaining of a

Student _____ Section _____ Time _____.

Teacher _____ Date _____.

Nature of Problem _____.

Action Before Referral	**Teacher/Student/ Administrator Conference**	**Action by Administration**
Conference with pupil _____	My planning period	Date _____.
Detention _____	is _____	Conference with pupil (warning/reprimand)
Phone call home _____	Student is in room	
Parent conference _____	_____	_____.
Letter to parents _____		Detention _____.
Guidance _____		Phone call to parents
Other _____		_____.
		Formal letter (copy in your mailbox) _____.
		Conference with parent being requested _____
		Referral to pupil personnel department _____
		Suspension (until conference) _____
		Corporal punishment
		_____.
		Other _____
Initials _____		

Figure 13.3. Referral and Feedback Form.

written record of the action taken, which can be very useful in building documentation or in conducting an analysis of trends in discipline problems and the types of action initiated by the administrator.

UTILIZING SPECIALIZED RESOURCES

In attempting to prevent and ameliorate student misbehavior, the administrator should organize all of the professional resources that are available to him. [16] The school counselor, psychologist, social worker, and nurse, as well as personnel in law enforcement and family assistance agencies, all possess specialized knowledge and skill which an administrator should try to utilize in working with students who are discipline problems. These specialists should not be involved in administering punishment to the student, but they certainly can make a valuable contribution to the diagnosing of the nature of a problem, and in the making of recommendations for remedial action.

For these specialists to make a maximum contribution, the administrator should consider organizing them into a pupil personnel committee for the purposes of studying and diagnosing severe student disciplinary problems and for offering suggestions about possible remediation. A deficiency in most approaches to student misbehavior is that they do not capitalize in an organized way on the various kinds of professional expertise which exist within the school and the community. The type of approach to student misbehavior that is needed is one in which the administrator takes responsibility for organizing and utilizing all of the different kinds of expertise which are available. Until the administrator assumes this organizational responsibility, the school's approach to student discipline problems is likely to be piecemeal, uncoördinated, and not very effective.

EVALUATING DISCIPLINARY POLICIES AND PROCEDURES

The disciplinary policies and procedures of many schools have been attacked in recent years by students, parents, and the courts. At the same time, the number and severity of discipline problems in the schools have increased. Both of these factors have made the job of trying to prevent or deal constructively with discipline problems a very difficult and frustrating one for the school administrator. As Ladd has noted, "Being an administrator trying to keep order in school must sometimes seem like being a modern physician trying to practice medicine in a country that has outlawed scalpels and hypodermic needles." [17]

While some administrators may feel that, on the basis of court rulings, there is little student misbehavior that they can regulate, the courts have never taken the position that the schools have no authority in this area. In fact, in the famous Blackwell case the court reaffirmed that "It is always within the province of school authorities to provide regulation, prohibition, and punishment of acts calculated to undermine the school routine." [18] In ruling *against* school disciplinary policies and procedures, the main thrust of the courts' decisions has been that the policies and procedures were not fair, reasonable, or clear. Therefore, every administrator should periodically evaluate the school's disciplinary policies and procedures to ascertain the extent to which they meet these criteria.*

Since *specific* discipline policies and procedures are frequently made at the building level, the school administrator is most likely to be concerned with evaluating the validity and effectiveness of these policies and procedures, rather than the ones established by the school board. However, there may be situations in which he will be requested to evaluate school board policies on student discipline, and suggest changes. In either case, the administrator will need defensible criteria upon which to make his evaluation. Due to the paucity of research on disciplinary policies and procedures, the criteria presented below are primarily based on a synthesis of recommendations in the professional literature and should therefore be discussed and analyzed before they are accepted. [19]

CRITERIA FOR EVALUATING STUDENT DISCIPLINE POLICIES AND PROCEDURES

1. **A school's discipline policies and procedures should be based on school board policy.** [†] School building policies and procedures, particularly those presented in student and faculty handbooks, should be examined to determine the extent to which they are in conformity with school board policies. In situations where there is doubt about a school policy or procedure, clarification should be obtained from the district administration and, if necessary, from the school board.

2. **There should be overall agreement among students, teachers, parents, and administrators about the philosophy and objectives of the disciplinary policies and procedures of a school.** If there is no overall agreement about the purposes of a school's disciplinary policies and procedures and why they must exist, they will be very difficult to enforce. This is par-

---

*A very helpful source for any administrator who wishes to evaluate his policies on student discipline and the school's code of student behavior is a publication by the Center for Law and Education, *Student Codes: A Packet on Selected Codes and Related Materials* (Cambridge, Mass.: Harvard University, 1971).

†The National School Boards Association has periodically published surveys of school board policies and procedures on discipline and attendance which are worthy of the administrator's consideration. For more information, write National School Boards Association, Waterford, Conn.

ticularly true for classroom "misbehavior." Unless the administrator has secured from the staff an agreed-upon, uniform, explicit designation of the kinds of behavior which can legitimately be considered discipline problems, some members of the faculty may feel free to provide their own interpretations. In the latter case there will undoubtedly be teachers who view students who question and argue as disrespectful and arrogant, while other members of the faculty will perceive the same behavior as stimulating and challenging. In circumstances involving student tardiness, some teachers may feel that if a student is late to class two or three times, the student's behavior is excessive; other teachers may not concern themselves at all with this kind of behavior. In the absence of a definitive discipline policy which has been developed with faculty, student, and parent involvement, identical student behavior may be viewed by some people as a problem, and by others as unimportant; as a result of this type of inconsistency, students may be treated unfairly.

Discipline policies and procedures are seldom popular. But if those who are going to be affected by the policies and procedures and those who are expected to implement them can understand and generally agree with their purpose and justification, then the possibility of adherence to them should be significantly increased.

3. **The school should maintain only those disciplinary policies and procedures which have an educational purpose, are administratively feasible, and are legally enforceable.** The more rules and procedures, the more difficult it will be to gain acceptance and adherence by students and teachers, and the more likely it will be that the administrator will have to devote a larger and larger portion of his time to interpreting and enforcing disciplinary rules and procedures.

In the past, schools have attempted to enforce rules on such items as hair length and style of clothing. These rules were unacceptable to many students and parents, for one reason or another, and ultimately, through court actions, have proved to be unenforceable in most situations. Therefore, it is important for the school to confine its regulations and procedures to those that are generally accepted and can be enforced. Three criteria which the New Jersey School Board has recommended be applied to every proposed rule should be considered by the administrator: "(1) Is the rule necessary for the orderly and effective operation of the school? (2) Does the rule involve some suppression of freedom? (3) If so, is the incidental restriction on . . . freedom any greater than is reasonably necessary for the orderly functioning of the school?" [20]

In determining which student behavior should be regulated, the faculty and administration should initially try to make a distinction between behavior which is disruptive and behavior which is distractive. *Disruptive* behavior may be defined as any action which prevents the continuation of an activity currently in process, such as teaching or learning. Fighting in class, throwing erasers, or refusing to keep quiet are examples of behavior which tends to disrupt a class.

Distractive behavior, on the other hand, may temporarily slow down a class activity but does not actually prevent it from continuing. Chewing gum while the teacher is lecturing, is an example of behavior which may be distractive but certainly not disruptive.

Although a school may choose to regulate and punish distractive behavior, the administrator should recognize that this decision will significantly increase the number of discipline problems with which he and the faculty must cope. It should also be understood by all concerned that in discipline cases the courts have, by and large, tended to apply the criterion of disruption rather than distraction. Although a school could, if it chose, administer minor punishments, e.g., chastening, to those students who engage in distractive behavior, more extreme measures such as suspension would probably not be upheld by the courts.

4. **Policies and procedures on student behavior should be stated in positive form as much as possible, and student responsibility rather than misbehavior should be stressed.** The emphasis on student behavior should be on that which is desired, not on behavior which is unacceptable. An example of this kind of emphasis is a statement in a student handbook disseminated by Barrington Consolidated High School, entitled "Bill of Rights and Duties."*

BILL OF RIGHTS AND DUTIES[21]

1. Because it is my right to elect student representatives to govern the student body . . . it is my duty to elect those who can lead us wisely and to give them my full cooperation.

2. Because it is my right to have free speech, assembly, press, and religion . . . it is my duty to allow others the same privilege.

3. Because it is my right to have free education and to choose subjects which interest me . . . it is my duty to use my privilege to the best of my ability.

4. Because it is my right to act with freedom . . . it is my duty to conduct myself so that I will not interfere with others.

*For a similar approach at the elementary level see Alfred A. Arth and Edward J. Lawton, "Building a Bill of Rights for the Elementary School Child." *Elementary School Journal* 73 (January 1973):200-203.

5. Because it is my right to participate in school activities . . .	it is my duty to do my best in these activities and to uphold the name of the school at all times.
6. Because it is my right to use school and public property . . .	it is my duty to care for and respect this property.
7. Because it is my right to enjoy all of these rights . . .	it is my duty to accept the responsibility of preserving these rights.

5. **The policies and procedures governing student behavior should be written in clear, understandable language and be presented in student, teacher, and parent handbooks which are reviewed at the beginning of each school year.** Rules and procedures which are not written are more easily misunderstood or forgotten. And rules and procedures which are not written in clear and understandable language can be misinterpreted or incorrectly applied.

Compounding these problems would be failure by a school to periodically review its rules and procedures with students, teachers, and parents. Every school should review its policies and procedures on student behavior at the beginning of each school year in order to refresh people's memories, clear up misunderstandings, and identify the need for change in current policies and procedures.

6. **The rationale supporting the rules and procedures governing student behavior should be clearly communicated to students, and the rules and procedures should be enforced fairly and consistently.** An understanding of the rationale behind the rules, and fairness and consistency in enforcement of rules and procedures are essential prerequisites to students' acceptance and compliance. In a study by Vredevoe, students reported that the following factors (in order of frequency) were important:

1. Interpreting the reasons and purposes of the rules
2. Fairness in enforcement
3. Treatment which recognizes maturity of student
4. Consistency in enforcement
5. Enforcement without embarrassment, whenever possible
6. Observance of rules by teachers
7. Opportunity to participate in making rules in areas where students are capable. [22]

It is interesting to note that students felt that if there were to be rules, they should be observed by the adults working in the school as well as the students. Of course, this may not always be feasible in school, but clearly it is a factor that is important to the students.

After an administrator has utilized the six general criteria for evaluating the school's discipline policies and procedures, he may want to make certain changes in them. The types of changes will depend on his particular situation, but should not be made without faculty, parent, student, and school board involvement. Participation by all parties who may be affected by revisions in a school's disciplinary policies and procedures is the key to successful implementation of needed changes.

A FINAL NOTE

Recent studies show a dramatic increase in certain kinds of criminal acts in the schools, such as assaults, vandalism, and narcotics. [23] In response to this troubling situation a growing number of schools have employed their own security officers [24] and some have experimented with various forms of technology, such as closed-circuit television and walkie-talkies. [25]

Even though the "good old days" were far from idyllic, there is little doubt that school discipline problems are becoming more numerous and severe.* Whether school security officers or technological aids will be successful in the long run in preventing student misbehavior is open to question. It is conceded that these measures may be temporarily necessary in some schools in order to control a bad situation. However, by their very nature these techniques tend to deal more with the symptoms of the problem than with its basic causes, and such methods run the danger of infringing on the civil rights of students.

It would appear that if a school is to make a significant reduction in student misbehavior, the administrator and faculty will need to identify and correct the basic causes of that misbehavior. Diagnosis is the first step; then alternative approaches to preventing misbehavior should be instituted. These approaches will be discussed in the next chapter.

Review
1. Explain how it is possible for an administrator to narrow or broaden the scope and nature of his responsibilities by changing the definition of what constitutes student misbehavior in school.
2. What are the purpose and steps of diagnosis in responding to student misbehavior?

*In Clifton Johnson's, *Old Time Schools and Schoolbooks* (New York: Macmillan Co., 1907), p. 21, it is reported that in 1837 over 300 schools in Massachusetts alone were broken up by rebellious pupils.

3. Identify the main hypothesized causes of student misbehavior. What is the rationale for investigating certain of these causes first, and others later?
4. How can an administrator work with teachers and other specialized personnel to reduce or prevent student discipline problems?
5. What criteria can an administrator use to evaluate and improve the school's disciplinary policies and procedures?
6. Cite those factors that *students* feel are important in regard to a school's disciplinary policies and procedures.

Notes

1. Ellwood P. Cubberly, *Public Education in the United States,* rev. ed. (Boston: Houghton Mifflin Co., 1934), p. 328.

2. George Gallup, "How the Public Views the Public Schools, *Phi Delta Kappan* 54 (September 1972):10. Also see *Phi Delta Kappan* 56 (September 1974):21.

3. *Vandalism and Violence: Innovative Strategies Reduce Costs to Schools* (Arlington, Va.: National School Public Relations Association, 1972).

4. Robert A. Stebbins, "The Meaning of Disorderly Behavior: Teacher Definition of a Classroom Situation," *Sociology of Education* 44, no. 2 (Spring 1971):217-36.

5. See Puran L. Rajpal, "Seriousness of Behavior Problems of Elementary School Boys," *Education* 92 (February-March, 1972):46-50; and Dale Findley and Henry M. O'Reilly, "Secondary School Discipline," *American Secondary Education* 2, (December 1971):26-31.

6. *Guidelines for Student Rights and Responsibilities* (Albany, N.Y.: New York State Education Department, n.d.), p. 30.

7. This list represents an adaptation and extension of factors suggested by George V. Sheviakov and Fritz Redl in *Discipline for Today's Children and Youth* (Washington: Association for Supervision and Curriculum Development, 1956).

8. Eugene R. Howard and John M. Jenkins, *Improving Discipline in the Secondary School.* A CFK Ltd. Occasional Paper 1972, pp. 2, 12.

9. Most of the conceptual work on diagnosis in the school has occurred in the field of counseling, and its application to administration has been extracted from the pioneer work of Francis P. Robinson. See Francis P. Robinson, "Modern Approaches to Counseling Diagnosis, *Journal of Counseling Psychology* 10 (Winter 1963):325-33. See also G. A. Koester, "The Study of the Diagnostic Process," *Educational and Psychological Measurement* 14 (1954):473-86.

10. For a description of how such records might be used, see William S. Amoss, "The Use of School Records in the Identification of Juvenile Delinquents" (Ed.D. diss., University of Tulsa, 1970).

11. There is evidence to the effect that school boards are becoming more specific in defining disciplinary policies and procedures. See *School Board Policies on Student Discipline* (Waterford, Conn.: National School Boards Association, 1971).

12. For an excellent study of the discretionary authority of the principal in this area, see Stanley A. Wignes, "Dimensions of the Discretionary Authority of the Secondary School Principal in Making Rules for Pupil Control." (Ed.D. diss., University of Minnesota, 1971).

13. Edwin J. Brown and Arthur T. Phelps, *Managing the Classroom—The Teacher's Role in School Administration* (New York: Ronald Press Co., 1961), pp. 121-24.

14. John S. Packard, "Pluralistic Ignorance and Pupil Control Ideology." An ERIC Report: Ed-055-054, 1971, pp. 109-11. Another instrument specifically designed for the elementary school which might be of interest to the elementary school administrator is described by Priscilla Pitt Jones, "A Method of Measuring Discipline Expectations," *Journal of Experimental Education* 36 (February 1967):39-45.

15. Reported in *NASSP Spotlight,* October 1972, a publication of the National Association of Secondary School Principals.

16. Carl F. Vampel, Jr., "Dealing with Youth Crime, a Cooperative Effort between the School and Law Enforcement Agencies," *American Secondary Education* 3 (December 1972):39-41.

17. Edward T. Ladd, "Regulating Student Behavior without Ending Up in Court," *Phi Delta Kappan* (January 1973):305.

18. Blackwell v. Issaquena, 363 F. 2 and 749 (5th Cir. 1966).

19. Two noteworthy exceptions are studies by Anne M. Laird, "An Analysis of the Discipline Policies and School Regulations in Representative School Districts in the State of Michigan to Determine the Extent to Which They Satisfy Current Legal Criteria" (Ph.D. diss., University of Michigan, 1969); and John P. Hansen, "An Analysis of Student Behavior Codes in American Secondary Schools with Regard to Certain Freedoms Guaranteed by the Constitution of the United States" (Ph.D. diss., University of Michigan, 1971).

20. *Policies That Clarify Student Rights and Responsibilities* (Waterford, Conn.: National School Boards Association, 1970), p. 6.

21. *The Roundup* [Student Handbook](Barrington, Ill.: Barrington Consolidated High School, n.d.).

22. Lawrence E. Vredevoe, *Discipline* (Dubuque, Iowa: Kendall/Hunt Publishing Co., 1971), p. 24.

23. John W. Powell, "School Security: An Emerging Professionalism," *American School and University* 44 (July 1972):12-15.

24. "The Problem of Discipline/Control and Security in Our Schools," Position Paper 1 (New York: National Urban League, 1971).

25. Dick Tunchen, "Television for Surveillance: An Overview," *Educational and Industrial Television* 4 (December 1972):11-12.

14

Responses to Student Discipline Problems

By implementing the recommendations discussed in the previous chapter, the school administrator should gradually be able to reduce the number and the severity of student misbehavior problems with which he is confronted. But despite this improvement, it seems reasonable to assume that in most schools there will continue to be student misbehavior of some type and degree. Two basic questions, then, are how should the administrator deal with student misbehavior after it occurs, and how can it be prevented from occurring again? The following sections will address these questions by analyzing punishment alternatives typically utilized by the school administrator, and by presenting several nonpunitive approaches for ameliorating student misbehavior and preventing its recurrence.

ANALYSIS OF PUNITIVE APPROACHES

In making a decision about punishing a student, an administrator generally chooses among several alternatives identified in figure 14.1.*[1]

---

1. **Verbal Punishment ("Chewing Out")**
2. **Detention (Student Must Stay After School)**
3. **Assigned Work Around the Building After School**
4. **Corporal Punishment**
5. **Suspension**
6. **Recommendation of Expulsion**

Figure 14.1. Punitive Responses to Student Misbehavior.

The possible alternative—"no punishment"—is apparently one which few administrators feel they can accept if a student has misbehaved, par-

*Other alternatives could also be listed, but the ones which seem to be mainly utilized by administrators are identified. Such actions as holding a parent conference or referring the student to a social agency should not be considered as punishment but as a nonpunitive approach to helping the student to deal with the causes of his misbehavior.

ticularly if serious violation of school rules and regulations has occurred. An administrator may feel that, given the violation of a rule, he must punish the student—if for no other reason than to indicate that the student's behavior is not condoned. Or the administrator may face strong expectations by a teacher or a parent that a student be punished for his misbehavior. Teacher and parental expectations that the administrator be a strong disciplinarian undoubtedly influence the decisions of many administrators regarding discipline alternatives. [2]

However, the school administrator should understand that, whatever else is achieved by punishment (and its effectiveness is debatable), it does not treat the basic *causes* of student misbehavior. At best, punishment may act to repress the misbehavior temporarily; it does not deal with its underlying causes. [3] An administrator may sometimes need to punish a student to set an example or to meet teachers' or parents' expectations. But he should not operate under the illusion that punishment will somehow remove the roots of a problem or that the student misbehavior will not recur. There is little affirmative evidence to show that punishment is an effective technique for preventing misbehavior from recurring, and much evidence to show the contrary. [4] In addition, there is the possibility that punishment may lead to undesirable side effects, such as an even more negative attitude on the part of the student toward school. [5]

If, however, an administrator feels that a student's misbehavior must be punished, there would appear to be four factors which should influence a decision relative to the type of punishment: (1) the cause of the misbehavior, (2) the severity of the offense, (3) the habitualness of the offender, that is, the number of times he has committed the offense, and (4) the personality of the offender, e.g., certain individuals may respond to punishment better than others. Also, in punishing a student, the school administrator would do well to heed the recommendation of the O'Learys: [6]

1. Use punishment sparingly.
2. Make clear to the student why he is being punished.
3. Provide the student with an alternative means of meeting his needs.
4. Reward the student for utilizing the alternative means.
5. Avoid physical punishment if at all possible.
6. Avoid punishing while you are in a very angry or emotional state.

The following sections contain a discussion of some of the more significant punishments used in response to student misbehavior, and the subject of due process.

CORPORAL PUNISHMENT

In deciding which type of punishment should be selected, administrators need to be aware of certain factors which could affect their decision. For example, there is now growing professional opinion that corporal punishment is not an appropriate or acceptable response to student misbehavior. Its effectiveness has been questioned by a number of authorities, one of whom has pointed out that

> It has been repeatedly observed that some children are paddled (spanked, whipped, hit) over and over again. The evidence implies that corporal punishment does not work. Some studies have shown that corporal punishment is not effective in reducing behavior problems. Others have indicated that schools using corporal punishment have more behavior problems.[7]

In recent years even teachers have become skeptical about the use and value of corporal punishment. Although earlier surveys showed that the majority of them were in favor of corporal punishment, an NEA task force has recommended its discontinuation.[8] The task force suggested that each state adopt the following law in regard to corporal punishment:

> No person employed or engaged by any educational system within this state, whether public or private, should inflict or cause to be inflicted corporal punishment or bodily pain upon a pupil attending any school or institution within such education system; provided, however, that any person may, within the scope of his employment, use and apply such amounts of physical restraint as to be reasonable and necessary:
>
> 1. to protect himself, the pupil or others from physical injury;
> 2. to obtain possession of a weapon or other dangerous object upon the person or within the control of a pupil;
> 3. to protect property from serious harm . . .[9]

Although proposed as a state law it would appear that this statement could be usefully adopted as policy on corporal punishment by individual schools and school districts.

In spite of growing professional opinion opposing corporal punishment and several court rulings which have raised questions about its use in the school, the Supreme Court has refused to accept a case which would permit the Court to pass judgment on the validity of corporal punishment and, as a result, its use is still legal in certain parts of the country.[10] Nevertheless, the administrator and faculty need to recognize that corporal punishment can be used only under limited conditions. These conditions have been identified by Hamilton:

> . . . From the purely legal point of view, even in states in which corporal punishment is permitted, a teacher who resorts to it assumes substantial legal risk. He is bound under the law, at least to

1. Act from good motives, and not from anger or malice.
2. Inflict only moderate punishment.
3. Determine what the punishment is, in proportion to the gravity of the offence.
4. Convince himself that the contemplated punishment is not excessive, taking into account the age, sex, and physical strength of the pupil to be punished.
5. Assume the responsibility that the rule he seeks to enforce is reasonable.[11]

In addition, the courts specified in a recent case that the school must warn students in advance of the kinds of behavior which warrant the use of corporal punishment, that an adult witness must be present when corporal punishment is administered, and that the parents can obtain a written explanation of the punishment, if they request one.

Although these particular guidelines were written for teachers, it seems safe to assume that they also apply to the school administrator.

SUSPENSION AND EXPULSION

Suspension and expulsion are two other punishment alternatives utilized by school administrators in cases involving extreme misbehavior. *Suspension* can be defined as the temporary removal of a student from school for a certain period of time, generally from one day to several weeks, depending on the offense. *Expulsion* involves removing a student from school on a more permanent basis, usually for at least a semester or longer, depending on the severity of the misbehavior.

Administrators employ the procedure of suspension in cases of repeated minor offenses by students, and for more serious student misbehavior such as smoking in school, or truancy. Expulsion is usually applied only to the *most* serious student misbehavior and is generally used by administrators as a last resort. In the case of either suspension or expulsion, however, there is considerable doubt about the effectiveness of removing a student from school as a method of disciplining him. As Phay and Cummings have observed, "School separation is a poor method. Students who misbehave usually are students with academic difficulties, and removal from the school almost inevitably adds to their academic problems."[12] Therefore, although suspension and expulsion may occasionally be necessary to protect the interests of other students, these methods are probably counterproductive in their effect on the students who are removed from school.

Though it seems clear that suspension and expulsion are disciplinary methods which may adversely affect the student who is removed, there undoubtedly will be times when an administrator may need to initiate these procedures in the case of emergency or extreme situations. The nature of these situations has been defined by the National Juvenile Law Center at St. Louis University as including the following types of student misbehavior:

1.   Assault or battery upon any other person on school ground
2.   Continual and repeated willful disobedience of school personnel legitimately acting in their official capacity, which results in a disruptive effect upon the education of the other children in school
3.   Possession or sale of narcotics or hallucinogenic drugs or substances on school premises.

The Center also suggests that consideration for suspension be given to occurrences of the following kinds of student behavior: (1) academic dishonesty, e.g., cheating or plagiarism, (2) theft from or damage to institution premises or property, (3) intentional disruption or obstruction of the educational function of the school, and (4) possession of firearms.[13]

It should be noted that most of the student misbehavior identified by the National Juvenile Law Center represent violations of the law, and an argument can be made that in such cases law enforcement agencies should administer punishment rather than the school.

DUE PROCESS

The school administrator needs to recognize that there is increasing social pressure, supported by court rulings, to require the school to provide the student with due process in cases of suspension and expulsion.[14]   Two types of due process need to be considered: (1) substantive, and (2) procedural. [15]

Substantive due process examines the question of whether the *purpose* of the rule or regulation which the student violated is fair, reasonable, and just. *Procedural due process* focuses on the question of whether the *procedures* used to remove the student from the school were fair, reasonable, and just.

In the past, due process was required primarily for expelling a student, but in some instances it has been required for suspension as well, particularly if the suspension was for an extended period of time.[16]   The procedures usually involve a hearing and the right of appeal by the student.[17]

In its publication, *The Reasonable Exercise of Authority*, the National Association of Secondary School Principals makes the following recommendations in regard to due process and disciplining students:

> Minor infractions of school rules should be handled informally by faculty members. Serious breaches of discipline leading to possible suspension or some other major penalty should be subject to a hearing, but suspension by the principal, pending the hearing, may be enforced where necessary.[18]

The publication goes on to say, in describing and recommending the nature of due process, that

A notice of the time and place of the hearing and of the exact nature of the charge must be given to the student a reasonable time in advance. . . . In all cases the accused must be allowed to be represented by someone of his own choosing. The hearing may be informal, though it need not be open; and the accused must be allowed to cross-examine witnesses and to present witnesses on his own behalf. The student's parents or guardian may attend. The panel [a committee formed to conduct the hearing] should be instructed to make findings of fact and submit these, together with its recommendations, to the principal promptly after the close of the hearing. The principal and subsequently the board of education should be guided by the report and the practical recommendations of the panel. Also, if the accused believes he was not accorded a fair hearing, he must be allowed to appeal on this ground; any other plan of action may result in school authorities being brought into court. [19]

The NASSP recommendations deal for the most part with due process when serious violations of discipline have occurred and an extended period of suspension is needed. Until recently many school administrators believed that for short term suspension, due process was not required. However, in 1975, the U.S. Supreme Court ruled that school administrators could not suspend students for any period up to ten days without "minimum due process."[20] Minimum due process was defined by the Court to mean that the administrator must provide for the accused student, prior to suspension, (1) oral or written notice of the charges against him, (2) an explanation of the evidence supporting the charges if they are denied by the student, and (3) an opportunity for the student to present his side of the story. The Court also indicated that longer suspension, expulsion for the remainder of the school term, or permanent expulsion may require more formal procedures, such as the right of the student to legal counsel.

The court's decision on due process does not appear to be inconsistent with earlier recommendations of the National Association of Secondary School Principals. In fact, an argument could be made to the effect that the decision did not go as far in some respects as the NASSP recommendations. The major import of the Court's decision was that it changed the status of due process for students, in the case of short term suspension, from a recommended practice to a legal requirement. While this legal requirement may pose unforeseen problems for some administrators, Justice White (speaking for the majority of the Court) stated, "We have imposed requirements which are, if anything, less than a fair-minded school principal would impose upon himself in order to avoid unfair suspension."*

(Another significant court ruling of which the administrator should be aware in administering suspension as a punishment for student misbehavior was given in the case of Mills v. the Board of Education.[21] In this case involving suspension, the court indicated that in addition to due process, the school system would need to provide an alternative form of education for the student while he was suspended. The district was also required to maintain the student in his regular classroom or provide him with other educational services while he was awaiting a hearing.)

It should be obvious that the time is coming when an administrator will no longer be able to simply remove a student from school without providing both due process and some means for that student to continue his education while he is not in school. The traditional practice of suspending a student from school for several days, during which the student falls farther and farther behind in his education, has always seemed counterproductive to many observers. Now it appears that this practice will be challenged in the courts and the main result may be a less indiscriminate and more reasoned use of suspension as a punishment by administrators.

NONPUNITIVE APPROACHES TO STUDENT MISBEHAVIOR

A major implication of the data and statements discussed in the previous sections is that the school administrator and faculty will need to concentrate more on the in-depth diagnosis and remediation of student discipline problems and less on the punishment of student misbehavior. While punishment may still have to be utilized at times in order to *temporarily* control or suppress misbehavior, or to meet teachers' or parents' expectations, it is at best a short-term solution to a problem which requires alternative methods. A model which has been designed to provide the administrator with an overview of several alternative approaches to student misbehavior is presented in figure 14.2.

As figure 14.2 indicates, the first step that an administrator should take cooperatively with teachers, parents, and others in response to student misbehavior is to try to diagnose the cause(s) of the misbehavior.† Student misbehavior doesn't just happen; it is caused by some condition(s).

*Two excellent articles on how a school can meet the challenges of due process are W. Richard Brothers, "Procedural Due Process: What Is It?" *Bulletin of the National Association of Secondary School Principals* 59 (January 1975):1-8; and George Triezenberg, "How to Live with Due Process," *Bulletin of the National Association of Secondary School Principals* 55 (February 1971):61-68.

†Possible causes of student misbehavior, and the process of diagnosis were discussed in the preceding chapter.

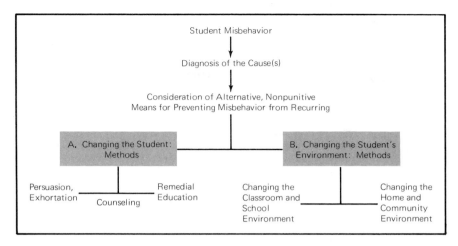

Figure 14.2. A Model for Responding
to Student Misbehavior.

It is important for an administrator to recognize that his diagnosis of the cause(s) of student misbehavior will greatly influence his choice of approaches to preventing the problem from recurring. If an administrator decides that the cause(s) of a problem rests within the student himself, then attempts to change the student will probably be made through one or more of the means identified in figure 14.2, part A. If, on the other hand, the administrator diagnoses the cause(s) of the problem as lying within the student's environment (either the school environment or the home and community environment), the administrator will try to change that environment. The essential point is that an administrator's perception of the causes of the misbehavior will determine to a large extent his selection of an approach to be employed in an effort to prevent the misbehavior from recurring.

A second factor which will influence the administrator's choice of the best approach to prevent student misbehavior from recurring is his *awareness* of alternative methods of responding to student misbehavior. Since punishment has already been discussed, the focus now will be placed on analyzing nonpunitive approaches. [22]

CHANGING THE STUDENT

Persuasion and Exhortation
Most administrators who are confronted with the "first instance" of a student's misbehavior respond with an approach other than punishment. Even

in the case of repeated misbehavior, many administrators attempt to change the student by trying to persuade him that it is not in his best interest to misbehave and by exhorting him to "do a better job."

An investigation of the educational literature uncovered no research evidence on the effectiveness of these disciplinary tactics. Undoubtedly, for some administrators, these approaches "work"—at least with certain students. For the most part, however, persuasion and exhortation do not appear to be very effective with students who are discipline problems, if one can judge by their repeated misbehavior. These methods typically are employed by administrators because the "let us reason together" approach is commonly valued in American society, and they are frequently unaware of any other type of nonpunitive techniques.

It would seem that before persuasion and exhortation could be effective in preventing student misbehavior from recurring, a correct diagnosis of the factors causing the misbehavior would have to be made, and the administrator employing these tactics would have to be perceived by the student as possessing a high degree of credibility.[23] If the causes of the student's problem have been incorrectly diagnosed, an administrator may be trying to persuade or exhort a student to do something which will not remove the basis of the misbehavior. And if an administrator is not perceived by a student as someone who can be believed and trusted, the student is unlikely to be persuaded or exhorted to do anything the administrator wants (if the student can avoid it).[24] Therefore, while persuasion and exhortation by an administrator in response to student misbehavior may be preferable to puntitive measures, the former techniques are dependent on certain conditions which may or may not be present in a specific situation.

Counseling

In working with students who misbehave, many administrators attempt to use counseling techniques. However, the administrator's success is dependent on adequate knowledge and skill in employing these techniques and on the perception of the students that the administrator is a counselor rather than a disciplinarian. Unfortunately, seldom is either of these conditions met. This does not mean that a school administrator should not use counseling techniques in working with student discipline cases. But most school administrators probably need to become more knowledgeable about these techniques before much success will be achieved. Perhaps a more realistic and effective approach for an administrator would be to utilize whatever counseling resources exist within the staff.

Individual and group counseling of students who engage in misbehavior has been tried by counselors in numerous situations, with varying degrees of success.[25] Caplan, for example, counseled several boys who had long records of conflict with school regulations. On the basis of pretest and post-test analysis, he found that the students he had counseled had improved significantly in self-congruence and in their citizenship ratings by teachers. [26] In another study, Arbuckle and Boy counseled a group of twelve students who were serving daily after-school detentions. They found that after counseling, the students received better citizenship ratings from their teachers and there was greater congruence between students' ideal and actual self-ratings. [27] In a third study, described by Webb and Eikenberry, a special program of group counseling was initiated with students exhibiting acting-out behavior in the classroom. By the end of the program of counseling the students were showing a significant change in their acceptance of school rules, and their teachers indicated that the students had changed from being "serious distracting elements" to "average participants" in the regular classroom. [28]*

Although such studies strongly suggest that counseling can be successful in improving student behavior, it should be noted that other research has revealed little or no change in student behavior as a result of counseling. [29] The degree of expertise of the pupil services team, the availability of their time, proper facilities and the extremity of the student misbehavior problems seem to be important considerations in determining counseling effectiveness. However, probably the most significant factor is the degree to which the counselors and other members of the pupil services team understand and accept the principle that they possess specialized expertise which can make a valuable contribution to ameliorating student behavior problems. Unless the pupil personnel workers wholeheartedly accept this concept, it is unlikely that they will make any significant contribution to improving student behavior.

Regrettably, it would appear from reports by both administrators and counselors that the role of the pupil services specialist in working with students who misbehave is not widely accepted. It should be pointed out, however, that not all counselors reject the role of helping to resolve student misbehavior problems. [30] Keating has emphasized that, "Except for the very severely emotionally disturbed, . . . the rehabilitation of emotionally disturbed children and adolescents should be part of the educative task of the school system. At the junior and senior high school levels, the school counselor should be the coordinator of the rehabilitative re-educative program." [31]

Since the attitude of the pupil personnel specialists may be the most significant variable affecting the success of a counseling program for students who misbehave, it is important that the school administrator work

*For an interesting study of group counseling with behavioral problems in the elementary school, see Jim Gumaer and Robert D. Myrich, "Behavioral Group Counseling with Disruptive Children," *School Counselor* 21 (March 1974):312-17.

with the pupil services team to help them develop an appropriate understanding of and attitude toward the contribution they can make to
ameliorating student misbehavior.

Remediation of Learning Problems

It is probably accurate to say that learning problems of one kind or another
are associated with most student misbehavior. Whether the learning
problems result from the misbehavior or cause it has long been a subject of
debate among educators. Unfortunately, research has not resolved the
debate.

It does seem reasonable to assume, however, that learning problems
play some role in regard to student misbehavior. The process seems to occur
in either of the two ways presented in figure 14.3. [32]

Figure 14.3. Some Possible
Relationships between Learning
Problems and Misbehavior.

As figure 14.3 suggests, learning problems might cause, as well as result
from, student misbehavior. Students who do not initially engage in
misbehavior or encounter learning problems may eventually become
discipline problems if sufficiently bored with school or if experiencing personal problems, and as a result of conflict with the school or of a loss of time,
may develop learning disabilities. Also, students who possess learning
disabilities of one kind or another and who experience resultant failure in the
classroom are more likely to feel frustration, anger, or boredom, and then
engage in misbehavior in order to vent their emotions. The misbehavior may
consist of talking back to the teacher, "fooling around" in class, or skipping
class or school. [33] That the latter misbehavior has its roots in learning
disabilities was poignantly brought out by one probation officer: "I found
that the biggest problem with youngsters getting into trouble, boys in particular, was that they didn't want to face not being able to read in class. They
would stay out of school, and their truancy would lead them into more
serious trouble." [34]

A constructive approach, therefore, to ameliorating student misbehavior would be for the administrator to investigate the possibility that the
student who is engaging in misbehavior is handicapped by some type of

learning disability or motivational problem, and if true, to involve appropriate school resources in remedial action. Depending on the nature of the learning disability, remediation might take several forms, including individual and small-group work, special classes, different materials, and other remedial approaches.[35]

It is conceded that remediation of student learning problems may be a long-term solution to a problem (i.e., student misbehavior) that demands some kind of immediate response from the administration. It is also possible that the administrator will be pressured by the expectations of teachers and others to take more immediate and punitive action when student misbehavior occurs. However, if the administrator hopes to have any significant success in preventing student misbehavior from recurring, he will need to investigate the possibility that student learning problems are causing or are a result of the misbehavior, and organize remedial assistance to correct these conditions.

CHANGING THE STUDENT'S ENVIRONMENT

Thus far, attention has been focused on nonpunitive approaches to changing the student in order to reduce or eliminate his misbehavior. However, it should be recognized that it may be difficult or even impossible for a student to change unless his environment changes. And, for many students, their environment may be the basic cause of their misbehavior.

A student's environment can be considered as composed primarily of two elements: (1) classroom and school conditions, and (2) home and community conditions. Figure 14.4 presents possible variables in the student's

---

Classroom and School Environment	Home and Community Environment
1. Teacher's attitude toward and expectations for the student.	1. Parents' attitude toward and expectations for the student and for the school
2. Teacher's style or methods of teaching.	2. Extent of crowdedness in the home
3. Classroom rules and policies	3. Attitude toward school held by siblings in the family and by the neighborhood peer group
4. Content of the subject being taught	
5. Textbook and other reading materials	4. Availability of alternative pursuits which are more attractive and rewarding to the student than is school
6. Size and composition of the class	
7. Student's seating assignment in the class	
8. School's schedule and total program of studies	

Figure 14.4. Possible Environmental Variables Affecting Student Misbehavior.

environment which individually or collectively may be causing his misbehavior and which may need to be changed before the misbehavior can be reduced or eliminated.

The list of variables identified in figure 14.4 does not, of course, exhaust all of the possibilities, but it should give the administrator a good indication of the numerous environmental factors which may be causing a particular student's misbehavior.

In general, it would appear that an administrator will be more likely to achieve success in trying to modify a student's classroom and school environment than his home and community environment. An administrator has more contact with and control over the school environment, and in many cases, there is very little that he can do about a student's home and community environment. This does not mean that efforts should not be made to influence the student's home and community environment in positive ways, and specific suggestions will be discussed later in the chapter.[36] Nevertheless, it would appear that the highest priority for changing a student's environment (if that is what is needed) should be given to attempts to bring about changes in his classroom and school environment. The nature of the changes would depend on the administrator's diagnosis of the causes of the problem, but two approaches which seem particularly promising for changing the student's school environment are discussed in the following sections.

Changing the Student's School Environment: Behavioral Modification

A relatively new approach to preventing student misbehavior from recurring is behavioral modification. Behavioral modification, defined simply, is an attempt to change the behavior of an individual who has misbehaved by changing the response of the person or persons who are reacting to the misbehavior.[37] The method is based on the premise that it is the response to the misbehavior which is the key factor that determines whether or not the misbehavior persists, rather than any antecedent or internal cause.

In the school situation a student's misbehavior typically provokes a response from a teacher or administrator. The response may range from a form of punishment to a suggestion of possible rewards for correct behavior. The behavioral modification method is based on the assumption that certain responses to student misbehavior will tend to prevent the misbehavior from recurring, while others will only encourage the student to persist in misbehaving.[38]

The behavioral modification approach would change the role of the teacher or administrator from that of punishing misbehavior to one of rewarding correct student behavior and ignoring misbehavior. Advocates of the approach do not entirely reject the use of punishment, but question its effectiveness unless used sparingly. They also believe in clear and consistently applied rules, preferably kept to a minimum.

Perhaps the best means of understanding the behavioral modification method would be to examine the instructions given to classroom teachers who were asked to employ this approach in working with student discipline cases:

GENERAL RULES FOR TEACHERS

1. Make explicit the rules as to what is expected of children for each period. (Remind of rules when needed.)
2. Ignore (do not attend to) behaviors which interfere with learning, unless a child is being hurt by another. Use punishment which seems appropriate, preferably withdrawal of some positive reinforcement.
3. Give praise and attention to behaviors which facilitate learning. Tell child what he is being praised for. Try to reinforce behaviors incompatible with those you wish to decrease. Example of how to praise: "I like the way you're working quietly." "That's the way I like to see you work." "Good job, you are doing fine." Transition period: "I see Johnny is ready to work." "I am calling on you because you raised your hand." "I wish everyone were working as much as 'X'," etc. Use variety and expression. In general, give praise for achievement, pro-social behavior, and following the group's rules.[39]

As can be seen by examining the instructions given to teachers, behavioral modification places a great emphasis on the teacher's rewarding students for behaving correctly, rather than paying attention to and punishing misbehavior. One of the underlying premises of the behavioral modification approach is that when a teacher or administrator reacts negatively to a student's misbehavior, that response only provides the student with the attention he is seeking, and therefore his misbehavior is likely to be repeated. On the other hand, if the student's misbehavior is ignored and the teacher's attention is focused instead on identifying (and rewarding) the response that is desired, the misbehavior will eventually be eliminated and the correct response will be strengthened.

It would appear that the behavioral modification approach offers school administrators a method they might use in working with students or one which they might try to encourage their teachers to utilize.[40] The approach has been tested empirically in a number of classroom situations, and it seems to be generally effective.[41] It should be noted, however, that with some exceptions, the method has been used primarily on student misbehavior in the elementary school, and therefore should be employed more cautiously in the secondary school. [42]

It should also be emphasized that behavioral modification has been criticized in some circles.* Probably the greatest obstacle to its effective utilization is that, when faced with student misbehavior, teachers and administrators will not find it easy to accentuate the positive and to ignore rather than punish the misbehavior. Nevertheless, there is now sufficient evidence of the merits of this approach to student misbehavior to motivate the school administrator to at least investigate it further for possible use in his own school. [†]

Changing the Student's School Environment: Alternative Educational Programs

The use of behavioral modification is an attempt to change the school environment of a student who has misbehaved by changing the teacher's or administrator's immediate response to the misbehavior. While this approach appears to show promise, many schools have tended to turn to alternative education programs for those students who persistently engage in misbehavior. Two educational alternatives which have been introduced are: (1) work-study programs, and (2) special classes or schools for chronic misbehavers.

Participation in work-study programs is, of course, not restricted to students who have misbehaved; many types of students participate in this forward-looking educational alternative which combines study in school with work on the job. [43] But for students who are not motivated by standard classroom activities and who, because of their boredom and frustration get into trouble, a work-study program seems to offer an alternative way of learning from which they can derive greater meaning and satisfaction. [44] Students in such a program usually attend formal academic classes in the morning and work at a job in the afternoon. An attempt is often made to relate the job to the academic activities being pursued in school, and vice-versa.

Although the work-study program seems to be a constructive alternative to punishment as a means of reducing student misbehavior, it is not without limitations. [45] Sometimes, due to child labor laws, participation in the program cannot begin until the junior year of school, and by that time a student may have dropped out of school, or his behavior may have become so chronic that he could not qualify for the program. Also, since there is careful screen-

---

*A review of these criticisms may be found in the *Phi Delta Kappan* 54, May 1973, pp. 593-97.

† An excellent book for the classroom teacher that could be used in an in-service program is *Behavior Modification: A Practical Guide for Teachers,* by James Poteet. (Minneapolis: Burgess Publishing, 1975.)

ing of applicants for the work-study program in order to maintain cooperative relationships with employers, the problem students who are most in need of this experience may not qualify for admission because of their extreme behavior. In addition, the program suffers because there are frequently insufficient jobs available in which to place students, or insufficient funds and other resources to do an adequate job of administering and supervising a large program.

For these reasons the work-study program has not totally met the need of an alternative educational experience for students who are turned off from school and who engage in misbehavior. But work-study programs still represent valid options in reducing student misbehavior and should be explored and utilized by the administrator to the greatest extent possible. [46]

Another approach to changing the school environment of students who have engaged in misbehavior is to provide them with special classes or, in some instances, placement in a special school. [47]

Ability-grouping has in many circumstances resulted in special classes for students who misbehave, because of the strong relationship between learning problems and student misbehavior. [48] In other situations, special classes have been specifically designed for "problem students." These classes emphasize the development of reading and study skills, and frequently include opportunities for individual and group counseling and discussion of vocational opportunities. The classes are generally smaller than regular classes and are taught by teachers who have been trained to work with these kinds of students. In addition, the school schedule set up for the students is usually more flexible. (The same characteristics are true of special schools for chronic misbehavers.)

The limited research that has been conducted on the merits of special classes or schools for students who engage in misbehavior suggest that they can be effective if the right conditions are present. [49] The "right conditions" include

1. **A teacher who wants to work with these kinds of students and who understands their strengths and limitations.** Although a teacher who has been especially trained for this type of work is desirable and may be required in certain states, the teacher's attitude and commitment to working with these students is probably the most important prerequisite.
2. **Careful screening and assignment of students.** Probably not every student who misbehaves can benefit from special classes or a special school, so potential applicants should be screened to make sure that the classes have a reasonably good chance of succeeding. In assigning students to special classes care should be taken to avoid putting people together who will stimulate or feed upon each other's misbehavior.

3. **Adequate resources to insure small classes (9-12), a good-sized room and sufficient materials and supplies.**

4. **Reasonable flexibility to depart from the school schedule, curriculum, and rules and regulations when it seems desirable in the eyes of the teacher to do so.** Special classes should be treated differently, and should not be expected to adhere to everything that the regular classes need to do.

5. **A relevant and worthwhile curriculum in the eyes of the students, teachers, and parents.** Whatever is going to be accomplished in the special classes has to be viewed first of all as interesting and worthwhile by the students. Unless that objective is achieved, the rest of the program will make little difference.

6. **Interested and cooperative parents.** The interest and cooperation of the parents are desirable, if not essential conditions for an effective program. Whether the parents are interested and cooperative will depend, of course, on their perception of whether the school is REALLY interested in them and their child, or is merely trying to "get rid of" a troublemaker.

7. **Interested and cooperative administration.** Unless the administration understands the purposes of this kind of program and is committed to securing the resources necessary for making it work, there is little possibility that such a program can be effective.

In some situations it may not be necessary for each and every condition to exist for a special class or school to succeed, but in general most of the conditions should be viewed as prerequisites to success. There will no doubt be problems (particularly, financial ones) that must be resolved in providing these conditions, but the school administrator is the one who is responsible for resolving these problems and moving ahead with the introduction, maintenance, and improvement of the special program.*

CHANGING THE STUDENT'S HOME AND COMMUNITY ENVIRONMENT

Many educators seem to believe that the causes of student misbehavior can be found in the student's home and/or community environment.[50] While this theory has a certain amount of evidence to support it, the administrator who tries to change a student's home or community environment is frequently likely to encounter difficulties.[51] For example, the administrator and the professional staff are typically occupied with myriad tasks at the school and may not have sufficient time to become well acquainted with a

---

*It should be emphasized that the ultimate goal of a special class or school should be to prepare the student so that he can eventually be reintegrated into the regular school program.

student's home and community environment. In addition, in many situations the administrator and many of the teachers don't even live in the community from which the school draws its students.

But the basic difficulty that an administrator will probably face in trying to change a student's home and community environment is that the school has very little control or influence over that environment. It may be that the following conditions in a student's home and community contribute to his misbehavior in school, but then the real question is, what can the school do about any of these conditions?

1. Large family living in a crowded home.
2. Both parents work and don't have much time to supervise children.
3. Older brothers and sisters did not finish school.
4. Street gangs exist in the neighborhood.
5. Undesirable influences on the student, such as drugs, exist in the neighborhood. [52]

Any or all of these home and community conditions may be causing a student's misbehavior at school, but the likelihood that an administrator and the professional staff can change any of them is small. This is not to minimize the importance of efforts to work with parents and various neighborhood groups to improve conditions in the home and/or community.* For example, individual and group counseling of parents of children with behavioral problems has been effective in some situations in ultimately improving student behavior. [53] Other schools have been successful in working out cooperative programs with community groups to improve the community. [54]

But the administrator will need to recognize that, in attempting to change a student's home and community environment, progress may be slow and limited. Consequently, his main efforts and those of the professional staff should be focused on diagnosing and taking action on possible environmental conditions existing within the classroom and the school which may be causing the student's misbehavior and over which the administrator has better control and can more easily bring about change.

OTHER APPROACHES

In addition to the methods discussed thus far, some schools have experimented with several other approaches to preventing and reducing student misbehavior. These include the use of a student ombudsman, [55]

---

*One particularly interesting and apparently successful program involving the use of the home-school-community worker is described by Walter L. Gant and Greta I. Gustavson, "Home-School-Community: A Catalyst," *Journal of the International Association of Pupil Personnel Services* 18 (March 1974):124-31.

grievance committees to hear and take appropriate action about students' concerns about their school environment,[56] and the use of "crisis rooms"[57] to help students calm down before returning to their regular classrooms. Since experience with and research on these approaches is limited, they will be identified in this chapter only for purposes of recommending further investigation by the reader.

A FINAL NOTE

Ladd has observed that "A sad but no longer rare spectacle is the school principal who used to keep order with reprimands, threats, and punishment but who finds them ineffectual today and becomes frustrated and angry."[58] The discussion and analysis in this chapter should have shown the school administrator that punitive responses to student misbehavior are largely ineffective in preventing that behavior from recurring—even though they may be temporarily necessary—and that nonpunitive remedies are available to prevent and reduce student misbehavior. Although the nonpunitive methods suggested may be perceived by some administrators as too time-consuming or not immediate enough in their impact, every administrator needs to recognize that there are few shortcuts to or panaceas for the prevention and reduction of student misbehavior. The nonpunitive approaches recommended in this chapter may not *eliminate* student misbehavior, but if implemented they could eventually reduce its recurrence significantly.

Review

1. Define the function of punishment. What are its advantages and disadvantages?
2. Identify the punishment alternatives that an administrator has available to him. What guidelines should an administrator follow in deciding on and implementing a punishment alternative?
3. Discuss those factors and guidelines that an administrator should consider in using corporal punishment with students who misbehave.
4. Under what circumstances are suspension and/or expulsion appropriate or inappropriate methods of responding to student misbehavior?
5. Define the terms "substantive due process" and "procedural due process" as they apply to student suspension or expulsion. Explain what is meant by "minimum due process."
6. Identify several nonpunitive approaches to changing a student who has misbehaved. Describe the advantages and disadvantages of each approach.

7. What are several nonpunitive approaches to changing the environment of a student who has misbehaved? What are the advantages and disadvantages of each approach?

Notes

1. Emery Stoops and Joyce King Stoops, *Discipline or Disaster* (Bloomington, Ind.: Phi Delta Kappan Educational Foundation, 1972), pp. 19-21.
2. For an example of this type of influence by teachers, see Donald Willower, "The Teacher Subculture and Curricular Change." An ERIC Report: Ed-020-588, 1968.
3. William W. Purkey, *Self-Concept and School Achievement* (Englewood Cliffs, N.J.: Prentice-Hall, 1970), p. 55.
4. For an extensive review of the research on this point, see R. L. Solomon, "Punishment," *American Psychologist* 19 (1964):239-53. For an opposing point of view, see J. A. Cheyne and R. H. Walter, "Punishment and Prohibition: Some Origins of Self-Control," in *New Directions in Psychology,* ed. T. M. Newcomb (New York: Holt, Rinehart & Winston, 1970), pp. 281-366.
5. N. H. Azrin and W. C. Holz, in *Operant Behavior: Areas of Research and Application,* ed. W. K. Honig (New York: Appleton-Century-Crofts, 1966), pp. 213-70. For a different point of view, see T. R. Rislen, "The Effects and Side Effects of Punishing the Autistic Behavior of a Deviant Child," *Journal of Applied Behavior Analysis* 1 (1968):21-34.
6. K. Daniel O'Leary and Susan G. O'Leary, *Classroom Management: The Successful Use of Behavioral Modifications* (Elmsford, New York: Pergamon Press, 1972), p. 152.
7. Charles T. McElvaney, *Statement on the Proposed New By-Law 741:2 Corporal Punishment* (Public Hearing of the Maryland State Board of Education, January 27, 1971), p. 4.
8. *Report of the Task Force on Corporal Punishment* (Washington, D.C.: National Education Association, 1972), p. 5.
9. Ibid, p. 30.
10. Ware v. Estes, 458 F. Supp. 1360 (1972).
11. Robert Hamilton, *Legal Rights and Liabilities of Teachers* (Laramie, Wyo.: Laramie Printers, 1956), p. 36. For more recent but essentially the same guidelines on administering corporal punishment, see Earl Hoffman, "The Classroom Teacher and School Law," *Educational Horizons* 49 (Winter 1970-71):33-39.
12. Robert E. Phay and Jasper L. Cummings, Jr., *Student Suspension and Expulsions* (Chapel Hill, N.C.: Institute of Government, 1970), p. 9.
13. Ralph Faust, *Model High School Disciplining Procedure Code* (St. Louis, Mo.: National Juvenile Law Center, 1971), pp. 4-5. Also see Phay and Cummings, *Student Suspensions and Expulsions,* pp. 15-23.
14. See *Givens v. Poe,* D. C. W. D., North Carolina; Charlotte, Div., 2615, (1972).
15. "Due Process of Law in School Discipline," *Inequality in Education,* July 1973, pp. 55-66.
16. Sullivan 333 F. Supp. 1172.
17. *Academic Freedom in the Secondary Schools* (New York: American Civil Liberties Union, 1968), p. 18. Also see 1973 edition, pp. 55-81.
18. Robert L. Ackerly, *The Reasonable Exercise of Authority* (Washington, D.C.: National Association of Secondary School Principals, 1968), p. 14.
19. Ibid., p. 15.
20. *Goss v. Lopez,* No. 73-898.
21. Reported in *Education USA,* a weekly newsletter published by the National School Public Relations Association, October 2, 1972, p. 25.
22. For additional alternatives, see *Report of the Task Force on Corporal Punishment,* pp. 28-29.
23. Behaviors that might convey the credibility are identified in a study by Rosa L. Baggett, "Behaviors That Communicate Understanding as Evaluated by Teenagers" (Ed.D. diss., University of Florida, 1967).

24. The norms of the reference group to which the student belongs are a major factor in this regard. See Albert K. Cohen, *Delinquent Boys* (Glencoe, Ill.: Free Press, 1955), chap. 4.

25. Peter E. Maynard et al., "Group Counseling with Emotionally Disturbed Students in a School Setting," *Journal of Secondary Education* (November 1969):358-65.

26. S. W. Caplan, "The Effects of Group Counseling on Junior High Boys' Concept of School," *Journal of Counseling Psychology* 4 (Spring 1957):124-29.

27. D. S. Arbuckle and A. W. Boy, "Client-Centered Therapy in Counseling Students with Behavioral Problems," *Journal of Counseling Psychology* 8 (Summer 1961):136-39.

28. A. P. Webb and J. Eikenberry, "A Group Counseling Approach to Acting Out Pre-adolescents," *Psychology in the Schools* I (October 1964):395-400.

29. See, for example, D. E. Zimpfer, "Expression of Feelings in Group Counseling," *Personnel and Guidance Journal* 45 (March 1967):703-8.

30. For a good description of procedures for introducing group counseling, see Irvin Hyman and Bud Feder, "Instituting Group Counseling in the Public Schools," *Psychology in the Schools* I (October 1964):401-3.

31. A. C. Keating, "Counseling with the Emotionally Disturbed," *School Counselor* 15 (March 1968):267-72.

32. For the model's theoretical basis, see John Dollard et al., *Frustration and Aggression* (New Haven: Yale University Press, 1939); that misbehavior is not the only outcome of aggression is suggested in a review of relevant research by Gerald R. Adams, "Classroom Aggression: Determinants Controlling Mechanics and Guidelines for the Implementation of a Behavior Modification Program," *Psychology in Schools* 10 (April 1973):155-67.

33. For an excellent review of research and possible causes of student attendance problems and a summary description of innovative attempts to improve attendance procedures in various schools, see D. Cornell Thomas, "A Comparative Study of Absenteeism at Kennedy and Olympus Junior High Schools" (Ed.D. diss., University of Utah, 1970), chap. 2.

34. Statement of former probation officer Jessie Jackson, reported in *Ebony*, November 1972, p. 67.

35. For further ideas on this subject, see John Gormley and Michael J. Mittoli, "Rapid Improvement of Reading Skills in Juvenile Delinquents," *Journal of Experimental Education* 40, no. 2 (Winter 1971):45-48.

36. For an example of an attempt by the school to effect change in the home, see "Final Report of the Evaluation of the 1969-70 School-Home Liaison: Programs and Patterns for Disadvantaged High School Students." An ERIC Report: Ed-063-446, 1967.

37. For a rather complete treatment of this topic, see Carl E. Thoresen, ed., *Behavior Modification in Education,* (Chicago: University of Chicago Press, 1973).

38. Vivian Hedrich, "Rx for Disruptive Students," *American Education* 8, no. 6 (July 1972):11-14.

39. Wesley C. Becker et al., "The Contingent Use of Teacher Attention and Praise in Reducing Classroom Behavior Problems," *Journal of Special Education* 1, no. 3 (Summer-Fall, 1967):287-307.

40. See Ronald E. Brown et al., "The School Principal as a Behavior Modifier," *Journal of Educational Research* 56, no. 4 (December 1972):175-80. See also Rodney E. Copeland et al., "Effects of a School Principal Praising Parents for Student Attendance," *Educational Technology* 12 (1972):56-59.

41. An excellent work (previously cited) which reviews the research on this approach is that by K. Daniel O'Leary and Susan G. O'Leary, *Classroom Management.*

42. See for use at the secondary level, Maureen O'Keefe and Marlow Sunaby, "Seven Techniques for Solving Classroom Discipline Problems," *High School Journal* 56 (January 1973):190-98.

43. United States National Advisory Council on Vocational Education, "Career Education for Everyone," *Vocational Guidance Quarterly* 20 (March 1972):183-87.

44. For an excellent description of a work study program for ninth- and eleventh-grade students who had been experiencing difficulties with school, see P. Muller, *First Year Report of the Work Experience Career Exploration Program* (WECEP) (Minneapolis: Minneapolis Public Schools, 1970).

45. Minneapolis Public Schools, "Work Experience Career Exploration Program (WECEP) Advisory Committee Report: Evaluation and Recommendations." An ERIC Report: Ed-068-651, 1972.

46. For a very good overview of a number of representative work study programs in the nation, see Steven M. Frankel et al., "Case Study of Fifty Representative Work Education Programs." An ERIC Report: Ed-081-997, 1973.

47. For an excellent description of how one school district organized special classes and a special school for these kinds of students, see "Alternative Learning Centers in Hartford Public Schools, Connecticut." An ERIC Report: Ed-068-590, 1972.

48. For a review of research which suggests possible disadvantages of ability grouping, see Warren G. Findley, *Ability Grouping: Status, Impact and Alternatives* (Athens, Ga.: Center for Educational Improvement, 1970).

49. For two different descriptions of special schools for students who are experiencing difficulties in the regular academic program, see Edward G. Dauu, "The Effect of a Special Curriculum and Separate Physical Facility on a Population of Unsuccessful High School Students" (Ph.D. diss., University of Michigan, 1969); and "Personal Interest and Practical Skills: Success," *NASSP Spotlight,* March 1972.

50. For a review of the theoretical basis for that point of view, see Clinard B. Marshall, *Sociology of Deviant Behavior,* rev. ed. (New York: Holt, Rinehart & Winston, 1964).

51. See R. Lynn, "Personality Characteristics of the Mother of Aggressive and Unaggressive Children," *Journal of Genetic Psychology* 99 (1961):159-64. Also see Naomi M. Serot and Richard C. Teevan, "Perceptions of the Parent-Child Relationship and Its Relation to Child Adjustment," *Child Development* 32 (February 1961):363-78.

52. Extracted from Sheldon Glueck and Eleanor Glueck, *Unraveling Juvenile Delinquency* (Cambridge: Harvard University Press, 1950).

53. For a description of one such program, see George H. Dee, "The Effects of Parent Group Counseling on Children with School Adjustment Problems" (Ph.D. diss., Arizona State University, 1970).

54. Hannah Shields, "You Have to Bend a Little," *American Education* 8 (July 1972):27-31.

55. Francis F. Barham, "The Educational Ombudsman: A Study of the Ombudsman in American Public Education" (Ed.D. diss., University of Virginia, 1973).

56. An example of such a committee may be found at Chesterton Senior High School, Chesterton, Ind.

57. See R. E. Stiaveili and D. E. Sykes, "Guidance Clinic: An Alternative to Suspension," *National Association of Secondary School Principals Bulletin* 56 (April 1972):64-71.

58. Edward T. Ladd, "Regulating Student Behavior without Ending Up in Court," *Phi Delta Kappan* 54 (January 1973):308.

15

Administration of the Pupil Personnel Services Program

There are many different kinds of students who attend school, ranging from the academically talented student to the special education student. The major objective of education should be to help each of these students achieve his maximum potential; the primary function of the pupil personnel services program should be to provide a set of specialized services which will aid the school and, ultimately the student, to accomplish that objective.[1]

Since a pupil personnel services program may be found in most schools, and the school administrator is usually the one who has overall administrative responsibility at the building level, he will need to be well informed about the many facets of this very important program. The intent of this chapter is to help the administrator better understand the objectives, personnel roles, administrative responsibilities, and issues and problems of two main components of pupil personnel services: (1) the counseling and guidance program, and (2) the social, psychological, and health program.

THE COUNSELING AND GUIDANCE PROGRAM

Although the counseling and guidance program is only one of the two components of pupil personnel services, it may constitute the only pupil personnel services offered in many schools. The basic purposes of the counseling and guidance program are to assist students to better understand themselves, and to realize their potentialities more fully.[2] In order to achieve these objectives the program should provide to the student, and to others who are working to help the student, a set of services, which are identified in figure 15.1.[3]

As an examination of figure 15.1 will show, the counseling and guidance program provides services to five groups.* The first and undoubtedly the most important group is the student body. The counseling and guidance program offers a set of services designed to help students understand themselves (appraisal), as well as their immediate and future environments (orientation,

---

*Although most of the services identified in figure 15.1 are as appropriate for the elementary school as for the secondary level, the reader who desires more information on guidance services at the elementary level should see Leonard Zudick, *Implementing Guidance in the Elementary School* (Boston: Houghton Mifflin Co., 1971).

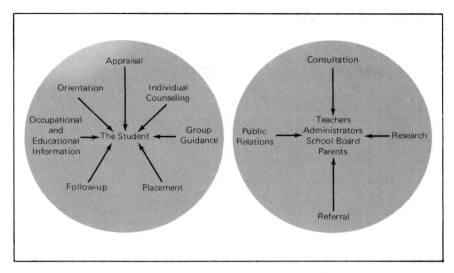

Figure 15.1. Counseling and
Guidance Services.

educational, and occupational information), and to reach decisions which
will fully utilize their present and future capabilities (individual and group
counseling and guidance). In addition, a good counseling and guidance program provides assistance to students seeking a job or a college which will be
appropriate for them (placement), and checks with them periodically after
they have left school to ascertain the effectiveness of the school's assistance to
them and their need for further help (follow-up).

While students are probably the primary recipients of counseling and
guidance services, the program also tries to provide help to other groups, as
figure 15.1 indicates. These services include *consultation* on ideas for maximizing students' potentialities; a *referral* source on ways to prevent and
ameliorate student problems; *research* on student aptitudes, interests, and
problems; and *public relations* activities to help people better understand the
counseling and guidance program. Teachers, administrators, school board
members, and parents can and should utilize these services to help them do a
better job in working with students. Frequently these groups do not make
adequate use of the specialized resources which the counseling and guidance
program can offer. Although the reasons for such underutilization are often
complex, it is the responsibility of the building administrator, in cooperation
with the guidance staff, to develop appropriate understanding and use of
counseling and guidance services on the part of teachers, parents, the school
board and other administrators.

THE ROLE OF THE COUNSELOR

Central to the effective utilization of counseling and guidance services is a broad understanding of the role of the counselor. The counselor is the transmitter of counseling and guidance services, much as the teacher is the transmitter of the curriculum. Though there have been many formulations of the role of the counselor, the most widely accepted conceptualization is the role description developed by the American Personnel and Guidance Association, presented in figure 15.2.

The APGA policy statement on the role of the counselor is a comprehensive one which should be useful to any school administrator. It clearly outlines the many facets and scope of the counselor's job, and identifies the various individuals and groups with whom the counselor works. It is a statement which should be studied by the school administrator and shared with

---

A. The Counselor's Responsibility to the Student

1. Demonstrates respect for the worth, dignity, and quality of the student's human rights.
2. Shows concern for and assists in the planning of the student's educational, career, personal, and social development.
3. Aids the student in self-evaluation, self-understanding, and self-direction, enabling him to make decisions consistent with his immediate and long-range goals.
4. Assists the student in developing health habits and positive attitudes and values.
5. Encourages the student to participate in appropriate school activities with a view toward increasing his effectiveness in personal and social activities.
6. Participates in the planning and designing of research that may result in beneficial effects to the counselee.
7. Assists the student in the development of an awareness of the world of work and in the utilization of the school and community resources to that end.
8. Helps the student to acquire a better understanding of the world of work through the acquisition of skills and attitudes and/or participation in work-related programs.
9. Encourages the student to plan and utilize leisure time activities and to increase his personal satisfaction.
10. Clearly indicates the conditions under which counseling is provided with respect to privileged communication.
11. Assists in the student's adjustment to school and evaluates his academic progress.
12. Makes referral to appropriate resources whenever his professional or role limitations limit his assistance.
13. Assists the student in understanding his strengths, weaknesses, interests, values, potentialities, and limitations.

Figure 15.2. The Role of the School Counselor. [4]   (continued)

B. The Counselor's Relationship with the Teacher

1. Views the teacher as a member of the guidance team.
2. Serves as interpreter of the school's guidance program to teachers and familiarizes them with the guidance services available.
3. Shares appropriate individual student data with the teacher, with due regard for confidentiality, and assists the teacher in recognizing individual differences in students, as well as their needs in the classroom.
4. Assists the teacher in making referrals to other appropriate school personnel, such as the remedial reading teacher, the school nurse, the school's learning disabilities specialist.
5. Supports teachers of vocational and/or cooperative programs offering students on-site work experience.
6. Cooperates with efforts of the middle school/junior high school and senior high school teachers to articulate academic course work for the benefit of the student entering the senior high school.
7. Maintains an objective and impartial view in teacher-student relationships, endeavoring to understand the problems which may exist and to assist in their solution.
8. Assists in the planning of classroom guidance activities and acts as a resource person for obtaining appropriate up-to-date materials and information.
9. Makes current job information available to the teacher about the myriad of careers and job opportunities during and beyond school.
10. Involves the teacher in conferences with students and parents, promoting a better understanding of the student and his development.

C. The Counselor's Relationship with the Administration

1. Recognizes that the administrator is the major member of the guidance team whose outlook, leadership, and support create the atmosphere for success in his important school services.
2. Serves as interpreter of the guidance program to the administration, familiarizing it with the guidance services available.
3. Works closely with the administration in planning, implementing and participating in-service training and other programs designed to maintain and promote the professional competency of the entire staff in curriculum development, in adapting learning activities to pupil needs, and in effecting positive student behavior.
4. Serves as liaison between the guidance staff and the school administration by preparing pertinent information regarding student needs and abilities or other data related to the guidance program and curriculum development.

D. The Counselor's Responsibility to the Parent or Guardian

1. Provides the parent/guardian with accurate information about school policies and procedures, course offerings, educational and career opportunities, course or program requirements, and resources that will contribute to the continuing development of the counselee.
2. Makes discreet and professional use of information shared during conferences.
3. Assists the parent/guardian in forming realistic perceptions of the student's aptitudes, abilities, interests, and attitudes as related to

Figure 15.2. Continued.   *(continued)*

educational and career planning, academic achievement, personal-social development, and total school progress.

4. Interprets the guidance program of the school to the parent/guardian and familiarizes him with the guidance services available.
5. Involves the parent/guardian in the guidance activities within the school.

E. The Counselor's Relationship with Significant Others

1. Maintains good communication with the office of the probate judge and with law enforcement agencies.
2. Retains a cooperative working relationship with community and social agencies.
3. Consults with students' previous counselors in order to utilize valuable knowledge and expertise of former counselors.
4. Maintains a close and cooperative relationship with the admission counselors of post-high school institutions.

Figure 15.2. Continued.

teachers, parents, students, and other relevant groups to develop their further understanding of the guidance program and the role of the counselor.[5] The role description should also be utilized by the administrator in discussions with the guidance department members on the extent to which the proposed role of the counselor is actually being implemented in the school and the degree to which improvement is needed.[6] For the administrator who is seeking direction on the role of the counselor in the school, the APGA policy statement should provide a valuable blueprint for bringing about desired change.*

THE ADMINISTRATOR'S ROLE IN THE COUNSELING AND GUIDANCE PROGRAM

Although in many schools the position of guidance director[7] has been created in order to accomplish certain administrative functions in relation to the counseling and guidance program, the school administrator is still responsible for providing overall leadership and administration to the program at the building level.

---

*Separate role descriptions have been developed for the elementary school counselor and for the middle/junior high counselor. An examination of these descriptions suggests that, for the most part, differences between them and the proposed role in figure 15.2 appear to be a matter of degree rather than of kind; therefore, the elementary and junior high roles are not presented in this section. Anyone who wishes more information on these two roles should refer to *Elementary School Guidance and Counseling*, March 1974 issue.

The leadership dimension of the administrator's role includes such responsibilities as: [8]

1. Assisting counselors to remove obstacles to the effective performance of their job, and helping them to utilize their specialized talents for improving education in the school.
2. Working with counselors to increase their awareness of unmet guidance needs of students, teachers, and parents; stimulating counselors to develop greater vision and creativity as to how these needs might be met.
3. Developing on the part of students, teachers, and parents a better understanding of the guidance program and the role of the counselor, and how these groups can best relate to that program and role.
4. Helping counselors to evaluate themselves and the guidance program on a regular basis in order to obtain information on effectiveness and to identify areas which are in need of improvement.

These are leadership functions which the building administrator should share with the guidance director, if the latter position has been established. However, the guidance director is frequently a counselor who may have little released time or professional training for carrying out the leadership functions identified above.* Therefore, in many cases the administrator may need to assume a leadership role relative to the counseling and guidance program, even if a guidance director is available.

Aside from the leadership dimension of the administrator's role in the counseling and guidance program, there are administrative responsibilities that he must perform in order for the program to be established and maintained at an appropriate level of effectiveness. These responsibilities include providing (1) sufficient and appropriately located office space, (2) an adequate budget for supplies, occupational and educational information, testing, and professional activities, (3) sufficient secretarial assistance, and (4) a reasonable counselor-student ratio. Of course, the definition of "sufficient," "appropriate," and "reasonable" will depend on local needs and conditions. However, the administrator should try to meet the standards covering these four areas of responsibility as recommended by authorities in the guidance field.

Recommended Standards: Office Space [9]

- Counselors' offices should be located near the main traffic patterns of students and be visible to the student body.
- Each counselor should be provided with an individual private office which will comfortably accommodate a desk, chair, two files, and two or three

---

*In larger school systems the likelihood is greater that the guidance director's job will be a full-time one. See Julian L. Biggers and David J. Mangusse, "The Work of the Guidance Administrator," *Counselor Education and Supervision* 12 (December 1972):130-36.

side chairs. The door to the office may have a window, but the window should be equipped with a curtain or shade to provide privacy.
- Counselors' offices should be made as soundproof as possible, in order to facilitate quiet, private discussions.
- Counselors' offices should be adjacent to one another in order to permit easy interaction among counselors, but arranged so that the traffic pattern does not become disruptive.
- There should be a reception area for the counseling suite, large enough to accommodate students waiting for their conference; one or two secretaries; departmental files; and a browsing area for students interested in reading occupational or educational information.
- There should be readily accessible facilities available for group guidance activities and for individual testing of students.

Recommended Standards: Budget, Supplies and Related Items

Different needs and financial factors make specific budget recommendations unrealistic. However, a few general recommendations can be offered: [10]
- A beginning or relatively new counseling and guidance program will need a proportionately larger budget than a well-established one.
- The larger the number of students served by the counseling and guidance program, the larger should be the budget.
- Within the total counseling and guidance budget the administrator should make sure that there are sufficient funds for the purchase of supplies, vocational and informational materials, tests, and for professional development.[11]

Recommended Standards: Secretarial Assistance

- There should be at least one full-time secretary for every three counselors in the department. Counselors engage in considerable correspondence which, along with general filing and conference notes, needs to be typed, thereby necessitating secretarial assistance. It is poor utilization of professional personnel to require a counselor to engage in these activities.
- A full-time receptionist should be employed for the counseling and guidance department in schools with an enrollment of 800 or more. Although one might think that a secretary could serve as receptionist, the two tasks are usually too demanding for a department with a thriving program. The receptionist may be expected to do some general clerical tasks along with making appointments, answering the telephone, and greeting people, but should not be given the major secretarial responsibilities.

Recommended Standards: Counselor-Pupil Ratio[12]

- The counselor-pupil ratio should be one full-time counselor for every 250 students.

- Experienced counselors might carry a higher counselor-student ratio; beginning counselors should probably be assigned a lower counselor-student ratio.
- Counselors whose clientele includes a higher proportion of behavioral and psychological problems should be assigned fewer students than the other counselors.

While the standards enumerated above represent the thinking of many authorities in the guidance field, it is recognized that the administrator may not always be able to implement or reach these objectives. Nevertheless, he should be striving toward these professional standards. For if the administrator lacks the professional vision of and deep commitment to providing the leadership and conditions necessary for a quality counseling and guidance program, such a program is unlikely ever to be achieved.

ISSUES AND PROBLEMS

The counseling and guidance program, like any other program in the school, is confronted periodically by issues and problems which, if not resolved, can reduce its effectiveness. The following three issues or problems seem common to many schools' counseling and guidance programs.[13]

1. The role of the counselor in resolving student discipline problems.

This is an issue which periodically causes friction in many schools. Students who misbehave usually need help, and there is a belief on the part of many administrators that the specialized skills of the counselor should be utilized to help these students change their attitude and behavior.

Most counselors, on the other hand, seem to feel that they should not be involved at all in working with discipline problems, at least not immediately after the student has engaged in misbehavior. Their position is that they are not "disciplinarians" and any association with a student who is a behavioral problem would tend to give them the image of administrators rather than of counselors, thereby making it more difficult to work with other kinds of students.[14]

It is in many respects unfortunate when the question of counselor involvement in helping to reduce student misbehavior becomes an issue or a problem in a school. In the first place, counselors should never be given the responsibility of disciplining students. That type of involvement is inconsistent with the role of the counselor and is a function which should be performed by the administration of the school. Neither should teachers and administrators refer for counseling any students who have *just* engaged in misbehavior. A referral to the counselor at that point is inappropriate and will make it unnecessarily difficult for him to work with the student later.

On the other hand, a counselor can and should be expected to contribute his specialized expertise so that misbehaving students can better understand themselves and the consequences of their behavior. Through individual diagnosis, counseling, and other guidance techniques, the counselor should also be able to help a student to develop a more positive attitude about himself and others, and ultimately to become a better school citizen.[15]

But the means by which the counselor and the student come together and the timing of their first conference are key factors to the success of this approach. If the counselor is to work with a misbehaving student in the manner indicated, then he or the student should be the one to initiate the conference, and it should not occur while the student is still subject to disciplinary proceedings. If a teacher or an administrator refers a student to a counselor and the conference takes place while the student is being considered for disciplinary action by that same teacher or administrator, there is a real danger that, in the eyes of the student, the counselor could easily become implicated in the disciplinary proceeding. In order for a counselor to work effectively with student misbehavior cases, his involvement needs to be separated as much as possible from the school's disciplinary measures.

There is little doubt that counselors can play an important role in assisting students who have behavioral problems. Failure to utilize counselors to help these kinds of students would mean that a valuable resource would go untapped. But the administrator needs to recognize that many counselors object to working with student behavior problems, because of their counseling philosophy or due to negative experience in the past. So unless the administrator, in conjunction with the counselors in the school, develops sensible policies and procedures for counselor involvement in working with student behavioral problems, a major issue or conflict may occur.

2. The role of the teacher in the counseling and guidance program.

Before formal counseling and guidance programs were introduced, the classroom teacher was expected to perform many guidance functions. Now, in most schools, the guidance role of the teacher is minimized and this responsibility is considered to be the province of the counselor and the guidance department. For example, many counselors appear to believe that teachers lack the specialized training and skills to play an important role in the counseling and guidance program.[16] Seemingly supporting this contention are many teachers who appear to feel that counseling and guidance is somehow separate from teaching, and that the school's formal counseling and guidance program obviates the need for them to become involved.[17]

In spite of limited support for the guidance role of the teacher, it would seem that the classroom teacher could make a valuable contribution to the total counseling and guidance program, and his resources should be organized by the administrator in such a way that they can be utilized by the guidance department for the good of the student. Specifically, the classroom teacher can and should be expected to perform the following counseling and guidance functions:[18]

   a. Study the individual student and become more aware of his needs, problems, and characteristics.

   b. Counsel with students on educational problems and, when sought out by students, on minor personal problems.

   c. Refer to counselors any students with social, personal, and vocational problems.

   d. Administer appropriate measurement instruments, e.g., standardized tests, to ascertain students' strengths and limitations.

   e. Utilize data from the school's testing program, the cumulative record, and suggestions from counselors in modifying the instructional and curricular program to meet the needs of students more adequately.

   f. Interact on a regular basis with counselors for the purpose of pooling perceptions and knowledge about students and about how they might be helped to improve.

In many schools, the question of the extent to which teachers should be involved in the counseling and guidance program has not been satisfactorily resolved. Obviously, teachers have other responsibilities, and many teachers don't possess a great deal of time or inclination for performing guidance functions. However, teachers can make a valuable contribution to the guidance program, particularly in the area of helping special education students, and it is the responsibility of the school administrator to help teachers better understand and accept their guidance role and to remove the obstacles to their carrying out that role effectively.

   3. **The role of the administrator in the evaluation of the counseling and guidance program.**

Evaluation of the performance of the school counselor and the effectiveness of the counseling and guidance program can present a problem. If the administrator tries to initiate evaluation procedures, he may encounter resistance. The counselors may infer that the administrator feels dissatisfied with their work, and may then become defensive. Or they may be opposed to any type of evaluation other than informal self-assessment.

Compounding these problems is the fact that much of the counselors' work is not conducive to evaluation. Counseling takes place privately and the nature of the conference is usually kept confidential. Also, many of the outcomes of counseling and guidance, particularly in the area of vocational guidance, may not be realized until the students have graduated from school.

In spite of these problems, however, the school administrator has a responsibility to evaluate all personnel and programs, including the counselors and the counseling and guidance program.* However, to carry out this responsibility effectively the administrator will need to be aware of the problems which may be associated with evaluation of counselors and the guidance program, and he will need to move cautiously and cooperatively with the counselors in developing evaluation criteria and procedures.[19]

PSYCHOLOGICAL, SOCIAL, AND HEALTH SERVICES †

Although in many schools the counseling and guidance services may represent the total pupil services program, a comprehensive program will also include psychological, social, and health services. These services are performed by the school psychologist, the school social worker, and the school nurse respectively, all of whom can offer specialized assistance to students, teachers, parents, and the administration, beyond that contributed by the school counselor.

The assistance which these other members of the pupil services team can offer a school is potentially of great value (particularly in regard to the growing concern about the needs of special education students), but that potential is frequently not achieved. Part of the problem lies in an inadequate understanding by administrators and teachers of the role of these pupil personnel specialists. A second important factor, though, is the way these services are organized and delivered. This section will attempt to develop a better understanding on the part of the school administrator of the role of the school psychologist, the school social worker, and the school nurse. Problems involved in the organization and delivery of their services will also be discussed.

THE SCHOOL PSYCHOLOGIST

Many school districts employ a school psychologist. He typically works out of the district's central office and divides his time among several schools. He may or may not be assigned a permanent office in each school building, and his schedule usually varies from week to week, depending upon the problems and needs of the schools with which he works. His role may be specifically defined and understood by the groups who could utilize his service, but this

*One approach (referred to as "results management") which merits investigation by the administrator interested in counselor evaluation, is described in ERIC Report Ed-086-914, "Progress Report: Pupil Personnel Services," 1973. This type of approach is described later in the chapter.

† It is recognized that there are other aspects to pupil personnel services in the schools, such as speech services. However, only those services most frequently offered at the building level are emphasized in this section.

specificity is frequently not the case. In too many schools the role of the school psychologist is not well defined, and certainly is not well understood by the school administrator. This is inexcusable, since there are excellent statements on the role of the school psychologist which, if studied and implemented by the school administrator and the staff, would help the school psychologist to achieve more of his potential usefulness to the school.

One such role description which merits review by the school administrator is presented in figure 15.3.

As the role description in figure 15.3 indicates, the school psychologist should be involved in a wide range of diagnostic, counseling, and program consulting activities. His services should be utilized by students, teachers, parents, and administrators.[20]

It should be noted, however, that whether or not his proposed role is actually implemented fully will probably depend as much on a clear and complete understanding of that role by the administrator as on any other factor.[21] If the administrator understands the role of the school psychologist and is committed to helping him fulfill that role, the potential for his making an important contribution to the school is more apt to be realized. If, on the other hand, the administrator possesses an inadequate understanding of this role or is not committed to helping the psychologist carry out his role, it is unlikely that he can operate effectively. In the final analysis, the administrator holds an important key to the psychologist's success in a school.

---

1. Counsels with individual students who are self-referred or referred by teachers, administrators, or community agencies, to help them develop behavior patterns and attitudes which are appropriate to students' environmental and developmental stages.
2. Gathers sufficient information from previous records and through observation and assessment, to determine how a student can best be helped.
3. Assists the school staff to develop criteria and referral procedures for identifying students who need the services of the school psychologist.
4. Assists teachers, administrators, and parents to develop a greater understanding of student behavior, and to create a special climate in the school which maximizes learning and personal growth for the student.
5. Consults with teachers, curriculum specialists, and administrators on possible ways to improve conditions necessary for effective student learning.
6. Encourages teachers and other professional educators to accept responsibility/accountability for (and to help students accept responsibility for) growth toward predetermined goals.
7. Identifies and utilizes remedial/corrective resources available within the school or community.
8. Serves as a liaison between school and community.

Figure 15.3. Role of the School Psychologist.[22]

THE SCHOOL SOCIAL WORKER

The school social worker's employment situation and work schedule are similar to that of the school psychologist in many respects. The social worker usually works out of the district's central office, dividing his time among several schools. His work schedule may vary from week to week, and he is viewed by many as a primary liaison between the school and the home. [23] His specific function is to provide assistance to "children who are having difficulties in using the resources of the school effectively." [24] The nature of his responsibility to the school can be conceived of as "a specialized service involving home and school case work with a minority of pupils whose school problems are primarily affected by family and neighborhood conditions." [25]

As with the school psychologist, the social worker's effectiveness has been hampered in many school systems by a poorly defined and poorly understood role. To partially remedy this problem a proposed role for the school social worker is outlined in figure 15.4 for the administrator's consideration.

---

1. Counsels with parents and students on problems of student adjustment to school.
2. Utilizes community resources in the process of working with children and parents.
3. Consults with staff members concerning community factors which may be affecting problems of student adjustment in school.
4. Collaborates with teachers, administrators, and noninstructional personnel in gathering and sharing information about students, designed to modify or resolve student adjustment problems.
5. Acts as liaison between the school and community agencies.
6. Cooperates with community agencies by providing pertinent information about a student's school adjustment and achievement.

Figure 15.4. Functions of the
School Social Worker. [26]

The proposed role described in figure 15.4 suggests that the school social worker can perform a variety of useful services for students, teachers, parents, and administrators that can, in turn, help all groups understand and capitalize on the contribution that the home and the school together can make to the educating of the student. Again, whether these services are fully and properly utilized will depend to a great degree on the school administrator. [27]   Given a school administrator who understands and is committed to implementing the role proposed in figure 15.4, the influence of the school social worker should be a significant one.

HEALTH SERVICES

The importance of providing health services in the schools has long been recognized in education, but the implementation of a program to that end has frequently been limited. Although the extent and quality of health services in the schools varies widely throughout the country, thereby making generalization difficult, the program in many school districts consists of no more than a part-time nurse whose time is divided among several schools, with perhaps only 1 1/2 days per week spent at each one.

The primary function of school health services is to assess and diagnose the health status of students in the school, and to work with teachers, parents, administrators, and others to promote better student health habits and practices. [28] The personnel for staffing a comprehensive school health services program should include a nurse, a physician, and a dental hygienist. Whether these personnel are employed full-time or part-time will depend on the size of the school or school district, availability of personnel, and—most importantly—the concept held by the educators of the district in regard to the role of each of these specialized workers.

Since the school administrator is, in most situations, more likely to have contact with the nurse than with any of the other health personnel, an understanding of the nurse's role is essential. Figure 15.5 presents a proposed role for the school nurse which defines the nature of his services.

---

1. Assesses and evaluates the health and developmental status of students in order to identify those who should be referred for medical diagnosis or treatment.
2. Interprets the health and developmental status of the pupil to him, his parents, and school personnel.
3. Interprets the results of medical findings concerning the pupil to him, his parents, and school personnel.
4. Counsels the pupil, his parents, and school personnel regarding plans for eliminating, minimizing, or accepting a health problem that interferes with his effective learning.
5. Motivates and guides the persons responsible for pupil health to appropriate resources.
6. Recommends to the administration modifications in the educational program when indicated by the health or developmental status of the pupil.
7. Serves as health consultant and resource person in the health instruction curriculum by providing current scientific information from related fields.
8. Uses direct health services as a vehicle for health counseling.
9. Serves as liaison among the parents, school, and community in health matters.
10. Serves as member of the placement committee for special education programs.

Figure 15.5. Role of the School Nurse. [30]

In recent years the health problems of students have increased dramatically. Drug involvement, venereal disease, nutritional imbalance, obesity, adolescent pregnancy, dental decay, and other problems all strongly point to the need for a full-time nurse and a comprehensive health services program in the schools. [29] The program should probably emphasize referral rather than treatment, and it should help students experiencing health problems to secure proper medical assistance.

Administrators need to recognize that the condition of a student's health affects his educational motivation and performance in school. The school nurse and other health services personnel can and should play an important role in helping a school to ameliorate students' health problems.

ADMINISTRATOR RESPONSIBILITIES

Unlike the guidance counselor, the other members of the pupil-services team are typically part-time workers in a school. They divide their time among several schools, and their work schedule is sometimes unpredictable. The part-time nature of their assignment in any particular school frequently results in their not being considered as regular members of the school faculty. Therefore, when it comes to office space, secretarial help, and a budget for materials and supplies, the school psychologist, the social worker, and (to a lesser extent) the school nurse are likely to be left to shift for themselves. [31] They may be able to rely on some secretarial help and budget assistance from the district office, but the support from that source may not be sufficient to meet their needs.

At the minimum, the school administrator is responsible for making sure that each of the pupil services specialists working in the building has an office, which may be shared with someone else but which should be available when the specialist needs it. It should be equipped with a file (which should not be shared), a desk, and sufficient side chairs so that the specialist may expeditiously proceed with his work. The administrator should also make available to each of the pupil personnel specialists sufficient secretarial assistance to supplement the clerical support provided at the central office. Reports and much of the correspondence can more easily be prepared at the school than at the district office. In addition, provision should be made within the school budget for purchase of those supplies and materials necessary for the psychologist, social worker, and nurse to operate effectively. Perhaps the best approach would be for the administrator to think in terms of a total pupil services program and budget.

Although the psychological, social, and health services components of the pupil services program cannot succeed without the administrator's carrying out the administrative tasks previously identified, the most important responsibility for the administrator is to provide *leadership*. Whether psychological, social and health services are administered by someone at the central office or at the building level, the program will not be successful without the leadership of the building administrator. Specifically, his leadership responsibility includes the following:

A. Help the school psychologist, social worker, and health workers to develop a better understanding of their roles and functions on the part of students, teachers, and parents. The functions and roles of these pupil services specialists are poorly understood in many schools. The building administrator who is willing to help develop an understanding on the part of others about these specialists' contributions to the school will do much to increase the effectiveness of the pupil services program.

B. Work with pupil services specialists to increase their awareness of the unmet psychological, social, and health needs of students, and stimulate the development of greater vision about how these needs might be met.

C. Work with pupil services specialists, guidance counselors, and other faculty members to help these groups see how they can work together more cooperatively and productively.

D. Assist each of the pupil personnel specialists to evaluate his own effectiveness and the overall usefulness of the pupil services program.

ISSUES AND PROBLEMS

The administrator needs to be aware of four major problems or issues that are associated with the delivery of psychological, social, and health services to the school. These are (1) inaccessibility, (2) underutilization, (3) inadequate coordination, and (4) difficulty of supervision.*

Inaccessibility

Because the psychologist, social worker, and nurse are usually part-time members of a school staff and have somewhat unpredictable work schedules, they are often not available to students, teachers, parents, or administrators when a problem arises. However, a person who is experiencing trouble frequently needs help immediately, or at least during the same day, and doesn't want to be told to wait until the next day or later in the week when the

---

*These problems or issues were identified by the writer in an interview survey of principals, teachers, and pupil personnel services specialists.

pupil services specialist is scheduled to arrive at the school. Although it is true that the pupil services specialist might be called to the school in response to a problem (if he can be located at another school or at his office in the central administration building), such calls are not generally made unless an extreme emergency exists. Consequently, in the eyes of many students, teachers, and administrators, the limited accessibility of part-time pupil services workers poses a restriction which severely hampers the effectiveness of the program.

The ideal solution to this problem would be the full-time assignment of a school psychologist, social worker, and nurse to each school. While an argument could be made that there is sufficient work for these specialists, even in a small school, financial considerations and a limited vision of their potential contribution often rule out this possibility. Certain steps, though, should be taken by an administrator to alleviate the inaccessibility problem.

1. The administrator should try to secure from each of the part-time pupil personnel specialists a commitment to an established work schedule at the school. In too many situations these specialists do not keep any scheduled office hours at a school and, as a result, others at the school do not know when their services are available. There may, of course, be times when a pupil services specialist will not be able to keep his office hours because of an emergency at another school. But generally it should be possible for all of the specialists to identify at the beginning of the year the hours when they will be at each school to make their services available.

2. The administrator should ascertain from each of the part-time specialists what their work schedule will be when they are not at the school so that they can be reached if an emergency arises. This information may be difficult to obtain because the pupil services specialist may not have his work schedule well organized, or he may be apprehensive that the information may be used for monitoring his performance. However, in spite of any resistance the administrator may receive when he seeks this information, he has an obligation to find out where the pupil services specialists are most likely to be located when they are not in the school.

3. The administrator should communicate at the beginning of the year to students, parents, and teachers the work schedule of the part-time pupil services personnel at the school and indicate the procedures to follow in order to reach these specialists at other times. If people in the school are to utilize the services of the pupil personnel specialists, then the schedule of their availability should be made common knowledge. And it is the administrator's responsibility to see that this information is communicated.

Underutilization

Judging from observation and comments by administrators and teachers, the services of the psychologist, social worker, and perhaps the nurse, are not being utilized to the extent that one might hope and expect. Many problems are not referred to these specialists simply because students, teachers, and administrators do not perceive that the specialists can be of any help, or because they are not sure how to work with them. Part of the problem lies in an inadequate understanding about the role of pupil services specialists and what services they can provide. The administrator can help ameliorate this problem by becoming better informed about the role of each of the pupil services specialists. But beyond that, he should take the initiative in helping the pupil services specialists to develop a better understanding of their role on the part of other people in the school.

The administrator will probably also need to take a look at the school's referral procedures to these specialists. Referral procedures represent the main mechanism for utilizing the services of the pupil personnel specialists. So if the referral procedures are inadequate or unclear, utilization of the pupil personnel specialists will be limited. In essence, a school's referral procedures should include the following characteristics:

1. The types of problems which can be referred to either the psychologist, the social worker, or the nurse should be explicitly defined to the school staff.
2. The person who makes the referral should be asked to state briefly the nature of the problem and his perception of its causes.
3. The faculty should know when the pupil services specialist will be at the school to receive the referral.
4. After the referral is received, there should be a preliminary conference between the individual submitting the referral and the pupil services specialist to determine the best plan of action for coordinating efforts.
5. An initial progress report by the pupil services specialist should be made within a week to the person who submitted the referral; a more complete report should be provided by the end of the semester during which the referral was initiated.

A referral form which incorporates most of these characteristics is presented in the chapter on student discipline and attendance problems.

Inadequate Coordination

Inadequate coordination of services is frequently a problem when two or more specialists are working with the same client. This problem is particularly prevalent in the pupil services program. All too often the psychologist, the social worker, the nurse, and the guidance counselor work independently, each specialist "doing his thing," with little or no attempt to coordinate efforts in a unified approach.

Although each of the pupil services specialists can make an independent contribution to the school, their efforts would be significantly strengthened through a coordinated, collaborative approach to delivering pupil services. [32] Methods for developing such an approach could include organizing the various specialists into a pupil services team, appointing someone to coordinate the efforts of the team at the building level (perhaps the guidance director), establishing regular meetings of the team to focus on collaborative efforts and using the case conference procedure in working with students who have problems. This type of an approach is especially appropriate for diagnosing and working with special education students.

It should be noted that the pupil services specialists may not be inclined or able to develop the team approach without administrative assistance. They may be used to working independently and may not see the need to work together in a collaborative effort. [33] Therefore, the administrator, himself, may need to take the initiative to organize the specialists into a pupil services team and appoint someone to lead that team.

It should be reemphasized that the administrator would do well to involve the pupil services specialists in developing the concept of the team and how it will function, if he desires their cooperation. The idea of the team should not be imposed on its members. They may harbor mixed feelings about its merits, having previously worked independently. [34] Those pupil services specialists who work out of the central office and spend only part-time in a particular building may also resist the notion of someone at the building level heading their team. It would be advisable, in this regard, for the administrator to define the main responsibility of the team leader as that of coordination rather than supervision. If the right team leader is chosen, he should be able to exercise supervisory responsibilities informally.

Once the team concept has been accepted, the team organized, and a leader appointed, then the scheduling of periodic meetings becomes important. [35] Finding a time when everyone can be at the meetings will be a difficult task for a team primarily composed of part-time specialists with different work schedules. However, despite the problems that may be involved, the administrator should insist that the team meet at least monthly and more often as the need arises. A team cannot function effectively unless it meets often enough to develop a common frame of reference and cooperative efforts in problem solving. A good way for the administrator to keep himself informed of the operation of the team is to request that its leader provide the administrator with a copy of the agenda and minutes for all team meetings. This procedure should result not only in the administrator's becoming better informed of the functioning of the pupil services team, but may also cause the team leader to become better organized if he knows that this kind of information is expected.

An important team activity which the administrator should try to promote on the part of the pupil services specialists is the case conference. The case conference can be described as a meeting at which the various pupil services specialists, with relevant others, try to understand the problems of a particular student by examining the perceptions and data which each can contribute about the student. By utilizing and pooling the information and expertise of all appropriate parties, an insight into the student's problem and a possible resolution for it may be obtained—perhaps not possible had only one of the specialists been working with the student independently.

Most pupil services specialists know about the case conference method, but because it requires someone to take the initiative to organize the conference, it is not used often enough. In order to promote its use, the administrator might assign his pupil services team leader the responsibility for organizing such meetings and then request that the team leader report to him each semester about how many case conferences were held, and with what success.

Since tradition, current practice, and the varied work schedules of the pupil services specialists all mitigate against a coordinated, collaborative team approach, it will take considerable vision, commitment, and human relations skills on the part of the administrator to achieve this goal. However, there is little doubt that such an approach is necessary for a totally effective pupil personnel program.

Supervision Difficulty

Perhaps the most perplexing problem for the school administrator in regard to the pupil services specialists is how best to supervise them. The problem is three-fold. First of all, each of the pupil services workers possesses specialized knowledge and skills which most administrators have not acquired and probably would have difficulty obtaining. The problems involved in trying to supervise personnel who perform tasks for which the supervisor himself is not proficient is readily apparent to all who have been in such a situation.

Secondly, the work performed by pupil services specialists is typically not visible to the administrator since it is frequently carried out in privacy. This aspect of the problem is further compounded by the part-time nature of the specialists' work schedules.

Thirdly, the pupil services specialists probably perceive their superior in the district office as their only "legitimate" supervisor and may resist efforts by anyone at the building level to supervise them.

This set of problems has tended in many schools to result in little or no building-level supervision of pupil services specialists. Of course, some supervision of these specialists is conducted by their superiors at the district level. But the latter individuals' concept of supervision may be limited, or they may be "spread too thin" by reason of the considerable number of people they have to supervise. Therefore, it would appear that if the pupil services specialists are to be supervised at the building level, the school administrator himself will have to design a system to accomplish the task.

Since the administrator is not an expert in pupil services and is involved with many other kinds of supervisory responsibilities, his best approach with the pupil services specialists may be to establish a system of "supervision by objectives." [36] This system of supervision would include the following steps:

1. Each pupil services specialist would be asked at the beginning of every semester to identify the objectives he hoped to achieve while working at the school. Proposed objectives might be requested for the areas of students, teachers, parents, and collaborative efforts. Objectives could be up-dated during the semester as a result of new developments.
2. At the end of each semester all pupil services specialists would prepare and submit a short report indicating the progress which had been made in achieving the previously proposed objectives, the evidence for such progress, and the problems which were encountered in trying to achieve the objectives.*
3. After the report is read by the administrator, he would meet with each pupil services specialist to review its contents and discuss the need for improvement. The report could be a vehicle for initiating follow-up supervisory activities.

In light of the problems previously discussed, it is unlikely that an administrator can or should engage in direct supervision of pupil services specialists. But he should institute a system of supervision which would help the specialist to evaluate his own performance and, at the same time, keep the administrator better informed of that performance. The supervision by objectives approach to supervision is such a system.

Review

1. Define the primary purpose of the pupil personnel services program and the counseling and guidance program.
2. Identify the kinds of services that the counseling and guidance program can provide to those groups who are associated with the school. What is the role of the administrator in developing appropriate use of those services?

*For a good example of how this can be done, see Charles T. Dykstra, "Accountability: The Monthly and Yearly Guidance Report," *School Counselor* 21 (November 1973):151-53.

3. How should the school administrator make use of the counselor role description developed by the American Personnel and Guidance Association?
4. In what ways can the administrator make a leadership and an administrative contribution to the counseling and guidance program?
5. What are three major issues or problems that are frequently associated with the counseling and guidance program? How can the administrator best prevent or ameliorate these problems?
6. In what ways can the administrator make a leadership and an administrative contribution to improving the psychological, social, and health services of the school?
7. Describe the major issues and problems that frequently are associated with the psychological, social, and health services of the school. How can the administrator best prevent or ameliorate these problems?

Notes

1. Bruce R. Amble and Richard W. Bradley, *Pupils As Persons* (New York: Intext Educational Publishers, 1973), p. 10.

2. American School Counselor Association, *Proposed Statement of Policy for Secondary School Counselors* (Washington, D.C.: American School Counselor Association, 1964), p. 4.

3. Figure 15.1 was developed from an extraction and synthesis of statements contained in *Policy for Secondary School Counselors* (Washington, D.C.: American School Counselors Association, 1964); and *The Development and Management of School Guidance Programs* by Robert L. Gibson et al. (Dubuque, Iowa: Wm. C. Brown Company Publishers, 1973), pp. 73-81.

4. "The Role of the Secondary School Counselor," *School Counselor* 21 (May 1974):380-86.

5. For examples of how this can be done, see *Promising Practices in School Counselor Role Communications* (Madison, Wis.: Wisconsin Department of Public Instruction, 1970).

6. For an example of the process one school utilized to redefine the role of its counselor, see Jane Bebb, "A Model High School Counseling Program." An ERIC Report: Ed-061-546, 1972.

7. For those who are interested in a good discussion of this position, see Herman J. Peters and Bruce Shertzer, *Guidance Program Development and Management* (Columbus, Ohio: Charles E. Merrill Publishing Co., 1969), pp. 144-46.

8. For an excellent monograph which describes the administrator's responsibilities in detail, see William A. Matthes and Robert Frank, "Strategies for Implementation of Guidance in the Elementary School." An ERIC Report: Ed-048-602, 1970, pp. 187-216.

9. For additional details on guidance facilities, see Don Twiford, ed., *Physical Facilities for School Guidance Services* (Washington, D.C.: U.S. Department of Health, Education and Welfare, Office of Education, OE-25013).

10. Herman J. Peters and Bruce Shertzer, *Guidance Program Development,* pp. 144-46.

11. Joseph W. Hollis and Lucile U. Hollis, *Organizing for Effective Guidance* (Chicago: Science Research Associates, 1965), p. 259.

12. For a review of recommendations on this topic and practical suggestions for lowering the counselor-pupil ratio, see Julian L. Biggers, "The Counselor Utilization Index," *School Counselor* 19 (November 1971):120-22.

13. For a description of some of the other problems associated with the counseling and guidance program, see John D. Swisher, "Counselors in Conflict," *School Counselor* 17 (March 1970), pp. 272-79. Also see J. D. Killian, "The Law, the Counselor, and Student Records,"

Personnel and Guidance Journal 48 (1970):423-32; and E. V. Daubner and Edith S. Daubner, "Ethics and Counseling Decisions," *Personnel and Guidance Journal* 48 (1970):433-42.

14. For an excellent discussion of the problem, see David J. Armor, *The American School Counselor* (New York: Russell Sage Foundation, 1969), pp. 109-16.

15. For an example of how this can be done, see T. E. Long, "A Challenge—Counseling High School Disciplinary Cases," *National Catholic Guidance Journal* 15 (1971):100-105.

16. See Stanley B. Escott, "The Counselor Teacher Relationship," *School Counselor* 11 (May 1964):215-20.

17. Armor, *American School Counselor*, pp. 116-19.

18. For an example of how one school involved the teacher in the guidance program, see Hal Simons and Dan Davies, "The Counselor as Consultant in the Development of the Teacher-Adviser Concept in Guidance." An ERIC Report: Ed-057-385, 1971. See also Edgar G. Johnson et al., *The Role of the Teacher in Guidance* (Englewood Cliffs, N.J.: Prentice-Hall, 1959).

19. For an excellent presentation of the evaluation process along with specific recommendations on evaluating a guidance program, see Dale G. Anderson et al., "Guidelines for Evaluation of Counseling and Guidance Programs." An ERIC Report: Ed-049-480, 1967. Other ideas are presented by Mary Jane Kidder in "Searchlight: Relevant Resources in High Interest Areas—Program Evaluation and Accountability." An ERIC Report: Ed-061-569, 1971. Also see Percy Sillin, "Evaluating an Elementary Guidance Program," *Guidance Clinic*, September 1973, pp. 7-10.

20. Robert D. Roberts, "Perceptions of Actual and Desired Role Functions of School Psychologists by Psychologists and Teachers," *Psychology in the School* VII (1970):175-78.

21. T. N. Clair and R. Klausmeier, "Dissatisfaction of Practicing School Psychologists with Their Profession," *Contemporary Education* 44 (October 1972):20-23.

22. Adapted from *Guidelines for Training Programs in School Psychology* (Washington, D.C.: National Association of School Psychologists, 1972), pp. 27-34; and Dean L. Hummel and S. J. Bonham, Jr., *Pupil Personnel Services in Schools: Organization and Coordination* (Chicago: Rand McNally & Co., 1968), pp. 157-58.

23. Herman J. Peters and Gail F. Farwell, *Guidance: A Developmental Approach* (Chicago: Rand McNally & Co., 1959), p. 421.

24. John C. Nebo, *Administration of School Social Work* (New York: National Association of Social Workers, 1960), p. 17.

25. Robert H. Mathewson, *Guidance Policy and Practice*, 3d ed. (New York: Harper & Row Publishers, 1962), p. 197.

26. Adapted from Charles Guzzetta, *School Social Work Leadership in the 1970's* (Tallahassee, Fla.: State University System of Florida, 1973), pp. 14-26; and Edward F. DeRoche, "Responsibilities of the School Social Worker," *Elementary School Principal* 43 (April 1964):50-52.

27. D. Benjamin and Z. Chapin, "The Principal and the Social Worker," *Educational Forum* 34 (November 1969):99-103.

28. Charles C. Wilson, *School Health Services* (Washington, D.C.: National Education Association and American Medical Association, 1964).

29. Marion J. Owen and Linda Sanders, "The School Nurse—A Job Description," in *Guidelines for Pupil Services* 11, no. 2 (Madison, Wis.: Department of Public Instruction, (February 1973), p. 61.

30. Lotta C. Ford, "The School Nurse Role—A Changing Concept in Preparation and Practice," *Journal of School Health* 40 (January 1970):21-24.

31. See, for example, Clair and Klausmeier, "Dissatisfaction of Practicing School Psychologists."

32. For an extended description of this approach, see Mary A. Sarvis and Marianne Pennekamp, *Collaboration in School Guidance: A Creative Approach to Pupil Personnel Work* (New York City: Brunner/Mazel, 1970).

33. The difficulties encountered by the members of a pupil services team in cooperating with each other and with the other professionals of the school are vividly described in Barbara K Thomas, "Collaboration of Pupil Services and Instructional Personnel," *Journal of School Psychology* 10 (March 1972):83-87.

34. See the following article on the problems which a pupil personnel services team may encounter: Richard J. Anderson, "Teamwork in Pupil Personnel Services: The Story of the 70's," *Journal of the International Association of Pupil Personnel Workers* 16 (March 1972):82-88.

35. For a good description of how a pupil services team can function, see Charles Sussman, "Guide to the Pupil Services Team Conference," *Journal of the International Association of Pupil Personnel Workers,* 17 (March 1973):75-87.

36. An example of this approach that was utilized with counselors (and could be adapted by other members of the pupil services team) may be found in a publication by Douglas S. Baugh, "Accountable Management for Effective Guidance Operation." An ERIC Report: Ed-058-588, 1971.

16

Administration of the
Student Activities Program

The student activities program, also referred to as the "extracurricular" or "cocurricular" program* has been an accepted part of American education for many years.[1] Initially introduced in only a few schools, in an attempt to provide for the recreational and athletic interests and needs of students, it is now an integral component of the total educational program in the vast majority of schools in the United States.[†]

While the overall responsibility for administering the student activities program is sometimes delegated to a student activities director, in most schools the building administrator is assigned this responsibility directly, and certainly is ultimately accountable. Therefore, it is extremely important for the school administrator to develop a comprehensive understanding of the various facets of the activities program so that it can be operated with efficiency and effectiveness. Included in this understanding should be knowledge about the objectives, scope, and organizational dimensions of the program, as well as its major problems. The administrator should also be knowledgeable about criteria and a plan for evaluating the program, because without regular assessment, improvement of the program is likely to be limited.

PURPOSE, OBJECTIVES AND SCOPE

The primary purpose of the student activities program should be to meet those school-related interests and needs of students which are not met—at least not to a sufficient degree—by the curricular program of the school.[2] The objectives of the student activities program may vary somewhat from school to school, depending on local conditions, but they should be logically related to the objectives of the overall educational program. Numerous statements of student activities objectives have been proposed during the

---

*The term, "student activities" will be used in this chapter, rather than the other terms, because in practice it seems to be the one which authorities prefer.

†Although some people may feel that the student activities program is or should be confined to the secondary school, the program has been recommended for the elementary school for some time. See Harry C. McKown, *Activities in the Elementary School* (New York: McGraw-Hill Book Co., Inc., 1938).

years, and an examination of these statements would suggest that the objectives of the program should be [3]

1. to help all students to learn how to use their leisure time more wisely
2. to help all students to increase and use constructively whatever unique talents and skills they possess
3. to help all students to develop new avocational and recreational interests and skills
4. to help all students to develop a more positive attitude toward the value of avocational and recreational activities
5. to help all students to increase their knowledge of and skill in functioning as a leader and/or as a member of a group
6. to help all students to develop a more realistic and positive attitude toward themselves and others
7. to help all students to develop a more positive attitude toward school, as a result of participation in the student activities program.

The key word in the statement of each objective is the word "all." The student activities program should be for *all* students, not just the more active and talented students; and the objectives of the program should reflect this priority.[4] While it may not be possible in some situations for all students to participate in the activities program, total participation should remain the objective to which a school aspires. A school that aims at a higher objective than may seem attainable is ultimately likely to accomplish more than the one with more "practical" goals.

It should also be noted that the objectives listed above are stated so that the emphasis is on *helping* the students, not on just providing an opportunity for them.[5] A school should be responsible for *more* than just providing an opportunity for students; it should be responsible for helping students *reach* whatever objectives that opportunity is supposed to engender. Those objectives should include the development of certain student attitudes, as well as knowledge and skills. Perhaps the most important objectives of a school's student activities program should be the development of a more positive attitude on the part of the student toward himself, others, avocational and recreational activities, and toward school in general. These attitudinal objectives will undoubtedly be difficult for the school to achieve but, if attained, are likely to show great carry-over value into the student's adult life.

To achieve the knowledge, skill, and attitudinal objectives of the student activities program, the school will need to provide a comprehensive range of student activities which includes the kinds of offerings presented in figure 16.1.

The activities identified under each major category in figure 16.1 are illustrative of possible types of student activities.[6] Of course, different schools offer different kinds of activities, depending on the needs and in-

Student Government and Publications	Performance Groups	Clubs and Organizations	Intramurals Boys' and Girls'	Athletics Boys' and Girls'
Student Council	Dramatics	Chess Club	Bowling	Basketball
Student Newspaper	Instrumental	Photography Club	Golf	Swimming
Student Annual	Vocal	Literary Club	Ping Pong	Tennis
Others	Debate	French Club	Others	Others
	Others	Others		

Figure 16.1. Major Activities Included in a Comprehensive Student Activities Program.*

terests of the students, as well as other conditions. However, two factors which are extremely important are the *vision* and *commitment* of the administration and staff to a comprehensive student activities program. Unless the administration and staff of a school have the vision to develop comprehensive objectives for the total student activities program and the commitment to invest their own time and energy to achieve those objectives, the program will probably be limited in scope and in its impact on the student body.

The main purpose of a student activities program should be to meet students' interests and needs. Without the vision and commitment of the administration and the staff, this purpose cannot be achieved. It should be emphasized that the administrator is the one who is responsible for generating that vision and commitment on the part of the staff (if they do not already exist).

ORGANIZATIONAL DIMENSIONS

The emphasis thus far has been on the objectives and scope of the student activities program and on the vision and commitment of the administration and staff. However, if the program is to succeed, it must also be well organized. Good organization will not insure the success of a program, but without it a program is likely to flounder.

In organizing the student activities program the administrator should consider the following principles.

1. **Each activity, as well as the total program, should have well-defined, written objectives.** The importance of establishing objectives for the *total* stu-

*The extent of these activities will differ according to whether the school is elementary or secondary.

dent activities program has already been noted. It is equally important for the administrator to work with teachers and students to define the objectives of each activity *within* the program. Activities without objectives lack direction and meaning, and are difficult to evaluate in terms of their effectiveness.

In developing the objectives for each activity in the student activities program, the administrator should make sure that they are stated in the form of outcomes, i.e., increased knowledge, skill, attitude, or participation, rather than in terms of the number of meetings of the activity.[7] The important thing is not how many meetings of an activity occur, but what the activity contributes in terms of increased student participation, knowledge, skill, or attitude change.

2. **Each activity should be directed by a well-qualified, interested advisor.** It is recognized that this is easier said than achieved, and that it may be stating an unattainable ideal for certain activities. However, obtaining well-qualified, interested advisers for the various components of the student activities program should be the objective to which the administrator is committed. He should do everything within his power to achieve, or at least be working toward, that objective.

To a large extent, the adviser of an activity is the key to its success.[8] A competent, interested adviser can provide leadership and spark to a student activity; a poorly-qualified, apathetic adviser can ruin it. Even a moderately-qualified and interested adviser may not be able to provide the leadership necessary for an activity to blossom and grow. It is conceded that there are problems in securing competent, interested advisers, and this problem will be addressed later in the chapter.

3. **There should be a written role-description for each adviser, as well as a developmental in-service program to upgrade competencies.** Each adviser to a student activity should have a written role description specifying the qualifications and responsibilities of the position, and the individuals and groups to whom the adviser reports.[9] Such a role description will provide direction to the adviser and can serve as a basis for evaluating the effectiveness of his work. In the absence of this kind of a role description the advisers will have to create their own definition of their responsibilities, and an evaluation of their effectiveness by the administrator will become difficult.

A developmental in-service program to upgrade advisers' competencies is essential, particularly if the administrator has been less than completely successful in recruiting well-qualified advisers. It seems peculiar that in-service education is provided for almost every other type of need, but apparently it is assumed that student activities' advisers are all well-qualified and are never in need of updating their skills.

A developmental in-service program for student activities' advisers should include learning opportunities for improving their skill in planning and organizing activities, decision making, communication, leadership, group dynamics and program evaluation. The in-service program should also regularly provide opportunities for all the advisers to discuss problems and ideas, and to learn from each other.

The student activities' advisers also can benefit from the experiences and recommendations of experts outside of the school who are working in this field. Membership and participation in state and national associations of student activities' advisers are probably the best ways of acquiring this assistance. The administrator should assume the responsibility of encouraging and stimulating this kind of professional growth.

4. **There should be written role descriptions for the student officers of each activity, and an in-service program should be offered to help them improve their competencies.** In many schools the student activities program seems to be based on the implicit assumption that the students who are elected or appointed to office will already be familiar with all aspects of their job, and that they need no training to help them carry out their responsibilities effectively. Though there may be exceptions, in general this assumption is unwarranted.

Students are seldom familiar with the various responsibilities of the office to which they are elected or appointed, and they usually need on-the-job training. They should be provided with role descriptions which identify the qualifications and responsibilities of their positions, and with an in-service program which will help them improve their leadership skills.* Specifically, they need help in improving their knowledge and skills in planning and organizing activities, decision making, communication, leadership, group dynamics, and program evaluation. They also need to participate in state and national student activities' associations, and the school should see that the professional literature which is available from these associations is accessible to the students.†

5. **The various organizational meetings that are held as part of the student activities program should be well planned.** With the possible exception of performance groups, intramurals, and athletics, there are many organizational meetings held during the year by various student organizations. Since students and advisers are usually busy, these meetings are frequently not well planned.

---

*An example of the type of role description needed for *all* student officers can be found in *Profiles of Student Council Officers* (Washington, D.C.: The National Association of Secondary School Principals, 1974).

† For example, the Office of Student Activities of the National Association of Secondary School Principals conducts workshops and publishes material for students involved in the student activities program of their school. The school administrator should see to it that representative students have an opportunity to attend these workshops and to receive materials published by the NASSP Office of Student Activities.

However, if the meetings of an organization are to be successful, then thought and time must be devoted to planning them. This includes a planning session between the adviser and the officers prior to the meeting, and a written agenda sent to the members of the organization before the meeting so that thought can be given to what will be discussed. Written minutes of the main points discussed and the actions taken during each meeting should also be sent to all members of the organization so that continuity between meetings is increased. The minutes will maintain a public record during the year (and from year to year) on what the student organization is accomplishing. These are basic management procedures which to some may seem like "red tape" but, if constructively applied, should increase the productivity of student organizations' meetings.

6. **A complete, written description of the total student activities program should be disseminated to students and other appropriate parties at the beginning of each school year.** The student activities program is for the students, and if they are to participate wisely, they need as much information as possible about the various aspects of the program. Perhaps the best approach for a school would be to publish a student activities handbook. Included in the handbook should be a description of each student group's purposes, objectives, types of activities, qualifications for membership and holding office, as well as the adviser's name, and who should be contacted about membership, or for more information. [10]

This type of handbook could be very helpful to students in choosing their participation in the student activities program, and could provide a valuable source of information to the student advisers, the administration, and the rest of the professional staff. It should be noted that the handbook would need to be updated periodically. This process would take time, and the cost of issuing the booklet at the beginning of each year may not be a minor expense. However, if the school is committed to informing its students about all aspects of the student activities program, ways will be found to resolve these problems.

7. **There should be a director of student activities and a student teacher advisory council for the total program.**[11] In too many schools the student activities program is composed of numerous groups and organizations, each seemingly going its separate way with very little overall program planning, coordination, or direction. As a result, there are conflicts in philosophy, use of facilities, membership criteria, and allocation of funds.

What is needed is a student activities director to take charge of the overall program, with an advisory group that can work with this individual in establishing policy for the total program and resolving significant disputes between student groups. The director should be an administrator or a teacher with released time, and at least one-third of his time should be devoted to carrying out leadership responsibilities.

The activities director should chair the student activities advisory council and be responsible for calling meetings, stimulating discussion, and problem solving. The membership of the council should include representation from students, as well as from the activities advisors, and should function in an advisory capacity with the director. Through this kind of an organizational structure, better direction and coordination for the overall student activities program should result.

8. **The total student activities program and each of the component activities should be periodically evaluated to ascertain effectiveness and to identify areas which are in need of improvement.** The student activities program is like any other program offered by the school in that it needs periodic evaluation. Ideally, the program should be evaluated yearly, but this may not always be possible. At the very minimum, however, the program and each of its constituent parts should receive a thorough evaluation every two or three years. For, as Frederick has observed, "It sometimes happens that particular activities are repeated year after year, not because of a genuine interest and need, but because we have always had them. The form lingers on after the spark of life has died." [12]

The school administrator (or the student activities director) is responsible for making sure that the student activities program is evaluated periodically, although he may not be the one who actually conducts the evaluation. In fact, the wise administrator will, in the evaluation of a program, involve advisers and student leaders who participate in that program. While it might become appropriate to call upon outside consultants in conducting the evaluation, the school administrator is the one who should initiate and bring to completion the periodic evaluation of the student activities program. If evaluation is neglected, it is the administrator who should be held accountable.

A number of excellent statements of recommended criteria are available to the administrator in evaluating a school's activities program. [13] Based on an examination of these statements, it would appear that the administrator should seek answers to the following questions in assessing the program:

a. Is the overall program and each specific activity meeting its objectives in terms of improving student knowledge, skills, attitudes and/or values? What is the evidence that objectives are being met?

b. What is the extent of student participation in the total program and in each activity? Are a majority of the students participating in the program? What is the evidence in regard to the degree of student participation?

c. What *kinds* of students are participating in the program, and what is the nature of their participation? Do the non-college-bound students participate to the same degree as the college-bound students, and if not, why not?[14] Do the girls participate to the same extent as the boys, and if not, why not? Do some students participate *too much* in the activities program?

d. Is the activities program well balanced and comprehensive, or do some activities dominate? Are there any student interests and needs that are not adequately met by the program?

e. Is the total program and each of the activities well organized? (Specific aspects of organization are discussed in this section.)

f. Are all aspects of the program supported sufficiently in terms of availability of facilities, funds, school time, personnel, and recognition? Or are some activities disproportionately supported?

These are questions that administrators should be asking periodically about the student activities program, and which they should be able to answer if they are fully meeting their responsibilities for evaluating the program. The methods of evaluating the program will vary from situation to situation but could include student questionnaires, interviews, analysis of participation data, and observation of organizational factors. If administrators do not feel competent in evaluation methodology, they should seek outside help, but they should not use their own lack of competency to avoid evaluating the program.

9. **Each of the student groups in the student activities program should be required to prepare an end-of-the-year summary status report to be disseminated to all appropriate parties.** If the student activities program is to be administered properly, information will be needed relative to the accomplishments of each student group. The general question that needs to be answered is, "What has happened to each student group during the year?" An end-of-the-year summary status report prepared by each student group would help answer that question.

The report need not be long (2-4 pages) and could be prepared cooperatively by the adviser to the group and the student officers. It should contain information on the progress, accomplishments, and major unresolved issues and problems evident at the end of the year. Copies of the report should go to the chief administrator of the school, the director of the activities program, and all members of the student group, for their information and reactions. Such a report would be valuable, not only in keeping people informed about the accomplishments and problems of each student group, but in pointing up the need for improvement or a new direction for a group to take. It would also give the administrator the kind of information he needs in order to administer the overall student activities program effectively.

MAJOR PROBLEMS OF THE
STUDENT ACTIVITIES PROGRAM

It is difficult to generalize about the student activities program because of the variations among schools, but it is safe to say that in most districts the program has not operated without problems. Some of the problems have been associated with a specific activity, while others have been rather pervasive throughout the program. In the latter category, the following two problems have persisted through the years: (1) Difficulty in obtaining well-qualified, interested advisers; and (2) Apathy on the part of many students—overinvolvement on the part of a few students.

PROBLEMS IN THE RECRUITING
OF ADVISERS

It was pointed out earlier that the adviser is a significant key to the success of any student activity.* A well-qualified, interested adviser can resuscitate a dying activity and can help a mediocre one to reach greater heights of achievement. A poorly-qualified and barely interested adviser, on the other hand, will be of little help to a student group and may cause it to deteriorate. Despite the fact that most, if not all administrators recognize the need for obtaining well-qualified, interested advisers, many administrators experience difficulty in securing them. This is particularly true for nonathletic student activities. What seems to be the nature of the problem?

One contributing factor is that in many schools certain advisers are paid for their sponsorship of a student activity, while advisers of other activities in the same schools receive no reimbursement for their time and effort.

For example, advisers to special interest clubs and organizations are frequently unpaid, while coaches of athletic and other performing teams and the advisers to publications receive compensation. [15] Although financial reimbursement should not be the sole motivating force in causing a capable individual to seek the advisorship of a student group, it is nevertheless an important factor, and the administrator should be realistic about it. Potentially well-qualified individuals who might be interested in sponsoring a student club or organization are likely to think twice before volunteering their time and effort for little or no compensation when they see other advisers receiving remuneration for their contribution to an activity.

Compounding the problem of compensation is the fact that in many schools the salary differentiation among advisers seems to be based more on

*For a vivid description of the importance of the adviser to a student activity, see Earl Reum, *Of Love and Magic: The Junior High/Middle School Student Council Adviser* (Washington, D.C.: National Association of Secondary School Principals, 1973).

the status of the activity than on the extent of actual responsibilities. Coaches of athletic teams, for instance, seem to be paid at a higher rate than advisers for intramural sports; advisers to public performance groups such as band or dramatics seem to be paid more than advisers to nonpublic performing groups, such as debate.

While there are additional steps that an administrator could take to secure more qualified and interested advisers for the student activities program (including the provision of better facilities and more funding and recognition for some of the groups), removal of the inequities in the advisers' salary structure would represent an important action toward improving the situation.

STUDENT APATHY VS. OVERINVOLVEMENT

A paradoxical situation which has plagued the student activities program over the years is the problem of student apathy vs. overinvolvement. In many schools a large percentage of the student body does not participate in the student activities program, and if one were to eliminate participation in athletics from the analysis, it might even be said that in most schools the vast majority of students do not participate in the activities program. [16]

School administrators and student activities advisers usually attribute a lack of participation on the part of students to "student apathy," which may provide a label for the situation, but fails to explain the cause(s). The question that the administrator and the staff need to investigate is, "*Why* is there student apathy?" or, "What is there about our program which fails to attract students in larger numbers?" Underlying reasons may include lack of information about the activities, poor scheduling, low status of certain activities, limited activities, restrictive admission requirements for membership in a group, (e.g., "C" grade point average) and an inadequate understanding of the values to be obtained from participating in the student activities program.*

Perhaps the place to begin in analyzing reasons for student apathy is with the nature of the activities program itself. Such an examination might reveal, as Graham has observed, that "those young people who stand to benefit most from social experience in the activity program have the fewest opportunities to participate, whereas those students who have the least to learn from an activity program have the most opportunity to participate." [17]

Although student apathy is a much greater problem than student overinvolvement, the latter should also be of concern to administrators.

---

*Jobs outside of school can also play a major role. See *NASSP Spotlight,* May 1974. For an earlier study, see Berthold G. Pauley, "Effect of Transportation and Part-time Employment," *Journal of Educational Research* 52 (September 1958):8.

Overinvolvement manifests itself in two ways: (1) certain students get involved in too many activities, reducing the effectiveness of their participation, and (2) in some schools or during a particular period of time, a few students may capture many of the top leadership offices in the activities program, thereby reducing opportunities for leadership growth by other students. Most administrators and student activities advisers seem to be aware of these problems and some have taken steps to remedy the situation by restricting the number of offices which can be held by any one individual.

The problem of student overinvolvement in student activities is not an easy one to resolve. [18] Even the question of what constitutes "too much" participation is not readily determined. Obviously, the situation will vary, depending on the student and his circumstances.

Part of the problem is that most schools don't even have a mechanism for monitoring the deleterious effect on the student of excessive participation in the activities program, with the possible exception of grade reports. Though grade reports might be useful as one indicator of the problem, grades can be affected by many variables. Perhaps the best steps a school can take are to keep better centralized records of the number of activities in which each student is participating, and to ask advisers, counselors, and teachers to be especially observant of those students who are involved in several activities during a particular nine-week period of time.

MAJOR PROBLEMS ASSOCIATED WITH SEVERAL SPECIFIC STUDENT ACTIVITY PROGRAMS

THE ATHLETIC PROGRAM

The athletic program has probably been the most successful of all the student activities, at least in terms of the number of students participating and the degree of esteem awarded it by the school and the community. It has undoubtedly maintained some students in school who would have dropped out without this interest, and the program has made it possible for certain individuals to obtain scholarships to college, and other kinds of recognition. It has also been a source of school spirit for many students, and a means of entertainment for a large number of communities. [19] However, the program has periodically been criticized and has had to face some serious problems. [20]

One of the more serious problems confronting the athletic program is the matter of poor sportsmanship on the part of players and spectators. [21] Poor sportsmanship by players usually manifests itself when they argue with the officials or become involved in fights with the opponents on the playing field. Poor sportsmanship on the part of spectators includes booing the officials, throwing articles onto the playing field, or fighting among the fans during or after a game. While the extent of the problem varies from school to school and, sometimes, from sport to sport, such behavior represents a serious problem that should be of concern to the administrator and the school staff.*

The approach to unruly behavior on the part of athletes and the student body should not be dependent solely on greater control or more security, but should also include a planned program of developing better student and player sportsmanship.[22] The objectives of the program should be to teach good, sportsmanlike attitudes and behavior to athletes and to the rest of the student body. A beginning step for achieving this goal would be for a school to develop a sportsmanship code similar to the one presented in figure 16.2.

---

1. *Show respect for the opponent at all times.*
   The opponent should be treated as a guest; greeted cordially on arriving; given the best accommodations; and accorded the tolerance, honesty, and generosity which all human beings deserve. Good sportsmanship is the Golden Rule in action.
2. *Show respect for the officials.*
   The officials should be recognized as impartial arbitrators who are trained to do their job and who can be expected to do it to the best of their ability. Good sportsmanship implies the willingness to accept and abide by the decisions of the officials.
3. *Know, understand, and appreciate the rules of the contest.*
   A familiarity with the current rules of the game and the recognition of their necessity for a fair contest are essential. Good sportsmanship suggests the importance of conforming to the spirit as well as the letter of the rules.
4. *Maintain self-control at all times.*
   A prerequisite of good sportsmanship requires one to understand his own bias or prejudice and to have the ability to recognize that rational behavior is more important than the desire to win. A proper perspective must be maintained if the potential educational values of athletic competition are to be realized. Good sportsmanship is concerned with the behavior of all involved in the game.
5. *Recognize and appreciate skill in performance regardless of affiliation.*
   Applause for an opponent's good performance is a demonstration of generosity and goodwill that should not be looked upon as treason. The ability to recognize quality in performance and the willingness to acknowledge it without regard to team membership is one of the most highly commendable gestures of good sportsmanship. With the fundamentals of sportsmanship as the points of departure, specific responsibilities and expected modes of behavior can be defined.

Used with permission of the American Association for Health Physical Education and Recreation Publications.

Figure 16.2. Fundamentals of Sportsmanship. [24]

*That the problem is not confined to the secondary level is made clear in a study by George Bovyer, "Children's Concepts of Sportsmanship in the Fourth, Fifth and Sixth Grades," *Research Quarterly* 24 (October 1963):16-18.

The code in figure 16.2 and other aspects of the sportsmanship program should be implemented in physical education classes, assembly programs, after-school practices, and through the example of coaches and other adults in the school. The school administrator can "show the way" through his own example at games, and by making clear to the coaches and the student body the importance which is attached to good sportsmanlike behavior. In the final analysis the administrator and the staff need to view the success of the athletic program not just in terms of how many games are won or lost, but of equal importance, in the amount of progress made by the athletes and the student body in learning better sportsmanship. [23]

A second major problem with which the athletic program has been confronted is the introduction of girls' sports. Traditionally, the athletic program has involved mainly boys, although girls have sometimes participated in certain sports, e.g., basketball. Recently, however, girls have indicated an interest in participating in many aspects of the athletic program, particularly noncontact sports. Their interest has, unfortunately, frequently been met by resistance from some schools, and much publicity and frustration has resulted.

The problem is a complicated one, overlaid in some instances with male chauvinistic thinking and excessive concern about protecting girls. The heart of the problem, however, is how to accommodate girls' athletics in the schools within existing physical facilities (which, in many places, are already in short supply for boys' athletics and the intramural program), and within an athletic budget which is under attack by critics as being too large. This is not an unresolvable problem, and many schools have done a rather good job of accommodating girls' athletics through tighter scheduling and budgeting.

Probably the best perspective that an administrator can adopt is to recognize that female students have as much right as male students to participate in sports and to have access to appropriate equipment, facilities, and coaching. (Title 9 of USOE makes this the law.) The goal should be to make sure that the athletic needs of both boys *and* girls are being met.

THE STUDENT COUNCIL

Most schools provide an opportunity for students to participate in decisions about school affairs, usually through the mechanism of a group called the student council.* It is generally comprised of student representatives who

---

*While the student council is traditionally perceived as a secondary school activity, it is also included in good elementary schools. For examples of student councils in the elementary school, see Jacqueline Butter, "Student Council Elementary Style," *Today's Education* 59 (September 1970):58-59. Also see Frank Emmerling, "The Student Council—A Vehicle for Self-Improvement," *National Elementary Principal* 46 (May 1967):67-69.

have been elected to their positions by the school's student population, and an adviser who is usually appointed by the principal. The council may meet during the school day, but frequently tends to hold its meetings after school. Meetings may consist of hearing reports from various subcommittees, passing motions recommending certain actions to the administration, and raising problems or questions which require discussion and possible further investigation.

Although the specific objectives of the student council are not the same in all schools, the following are recommended:

1. To promote the general welfare of the school.
2. To foster, promote and develop democracy as a a way of life.
3. To teach home, school, and community citizenship.
4. To provide school experiences closely related to life experiences.
5. To provide learning opportunities through the solution of problems which are of interest and concern to students.
6. To provide training and experience in representative democracy.
7. To contribute to the total educational growth of boys and girls. [25]

There is little doubt that a student council can become an important and valuable force in the school. However, for it to be successful, certain problems and crises must be averted or resolved. One of the major problems or issues which many student councils and administrators encounter is how much authority should be granted to the student council. That is to say, should the student council be an advisory group with authority only to make recommendations, or should it be given decision-making authority? This question has troubled schools for a number of years, but it became a fundamental issue with the advent of student activism in the late 1960s. [26]

Actually, there should be no confusion in an administrator's mind about the answer to the question of the extent of the student council's authority.* The building administrator is the one who is legally accountable to the school board for administering the school. Therefore, the student council can legitimately be given only the authority to offer recommendations in regard to how the school should be run. It is true that an administrator can delegate certain decision-making responsibilities to the student council, but final decision-making authority cannot be delegated to such a group unless the school board provides for a departure of this kind from normal procedure. [27]

An initial step that an administrator should take to avert the authority issue from coming to a head is to develop an understanding on the part of the entire student council and its adviser of the legal requirements and restric-

---

*The question is also discussed in the booklet by Earl Reum and Oneta Cummings. *The Effective Student Council in the Mid-Seventies* (Washington, D.C.: The National Association of Secondary School Principals, 1973).

tions of the administrator's position, and the main function of the council in light of these factors.[28] This should be done in such a way that the importance of the recommending role of the council is stressed while at the same time it is being indicated that the council does not have a final decision-making role. Administrators should recognize, however, that regardless of the importance they attribute to the recommending role of the council, their reactions to its recommendations will communicate more than any statements they may make about the council's usefulness.

If the student council is to play an important role in the school, the administrator will need to exercise extreme caution in rejecting its recommendations. Of course, this does not mean that recommendations which are clearly illegal or not in the best interest of the school must be accepted, although discerning which recommendations to accept and which to reject because of the latter criterion will take considerable administrative judgment and wisdom. Administrators should realize that they will probably have to compromise sometimes, and in certain instances take risks in accepting recommendations which they believe to be impractical. At times however, the only way the students can appreciate the judgment of the administrator is if they are permitted to make their own mistakes.

The scope of many student council programs is another major problem. If one examines the general purposes of the student council set forth earlier, a rather broad mandate for taking action to improve the total environment of the school seems to be implied. However, if one looks at the actual activities of many student councils, the main thrust appears to be limited to fund-raising, organizing and promoting social affairs, and occasionally coalescing to promote some particular school issue, such as a new smoking lounge.[29] What seems to be lacking on the part of these student councils—and, perhaps, on the part of the school administration as well—is a deep understanding of the potential purposes and scope of the student council in a school and the kind of program that would accomplish these purposes.

Administrators should assume leadership responsibility for helping to resolve this problem, if it occurs. They should, in their own minds, be clear about the purposes of the student council, and they should make equally sure that the student council and its adviser are also clear about the purposes of the organization. Then they should work with the adviser, who in turn should work with the members of the council to develop a program each year that will accomplish those purposes.

While it is probably true that some administrators prefer a student council that confines its program to organizing social events, the administrator who is truly interested in capitalizing on and encouraging the interests and skills of the students will help them to develop a more far-reaching program. Such a program should have as its main purpose the improvement of the educational and social environment of the school and the community. Included in this program might be the following kinds of activities:

1. Conducting remedial classes in a disadvantaged neighborhood
2. Refurbishing a community center for youth and adults
3. Setting up a city-suburb exchange program
4. Meeting with the principal to recommend new courses for the school's curriculum
5. Arranging for an after-school series of school lectures on "Black Militancy and White Power"
6. Developing a form for evaluating class instruction
7. Organizing a student-led seminar on contemporary issues to be offered in summer school, without grades or credits
8. Setting up a corps of student tutors to help slow learners in the school
9. Developing student-written individualized learning materials
10. Meeting with community leaders to plan for more effective use of community resources
11. Meeting with parents to explore school problems as parents perceive them
12. Making a proposal to the school board for the hiring of teacher aides. [30]

Participation in these and similar activities by the student council should help it to achieve its general purposes, make a significant contribution to the school, and ameliorate the two-pronged problem of student apathy and criticism of the council that "it never does anything worthwhile." [31] Such a program should attract student participation, provide valuable learning experiences for students, and greatly improve the image of the student council in the school. Given a complete understanding of its purposes and the nature of its authority in the school, as well as continuous encouragement and assistance by the administration and the staff, the student council can become an important force for school and community improvement.*

THE STUDENT NEWSPAPER

Every school should sponsor a student newspaper as a part of its activities program. A student newspaper can provide valuable learning experiences for those students who serve on its staff, and can act as a source of information

---

*The individual who is interested in student government alternatives to student councils should look at *Student Structures: Moving Toward Student Government* (Washington, D.C.: National Association of Secondary School Principals, 1974).

about student perceptions, student functions, and school and community activities and problems. The newspaper's basic purpose, in addition to providing journalistic learning experiences for students, is to inform the student body and other school personnel about events in the school and community which may be of interest to students and to the professional staff.

In spite of its potential and frequently realized worth, the student newspaper has been a source of considerable controversy in recent years. Editorials attacking the administration and faculty and criticizing certain school practices and programs have appeared in some student newspapers. The use of obscene language, and pictures of questionable taste in some student newspapers have also caused problems for school administrators and newspaper advisers. And, finally, the initiation of an "underground" student newspaper in a number of schools has troubled many administrators.*

Administrators have tended to react to these problems in several different ways. Some administrators have tried to ignore such problems in the hope that they would eventually disappear. Their success has been mixed. Some administrators have responded by initiating procedures designed to censor in advance any undesirable (from the administrator's point of view) language, pictures, editorials, or articles. [32] These administrators have also tried to stop the distribution of student underground papers in school, and, in some instances, away from the school grounds.

While it is difficult to assess the effectiveness of these efforts, it is worth noting that students have achieved considerable success in their court challenges of unnecessary administrative censorship and restriction of their publications. Although the case law is still in somewhat of a flux, the courts have generally upheld students' rights to publish material, with the following exceptions:

1. *Libelous Material*—that which may result in defamation of character, such as a statement concerning a person which may unnecessarily expose him to hatred or contempt, or which could have a tendency to injure him professionally.
2. *Obscene and profane material.* Generally the courts have been more restrictive as to the language and pictorial representations from younger students than those from college students.
3. Material which would tend to *incite to disruption* the educational process of the school.
4. Material which would *clearly endanger the health and safety* of the students. [33]

*The underground newspaper can be defined as a non-school-sanctioned student newspaper put out by students who typically feel that what they have to say about the school, the community, or a larger issue would not be approved by school authorities for inclusion in the "official" student newspaper. And they are usually, though not always, right in this perception. For more information, see Thomas George, "A Legal Analysis of the Underground Press," an ERIC Report: Ed-062-694, 1972.

If the administrator or the journalism adviser of a school is going to censor some aspect of a student publication, it would appear that such censorship should be based on one or more of the above-identified four categories.

An approach employed by some schools which seems to be successful in resolving publication problems is to establish a publications advisory committee. [34] Such committees are generally composed of the advisers for the newspaper and yearbook, the student editors of each of these publications, one or more representatives from the faculty and from the administration, and sometimes a representative from the local newspaper. The committee membership should be broadly based in order to capitalize on the capabilities and insights of a number of people who can contribute valuable ideas for the improvement of school publications.

The main purposes of the advisory committee are to develop policies and procedures concerning student publications in the school, to evaluate various aspects of the publications program, and to act as a hearing board for people who have complaints about school publications. The committee's actions are advisory to the principal of the school, who may or may not be a member of the committee. The primary advantage of such a committee is that it serves as a focal point for the fostering of a continuous examination and upgrading of student publications, while providing a less emotional and more thorough process of resolving complaints and controversy surrounding student publications.

Although there is little doubt that guidelines and committees can help to promote good journalism in schools—and to avoid controversy—the administrator should recognize that all controversy is not necessarily bad, and in some instances it may represent a desirable learning experience for students. Perhaps this perspective has been best expressed by the Civil Liberties Union, which stated in its landmark pamphlet, *Academic Freedom in the Secondary School:*

> The student press should be considered a learning device. Its pages should not be looked upon as an official image of the school, always required to present a polished appearance to the extramural world. Learning effectively proceeds through trial and error, and as much or more may be sometimes gained from reactions to a poor article or a tasteless publication as from the traditional pieces, groomed carefully for external inspection. [35]

A FINAL PERSPECTIVE

The quality of a student activities program is primarily dependent on the vision and commitment of those people who are associated with the program.

Any student activities program will, over a period of time, encounter certain problems. However, given proper leadership—particularly by the student officers, faculty advisers, and the principal of the school—these problems can be resolved, and the student activities program can make an important contribution to meeting school goals and student needs. [36]

Review

1. What are the purpose, objectives, and scope of the student activities program?
2. Cite two characteristics of the administration and the staff which are most important to the success of the student activities program. Why are these two aspects important?
3. What principles should the administrator follow in organizing or evaluating the organization of the student activities program?
4. Indicate the importance of continuous evaluation of the student activities program. What kinds of questions should the administrator be asking?
5. Define the major problems of the student activities program. What factors seem to contribute to the problems, and how can the administrator prevent or ameliorate the problems?
6. Discuss the major problems associated with the following student activities, the factors contributing to these problems, and ways that the administrator can prevent or ameliorate them.
   a. The athletic program
   b. The student council
   c. The student newspaper

Notes

1. For a description of the early evolution of the student activities program, see E. D. Grizzell, "Evolution of Student Activities in the Secondary School," *Educational Outlook* (November 1926):19-31.

2. Robert W. Frederick, *The Third Curriculum* (New York: Appleton-Century-Crofts, 1959), p. 58.

3. For examples of other statements of objectives, see Harry C. McKown, *Extracurricular Activities* (New York: Macmillan Co., 1952), pp. 13-16.

4. For an excellent and still relevant statement of the rationale supporting this position, see Ellsworth Thompkins, "Extra-Class Activities for All Pupils," *Federal Security Agency* (1950), pp. 1-3.

5. Most studies have found that a majority of the students do not participate in school activities if one excludes the athletic program. See for example, Kenneth J. Bourgon, "Which Students Are Active?" *School Activities* 38 (May 1967):15-19.

6. See M. E. Rizzo, "Active Activity Program," *The Clearing House* 44 (November 1969):184. Also see Robert L. Buser, "Student Activities in the Schools of the Seventies," *Bulletin of the National Association of Secondary School Principals* 55 (September 1971):1-9.

7. For an example of how to do this, see Lester R. Grum, "Evaluation of an Activities Program," *School Activities* 26 (April 1955):243-47.

8. See Gerald M. Van Pool, "The Student Council," *Bulletin of the National Association of Secondary School Principals* 48 (October 1964):42-53.

9. For example, see Grace Graham, *Improving Student Participation* (Washington, D.C.: National Association of Secondary School Principals, 1966), pp. 35-44.

10. An excellent example of this type of handbook is the one developed by Princeton High School, Cincinnati, Ohio.

11. A sample description of the duties and responsibilities of the student activities director may be found in Earl Reum, "The Responsibilities of the Multi School Activities Coordinator," *School Activities* 5 (Spring 1970):86.

12. Frederick, *The Third Curriculum,* p. 121.

13. For examples of evaluation criteria for determining whether an activity should be initiated or continued, see Harl R. Douglas, *Modern Administration of Secondary Schools* (New York: Ginn & Co., 1963), p. 204. For criteria to use in evaluating the total activities program, see Arthur C. Hearn, *Evaluation of Student Activities* (Washington, D.C.: National Association of Secondary School Principals, 1966).

14. For example, see James W. Bell, "A Comparison of Dropouts and Non-Dropouts on Participation in School Activities," *Journal of Educational Research* 61 (Feburary 1967):248-51.

15. For evidence of this problem, see Glenna J. Scheer, "A Study of Senior High Student Councils in the State of Texas" (Ed.D. diss., North Texas State University, 1971), p. 85.

16. Bourgon, *"Which Students Are Active?"*

17. Grace Graham, "Do School Activity Programs Build Better Intergroup Relations?" *School Activities* 38 (February 1967):6-7. Also, for an extensive review of various approaches for getting students involved, see James E. House, "A Study of Innovative Youth Involvement Activities in Selected Secondary Schools in Wayne County, Michigan" (Doctoral diss., Wayne State University, 1969).

18. See Neil F. Williams, "Encouraging and Limiting Participation in School Activities," *School Activities* 35 (November 1964):19-21.

19. For example, see James Coleman, *Adolescents and the Schools* (New York: Basic Books, 1965), p. 40.

20. For an excellent review of research on problems confronting the athletic program in the schools, see Michael Feldman, "Some Relationships between Specified Values of Student Groups and Interscholastic Athletics in Selected Schools" (Ed.D. diss., University of Massachusetts, 1969), pp. 15-40. Also see *Phi Delta Kappan,* October 1974, entire issue devoted to problems of the athletic program.

21. National Council of Secondary School Athletic Directors, *Crowd Control for High School Athletics* (Washington, D.C.: The Council, 1970).

22. See Harold Meyer, National Council of Secondary School Athletic Directors, *Crowd Control for High School Athletics* (Washington, D. C.: The Council, 1970), pp. 9-14.

23. Ibid., pp. 10-11.

24. For evidence that a great deal of improvement is needed, see Feldman, "Some Relationships," pp. 100-114. Also, for the administrator who is interested in evaluating his total athletic program, see "Cardinal Athletic Principles," *Journal of Health and Physical Education* 18 (September 1947):435 and 557-58, for an excellent and still relevant statement of Standards.

25. George E. Mathes, "The Student Council—A Vital Force?" *The Student Council Handbook* (Washington, D.C.: National Association of Secondary School Principals, 1967), p. 116. For an excellent study on the same aspect, see Lawrence M. LeKander, "Student Participation in Secondary School Government: An Analysis of Purposes, Values, and Practices" (Ed.D. diss., University of California, 1967).

26. See Oscar F. Mussman, "A Study of the Student Councils in Selected Secondary Schools to Identify Differences of Their Roles as Perceived by Principals and Students" (Ed.D. diss., University of Nebraska, 1970).

27. For a somewhat different point of view, see James B. Conant, *Recommendations for Education in the Junior High School Years* (Princeton, N.J.: Educational Testing Service, 1960).

28. Gerald M. Van Pool, "The Student Council," *Bulletin of the National Association of Secondary School Principals* 42 (October 1964):42-53.

29. See Kent M. Keith, "Will Student Councils Die?" *Student Life Highlights* (November 1969).

30. Allan A. Glatthorn, *The Principal and the Student Council* (Washington, D.C.: National Association of Secondary School Principals, 1968), pp. 44-45.

31. For information on additional Student Council projects, see *A Guide to Student Council Projects* (Washington, D.C.: National Association of Secondary School Principals, 1971).

32. Although questions have been raised about the objectivity of the report, examples of administrator censorship of student publications are reported in *Captive Voices—High School Journalism in America* (New York: Shocken Books, 1974).

33. For an in-depth treatment of the legal aspects of censorship, see "Freedom of the Scholastic Press: Landmark Legal Cases," *Albany Law Review* (New York: Albany Law School, 1970).

34. For an earlier proposal of this type of committee, see Franklin A. Miller et al., *Planning Student Activities* (Englewood Cliffs, N.J.: Prentice-Hall, 1956), pp. 437-39.

35. American Civil Liberties Union, *Academic Freedom in the Secondary School* (New York: American Civil Liberties Union, 1968), p. 12.

36. For the administrator who is interested in further reading on this topic, an excellent source is *Student Activities in the Secondary School: A Bibliography* (Washington, D.C.: National Association of Secondary School Principals, 1974).

Part 5

The School and the Community

17

School-Community Relations: Community Structure and Involvement

A school is not an independent or isolated entity; it operates in a social context, an important element of which is the local community. [1] The school draws its students from the local community and depends on the community for much of its financial and social support. The community exercises its power over the school primarily through the school board, which has authority to establish policies and approve financial expenditures. The community also exerts its influence on the school informally through parents' groups and individual contacts. [2] Because of these factors every administrator needs to develop a good understanding of and competency in building and maintaining effective school-community relations.

UNDERSTANDING THE COMMUNITY

THE SCHOOL ADMINISTRATOR'S COMMUNITY

The school community can be thought of as encompassing the total geographical area and population of a school district, or as comprised of the more immediate area and population within an individual school's boundaries. While a school administrator needs to understand the total community, he needs particularly to understand and develop good relationships with the immediate community that the school serves. It is the immediate community that is sending its children to the school, and it is the people in this community with whom the administrator is likely to have the greatest contact. They are also the ones with whom the administrator needs to communicate the most, since their opinions about the school are likely to be most influential.

The most important step that an administrator can take initially to develop good school-community relations is to study and better understand the school's immediate community. [3] A community is a very complex unit, but there are four elements to which the administrator should pay especially close attention. Those elements are presented in figure 17.1.

In trying to develop a better understanding of the immediate community served by the school, the administrator first needs to study the kinds of people who reside in that community.[4] Examples of questions which might guide his study include the following: What percentage of the people in the immediate community are parents/nonparents? What is the socioeconomic

Factor 1:	Factor 2:	Factor 3:	Factor 4:
		Methods of Communication People Use	Expectations and Attitudes
People	Places Where People Meet		
Examples	*Examples*	*Examples*	*Examples*
A. *Individuals:*	Homes	Face-to-Face	Attitudes about
Parents/nonparents	Churches	Telephone	children
Professional/laboring	Supermarkets	Letter	Expectations for the
class	Cocktail parties	Newsletter	school
Welfare clients	Coffees	Radio	Attitudes towards
Working mothers/	Organizational meetings	TV	school effective-
fathers			ness
Informal leaders			Interest in and avail-
B. *Groups:*			ability for working
Parents' organizations			with the school
Social and fraternal			
groups			
Informal groups (cof-			
fees, bowling teams)			

Figure 17.1. Major Community Elements.

background of the people? What percentage are professional, in contrast to blue-collar workers? How many are on welfare? In how many instances are both parents working outside the home? Who are the informal leaders of the community? What percentage of the parents move each year? What percentage of the parents represent minority groups?

The answers to the above questions can usually be obtained from a school census and/or from a separate school survey, and should help the administrator develop a more accurate and complete understanding of the characteristics of people in the community served by the school.

A school administrator also needs to become knowledgeable about the different groups and organizations to which the people in the immediate community belong. The particular groups and organizations about which an administrator needs specific information are those which have a special interest in education and in the school. These would be the groups or organizations who discuss education from time to time in their meetings and who may even have a subcommittee for educational matters.* Figure 17.2 identifies groups and organizations about which the administrator should be knowledgeable.

*For an understanding of the power structure of a community, an excellent source is Michael Aiken and Paul Mott, eds., *The Structure of Community Power* (New York: Random House, 1970).

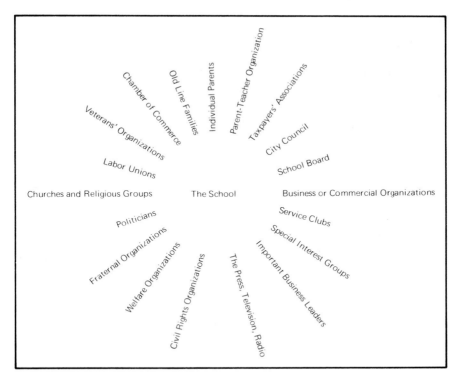

Figure 17.2. Community Groups and
Organizations with a Special Interest in
Education. [5]

At the minimum, an administrator should try to meet the leaders of the
major groups and organizations in the immediate community the school
serves and learn their points of view about education and about the school. [6]
The administrator should be well enough acquainted with each group so that
he can communicate easily with its leaders in a time of crisis and can utilize
whatever expertise the members possess for improving the school program.

In addition to studying the types of individuals and the major organizations in the community which the school serves, the administrator needs to
become more aware of the different places where people in the community
meet, and of the various methods of communication they use in discussing
education and the school. These meeting places—whether they be churches,
local barber shops, or coffee-klatches—are a part of the informal structure of
the community. By familiarizing himself with the informal structure of a
community, the administrator will be in a better position to ascertain what

people are thinking and saying about the school, and he can also use the informal structure for communicating information about the school. [7]

The objective of an administrator in regard to the ways people receive information about the school is to be aware of these channels so that he can capitalize on them when *he* tries to communicate information about the school or needs to find out what people are thinking. For example, if people in a community pay more attention to news about the school that they hear on radio or television than information they receive from the school newsletter or the city newspaper, the administrator should be aware of this reality and take it into consideration in his communication practices. An understanding of the ways in which the people in a community receive information about the school is essential for an administrator who wants to develop effective communication with the community.

The fourth and perhaps most important element of the community about which a school administrator needs to become knowledgeable is the educational expectations and attitudes of its people. [8] In most situations the community is not, of course, a homogeneous entity, and the administrator is unlikely to discover that everyone holds identical educational expectations and attitudes. Most communities comprise diverse people and groups who are likely to hold somewhat different expectations and attitudes about education and the schools.

Regardless of this diversity, however, the school administrator should try to understand the expectations and attitudes of the people in the community, for community expectations constitute standards by which the people in the community evaluate the performance of the school.* The current attitude of people in the community toward students and the school reflects citizens' feelings about how effectively the school is meeting community expectations. Therefore, the school administrator needs to become knowledgeable about both the educational expectations and the attitudes of people in the community. As a result of such knowledge, he will be in a better position to recognize the direction that the community would like to see education take in the school, and citizens' feelings about how successful the school has been in meeting their expectations.

MAJOR PROBLEMS IN SCHOOL-COMMUNITY RELATIONS

The administrator should understand that school-community relations have never been completely trouble-free. From the very beginning of education in

*While some administrators may feel that they already understand the expectations and attitudes of the people in their community, mounting evidence to the contrary would make that assumption questionable. Data on this point were collected in a study by Joel Milgram and John Hill, "The School Official Who Can Best Estimate Parental Approval or Disapproval of New Programs," 1972. N.P.M. Also see Gary L. Kesl, "Perceptions of the Community Power Structure of Selected Communities" (Ph.D. diss., University of Miami, 1972).

this country there have been periodic differences and conflicts between the school and the community. In most communities these differences and conflicts have usually not been severe, but in some periods school-community conflict has seemed to be rather widespread.

Although the basic causes of problems in school-community relations are complex and may vary according to the nature of a community and a school, it would appear that two general factors are at work: (1) professional challenges to community norms, and (2) community challenges to professional norms.* The first factor concerns those efforts by educators to change the educational program or system—efforts which in many instances have conflicted with community norms. Integration, sex education, open education, and modular scheduling are only a few of the innovations that educators have tried to introduce which have, in one way or another, challenged the norm structure of many communities. When a community feels that its schools are going beyond or against community expectations and norms, it tends to react negatively, thereby causing difficulties in school-community relations.

A second general factor which has caused problems in school-community relations is intensified efforts by many communities to ascertain and evaluate what is going on in the schools. These efforts have tended to challenge the professional norms of many educators, whose motto seems to be, "Trust us, we're the experts."

Increasing numbers of parents and other community citizens, however, have indicated that they no longer accept the word of educators that "everything is going all right." These community people want to see the *results* of the school's effectiveness, and in many cases, they want to be personally involved in the decision-making processes of the school. An administrator should not assume that all of the people of a community possess these attitudes. But he should recognize that there is a growing trend in this country toward greater expectations on the part of many citizens to become involved in school decision making and for the school to be held accountable for its educational effectiveness. †

These problems in school-community relations will not be easily ameliorated. It would appear, however, that more effective communication between the school and the community, and greater community involvement, are necessary prerequisites. The remainder of this chapter will focus on ways in which the school administrator might more effectively involve the com-

---

*An analysis of the causes of problems in school-community relations is discussed more fully in *Conflict, Controversy and Crisis in School Administration and Supervision* by Richard A. Gorton (Dubuque, Iowa: Wm. C. Brown Company Publishers, 1972), chap. 2.

†A group that recently organized for this purpose is the National Committee for Citizens in Education, which has its national headquarters in Columbia, Md., and local chapters in many communities.

munity in the school; the following chapter will discuss school communication and the school's public relations program.

INVOLVING THE COMMUNITY

Many observers believe that a key to improving school-community relations is greater parent and public involvement in school affairs. [9] While few educators would argue that parent and public involvement is unimportant, there continue to be considerable confusion and uncertainty among school administrators about the concept of involvement and how to utilize it in improving school-community relations. [10] The confusion and uncertainty seem to revolve around three basic questions: (1) What are the purposes of involvement? (2) What types of involvement are possible? and (3) What are the problems associated with parental and community involvement in the schools, and how can these problems be overcome? The following sections will take up each of these questions and attempt to present and discuss the ideas and issues involved.

PURPOSES OF INVOLVEMENT

Many administrators have experienced difficulty in understanding the concept of involvement, and in implementing a program of parental and community involvement in the schools, because they were not clear about the purposes which such involvement should achieve. Involvement has been presented so positively in the educational literature that it has frequently seemed to be the main objective of school-community relations rather than a means of improving education.

Although involving parents and the public in the schools represents an important task, the school administrator should understand that in the final analysis, involvement should be viewed primarily as a means rather than an end. Any involvement of others—regardless of the form it takes—should ultimately result in improving education, if the involvement is to be judged worthwhile. [11]

While the reasons for involving parents and other groups in school affairs will vary somewhat, depending on the nature of the involvement, there appear to be three main reasons for involving them: [12]

1. Through involvement, parents and other citizens will become more knowledgeable about school affairs, and as a result, they will become

   a. better informed about what students are learning in school

  b. more understanding of the problems that the school faces

  c. more supportive of efforts by the school to improve the educational program

2. Through participation by parents and other citizens, the school will receive ideas, expertise, and human resources, all of which will help the school to improve.

3. Through involvement, parents and other citizens will be in a much better position to evaluate the school fairly and effectively.

Perhaps Don Davies made the best summary statement of these objectives when he maintained that, "Meaningful citizen involvement can strengthen confidence in and commitment to the school, while making schools more responsible to citizens' diverse concerns." [13]

It should be pointed out that in the case of all three objectives, several assumptions are made. First of all, it is assumed that parents and other citizens need to become more knowledgeable about school affairs, that involvement of some kind is the best means of their becoming more knowledgeable, and that greater knowledge will result in more understanding and support on their part. The second objective assumes that parents and other citizens possess ideas, expertise, or skills which would be helpful to the school, and that they are willing to make these contributions to the school. The third objective assumes that parents and other citizens need or want to evaluate the school, and that they will do a more accurate job of evaluating the school if they are in some way directly involved in what the school is doing. And finally, all of the objectives assume a reasonable degree of cooperation and commitment on the part of the administrator, the faculty, and the community to the concept of involving parents and other citizens in the school.

The assumptions underlying the objectives of involvement may or may not be tenable, depending on the community and the school. Whether or not they are tenable will, of course, have a bearing on the success of any program of community involvement in the school.

While much will depend on the characteristics of the community and the faculty, possibly the most important variable is the school administrator himself. If he believes in the value of community involvement, he will seek to create the conditions necessary for its success. If, on the other hand, he lacks a strong conviction about the importance of community involvement, and the skill to introduce it, he is likely to feel that its objectives are not necessary, possible, or worthwhile pursuing. The administrator's own attitude and competency are two very significant factors. [14]

TYPES OF PARENTAL INVOLVEMENT*

Up to this point, we have discussed the concept of involvement, without identifying various ways in which a school might involve parents. Although there are many ways to involve parents in a school, these are organized into six different categories in figure 17.3. [15]

1. Member of an organization such as PTA	2. Committee member to study problems, offer recommendations, or make decisions	3. Evaluation of some aspect of the school through responding to questionnaire or by observation
4. Resource person for classes	5. Helper in the library, classroom, etc.	6. User of school facilities

Figure 17.3. Types of Parental Involvement.

Each of the types of parental involvement identified in figure 17.3 can potentially benefit both the school and the parents. The school can gain from the contributions made by parents through their involvement; parents can derive satisfaction from their involvement. [16] In order that the school administrator may better understand the nature of the types of involvement listed in figure 17.3, a capsule description of each is provided below.

Parents' Organizations

Probably the most typical type of formal parental involvement is membership in a school-related parents' organization, the best known of which is the Parent-Teacher Association (PTA). The PTA was organized in 1897 and now has local chapters in every state. Its overall objectives are to

(1) promote the welfare of children and youth in home, school, church and community, (2) raise the standards of home life, (3) secure adequate laws for the care and protection of children and youth, (4) bring into closer relation the home and the school, that parents and teachers may cooperate intelligently in the education of children and

---

*The following discussion will focus for the most part on *parental* involvement, although many of the ideas are also appropriate for other community citizens. Also, community control and decentralization will not be discussed directly because these types of involvement deserve more extensive treatment than is possible in this book. The reader is referred to an article by Marilyn Gittell for an excellent entry point into the literature on these topics. See "Decentralization and Citizen Participation in Education," *Public Administration Review* 32 (October 1972):670-86.

youth, and (5) develop between educators and the general public such united efforts as will secure for all children and youth the highest advantages in physical, mental, and spiritual education.[17]

Until recently, the PTA was considered by many to be little more than a coffee-and-cookies group who met several times a year to hear speeches and to discuss buying additional equipment for the school. As Koerner observed, "It [PTA] is chiefly useful to the administrator for raising money for special projects and persuading parents who are interested enough to attend meetings that the local schools are in the front ranks of American education." [18]

This situation has changed to some extent, however, and many PTA's have become very active in trying to bring about improvement in the education of children.* The new motto of a number of these organizations is "PTA—Parents Taking Action." While traditionally the PTA had not included students, many groups are changing their name and composition of membership to include students, referring to themselves as Parent-Teacher-Student Association (PTSA).

Whether a parents' group refers to itself as PTA, PTSA, or simply PA (Parents' Association), it would seem that parental involvement in some type of an organization associated with the school is a desirable goal for the school administrator. Through such involvement, parents can develop a better understanding of what goes on in the school and can make a useful contribution to improving education. While the performance record of parents' organizations is mixed, and they can be an irritant to a school administrator if they overextend their authority, they can play a valuable role in helping the school and parents to improve educational opportunities for children. However, much will depend on the vision and commitment of the school administrator. As one PTA president noted, "The PTA in a school is just as good as the principal wants it to be." [19]

Committee Member

Membership on a school committee is another type of parental involvement which an administrator should encourage. For example, parents might serve on committees to improve the homework policy, extracurricular activities, school-plant planning, and the school schedule and calendar. Unfortunately, in many schools the committee method of reaching decisions is either underutilized or makes little or no provision for involving parents. This is regrettable since in any community there are usually parents who possess the

*At its annual meeting, Spring 1972, the National PTA approved an important amendment to its bylaws. It discarded the previous section of the bylaws which said that local chapters should "cooperate with schools . . . in ways that will not interfere with the administration" and in its place substituted the statement that PTA intends to "seek to participate in the decision-making process establishing school policy."

available time and expertise to serve on committees *if* the school administrator is interested enough in their involvement to seek them out and encourage them.

It should be noted that parental involvement on school committees has frequently been perceived as a frustrating experience by both the administrator and the parents. [20] On one hand, parents have sometimes felt that they were not "meaningfully involved" on the committee and that the decision had already been made by the administrator. On the other hand, some administrators have felt that the parents expected too much from their involvement and tried to exceed their authority.

Although an administrator will never be able to eliminate all of the problems associated with parents' participation on school committees, most of these difficulties can be avoided if the administrator takes the following steps:*

1. Clearly defines and communicates to all members, in advance, the objectives, function, scope, and authority of the committee. If it is only an advisory committee to develop recommendations to submit to the administrator, then that function should be made clear to all participants.
2. Keeps all members of the committee well informed before, during, and between meetings, as to what is transpiring. Advance agendas and minutes of each meeting are minimum requirements.
3. Utilizes to the greatest extent possible the individual interests and talents of the members of the committee. There is little to be gained by either the school or the participants if the latter's potential contributions are not fully utilized. [21]
4. Rewards members of the committee for their individual and total contributions at every available opportunity. Committee work is frequently tedious, and periodic recognition of the value of the committee's work by the administrator will pay important dividends.

Evaluator

Although some administrators may recoil at the prospect of involving parents in the evaluation of a school, it should be recognized that, in one way or another, parents evaluate the school all the time. They may not evaluate the school in any scientific or formal sense, but parents do make evaluative judgments on the worth of different aspects of the school program. The real question to which administrators need to address themselves, then, is

*For further ideas on establishing and working with advisory committees, see *Policies for Better Advisory Committees* (Waterford, Conn.: National School Boards Association, 1972). Also see *Citizens Advisory Committees* (Arlington, Va.: National School Public Relations Association, 1973).

whether it is better to allow parents to continue to make informal kinds of evaluative judgments (about which the school may not be aware and which in many instances are based on inadequate information and limited contact with the school), or to involve parents formally in some type of systematic evaluation of the school's program. While the question is stated rhetorically and the answer is, hopefully, obvious, it is surprising how many administrators continue to behave as though the absence of a formal program of evaluation by parents means that parents are not evaluating the school.

An administrator needs periodic, systematic, evaluative feedback from parents regarding their perceptions, feelings, and ideas as to the effectiveness of the school and how the school program could be improved. "Periodic" evaluation means, in this context, at least once a year, and "systematic" means that an attempt should be made to secure representative parents' viewpoints in the evaluation. A school administrator needs this kind of information if he is to keep himself accurately informed on what parents are thinking and in order to correct any inaccurate perceptions on their part. He can also find such information helpful in identifying aspects of the school program which may need improvement. Despite the fact that most parents are not professionally trained in education, they can nonetheless contribute valuable ideas for improving the school. The administrator should attempt to capitalize on this potential source of ideas.

Although many administrators try to involve parents in evaluating the school, these efforts are often informal or initiated only after the development of a serious problem in school-community relations. Informal contacts with parents and the community are necessary and desirable, but they cannot adequately substitute for a formally organized program of securing evaluative community feedback. In addition, the best time to obtain community input is *before* a problem reaches the crisis stage, not at the point of crisis. Periodic surveying of parental and community sentiment can alert a school administrator to a developing problem and may suggest a possible means of avoiding a crisis.

There are various alternatives which an administrator might consider for involving parents in evaluating the school, but two techniques particularly merit his attention. The first is the questionnaire method. Utilizing this approach, an administrator (perhaps with consultant help) can design a questionnaire which asks for parents' reactions to or perceptions of the school program. The questionnaire can be long and comprehensive or short and specific, covering only a certain aspect of the school. An example of a short questionnaire is presented in figure 17.4

A questionnaire can be sent to all parents or to only a random sample. In most cases a questionnaire study will provide the school with valuable information, although it should be noted that its usefulness will depend as

Grade of your Child _____ School _____ Boy _____ Girl _____

We would like your reactions to our new homework policy. Please indicate your feelings as to its good points and any areas needing improvement, and then mail this form back to the school.

Good Points

Areas Needing Improvement

(Please return by Monday. Thank you for your help.)

Figure 17.4. A Short Questionnaire For Parents.

much on the care with which it is designed as on the cooperation of the parents.*

Another good technique for involving parents in the evaluation of the school is the interview. An interview might be used as a follow-up to a questionnaire, or it may be used instead of the questionnaire, depending on the administrator's objectives. Usually it will not be possible to interview all parents on a single matter, but through sampling procedures and in-depth interview techniques, the administrator should be able to secure representative views from parents. Interviews may be conducted either at the school, in the home, or by telephone. Provided with in-service training, teachers, counselors, and administrators should be able to conduct the interviews and obtain valuable information for the school. [22]

Regardless of the particular technique or approach used, it is important for the administrator to recognize that securing parents' assessment of the school on a regular basis is essential. Parents will be evaluating the school whether or not the administrator thinks it desirable for them to do so. The task for the administrator is to plan, design, and implement evaluative procedures for parents which will aid in eliciting information and ideas for the improvement of the school program.

Resource Person, Helper

An excellent means by which the school can involve parents and the community at large is by encouraging them to serve as resource people or helpers. There are many people in most communities who possess skills, knowledge, or ideas which might be made available to the school. Professional workers, craftsmen, individuals who have traveled, and those who have a particular area of expertise could serve as resource people and offer a great deal to supplement a school's curriculum. In addition, many housewives and older or retired people have time available and are willing to serve as helpers or aides to the school in the classroom, library, cafeteria, or guidance office.

Involvement of parents and community members as resource persons or helpers in the school is on the increase, according to a nationwide survey by the National School Public Relations Association. The authors of a survey of some 400 schools concluded that, "The rapid gain and spread of volunteer programs in the last several years is a strong indication that the values gained from such programs outweigh the drawbacks." [23]

Although all of the schools surveyed felt that the volunteer program was effective, a number of problems were reported, including staff resistance, irregular attendance by volunteers, high dropout and turnover rates, im-

---

*An excellent source for the administrator who is interested in using the survey method with his community is a book by James A. Conway et al., *Understanding Communities* (Englewood Cliffs, N.J.: Prentice Hall, 1974). See chaps. 5-12.

proper use of volunteers, inadequate communication, and recruitment problems, particularly in low-income areas. The authors of the survey felt, however, that these problems could be avoided or overcome by "careful planning, good coordination, effective training of both volunteers and staff, and periodic evaluation and recognition of volunteer efforts."

In all too many situations the community is still a relatively untapped source of knowledge and assistance. The school administrator has the responsibility of surveying the community to discover the different types of resource people and helpers that might be available. Then, through careful planning and appropriate training for staff members, as well as community volunteers, he should institute a program for capitalizing on these resources for the improvement of the school program.*

User of School Facilities

Possibly one of the best ways to gain parents' and other citizens' support for the school is to involve them in the use of school facilities. People who use the school building are usually more likely to support the school than those who have little or no opportunity to use the facilities maintained by their tax money.

The imaginative administrator can find a variety of ways in which to involve parents and other members of the community in the use of school facilities. Probably the most widely known method is the "lighthouse school" approach. [24] In this approach the school building is kept open and *lighted* at night, and educational and recreational programs are offered by the school to members of the community. Participants may be charged a minimum fee, or the entire expense may be assumed by the school district as an investment in community goodwill and adult education. The objectives of this type of program are to provide

1. An educational center where members of the community can study and learn.
2. A neighborhood center for cultural and recreational activities.
3. A center for social services.
4. A center for utilizing school and community resources to help citizens solve neighborhood problems. [25]

Although such programs are usually administered by the district office, the building administrator can help make them a success through his cooperation and leadership. In addition, by periodically making himself visible at the school while these programs are in process, the administrator can extend his knowledge of and acquaintance with the community, and indicate his support of this type of community involvement.

---

*For a very practical discussion of how to introduce and implement a program for utilizing community volunteers, see "How to Initiate and Administer a Community Resource Volunteer Program." An ERIC Report: Ed-081-061, 1971.

In a more direct sense, an administrator has an opportunity to involve community groups in the use of school facilities when he responds to their requests for the use of rooms in the building, (at the end of the school day or on weekends). Many groups, such as scouts or local drama players, may request the administrator's permission to use school facilities after school hours. The ultimate authority for granting this permission may be the central office, depending on school board policy. However, the school administrator can act as either a facilitator or an impediment in securing permission for use of the facilities. Certainly, the school administrator's attitude and behavior in this kind of a situation can either evoke considerable good will or create ill will on the part of these community groups.

Another opportunity for community use of school facilities on which more administrators should capitalize, is that of inviting retired people to view student activities as the school's guests. Retired people often have limited financial resources and social outlets, and appreciate complimentary passes to watch athletic, dramatic, and music activities at the school. Some schools issue a "Golden Age School Activities Pass" to retired people in the community. This type of effort by a school can deliver dividends in increasing community good will, and it offers at the same time, a service to the retired people of the community who have supported the schools for so many years with taxes. [26]

It should be noted that involving the community in the use of school facilities will not always be an easy task for the school administrator. Financial problems on the part of the district, lack of vision on the part of the school board and teachers, and inadequate cooperation from the custodial staff are three major obstacles which may have to be overcome by the school administrator. However, if an administrator really believes that the schools are for all the people in the community, and if he is willing to exert his energy and time to resolve serious problems, then a program of community use of school facilities should be possible and, in any event, remains desirable.*

INVOLVING PARENTS: PROBLEMS

PARENTAL APATHY

Although community participation in the school has value, the administrator should recognize that it is not without attendant problems. An initial barrier which may confront a school administrator who wishes to involve parents in the school is parental apathy. Ironically, despite the great emphasis recently on parental involvement, many administrators who have tried to involve parents report that they have encountered considerable apathy. For example,

*An excellent article on the steps to be taken in establishing a community school is by Tony S. Carriblo and Israel C. Heston, "Strategies for Establishing a Community Education Program," *Phi Delta Kappan* 54 (Nov. 1972): 165-67.

questionnaires sent to parents may not be returned, and meetings of parents' organizations are often poorly attended. A common complaint of many administrators is that parents are indifferent about school unless a controversial issue arises; otherwise, most parents seem to prefer to remain uninvolved in school affairs.

Realistically, a school cannot accommodate the active involvement of *all* parents and there will always be a number of them who simply do not care to participate in school affairs, regardless of how much effort the school expends in that direction. The school administrator should also realize that many parents are occupied with full-time jobs and, at the end of a long day, various leisure activities compete with the school for the available time of parents. (For example, how many school administrators, if given a choice, would decide against a relaxing evening at home, watching television, reading, or engaging in another type of leisure time activity with the family, in favor of attending a meeting at the school?) Although most parents are interested in the school and many of them might be willing to become more active in working to improve it, the administrator needs to recognize that a number of alternative activities are competing for parents' available time.

A school administrator who is faced with parental apathy needs to approach this situation as he would any other problem: by attempting to define more precisely the nature of and reasons for the problem. A thorough diagnosis may reveal that parent apathy is only a symptom, rather than the problem itself.

The initial question which the administrator needs to ask is, "Why are parents apathetic?" Until the administrator attempts a systematic investigation of the reasons for parental apathy, he is unlikely to make much progress in ameliorating it, and any actions he takes may be based on an incorrect diagnosis of the causes of the problem. An effective solution to a problem must be preceded by a correct diagnosis of the causes. The administrator, by trying to hypothesize as to the causes of parent apathy and then collecting data from parents on the hypotheses, is engaged in the processs of diagnosis. [27] This process should provide direction for a possible solution to parent apathy.

Figure 17.5 presents a questionnaire which an administrator can use to ascertain the reasons for parental apathy and the perceived importance of those reasons.

As figure 17.5 suggests, the reasons behind parental apathy may be complex. Parental apathy should be viewed as a *symptom* of limited parental involvement in the schools, but not as its cause. Actually, parental apathy may be only a convenient label which many administrators have used to affix blame on parents for not responding better to the school's attempts to involve them. Again, the basic question that the administrator needs to ask is, "*Why* are parents apathetic?"

	Parent's Response				
Reasons from Parent's Perception	Not Important	Of Some Importance	Fairly Important	Very Important	Extremely Important
1. Not enough time	_____	_____	_____	_____	_____
2. Not sure how to get involved	_____	_____	_____	_____	_____
3. Not sure the school really wants parents to get involved	_____	_____	_____	_____	_____
4. Not sure that I have the necessary skills and knowledge to get involved in school affairs	_____	_____	_____	_____	_____
5. No need to get involved; teachers and administrators already know what is best	_____	_____	_____	_____	_____
6. Have previously had poor or bad experience when I became involved in school decision making	_____	_____	_____	_____	_____
7. No one has ever encouraged me to become involved	_____	_____	_____	_____	_____
8. _____					
	_____	_____	_____	_____	_____
9. _____					
	_____	_____	_____	_____	_____

Figure 17.5. Factors which May Restrict Parental Involvement in the Schools. [28]

A related question which also should be raised by a school administrator as he investigates parental apathy is, "Do the professional staff and I really want parents to become *significantly* involved in school affairs, and if we do, are we willing to work *hard* to secure that kind of involvement?" Involving parents is a time-consuming, demanding, and at times frustrating task. Unless the administrator and the staff are truly committed to parental involvement, it is not likely to be successful.

Many parents believe, rightly or wrongly, that the school wants them to be involved only in busywork or in providing support for the school, rather than in evaluating the effectiveness of the school or participating in school decision making. If an administrator wants to combat parental apathy, he will probably need to provide more meaningful opportunities for parents to participate in school affairs. [29] Most people are apathetic about taking part in a given activity unless they feel that they can make a significant contribution.

PARENTAL "OVERINVOLVEMENT"

Although parental apathy can be a troublesome problem for a school administrator who is sincerely committed to participation by parents in the schools, an equally difficult (though opposite) problem for some administrators is parental overinvolvement. The latter problem can take many forms, but it may be defined as parental involvement which tends to interfere with the operation and administration of the school by the professional staff and the administrator. [30] Figure 17.6 presents some examples of parental overinvolvement, as perceived by many administrators.

---

1. Censorship of books or materials in the school by individual parents.

2. Efforts by individual parents or by groups of parents to become "excessively" involved in decision making about school policies and procedures.

3. Attempts to modify the school curriculum (e.g., ban on sex education) by pressure groups.

4. Regular or constant complaints by individual parents or parents' groups.

Figure 17.6. Types of Parental Overinvolvement.

It should be noted that parental overinvolvement is a value judgment that is in "the eyes of the beholder." What is considered to be "overinvolvement" by one administrator may be seen as appropriate or justifiable involvement by other observers. For example, a particular activity which might be part of no. 2 in figure 17.6 may be perceived as legitimate and reasonable by parents, and yet may be perceived by the school administrator and the professional staff as representing "overinvolvement" on the part of the parents and interference with the operation of the school.

As problems of the schools have recently attracted increased attention from the media, parents have become more concerned about the quality of education and, as a consequence, many of them have tried to become actively involved in school affairs. Depending on the nature of that involvement and the concept of parental involvement held by the school administrator and the professional staff, conflicts are possible.

Part of the problem is that active involvement by parents who have tended to question the school's effectiveness or who have attempted to develop a larger role for themselves in school decision making represents a threat to many school administrators and their professional staffs, and they respond negatively. In some cases, much of the administrator's concern about parental overinvolvement is caused by his own lack of willingness to be evaluated by parents and to share decision-making responsibilities with them. On the other hand, there is legitimate administrative concern in connection with certain types of parental involvement, such as attempts at censorship or the use of protest tactics by special interest groups.

According to Wirt and Kirst, the following factors are characteristic of special interest groups who use protest against the school: [31]

1. The use of protest indicates that regular channels for handling grievances and complaints are not functioning effectively for the special interest group.
2. The special interest group that uses pressure will try to publicize their demands through communications media in hopes of attracting allies and supporters.
3. The special interest group that uses pressure will try to dramatize issues and problems rather than to present "objective" data.
4. Working with a special interest group that uses pressure can be a difficult and frustrating task for the school administrator.

Despite the difficulties in working with a special interest group that uses pressure tactics, the administrator should not assume that the demands of the group are without merit or that pressure by a group is necessarily bad. Historically, in our society necessary change has frequently been brought about *only* after the use of pressure. While not every kind of method can be justified, pressure tactics may be needed in certain situations in order to bring about needed change. And, regardless of the methods used, the demands of a group should be considered on their own merits, separately from the tactics employed.

If an administrator is concerned about special interest groups who use pressure tactics, or any other type of parent overinvolvement, the following possible causes of that overinvolvement should be investigated:

1. The regular channels for parental involvement and resolution of grievances and complaints are not functioning effectively.
2. A misunderstanding. Perhaps the parents were not briefed clearly enough by the school as to the limits of their or the school's authority.

3. An unrealistic or inappropriate notion of the value and concept of parental involvement on the part of either the parents or the administration, or both.
4. An honest difference of opinion between the school administration and the parents on the role of parents in school affairs.

Parents' overinvolvement can create serious problems for the school. The school administrator's role in response to parental overinvolvement should be to investigate its possible causes and take whatever action seems appropriate and feasible in light of local circumstances.

A CLOSING PERSPECTIVE

Effective community involvement will not be an easy objective to achieve. There will be frustrations and problems which must be overcome, and little success will be experienced without considerable hard work and persistence on the part of the administrator. However, given an administrator with a strong commitment to and broad vision of the potential usefulness of community involvement, a successful program of community participation in the schools is attainable.

Review

1. Describe the relationship between the school and the community. List those aspects of the community about which the administrator needs to be knowledgeable.
2. Discuss two major types of conflict in school-community relations. What kinds of conditions seem to contribute to these conflicts, and how can the administrator prevent or ameliorate them?
3. Why is it important for the school to involve parents and other citizens in school affairs? What should be the main purpose of this involvement?
4. Explain the primary purpose, advantages and disadvantages, and the role of the administrator in each of the types of parents' involvement described in this chapter.
5. What are the two main problems that an administrator might encounter in trying to involve parents? How can he best prevent or ameliorate these problems?

Notes

1. William O. Stanley et al., *Social Foundations of Education* (New York: Holt-Dryden Books, Henry Holt Co., 1955), p. 81.
2. Neal Gross, *Who Runs Our Schools?* (New York: John Wiley & Sons, 1958).

3. For an early but still relevant introduction to the basic concepts for studying and understanding a local community, see Lloyd A. Cook and Elaine F. Cook, *A Sociological Approach to Education* (New York: McGraw-Hill Co., 1950). For a more recent approach, see Daniel Weiter and Jean Guertin, *School-Community Relations: Some Aids to Analyzing and Planning for the School Administrator* (Santa Monica, Calif.: Systems Development Corporation, 1971).

4. For a good description of how to carry out this study, see Gene C. Fusco, "Working with Organized Groups: Improving Your School-Community Relations Program." An ERIC Report: Ed-021-328, 1967.

5. Richard A. Gorton, *Conflict, Controversy and Crises in School Administration and Supervision* (Dubuque, Iowa: Wm. C. Brown Company Publishers, 1972), p. 23.

6. An excellent description of the objectives and influence of a number of these groups can be found in R. Campbell et al., *The Organization and Control of American Schools* (Columbus, Ohio: Charles E. Merrill Publishing Co., 1970), chaps. 12, 13.

7. An interesting study which revealed that the people in a community received their information more from informal than from formal channels was conducted by Donald G. Marcotte, "The Dyadic Relationship of Selected Variables in the Process of Communication from the School to the Public" (Ph.D. diss., Purdue University, 1971).

8. For help in this area, see Robert P. Bullock, *School-Community Attitude Analysis for Educational Administrators* (Columbus, Ohio: Ohio State University, 1959).

9. For an excellent discussion of the long history of citizen participation in school affairs, see Gordon McCloskey, *Education and Public Understanding* (New York: Harper and Row, 1959).

10. *Toward More Effective Involvement of the Community in the Schools* (Dayton, Ohio: Institute for Development of Educational Activities, 1972).

11. For research on the positive outcomes of involvement, see Herbert J. Schiff, "The Effects of Personal Contactual Relationships on Parents' Attitudes toward and Participation in Local School Affairs" (Ed.D. diss., Northwestern University, 1963).

12. See also Luvern L. Cunningham, "Community Involvement in Change," *Educational Leadership* 27, no. 4 (January 1970):363-66.

13. Don Davies, "The Emerging Third Force in Education," *Inequalities in Education* 15 (November 1973):5.

14. For evidence on this point, see Donald R. Eells, "Are Parents Really Partners in Education?" *Bulletin of the National Association of Secondary School Principals* 58 (January 1974):26-31.

15. See Suburban Area Study Group, "The Schools and the Community: A Communications Study." An ERIC Report: Ed-026-716, 1966.

16. Ibid., p. 10.

17. *PTA Magazine* 66, no. 1 (September 1971).

18. James Koerner, *Who Controls American Education?* (Boston: Beacon Press, 1968), p. 148.

19. "The Value of the PTA," *Today's Education* 58 (May 1969):31.

20. In at least one school district a parental advisory committee won from the courts the right to "meaningful participation" in the making of certain types of school decisions. Reported in *Phi Delta Kappan* (January 1973):343.

21. The consequences of not taking these steps are fully detailed in Donald P. Conde, "A Conceptual Analysis of Public Participation in the Decision-Making Functions of the Public Schools" (Ed.D. diss., University of Massachusetts, 1969).

22. For an example of how this was successfully done in one situation, see William D. Aldridge, "Changing Public Attitudes toward School Policies and Programs through a Planned Program of Citizen Interviews by Teachers" (Ed.D. diss., University of Oregon, 1967).

23. National School Public Relations Association, *School Volunteers* (Arlington, Va.: National School Public Relations Association, 1973).

24. W. Fred Totten and Frank Manley, *The Community School* (Galien, Mich.: Allied Education Council, 1969). For a future-oriented view of community use of the school, see Ted Gordon et al., "The Community Education View of Health, Physical Education and Recreation," *Phi Delta Kappan* 54 (November 1972):179-81. For an indication of the early roots

of the approach, see Clarence A. Perry, *Wider Use of the School Plant* (New York: Russell Sage Foundation, 1910).

25. John R. Hughes, editor, "The Community School and Its Concept." An ERIC Report: Ed-073-531, 1972.

26. For an interesting idea on how one school involved local senior citizens, see "Senior Citizens Share Fun Festival," *NASSP Spotlight,* May 1973.

27. Examine the following newsletter for a number of possible hypotheses: *It Starts in the Classroom,* a public relations newsletter for classroom teachers, published by the National Association of Public Relations, September 1972 issue.

28. Identified in a study by James Smith, "The Relationship between Parents' Attitude toward the School and Their Involvement in School Decision-Making" (Specialist field project, University of Wisconsin—Milwaukee, 1973).

29. Barbara Schram, "Some Basic Guidelines for Building Parent Participation Groups to Effect Change in the Public Schools." An ERIC Report: Ed-009-445, 1968. For a good example of how an administrator attempted to improve parental involvement, see George T. Frey, "Improving School-Community Relations," *Today's Education,* 60, no. 1 (January 1971):14-17.

30. For a review of the literature on the problem and a study of how the problem manifested itself in one school district, see Frank L. Heesacker, "Public Influence on the Teacher in One Oregon School District" (Ed.D. diss., University of Oregon, 1967).

31. Frederick M. Wirt and Michael W. Kirst, *The Political Web of American Schools* (Boston: Little, Brown & Co., 1972), pp. 57-59.

18

School-Community Relations:
Communication and Public Relations

Most administrators have long recognized the importance of effective school-community communication and the desirability of maintaining good public relations. Unfortunately, in too many situations, communication has been primarily *from* the school *to* the community (with little attempt to secure feedback), and the objective of the school's public relations activities has been to "sell" the school program.

School-community communication and public relations should be cooperative processes which are both honest and responsive. In the case of school-community communication, each party has something of value to communicate to the other and needs to seek feedback on whether its own message is being received and understood accurately. A school's public relations program must reflect honesty and integrity in all of its interfaces with the community in order to retain its credibility, and the confidence and support of the community. In the following sections, a number of different aspects of school-community communication and the school's public relations program will be explored.

SCHOOL-COMMUNITY RELATIONS: COMMUNICATION

TYPICAL COMMUNICATION PRACTICES

Traditionally the school has, for the most part, used two main methods of communicating with its immediate community: (1) the school newsletter, and (2) the PTA or parents' meeting. (The telephone and individual conferences are two other means of communication used by the school on a *limited* basis to communicate with parents or other members of the community.)

The school newsletter has taken several forms, depending on the school and the school district. It may be an informational bulletin developed and disseminated by the district office, describing noteworthy activities occurring in all the schools in the district. Or an individual school may publish its own newsletter, describing in more detail and to a greater extent than would be possible in a district newsletter, the major activities and happenings in that school that might be of interest to parents. The newsletter may be a semimonthly commercially printed news bulletin mailed to parents, or it may consist of an occasional, mimeographed information sheet sent with the students to the home. The school newsletter may be perceived by parents and the community as informative and worthwhile, or it may be perceived as containing little or nothing that is newsworthy or important.

A second major means by which schools try to communicate with parents and the community is through PTA or parents' meetings. At parents' meetings, information about some aspect of a school's program is usually disseminated, and there are opportunities for two-way communication between school personnel and parents. The meetings may be scheduled on a regular basis or they may be scheduled only irregularly. The meetings may be well attended by both teachers and parents, or by only a small percentage of parents and teachers. The programs at the parents' meetings may be informative to parents, or they may be perceived as presenting little or no real information about what is happening at school. [1]

Regardless of the type of school newsletter and parents' meetings, it is clear that they reflect an attempt by the schools to communicate with the parents and the community.* The questions which need to be raised, however, are: to what extent are the school's communication practices with parents and the community effective, and how could they be improved?

Although there is a paucity of research data on the effectiveness of school communication practices with parents and the community, observation and analysis of available studies would suggest that many schools are engaging in ineffective communications practices. Criticisms have generally focused on the following aspects: [2]

1. **Information disseminated by many schools has tended to be primarily self-promoting and not relevant to the immediate needs and concerns of the parents and the larger community.** This criticism is directed in part to the practice of communicating only the "good news" (e.g., National Merit Scholarships, the latest federal grant), while omitting the less desirable news (such as the truancy rate, or problems of vandalism or litter at the school).

The school should attempt to communicate to the home *both* favorable news and information about general problems. In most situations, news about problems will reach the home one way or another regardless. Therefore, for purposes of increasing accuracy, and informing parents of steps that are being taken to alleviate troublesome conditions, the school should be as candid about its "blemishes" as possible. This would include factual information about the *nature* of a problem, what the school is trying to do about the problem, and what contributions parents and the community might make toward ameliorating the problem.

Criticism is also directed at the tendency of schools to disseminate

*It is recognized that there can be innumerable variations of the newsletters and parents' meetings described.

predominantly that information which school officials *think* parents and the community should receive, without securing *feedback* from these groups on what they *actually want to receive*. In a good school-community communication program *both* types of information are disseminated. [3]

2. **Communication from the school to the community is limited to those special instances when a school needs the community's support, such as in a bond referendum, or when a major crisis or problem occurs.** Otherwise, most schools' communication to parents and the community is sporadic. That the public would like to receive more information about the schools was indicated by a Gallup survey which revealed that the majority of both public and nonpublic school parents were desirous of knowing *more* about the schools in their community. Specific areas included were: (1) the curriculum, (2) qualifications of teachers, (3) current methods of teaching, (4) how the schools are administered, and (5) problems of discipline. [4]

3. **The school's dissemination procedures are not reliable in many instances.** School newsletters which are not mailed directly to the home are frequently lost or destroyed by students, who are being used by the school as information carriers. Parents' meetings and parent-teacher conferences are often poorly attended and are an ineffective means of communicating with a large number of parents. Consequently, unless the information which a school wishes to communicate to parents is actually *mailed* to them, it is, in many cases, unlikely to be received.

4. **The school has not sufficiently utilized means of communication in addition to the newsletter and parents' meeting for transmitting information to parents and the larger community.** [5] Other means of communication include radio, television, the newspaper, and regular parent and community visitations to the school.*

5. **The school has not tried hard enough to ascertain the extent to which its messages are being received, understood, and acted upon by parents and the community as intended by the school.** [6] Conspicuously absent is a school plan for systematically and periodically seeking feedback from parents and the community on how they are reacting to the information which the school is communicating to them.

While poor communication practices are not characteristic of all schools, ineffective or inadequate messages and methods exist to a sufficient degree to cause concern among many parents, members of the community, and educators. Therefore, in the following section, ideas and recommendations will be presented to help school administrators improve their communication effectiveness with parents and the community.

---

*For an interesting report of how a school principal made effective use of the news media, see Del Harding, "How to Capitalize on News Media" *NASSP Bulletin* 58 (January 1974):43-49.

IMPROVING SCHOOL-COMMUNITY COMMUNICATION

THE MESSAGE

One of the most important aspects of communication is the message. In school-community communication there are potentially several types of messages. There is the message that the school wants to communicate, there is the one that the community wants to receive, and there is the actual message received by the community. Conversely, there is the message that the community *wants* to communicate to the school, there is the message the school wants to receive from the community, and there is the actual message received by the school. Complex? Perhaps, but school administrators should be aware of these six types of messages, and they should recognize that, to the extent to which the various messages within each set are congruent with each other, communication may or may not be effective.

For example, a school may have a message that it would like to communicate to the community. However, the community may not be interested in that particular topic and may want the school to communicate with it on a different topic. When this happens, communication between the school and the community becomes impaired. Too often this kind of situation exists because the school is not sending to parents and the larger community the types of information they would like to receive. (Of course, there are times when a school *should* send a particular message to the community regardless of whether or not the community wants to receive it, if the message is in the community's best interests.)

An important first consideration in improving school-community communication is for the school administrator to find out what kinds of messages and information parents and the community wish to receive. He can begin developing a better understanding of the types of messages he should send by means of a study of community expectations for communication from the school. (A survey periodically administered to all or a sample of parents and other people in a school's immediate community would ascertain many of their communication needs.)

In conducting such an investigation the administrator should be aware of existing research studies on parental expectations for school communication. For example, in a fourteen-school study Anderson found that parents from the central city, city fringe-suburban, rural and urban areas all agreed that they wanted to receive "frequently" from the school eight different types of information. These categories listed in order of their importance to the parents were: (1) the grades and achievement of the parents' son or daughter, (2) discipline problems involving their child, (3) the child's personal weaknesses or physical handicaps, (4) the child's talents and abilities, (5) a schedule of school events, (6) graduation requirements (7) career information, and (8) information on the school's rules and regulations. [7] In addition, parents' responses pertaining to desiring information on "the needs and shortcomings of the school" tended toward "frequently."

Anderson found also that although parents from all four population classifications generally agreed on the frequency with which they desired communication from the school on the items listed above, there were additional types of information which some groups wanted more frequently than other groups. For example, *suburban* area parents wanted to receive frequent reports from the school on new ideas and procedures of instruction being used or considered. Parents in the *central city* wanted frequent communication about their children's intellectual capacity and on the results of activity competition. Parents of children in schools located in *rural* settings wanted to receive frequent information from the school on (1) needs and shortcomings of the school, (2) the intellectual capacity of their children, (3) school activities and the results of activity competition, and (4) athletic events results. Parents of children attending *urban* schools wanted frequent communication on the latter three items, as well as reports on new ideas and procedures of instruction being used or considered, the goals and objectives of the school, and the guidance program.

School administrators who are seeking insight into parents' expectations for information from the school should find the results of Anderson's investigation helpful. His research revealed the kinds of information that parents, regardless of population setting, want to receive from the school, as well as specific types of information particularly valued by parents in certain areas. However, his findings should be used only as a general guide to parental expectations for school communication, not as a substitute for the administrator's own specific investigation. Any school administrator who is interested in improving a school's communication effectiveness should conduct his own study of parents and other residents in the school's immediate community to ascertain their communication needs.

School-community communication should be a two-way process. The school has something important to communicate to parents and other residents of the immediate community, and the school's professional personnel should recognize that the community and parents have something important to communicate to the school.

While there are many kinds of information which a school should be seeking from parents and other citizens, it should attempt to obtain the following information on a regular basis:

1. What are the expectations of parents and other citizens in regard to the types of educational programs the school should offer?
2. What elements do parents and other citizens perceive as the strengths of the school?
3. Which aspects of the school program would parents and other citizens like to see changed?

4. To what extent are parents and other citizens receiving the types of information they desire from the school?
5. To what degree are parents and other citizens satisfied with the *means* by which the school communicates information?

Too often the school seems to be interested primarily in getting its message across to parents and other citizens while giving little or no priority to ascertaining the message they want to receive or the message they would like to communicate to the school. If the school is to improve its communication effectiveness with the community, the administrator must give as much priority to developing a better understanding of the communication needs of the community as he does to communicating what the school wants the community to know.

THE MEDIUM

According to Marshall McLuhan, "The medium is the message." Even if McLuhan's observation was overstated, the administrator who wants to improve a school's communication effectiveness with parents and other citizens should examine the means by which the school is trying to send its message.

The best way to start would be to review the research on parents' preferences for how information from the school should be communicated to them. Again, the findings from Anderson's study are instructive.[8] Anderson asked parents to select, from among twenty-one different kinds of communication media by which they might receive school information, those communication channels by which they preferred that the school communicate information to them. The responses by parents concerning the relative importance of various types of media which might be used by the school revealed some definite preferences for certain channels of communication. Although choice of media differed somewhat according to the nature of the information and the population classification under consideration, there was considerable agreement among the parents in the total sample.

For example, in all of the four classifications of population, the town or city newspaper was selected as the parents' preferred means of school communication for the following types of information: athletic event results, new building programs in progress, new building programs being considered, facility remodeling, budget information, professional meetings attended by school officials, national education issues, needs and shortcomings of the school, and strengths of the school. Face-to-face conferences between school personnel and parents were preferred for communication of information about discipline problems, talents and abilities, and physical weaknesses or handicaps of the son or daughter, as well as about class content.

Parents in all four population classifications generally indicated that the local newspaper represented their highest preference as a source for receiving information about the school; the school'bulletin and the school newspaper represented their second and third choices, respectively. Face-to-face conferences, radio, letters, board meetings, school policy books, television, notes or special reports, calendars of events, the telephone, report cards, and group meetings varied greatly as to parental preference, depending on the type of information being considered.

While the findings from Anderson's study should not be generalized as referring to all school settings, they can serve as a guide to parental preferences for certain channels of communication.* However, as valuable as Anderson's research might be, the school administrator should still conduct his own investigation on parental preferences for school communication methods. This study might include ascertaining parents' preferences for the alternative channels of communication identified in Anderson's research. The important question which the administrator should try to answer is, by what methods would parents prefer that the school communicate information to them?

As the administrator examines the means by which the school communicates information to parents, he should also investigate to determine whether the information is attractively packaged and the degree of reliability with which it reaches the intended recipients of the message. The "printed word" is one of the principal methods by which most schools try to communicate a message of general interest to parents. Frequently, the information to be communicated is mimeographed or dittoed, and copies are given to the students to be taken home to the parents at the end of the day. Parents complain that all too often the information does not reach them because it is lost or thrown away before the students reach home. Even in those cases in which the information arrives at the home, however, the format, typing, and quality of reproduction of the message may be unattractive, perhaps illegible, and not conducive to stimulating the parents to read the school's message.

While there are times when a school probably cannot avoid communicating printed information through a dittoed sheet or by the student carrier, the administrator should try to limit their use. If the information which the school would like to communicate to parents is important and represents something that parents definitely should read, then the school should make every effort to communicate this information in an attractive, readable form. A publication which the administrator should find useful for

*It should be noted that the parents' preferences (or lack of them) for a particular medium are dependent, at least in part, on the degree to which the school has utilized that method. If, for example, a school never uses television for communicating school news, parents may not be aware of its potential.

improving the format and packaging of the information he sends home to parents is *Putting Words and Pictures About Schools Into Print*.[9]

A case can also be made that a school should make every effort to *mail* important printed information which it wishes to communicate to the home. Utilizing the student as a messenger to the home has not been a particularly successful practice in most school situations, for the reasons mentioned above. By mailing a message to the home, the school can be assured that the information will probably reach the parents. A bulk mailing permit is not an expensive item for a nonprofit organization such as the school, and the total cost of mailing information home from the school should not result in an exorbitant expense. The main question the administrator needs to ask is, "How important is it that the information the school is trying to communicate to the parents be received by them?" If it is important, then the administrator should strongly consider mailing the information to the home.

FEEDBACK

That communication should be a two-way process is a point that has already been made. The school should realize that it is just as important to ascertain what parents and other citizens have on their minds as to communicate messages to these publics. The specific kinds of information which the school should be seeking have already been identified. But a problem for many school administrators seems to be *how* to obtain feedback from parents and other citizens. While there are numerous approaches which administrators could employ to seek feedback, three methods in particular will be recommended.

One is to include space for feedback comments, suggestions, or questions in the printed information which the school disseminates. An example of this method is presented in figure 18.1.

The administrator can tailor this approach to the kind of feedback he desires. If he wants specific feedback on the content of a message he is sending to the parents, he can design his questions accordingly. If, on the other hand, he is interested in more general or open-ended feedback, a portion of the newsletter can be designed with that purpose in mind. Using part of the school's information bulletin for the purpose of seeking feedback from parents and other interested parties would seem to be a relatively easy, low-cost means.

A second approach which a number of schools have utilized in order to secure feedback from parents is the Parents' Invitation to Visit the School Program. This method differs from the traditional Parent-Teacher Conference Program or the Back-to-School-Night Program in that a smaller group of parents is involved, the discussion is less formal, and the meeting

How Come?

?

Do you ever wonder why certain things are done or are not done? Or why some things are done the way they are?? If so—and you have never had the time or opportunity to find out—use the form below and a reply will be mailed to you.

How Come: _____

_____

_____

Name: _____

Address: _____

Mail to: School District No. 1
8060 N. 60th Street

Figure 18.1. An Example of a Method
for Obtaining Feedback. [10]

does not focus on the problems or achievements of specific children. The primary purpose of the Parents' Invitation to Visit the School Program is to provide an opportunity for a small group of parents to meet with the school administrator in an informal atmosphere to share ideas and perceptions. The meetings usually take place during school hours on a biweekly basis and an attempt is made by the school to schedule as many of these meetings as possible during the year. An example of how such meetings are organized and implemented is presented in figure 18.2.

Reports from schools and parents who have employed this approach are generally favorable. One thing, though, that the administrator himself should try to avoid during these meetings is dominating the discussion and concentrating too much on "selling" the school's program. The primary purpose of this kind of meeting should be to provide an opportunity for parents to present *their* ideas, questions, and concerns—not just a forum for the administrator.

Care to spend an hour or so at Dean School on a Thursday morning, sipping coffee and sharing your ideas and opinions with the principal? Want to offer a parent's perception of the school scene? Looking for answers to questions raised by some educational trend or practice or development?

Starting Thursday, February 24, and continuing through May, small groups of parents will be invited to Thursday morning coffees with the principal. These "sip and share" sessions will be held in the main lobby of the Dean School and will begin at 10:00 a.m. If you would be interested in attending one or more of these meetings, please indicate below and have your child return the slip to school. You will then be contacted by phone to arrange for a specific date convenient to you.

Figure 18.2. Parents' Invitation to
Visit the School. [11]

While the previous two methods can provide useful feedback to a school, they do have shortcomings. The feedback portion of the newsletter allows only a limited amount of space for a response, and visits to the school are not convenient for all parents. This does not mean that the administrator should reject these means of obtaining feedback. They should definitely be employed. However, the administrator may need to utilize, in addition, a more comprehensive and systematic method of obtaining feedback from parents and the general public. If an administrator really wants to know what parents or other relevant groups in the community think about some aspect of education, an attempt should be made to survey them periodically through some type of a formal questionnaire, followed by a sample of in-depth interviews.* An example of such a survey is presented in figure 18.3.

The school survey is perhaps the most systematic and complete feedback approach. It can be designed for a variety of purposes, and it can provide a great deal of useful information.† It is probably the most costly of the feedback methods recommended in this chapter, but its expense can be justified on the basis of the valuable information it generates.

RELATIONSHIP WITH THE NEWS MEDIA

The relationship between the school administrator and the news media has frequently been one of ambivalence and suspicion. Often the administrator perceives the reporter as a nuisance who is interested only in exposing the school's shortcomings. On the other hand, the reporter may see the ad-

*For a description of how to conduct those interviews by telephone, see Donn R. Wilshaw and R. H. Hardick, "Instant Survey: New Answer to an Old Problem," *School Management* 17 (November-December 1973):30-32.

† The administrator who would like assistance in designing a survey should see The National Public Relations Association, *How to Conduct Low Cost Surveys* and *Policy and Survey Research* (Washington D.C.: National Public Relations Association.)

Presurvey

Objective: To improve the present public relations and communications program between home and school.

Survey Data:
1. Person completing survey: Mother _____ Father _____ Guardian _____
2. In what grade level(s) are your children? 7 _____ 8 _____ 9 _____

--- --- --- --- --- --- --- --- --- --- --- --- --- --- --- --- --- --- ---

Instructions:
Place a check (√) on the line indicating your preference with regard to the following questions and statements:

3. Have you received our November school newsletter? Yes _____ No _____
4. If "yes," how effective do you think it is in getting information about our school to our parents? (Check one.)

1 _____	2 _____	3 _____	4 _____	5 _____
very poor	poor	average	good	very good

5. When your child started junior high school, did you attend the orientation meeting for parents? Yes _____ No _____
6. If "yes," how useful do you think the orientation was for parents?

1 _____	2 _____	3 _____	4 _____	5 _____
very poor	poor	average	good	very good

7. Do you know about the Jerstad-Agerhold Junior High School Advisory Council of parents, teachers, and administrators? Yes _____ No _____
8. If "yes," please rate their effectiveness in getting information to our parents. (Check one.)

1 _____	2 _____	3 _____	4 _____	5 _____
very poor	poor	average	good	very good

Figure 18.3.* Jerstad-Agerholm Junior High School. [12]

ministrator as one who is secretive, defensive, and less than responsive to the public's right to be informed about what is happening in the schools. While neither point of view is valid, there is enough truth in both perceptions to create grounds for a poor relationship. This is unfortunate, since the news media does have a responsibility to obtain accurate information about the schools for the public, and administrators could more effectively utilize the news media to provide the public with information about various aspects of the educational enterprise.

The problem of a poor school-news media relationship does not lend itself to any simple solution. However, it would appear that greater openness and candor by the administrator would be helpful. Specifically, he should attempt to follow the ten guidelines recommended by Bruton: [13]

*Only sample questions are used to illustrate the nature of the survey.

1. Don't ever tell a lie . . . and that includes telling the technical truth designed to lead the reporter in reaching the wrong conclusion. An admission may put a school in a bad light, but not nearly so bad as it and you will be in if facts come to light after your untruthful denial. (Witness the Watergate situation.)

2. Try to be open in answering press questions. The right of students and staff members to privacy is protected by law and by common courtesy, but most questions can be answered without problems. The possibility of being misunderstood, the fact that an incident reflects badly on the school (perhaps unfairly), or the chance that any discussion of facts in a case may raise tensions in a school or community are not sufficient reasons to respond, "No comment" to press inquiries. If the press is doing its job, it will tell a story it feels needs to be told, whether you help or not. You have a responsibility to do all you can to see that it is told fully and correctly.

3. Don't talk off the record. A reporter is not there to satisfy idle curiosity. If it's not fit to print or broadcast, it's not a fit subject for discussion.

4. Regularly and systematically offer news and feature story ideas to the press. Don't be discouraged because your first half-dozen or dozen ideas are brushed off with no coverage or only a few lines. Keep trying. Not only is the law of averages on your side, but if you are alert, you will be sharpening your skills in identifying what makes a good story.

5. Spend as much time as necessary explaining an idea or program to get it understood. A percentage of the people who feel they are misquoted are really people who didn't make clear what they were trying to say.

6. Keep your head about errors. If a story has an error, decide whether the error invalidates the main idea of the story. If it doesn't invalidate the whole thing, you would probably still want to let the reporter know about it so the mistake won't reoccur on subsequent articles—but don't make a federal case out of it. A correction or a retraction on this level does more harm than good. If the mistake does serious harm (says the school play will be Friday when it is Thursday) or makes the whole story erroneous (says the school board is thinking of closing down one of the high schools when they have decided not to do so), ask for a correction. You'll probably get it. If a reporter does a good job on a story, tell him.

7. Don't be afraid to be interviewed. I have never known a professional reporter who knowingly and purposely misquoted anyone. He may attempt to get your true feelings on a subject plainly on the line while you would prefer to have your opinions not too clear, but he's not going to say "red" when you said "green."

8. Level with the reporter about your thoughts about the impact of facts. If a story or an aspect of a story will do undue harm to

someone or some program, tell the reporter. If timing can be an important factor to help or harrass you, explain that. The reporter retains decision on how he handles the story, but it can't hurt him to know possible consequences. It could affect how he handles the assignment.

9. If you don't know an answer, say so. If you know who does know, refer the reporter to the source, but don't shuttle him just because you don't want the responsibility for the answers. If you don't know and don't know who does, agree to try to find out and call back, and do it.

10. Find out the reporter's time-deadline requirements and try to cooperate. You need not drop everything for the press and, indeed, often you have more pressing responsibilities. But perhaps you can spare sixty seconds before his deadline, or assign someone else to help, or decide when you have time for the press before it's too late.

The recommendations advanced by Bruton may not be easily implemented in all situations, but they are basically sound. While some administrators may feel that reporters are the ones who need to improve and not themselves, it seems clear that as administrators we need to put our own house in order before turning our attention to others. (A booklet which contains many other good ideas for the administrator who is interested in improving his relationship with the press is published by the Pennsylvania School Boards Association and is recommended for the administrator's consideration. [14])

FINAL COMMENT IN IMPROVING SCHOOL-COMMUNITY COMMUNICATION*

Communication between the school and the community should be on a regular basis. The school has frequently been criticized because its communication with the community has been irregular, and then only at times of importance to the school, e.g., a bond referendum. Many administrators behave as though it is not too important for the school to communicate regularly with parents and the rest of the community. However, as Bortner has observed, "The community will acquaint itself with and express opinions about its school whether the school attempts to keep the people informed or not." [15] Regular and full communication between the school and the community is an important prerequisite for developing more accurate information on the part of both and, as a result, a more positive attitude toward each other. [16]

*For additional ideas on school-community communications, see *Communication Ideas in Action* (Washington, D.C.: National School Public Relations Association, 1971).

THE SCHOOL'S PUBLIC RELATIONS PROGRAM

PURPOSE AND OBJECTIVES

Most administrators would agree that it is essential that a school and school district maintain an effective program of public relations with the community. An initial problem, however, is that the term "public relations" in this context is subject to different interpretations, three of which are presented below:

1. The purpose of a public relations program is to *sell* the educational program to the people of the community, so that they will take pride in and support their schools. (To do this, the public relations program should widely publicize the strengths of the existing school program.)
2. The purpose of a public relations program is to *interpret* to the people of the community the educational program that is in operation so that the people will have a better understanding of what the schools are doing and will support the school program. (To do this, the public relations program should explain purposes and procedures in reporting both the strengths and weaknesses of the existing school program.)
3. The purpose of a public relations program is to encourage community interest and *participation* in the school program. (To do this, the public relations program should solicit and utilize appropriate information, advice, and assistance of interested community groups and individuals in many aspects of school operations. It should also report and explain both the strengths and weaknesses of the existing school program.)[17]

Although there are probably few administrators who would *publicly* admit to subscribing only to the first concept of school public relations, the behavior of many administrators suggests that the other concepts have little appeal to them. Seldom does one find an administrator who reports to the community both strengths *and* weaknesses of the existing school program. While the concept of encouraging community interest and participation in the school program has received considerable attention in the educational literature and at conventions and conferences, the number of schools implementing the concept in full measure is less than overwhelming. The fact of the matter is that in practice most administrators have not accepted fully the concepts of public relations as defined in nos. 2 and 3.[18]

Perhaps the failure by most administrators to endorse and implement the latter two concepts can be attributed to a misunderstanding of how one gains support of the school by the public. If administrators are really interested in community pride in and support of the schools, the most effective way to achieve this objective is to be completely open and candid in reporting to the community on the effectiveness of various aspects of the school program and to encourage and utilize community participation whenever appropriate and feasible.[19] Attempting to "sell" the educational program to the people of a community by publicizing only the strengths of the existing school program will strain the believability of a school's communication and will eventually seriously erode its credibility. As Hughes has perceptively observed, ". . . To expect people to 'buy' simply because educators are selling is unrealistic. The terms buying and selling are used advisedly; it is recognized that any successful program will have to be the result of mutual planning, mutual understanding, and mutual trust."[20]

The administrator should keep in mind that an essential requirement for effective communication and public relations is credibility. If a school continues to emphasize only the strengths of its program while isolating itself from community involvement, it runs the risk that the public will begin to ignore, suspect, or fail to believe what the school says. As noted in the publication, *Ideas for Improving Public Confidence in Public Education,* "School officials must report successes and failures honestly and realistically. This must be an on-going policy."[21]

The best kind of public relations program is one based on an open dialogue with the public on the strengths, weaknesses, and problems of the school, creating and maximizing opportunities for community groups and individuals to give information, advice, and assistance to the school. The specific objectives of such a program have been identified by Kindred:

1. To develop intelligent public understanding of the school in all aspects of its operation.
2. To determine how the public feels about the school and what it wishes the school to accomplish.
3. To secure adequate financial support for a sound educational program.
4. To help citizens feel a more direct responsibility for the quality of education that the school provides.
5. To earn the good will, respect, and confidence of the public in professional personnel, and services of the institution.
6. To bring about public realization of the need for change and what must be done to facilitate essential programs.
7. To involve citizens in the work of the school and the solving of educational problems.
8. To promote a genuine spirit of cooperation between the school and community in sharing leadership for the improvement of community life.[22]

ORGANIZATION OF THE PUBLIC RELATIONS PROGRAM

Public relations is not something that just happens. As Bortner has noted, ". . . the school does have a choice: between unplanned and planned public relations, between disregarding or developing an organized public relations program designed to promote community understanding and support." [23]

In order to achieve the objectives of a planned public relations program, people and resources will have to be organized. The final organizational design should clearly identify the various individuals and groups who are involved in the public relations program and the nature of their responsibilities.

While administrators in small school districts are primarily responsible for their school's public relations program, in many medium-to-large school districts a public relations or public information officer directs and coordinates the school district's public relations program. The public relations role of the school administrator in a district that has a public relations officer may be significant or quite limited, depending upon how he and the public relations officer conceive of that role. Generally, the public relations officer will view the school administrator as playing a potentially important role in public relations, although a role definition or in-service training to carry out the administrator's responsibilities in this area may be lacking. Regrettably, there is also some tendency on the part of school administrators in larger districts to feel that public relations is something that is solely in the public information officer's province and should involve other administrators only if a problem develops at their school.

Regardless of whether or not a district employs a public relations officer, the building administrator should be a key figure in the public relations program. It is at the building level that the success or failure of the public relations program is likely to be determined, and the school administrator is a crucial variable influencing that determination.

Although there are many different facets to the school administrator's role in public relations, he should attempt to perform the following tasks in cooperation with other members of the professional staff and representatives of the school community:

1. Develop or update the philosophy and objectives of the school's public relations program. Without clear specification and an understanding of the philosophy and objectives of the program on the part of everyone, it will tend to flounder or go off into different directions.

2. Identify and define the public relations role of the administrative team, the professional and certified staff, the students, and the community. Public relations should be the responsibility of all

people who are associated with the school. However, the administrator will need to define the precise nature of that responsibility, particularly for the personnel who work in the school.

3. Plan and implement a set of public relations activities which will accomplish the goals of the program. The nature of these activities will depend on the types of objectives adopted for the program, but a well-planned, comprehensive set of activities will be needed.*

4. Evaluate the school's current public relations program on a periodic basis to ascertain the need for adding, modifying, or eliminating public relations activities. The questions which the administrator should ask about the school's public relations program are, "What are we now doing that we could be doing better?" "What new activities are needed?" "What activities are unproductive?"

In conceptualizing the type of public relations program most desirable for a school, the administrator needs to recognize that there are many factors which affect the public's attitude toward the school.[24] In a broad sense, almost everything that happens in or to a school can potentially affect the public's attitude. While the administrator cannot always control or influence events or forces in the larger society which may affect the public's attitude toward the school, he can at least try to do something about those conditions that are associated with the school and which may affect public relations. A number of school-related factors which can potentially influence the public's attitude toward the school are presented in figure 18.4.

An examination of figure 18.4 suggests almost everything that the school does may affect the public's attitude toward it. As Charters has noted, "Every aspect of the school, every remark by an employee of the school, every communication with the home, every subject taught, every service to the community, even the janitor's appearance . . . is believed to affect public relations either favorably or unfavorably."[25]

Three factors which can particularly affect a school's public relations image are the ways in which parent-teacher conferences are conducted, the manner in which the school responds to telephone calls, and the general receptivity of the school office to visitors, whether they be parents or other adults. A courteous, friendly, and helpful approach in these situations will contribute greatly to a favorable public perception of the school; the expression (whether intended or not) of an impersonal, condescending, or disinterested attitude will lead to a negative view of the school. It is the

---

*For an excellent description of examples of public relations activities which can be initiated, see Ann Barkelew, "Organizing the School and the District for Public Relations," *Thrust for Educational Leadership* 3 (October 1973):20-21. Also see Larry Ascough, "Trends in Building-Level PR," *NASSP Bulletin* 58 (January 1974):69-70, 80-88.

Classroom Factors	General School Factors	School-Community Factors
1. Teacher-student relationship	1. Type of educational program	1. Receptivity and friendliness of school personnel to parents and visitors
2. Homework policy	a. program of studies	
3. Grading policy and procedures	b. teaching staff	2. Effectiveness of the school in resolving school-community issues and problems
4. Classroom discipline	c. student activities program	
5. Friendliness and communicability of the teacher to the parents	2. General school discipline	3. The accuracy and completeness of information about the school as it is transmitted to parents
	3. General atmosphere in the school	
	4. Appearance of the school building, inside and outside	4. The accuracy and completeness of information the school has about the community

Figure 18.4. School-Related Factors which Affect the Public's Attitude Toward the School.

administrator's responsibility to impress on all school employees the importance of positive contacts with parents and the community.*

While the contribution of school employees to public relations can be significant, probably the single most important public relations agent for the school is the student. [26] Most of the factors identified in figure 18.4 affect the student in some way, and it is through the student that parents and the larger community gain many of their impressions about the school. Therefore, the school administrator should give high priority to policies, procedures, and programs that will result in the development of positive student attitudes and accurate student information about the school and its personnel.

EVALUATING THE SCHOOL'S PUBLIC RELATIONS PROGRAM

The first step an administrator should take to improve a school's public relations program is to evaluate the current program's effectiveness, since periodic evaluation of any program is required for continued improvement.

---

*An excellent filmstrip and tape cassette which identify the public relations role of everyone in the school, and which could be used in an in-service program is *A School Is People,* produced by the National Public Relations Association, Washington, D.C. (1971).

To evaluate a school's public relations program the administrator will need criteria and assessment procedures. Of the many attempts to design criteria for evaluating a school's public relations program, those developed by Bainbridge [27] would appear to be among the most useful for a school administrator. These criteria are stated in the form of a checklist which can be used to analyze the status of a school's underlying public relations philosophy and objectives and the frequency with which certain policies and practices are employed. The specific areas covered by the checklist include (1) information service, (2) curriculum, (3) extracurricular activities affecting the community, (4) other school activities affecting the community, (5) faculty contacts with the community, and (6) community use of buildings and equipment. The final section of the checklist is designed to assist the school in evaluating the total public relations program and its results.*

Whether the administrator uses a checklist such as Bainbridge's or another assessment procedure, it is important that he recognize the need for periodic, systematic evaluation of the school's public relations program. In evaluating the program, the administrator should try to secure representative perceptions from every group associated with the school, including students, parents, teachers, and classified employees. If public relations is the responsibility of everyone in the school, and if the public is considered to include everyone in the community, then representatives of these individuals and groups should all be actively involved in assessing the effectiveness of the school's public relations program.

However, the leadership and impetus for evaluating a school's public relations program should come from the administrator. He must feel strongly about the need for periodic and systematic evaluation, or it probably will not occur. And if a school's public relations program is not evaluated and upgraded, it is the school administrator who should be held accountable for the consequences of a negative or apathetic public attitude toward the school.

A FINAL NOTE

School-community public relations and communication are important tasks for the school administrator. These activities should focus on giving an accurate, candid, and complete picture of the school's strengths *and* problems, and should provide ways by which members of the community can communicate to the school their perceptions and needs. The goal of the

*The National School Public Relations Association also has prepared evaluation standards which should be considered by the school administration. Write to the Association at 1201 Sixteenth Street, NW, Washington, D.C.

school administrator in performing these tasks should not be to manipulate public opinion, but to develop understanding, perspective, and commitment on the part of the community. Only the achievement of the latter goal will maintain school credibility and community support over the long run.

Review

1. What are the main conditions necessary for an effective public relations program and effective school-community communication?
2. Describe several criticisms that have been made of the communication practices of the school. How can these practices be improved?
3. Describe recommended guidelines an administrator should follow in his relations with the news media.
4. Define three different concepts of the function of a school's public relations program. Which is the best approach?
5. Identify the objectives of a good public relations program. Discuss the school administrator's role in helping to achieve those objectives.

Notes

1. For an example of a successful parent meeting, see Dale L. Berne, "Parent Night: A Unique Concept in Community Involvement," *The Clearing House* 47 (April 1973):459-62.

2. One particularly valuable study which documented most of these practices in a large school system was conducted by Thomas R. Williams, "Urban Schools and External Communications," *Administrator's Notebook* 17 (January 1969).

3. William Banach, "Listen Before You Leap," *School Management* 18 (April 1974):34-35.

4. George Gallup, "Sixth Annual Gallup Poll of Public Attitudes toward Education," *Phi Delta Kappan* 56 (September 1974):25.

5. For a comprehensive review of these kinds of communication media and their possible use by the school, see Kenneth Winfield, "A Summary of Reported Research Studies Dealing with Selected Mass Media of Communication and the Implications of the Findings for School-Community Relations Programs" (Ed.D. diss., Temple University, 1965). Also see Anthony F. Pinnie, "Reported Research Studies Dealing with Printed Mass Media of Communication, and The Implications of the Findings for School-Community Relations Programs" (Ed.D. diss., Temple University, 1965).

6. See Robert R. Spillane, "Fostering Communication in Education," *Phi Delta Kappan* 55 (November 1973):182.

7. Richard A. Anderson, "Home School Communications: Information and Media Preferred by Parents of Selected Colorado High Schools" (Ed.D. diss., Colorado State College, 1967, reviewed by Richard A. Gorton, "Comments on Research," *NASSP Bulletin* 56 (February 1972):98-101).

8. Ibid. A later study which found for the most part similar findings was conducted by Anne M. Marnix, "School-Home Communications: Information and Media Preference of Parents of Secondary School Students" (Ph.D. diss., University of Oregon, 1971).

9. *Putting Words and Pictures about School into Print* (Washington, D.C.: National Public Relations Association, 1972).

10. Edited from material employed by Brown Deer Public Schools. Used with permission.

11. Ibid.

12. Edited from material employed by Jerstad-Agerhold Junior High School. Used with permission.

13. Al Bruton, "The School Administrator and the Press: Is Co-existence Possible?" *Thrust for Educational Leadership* 3, no. 1 (1973):15.

14. *Public Relations for Principals: A Guide for the Pennsylvania Administrator* (Harrisburg: Pennsylvania School Boards Association, 1971).

15. Doyle M. Bortner, "The High School: Responsibility for Public Relations," *Bulletin of the National Association of Secondary School Principals* 40 (September 1960):7.

16. See George D. Harrish, "A Study of Citizen Participation in the Educational Decison-Making Process as Perceived by Parents from a Lower Socio-Economic Neighborhood" (Ph.D. diss., Michigan State University, 1970).

17. Part of a study reported in *The Classroom Teacher and Public Relations* (Washington, D.C.: NEA Research Division, 1959), p. 10.

18. For an excellent discussion of this point, see M. Scott Norton, "School-Community Relations—New Issues, New Needs," *The Clearing House* 44 (May 1970):538-40.

19. *Ideas for Improving Public Confidence in Public Education* (Washington, D.C.: National Public Relations Association, 1971).

20. Larry W. Hughes, "Know Your Power Structure," *American School Board Journal* 154, (May 1967):33-35.

21. *Ideas for Improving Public Confidence in Public Education,* p. 18.

22. Leslie W. Kindred, *School Public Relations* (Englewood Cliffs, N.J.: Prentice-Hall, 1957), pp. 16-17.

23. Bortner , "The High School," p. 7.

24. For an early analysis of this point, see W. W. Charters, Jr., "In a Public Relations Program Facts Are Never Enough," *Nation's Schools* 53 (February 1954):56-58.

25. W. W. Charters, Jr., "Public Relations," in *Encyclopedia of Educational Research,* ed. Chester Harris (New York: Macmillan Co., 1960), p. 1075.

26. See Harold Van Winkle, "Good Schools Tell Their Story," *Administrator's Notebook* 5 (December 1956):87.

27. F. W. Bainbridge, Jr., "The Growth and Development of Public Relations in Public Secondary Schools of the United States." Doctoral diss., Indiana University, 1950.

Part 6

Career Considerations

19
Career Assessment

The pursuit of a successful career in school administration involves at least two major elements: (1) understanding and capitalizing on career and employment opportunities, and (2) possessing needed competencies and professional ethics. These aspects will be discussed in this chapter, along with factors involved in obtaining a position in school administration and planning for the first year.

CAREER AND EMPLOYMENT OPPORTUNITIES IN SCHOOL ADMINISTRATION

CAREER OPPORTUNITIES

When one considers career opportunities in school administration,* the principalship is usually the first and most frequently cited position. Although the principalship is perhaps the most important position in the administration of a school, there are a number of other positions with administrative or quasi-administrative responsibilities with which the reader should also become familiar. Examples of these positions are identified in figure 19.1.

		Entry Positions		
Assistant	Dean of	Administrative	Administrative	Department
or	Students	Intern	Assistant	Head
Vice-Principal				or
				Unit
				Leader
		Advanced Position		
		Principal		

Figure 19.1. Examples of Career Positions in School Administration.

*The reader should keep in mind that throughout the book a distinction has been made between district administration and school administration, the latter being the administration of a school.

389

It should be noted that most people seeking their first job in school administration do not begin as principals.[1] An exception would be the person who moves from a teaching position to a principalship in a small school district. The more typical career pattern is for an individual to begin a career in administration by assuming one of the entry positions identified in figure 19.1, e.g., administrative intern, assistant principal. These positions can offer valuable experience and training for more advanced roles in school or district administration and can in many instances provide sufficient personal satisfaction and reward so that they become permanent career positions.

The entry positions in administration represent important components of the administrative team of a school or school district, and the individuals occupying them should have opportunities to make useful contributions to the success of the school program. It should be emphasized that no one should consider an entry position as *merely* a stepping stone to a higher place in the administrative hierarchy. An entry position offers a potentially valid career in and of itself, rather than as a temporary stopping-off point before a move on to a more advanced position.

However, even if a person decides that it is really the *principalship* or a position in district administration to which he/she aspires, it would be desirable for that individual to first obtain as much experience as possible in one or more of the entry positions in school administration. For example, a person who is now a teacher might seek the position of department head or unit leader in a school. Such a position, quasi-administrative in nature, could give one considerable experience in the administrative processes of goal setting, planning, organizing, and working with adult groups. It could also provide practice in supervising and evaluating teachers, if such responsibilities are associated with the job. All of these experiences constitute potentially valuable training in administration. Certainly, the experiences gained through being a department head or unit leader could be useful later when a person becomes a principal and interacts with the people occupying those positions.

Or an individual might prepare for the principalship by seeking on-the-job training as an administrative assistant, an assistant principal, a vice-principal, or a dean of students.* Unlike the department head, who generally teaches three or more classes, these other entry posts are usually full-time administrative positions. Typically they differ in types of responsibilities associated with each position, but they all offer potentially useful training for more advanced careers in administration. The problem is that none of these

*See chapter 5, The Administrative Team, for a description of these positions.

positions itself offers the kind of *broad* on-the-job training that a principal really needs.

For example, although there are exceptions, the administrative assistant's role is frequently managerial in nature, concerned with budgeting, plant management, or student discipline, with little or no responsibility in the areas of instructional improvement and curriculum development. The primary duties of the assistant principal, vice-principal, and dean of students are usually confined to student discipline and attendance. Instructional improvement, curriculum, and budgeting are responsibilities which are seldom associated with these positions, although that situation is changing to some extent. It is true that in larger schools with two assistant or vice-principals, one of them may be assigned responsibilities for instructional improvement and curriculum development, but in such cases the individual occupying that position receives little experience in the other aspects of the principalship.

Perhaps the best on-the-job training for the principalship, at least in terms of breadth, is the administrative internship. The internship has existed in education for a long time, in one form or another.[2] But it wasn't until the early 1960s, when Lloyd Trump and others proposed the administrative internship as an important training vehicle for those interested in school leadership, that it assumed major stature. Since then, thousands of individuals have used this approach as on-the-job preparation for the school principalship, and many school districts now sponsor their own internship program, often in cooperation with a nearby university.

Although the nature of experiences which an intern receives may vary from district to district, the intent of most programs is to provide a person with as much exposure to and actual experience in the various facets of the principal's job, as possible. Therefore, anyone who plans to become a principal (or for that matter, any of the full-time administrative positions in the school) should investigate the possibility of securing an administrative internship in a school in the district or in another district which offers such an opportunity.

By participating in an internship the prospective administrator will be able to test and apply the conceptual tools which were acquired through course work, before occupying a full-time position in administration.[3] The prospective administrator who arrives at a first job in school administration without an internship or some type of field work may be likened to a beginning swimmer who approaches a first experience in the water on the basis of only class lectures, films, and independent reading. Formal course work is essential, but a supervised internship is a desirable and important complement to the initial professional development of any prospective school administrator.

EMPLOYMENT OPPORTUNITIES

Before one decides on a career in school administration, that individual should thoroughly investigate the employment opportunities.

Until recently, it was assumed by those entering the field of administration that if state certification could be obtained, there would be little or no problem in securing a job.* Many people, including those responsible for preparing administrators, believed that if an administrative aspirant was willing to move to a new situation or wait until a vacancy occurred in his or her own district, it would be simply a matter of time before a job in administration could be secured. It has also been implicitly believed by many that once a person acquired an entry position in administration, it would not be long before an opportunity to become a principal would present itself.

Whether there was ever a close relationship between these beliefs and reality is debatable. Until recently there has been a paucity of data on employment opportunities, which unfortunately tended to encourage an optimistic viewpoint on job possibilities in school administration. In the early seventies, however, a rather important booklet by Donald Mitchell, *Leadership in Public Education Study,* was published, presenting statistics that cast considerable doubt on the previously optimistic beliefs about employment opportunities in administration.[4]

On the basis of a questionnaire sent to state certification authorities across the country, it was found that, in more than half of the thirty-nine states from which responses were obtained, more people were qualified to take the position of principal than there were openings. In fact, five states indicated that *many* more people were qualified for principalships than there were openings. Twelve states replied that there were a sufficient number of qualified people for the openings for principals; only four states indicated a shortage of qualified people for principalship vacancies. Although the data were not analyzed according to elementary or secondary openings, it seems fair to conclude from the findings of this study that most states have a surplus of individuals certified for the principalship, and that a person contemplating a career as a principal should therefore recognize that there may be extreme competition for a job. It should be noted that even this situation is likely to worsen as a result of the decline in student enrollment in the schools.

While the available data do not suggest a very rosy employment picture in school administration, several factors mitigate the severity of the overall outlook. First, observation would suggest that employment opportunities for a prospective principal appear to be better in certain states than in others.

---

*The reader who is interested in certification requirements for administrators and supervisors in the different states should check in a library for Elizabeth H. Woellner, *Requirements for Certification* (Chicago: University of Chicago Press, 1975).

The Mitchell study did not report by state the employment opportunities for the principalship; as a consequence the reader will have to do some investigating in this regard. Usually state departments of public instruction are a good source of general information on employment opportunities in school administration, and individual professors within a school of education may be especially good sources for such information. (Since Mitchell's study indicates that in most states there is a surplus of certificated people for available vacancies in the principalship, steps should be taken before an individual is very far along in a preparatory program to ascertain exactly what the situation is in a particular state or area.)

A second reason for investigating the local employment situation in school administration is that it may have changed since the Mitchell study. For example, there is some indication that the turnover rate in the principalship is increasing as a result of the many problems and pressures that have become a part of a principal's job. Consequently, there may be more early retirements, resignations, and advancements to central office positions than was formerly the case. Also, recent laws and court cases on sex and racial discrimination may provide greater job opportunities in school administration for women and members of minority groups. Although the evidence supporting these potential trends is fragmentary and contradictory, it is possible that conditions associated with the principalship, along with federal equal rights legislation, will create more employment opportunities (at least for certain groups) than the Mitchell data suggest.

Finally, it needs to be emphasized that Mitchell's study refers only to a likely surplus of *certificated* people for available vacancies in the principalship. In other words, there is a surplus of people who meet the minimum employment standards to become a principal. This says nothing about employment opportunities for those individuals who *exceed* state standards, or who possess or acquire competencies and personality characteristics which would place them above the average candidate for a principalship. While there may be a surplus of minimally qualified people for the principalship, it would seem reasonable to assume that there will continue to be employment opportunities for those who possess training beyond that of the average candidate for an administrative position, or who reveal outstanding leadership capabilities.

NEEDED COMPETENCIES AND PROFESSIONAL ETHICS FOR SCHOOL ADMINISTRATION

RECOMMENDED COMPETENCIES

One important theory concerning the competencies needed by administrators has been advanced by Katz, who feels that the three basic skills needed by administrators are (1) technical, (2) human, and (3) conceptual.[5] Technical skills are those which the school administrator must possess to perform such tasks as budgeting, scheduling, staffing, and other similar administrative responsibilities. Human skills refer to interpersonal skills needed to work successfully with people in one-to-one or group settings. Conceptual skills are those which the school administrator needs in order to see the "total picture" and the relationships between and among its various parts. Katz believes that the relative importance of these basic skills depends on the level of administrative responsibility, with higher level administrators (e.g., superintendents) requiring more conceptual than technical skills, and lower level administrators, (e.g., principals) needing more technical than conceptual skills.[6] Human skills, however, are important at all levels of administration.

In another context, Gorton has proposed four types of competencies which appear to be essential for school administrators who want to function as leaders.[7] The four, identified in question form, are:

1. Does the administrator have the ability to identify accurately the problems which need to be corrected in the school?
2. Does the administrator possess vision as an educator? Does he/she recognize, understand, and see the implications of the various trends and social forces which are and will be affecting education and the larger society?
3. Does the administrator feel a stong need to be a leader? Does he/she have a strong drive to set and achieve new goals? Does he/she seek out opportunities to exercise leadership?
4. Is the administrator willing to assume a degree of risk in initiating leadership—and to face resistance, opposition, and personal or professional criticism?[8]

In addition to the concept described above, research on leadership and numerous personal reports from administrators are helpful in suggesting those competencies that a person should possess or acquire in pursuing a career in school administration.[9] Rather than reviewing all of these studies and reports, a self-assessment questionnaire has been developed, based on a synthesis of this information, and is presented in figure 19.2.

In responding to the questions in figure 19.2, the reader should pay particularly close attention to examining the evidence used in determining the rating of the extent to which he/she possesses each of the traits. It is usually difficult for anyone to be completely objective or knowledgeable about his/her own strengths and weaknesses. Therefore, before answering such a question as, "Are you a problem solver as well as a problem

	Uncertain	Rarely	To Some Extent	To a Large Extent	Almost Always
1. Are you objective about yourself and about others? Evidence?	___	___	___	___	___
2. Do you possess ideas and convictions about improvements needed in education and the direction that education should take in the future? Evidence?	___	___	___	___	___
3. Are you a problem solver as well as a problem identifier? Evidence?	___	___	___	___	___
4. Are you a hard worker, strong on perseverance? Evidence?	___	___	___	___	___
5. Do you possess considerable self-initiative? Evidence?	___	___	___	___	___
6. Do you like responsibility? Evidence?	___	___	___	___	___
7. Are you interested in continuous self and professional improvement? Evidence?	___	___	___	___	___
8. Do you possess a good capacity to learn, to "catch on"? Evidence?	___	___	___	___	___
9. Do you have the ability to plan and organize a job? Evidence?	___	___	___	___	___
10. Are you interested in detail work and in paper work? Evidence?	___	___	___	___	___

(continued)

Figure 19.2. Self-Assessment Questionnaire for Prospective School Administrators.

	Uncertain	Rarely	To Some Extent	To a Large Extent	Almost Always
11. Are you well organized? Evidence?	___	___	___	___	___
12. Are you a good decision maker? Evidence?	___	___	___	___	___
13. Are you an articulate and effective speaker in front of a group, or as a member of a group, or as a leader of a group? Evidence?	___	___	___	___	___
14. Are you able to influence others, to change their thinking? Evidence?	___	___	___	___	___
15. Are you able to work well with parents, students, peers, superiors? Evidence?	___	___	___	___	___
16. Do you have the capacity to compromise and to be flexible? Evidence?	___	___	___	___	___
17. Do you possess the ability to know when to compromise and to be flexible? Evidence?	___	___	___	___	___
18. Do you have the ability to mediate conflict, to reconcile differences among others? Evidence?	___	___	___	___	___
19. Do you possess a high tolerance for frustration, anxiety, challenges to self by others? Evidence?	___	___	___	___	___
20. Are you relatively free of personal problems or "hang-ups"? Evidence?	___	___	___	___	___

Figure 19.2. Continued.

identifier?" the reader should think about his/her experiences in situations which called for problem solving and perhaps even discuss professional problem-solving capabilities with others who may be more objective in their perceptions.

It should be pointed out that a prospective administrator is unlikely to possess *all* of the traits identified in figure 19.2. In fact, it is doubtful whether the vast majority of current school administrators possess all of these traits to a large degree. But each of the traits identified in the self-assessment questionnaire is an important characteristic for an administrator to possess or acquire. Without having a majority of these traits, he/she will not be likely to succeed in exercising leadership in the school. Therefore, the reader should make every attempt to complete conscientiously the Self-Assessment Questionnaire for Prospective School Administrators, and then seek improvement wherever needed.

PROFESSIONAL ETHICS

It was emphasized in the previous section that prospective school administrators should either possess or acquire certain basic competencies if they expect to pursue a successful career in school administration. However, competencies are only one prerequisite to success. If a person is to be successful in administration, that individual also needs a set of ethical beliefs or standards for guidance or direction in the appropriate use of competencies. Without such beliefs, a person's competencies may be misused or misdirected, and the school will not receive the best kind of leadership. Therefore, every administrator should attempt to maintain high professional ethical standards in order to make a more positive contribution to the improvement of education in the school.

Although there are various sources to which a prospective administrator might turn in an attempt to enhance his/her professional ethics, the national administrators' associations recently developed a set of recommended guidelines which have much to commend them. The standards were developed on the basis of considerable involvement and input from school administrators throughout the nation, and represent the best thinking of practitioners on this important subject. They are presented in figure 19.3 for the reader's study and consideration.

The standards identified in figure 19.3 constitute a positive response to the need for ethical guidelines for school administrators. They should provide all administrators with a basis for directing their actions, and serve also as evaluative criteria by which administrators can determine whether or not they are acting ethically in professional matters.

An educational administrator's professional behavior must conform to an ethical code. The code must be idealistic and at the same time practical, so that it can apply reasonably to all educational administrators. The administrator acknowledges that the schools belong to the public they serve for the purpose of providing educational opportunities to all. However, the administrator assumes responsibility for providing professional leadership in the school and community. This responsibility requires the administrator to maintain high standards of exemplary professional conduct. It must be recognized that the administrator's actions will be viewed and appraised by the community, professional associates, and students. To these ends, the administrator subscribes to the following statements of standards.

The educational administrator:

1. Makes the well-being of students the fundamental value in all decision making and actions.
2. Fulfills professional responsibilities with honesty and integrity.
3. Supports the principle of due process and protects the civil and human rights of all individuals.
4. Obeys local, state, and national laws and does not knowingly join or support organizations that advocate, directly or indirectly, the overthrow of the government.
5. Implements the governing board of education's policies and administrative rules and regulations.
6. Pursues appropriate measures to correct those laws, policies, and regulations that are not consistent with sound educational goals.
7. Avoids using positions for personal gain through political, social, religious, economic, or other influence.
8. Accepts academic degrees or professional certification only from duly accredited institutions.
9. Maintains the standards and seeks to improve the effectiveness of the profession through research and continuing professional development.
10. Honors all contracts until fulfillment or release.

This *Statement of Ethics* was developed by a task force representing The National Association of Secondary School Principals, National Association of Elementary School Principals, American Association of School Administrators, Association of School Business Officials, American Association of School Personnel Administrators, and National Council of Administrative Women in Education. Used with the permission of the National Association of Secondary School Principals.

Figure 19.3. Statement of Ethics for School Administrators. [10]

THE NEW ADMINISTRATOR

The person who possesses the competencies and professional ethics already identified should be able to pursue a career in school administration successfully. However, because of a lack of knowledge about how to proceed, some individuals may experience difficulty in obtaining a position in school administration; and some may encounter problems during the first year on the job because of inadequate planning and misplaced priorities. Guidelines for avoiding or, at least, ameliorating these problems will be discussed in the following sections.*

OBTAINING A POSITION

The immediate objective of the person who has completed an administrator preparation program and obtained certification, and is ready to begin a career in administration, is to secure a position. Since career opportunities in educational administration are limited in most states, obtaining a position will not be an easy objective for the prospective administrator to achieve. However, if one has performed well in a preparatory program, possesses the kinds of qualities necessary for success in school administration, and is persistent, that individual's chances of securing a position in administration should be greatly improved.

The first step that a person should take in seeking a position in educational administration is to register with a university placement office. Usually any student attending a college or any graduate of a college can register with its placement office and utilize the placement services. Once registered with a placement office, an individual will receive vacancy notices such as those shown in figure 19.4.

Seldom will a placement notice provide all the information about a position that one might desire. However, sufficient information is usually supplied for the applicant to make a decision on whether follow-up action should be taken regarding the notice. If the position is of interest, the individual should contact the placement office and request that a copy of his/her credentials be sent to the school district. The prospective administrator should also write to the school district expressing an interest in the vacancy, and advising that placement papers are being forwarded to the district's office. In the letter a statement of the reasons for the applicant's interest in the position should be included together with a brief description of his/her qualifications with reference to any special factors of which the

---

*It is recognized that, to some readers, the ideas discussed in these sections will seem obvious or rather pragmatic in nature. However, contact with new administrators indicates that many need practical guidelines on how to obtain a position in administration and what to expect during the first year.

1. Assistant Principal Vacancy in Medium-Size School District

   Requirements
   a. Master's Degree and certification as an administrator
   b. Three years of successful teaching experience
   c. Open and warm personality, ability to lead others, ability to work well under pressure

   Benefits
   a. Salary range is $15,000—$18,000 for a 40-week contract
   b. Full retirement contribution, health-and-life-insurance contributions

2. School Principal Vacancy in Small School District

   Requirements
   a. Master's Degree and administrator certification
   b. Five years of teaching experience; some experience as an assistant principal desired
   c. Competency in school management and human relations

   Benefits
   a. Salary commensurate with experience and responsibilities
   b. Friendly community with good opportunities for hunting and fishing

Figure 19.4. Examples of Placement Notices in Educational Administration.

school district should be aware. If the district is interested, the applicant will usually be contacted within several weeks about the scheduling of an interview.

Information on job vacancies in educational administration can also be obtained from the state employment office (which may have an educators' employment division); private employment agencies; the city newspaper, which may carry vacancy notices; and also from the personnel office in the beginning administrator's own school district. Another potential source of information on administrative vacancies may be the professor who served as the student's adviser in the university's administrator preparation program. The prospective administrator should take the initiative to explore and maintain contact with all possible sources of information on administrative openings. Rarely will a school district contact the prospective administrator first; he/she will have to exert initiative and persistence to obtain a position.

An important factor which will greatly influence the number and type of vacancies available is the prospective administrator's geographic mobility. Many vacancies for beginning administrators occur in small school districts, and in districts located at a distance from metropolitan areas. An individual who, for whatever reason, is unable or unwilling to move to these districts, or who will consider a vacancy only if it is in his/her own district or in a metropolitan area, has significantly restricted opportunities for employment.

The more mobile the prospective administrator can be, the more likely is the applicant to obtain a position.

Once a prospective administrator has applied for a vacancy and has been contacted by the school district for an interview, that person should take time to plan for the meeting. An individual who has been scheduled for an interview can usually assume that he/she is among several persons who are being strongly considered for the vacancy. Generally, the school district will give considerable weight to the results of these interviews in reaching a decision on candidate selection. It is therefore essential that a candidate plan carefully for the interview.

Planning for an interview is really no different than planning for any important conference or meeting. First of all the candidate needs information about the situation itself, in this case the school and the school district where the vacancy has occurred. Prior to the interview, the prospective administrator should attempt to visit the school, talk with the administrator who is leaving, and try to become familiar with the school district and the community. The information and impressions that are gained will be invaluable in the planning for the interview.

Secondly, the candidate should determine the objectives he/she wants to achieve during the interview, and then define the questions and comments which need to be offered in order to achieve those objectives. In addition to thinking about objectives and questions, time should be spent in trying to anticipate the kinds of questions which the *interviewers* will ask. While it may be impossible to anticipate every question that may be raised, the more questions that are anticipated and considered prior to the interview, the greater is the likelihood that the interview will be a success.

During the interview the prospective administrator should try to remain calm and poised. An individual may experience some nervousness, which is perfectly natural and shouldn't cause a problem as long as he/she doesn't overreact. The candidate should concentrate on listening carefully to the interviewer's comments and questions and if a question or comment isn't understood, the interviewer should be asked for clarification or elaboration. The candidate should not attempt to respond to a question or comment unless it is clearly understood.

In answering questions or making observations the prospective administrator should be perfectly candid. Rather than presenting what he/she thinks the interviewer would like to hear, the candidate's own views should be given. This approach may cost an individual a particular job, but it is far better that the applicant be candid at the outset, since discrepancies in philosophy or approach will probably surface later and cause difficulties. This does not mean that one should be dogmatic or argumentative during an interview. However, there should be a frank and full exchange of views.

At the conclusion of the interview the candidate will usually be told that he/she will be contacted in the near future with regard to the school district's decision. If the applicant does not hear from a representative of the district within two or three weeks, contact should be made with the district's office to inquire as to when a decision will be reached. During this interval, however, the prospective administrator should be exploring other alternative employment possibilities until an actual contract is received and the offer accepted.

THE NEW SITUATION: ORIENTATION

Having accepted a position, the new administrator will need to become oriented further to the school, school district, and the community (unless, of course, the position is in his/her own district). The administrator may already have had an opportunity to meet several associates, and to visit the community; but there probably remains considerable orientation to be acquired before school begins in the fall.

In this endeavor the new administrator should attempt to secure and thoroughly read student and teacher handbooks, and copies of the student newspaper. A careful examination should also be made of the school board policies and district office manual of procedures, if one exists. All of this information should contribute to the process of familiarizing the new administrator with current school and district problems, policies, and procedures.

Next, individual meetings should be scheduled with the superintendent, and relevant members of the central office staff. The new administrator's meetings with the superintendent and the central office staff should be for purposes of getting better acquainted and ascertaining how all parties can work together cooperatively. One topic for discussion might be the district's master contract.

The beginning administrator should also schedule individual meetings with the school's assistant principal, department heads and/or unit leaders, the cook, the head secretary, and the head custodian. It is particularly important that an administrator pay attention to becoming acquainted with the latter three individuals, since they can play a significant role in the administrator's success or lack of it, yet are frequently overlooked. And the new administrator should see student and parent leaders who are available and interested in conferring with him.

During these initial meetings the administrator should focus primarily on developing a good personal relationship with the people with whom he/she will be working at the school, reviewing proposed activities and possible problems, and also indicating a receptivity to meeting with them again whenever the need arises. One should not attempt to cover too much in these first meetings. For example, unless the subject comes up naturally, the administrator should wait until later to ascertain people's role expectations. It will be more appropriate to discuss these topics after the new administrator and the other school personnel have become better acquainted.

While becoming better informed about the school district and school personnel, the new administrator should also be trying to become better oriented to the school community. Although he/she may have toured the community when interviewing for the vacancy, the administrator's knowledge of the community at this point is probably rather superficial.

A good starting point for orientation to a community is a drive around the neighborhoods and commercial areas surrounding the school within a half-mile radius. Such a drive should yield valuable impressions about the types of neighborhoods that are adjacent to the school, potential safety problems for students, extent and kinds of recreational opportunities for students, and possible student "hangouts." The latter may include cafes, drugstores, poolhalls, and similar places where students might congregate before or after school. Such places frequently represent the "community" from the student's point of view, and the new administrator needs to become more aware of that community.

The administrator should also try to become acquainted with the neighborhoods of those students who have to travel a long distance to the school. These students and their parents may feel isolated from the school, and the administrator should become more knowledgeable about their situation. If school is still in session in the spring when the administrator is hired, riding a school bus might be considered to achieve this objective.

As the administrator visits various neighborhoods of the community, any opportunities to meet the residents, particularly parents, should be capitalized on. There probably won't be time to meet too many parents, but the administrator should take advantage of those opportunities that present themselves in the situation.

Perhaps one of the better ways for a new administrator to become informed about the culture, norms, problems, and personalities in a community is to read the local newspaper, back issues of which are generally to be found in the local library. By browsing through the copies of the newspaper published during the preceding year, the new administrator should be able to become familiar with many important aspects of the community, including its significant groups and leaders, its problems and issues, and dates of special local events. Also generally found in the library is pertinent information about the community's governmental structure. Without question, the local library is potentially a very useful source of material for orienting a new administrator to a community.

PLANNING FOR THE OPENING OF SCHOOL*

In one sense, the orientation activities that have been described can be considered a part of planning for the opening of school. However, before mid-August the administrator should make some additional plans in regard to the start of the school year. [11] Although "get-acquainted meetings" with student, teacher, and parent leaders should already have been held by the administrator, it is important for him/her to meet with them again to plan activities to be held prior to the opening of school and during the first few weeks after school has started.

The administrator should also meet with the assistant principal (if one is assigned to the school) and with the department chairpersons or unit leaders to plan the workshop which usually takes place two or three days before school begins. Information should be solicited from these people about the type of workshop presented in the past at the school, and they should be encouraged to offer suggestions on how it could be improved. The new administrator will certainly have his/her own ideas on what should be included in the workshop, and these ideas should be presented and reactions sought.

Topics for inclusion in the workshop will depend to a great extent on local circumstances. However, the administrator should recognize that the total staff will be using this opportunity to "size up the new administrator," and will be listening carefully to what that individual has to say during the workshop. Although the new administrator will want to make a good impression, he/she should try to avoid raising people's expectations too much and should refrain from the temptation to promise more than can be delivered. [12] Also, it would be preferable to postpone reviewing one's own educational philosophy and expectations for the staff unless specific questions about them are raised. Until the new administrator and the total staff become better acquainted, discussions about educational philosophy and expectations could be misinterpreted.

During the workshop, the new administrator should project an image as that of someone who will try to work cooperatively with people to resolve problems, who is friendly, warm and professional in interpersonal relationships, and who is well organized and a hard worker.

In planning for the workshop the beginning administrator should take into consideration the needs of new teachers who will be attending the meetings, and the needs of the total staff for enough time to do individual planning for the first day of school. He/she should also plan for some form of activity which will provide an opportunity for the members of the staff (and perhaps their families) to socialize with each other. The preschool workshop should consist of more than just professional meetings.

---

*Most of the ideas in this section are more germane for the principal than for the assistant principal, although the latter will need to be aware of a number of those recommended.

In planning for the opening of school, meetings should also be scheduled with the school secretary, head custodian, chief cook, and student and parent leaders (such as the president of the student council, the editor of the student newspaper, and the president of the PTA). These meetings should be devoted to a review of proposed activities for the opening day and the first month of school (with a discussion of problems to be resolved), and steps which need to be taken prior to those activities. Careful planning before school opens will eliminate many problems that might otherwise arise later.

The new administrator should also check on a number of important operational details at least several weeks prior to the beginning of school. These include ascertaining whether the items enumerated in figure 19.5 still require attention.

---

1. **Development of the Master Schedule for the School.** Has it been completed? Does it need updating?
2. **Employment of Teachers.** Do additional teachers need to be hired?
3. **Allocation of Classroom Furniture and Textbooks.** Does each classroom have sufficient classroom furniture and textbooks to accommodate the number of students assigned to the room?
4. **Distribution of Teacher Supplies.** Has each teacher been allocated adequate supplies for the first week of school?
5. **Maintenance of the Building.** Have those aspects of the school which have been in need of repair been fixed? Has the school building itself been cleaned and floors waxed?
6. **Planning for the Cafeteria Program.** Have preparations been made to provide hot lunches on the first day of school?

Figure 19.5. Checklist: Planning for the Opening of School.

The checking on some of these details may be delegated to the assistant principal, if there is one. However, the principal still retains the ultimate responsibility for making sure that everything operates smoothly on the first day of school. While the new administrator may view himself/herself as an instructional leader, the staff's initial judgment will be based on their evaluation as to whether this "newcomer" is an efficient administrator. The events of the first day of school will greatly influence their evaluation.

PRIORITIES DURING THE FIRST YEAR

Regardless of whether or not the administrator is new, he/she will be expected to meet certain responsibilities. These include visiting classrooms; holding faculty meetings; conferring with individual students, teachers, and parents; developing a school budget, and many other tasks delineated in previous chapters.

The effectiveness with which these tasks are accomplished will depend in part on the type of role that the new administrator adopts. According to Lipham, the administrator is "the individual who utilizes existing structures or procedures to achieve an organization goal or objective."[13] Lipham goes on to state that "The administrator is concerned primarily with maintaining, rather than changing established structures, procedures, or goals."[14] The leader, on the other hand, is defined by Lipham as "concerned with initiating changes in established structures, procedures, or goals; he is a disrupter of the existing state of affairs." Leadership, to Lipham, is "the initiation of a new structure or procedure for accomplishing organizational goals and objectives."[15]

A case can be made that, during the first year, a new administrator should *not* function as a leader, as defined by Lipham, but should concentrate on administering the school. A new administrator needs to complete at least one year on the job becoming familiar with the school situation, before being in a good enough position to know what changes should be made and how they might best be accomplished. Also, a new administrator should take the time to become competent in performing administrative tasks before beginning to initiate changes in existing procedures and policies.

Of course, a new administrator may be forced to institute changes during the first year in response to a problem whose solution cannot or should not be delayed. However, as much as possible during the first year, the administrator should avoid initiating major changes in established structures, procedures, or goals, or in any other way disrupting the existing order of affairs. To the extent feasible, such leadership activities should be postponed until the new administrator becomes more knowledgeable about the school situation.

The priorities that a new administrator should concentrate on during his/her first year are presented below.

1. *Obtaining a good understanding of all aspects of the educational program and the social context in which the school operates.* During the first year, the new administrator needs to become very familiar with what is going on in the school, and why things are done the way they are. He/she also needs to continue to learn about school district procedures and how the school relates to the total community.

2. *Developing a good interpersonal relationship with other people.* This includes students, parents, and central office personnel, as well as the teachers in the school. The new administrator's first year will be a busy one

with many tasks to accomplish, but never so busy that there isn't enough time to see students, teachers, parents, and other relevant people. These individuals will determine the success of the beginning administrator more than any other factor.

3. *Attaining a well-organized and smoothly operating school.* Most of the people with whom the new administrator will have contact will tend to view him/her as an administrator, rather than as a leader. If both roles can be performed effectively, people will be pleased; but first of all competency as an administrator must be shown. This can be achieved by running a well-organized, smoothly operating school. Having obtained this objective, the new administrator can begin to function in the role of leader if he/she possesses the qualities needed for leadership. [16]

A CONCLUDING NOTE

For the individual interested in a new position in school administration, securing a job and planning and establishing priorities for the first year will require careful organization, persistence, and clear thinking. The administrator's first year will undoubtedly be a useful learning experience but, at the same time, the new administrator should realize that people will expect effective performance regardless of whether or not the individual is new to the position. Two major factors which will tend to demonstrate the administrator's effectiveness are his/her response to the problems which are associated with the school situation, and the efforts made by the administrator to pursue continuing professional development. The next chapter will focus on problems of school administration and the need for continuous professional growth.

Review
1. Analyze the advantages and disadvantages of various entry positions in school administration.
2. What is the nature of employment opportunities in school administration? What are the implications of this situation for an individual who is interested in pursuing a career in school administration?
3. Identify the administrator competencies recommended by Katz and Gorton and describe the implications of these ideas for the professional development of the administrator.
4. Assess yourself in regard to the extent to which you possess the traits identified in figure 19.2 and the ethical standards identified in figure 19.3. What are the implications of your assessment?

5. What steps should an individual take and which factors should he/she be aware of in:
   a. Seeking a new administrative position?
   b. Becoming oriented to a new administrative situation?
   c. Planning for the opening of the school?
6. Why is it important for an administrator to determine his/her priorities in a new situation? What would appear to be reasonable first year priorities for a new administrator?

Notes

1. See, for example, John Hemphill et al., *Report of the Senior High Principalship* (Washington, D.C.: National Association of Secondary School Principals, 1965), p. 35. See also Department of Elementary School Principals, *The Elementary School Principalship: A Research Study* (Washington, D.C.: The Department, National Education Association, 1968), pp. 12-15.

2. For an excellent review of the origins and various aspects of establishing and administering an internship program, see Don R. Davies, *The Internship in Educational Administration* (Washington, D.C.: Center for Applied Research in Education, 1962). Also see T. F. Flaherty, "Theory and Practice Yields Qualified Administrators," *Education* 93 (November 1972):128-29.

3. For more information on internships, see *Internship Programs in Educational Administration* (Arlington, Va.: Educational Research Service, 1974).

4. Donald P. Mitchell, *Leadership in Public Education Study: A Look at the Overlooked* (Washington, D.C.: Academy for Educational Development, 1972).

5. Robert L. Katz, "Skills of an Effective Administrator," *Harvard Business Review* 33, no. 1 (January-February 1955):33-42.

6. Ibid., p. 42.

7. Richard A. Gorton, *Conflict, Controversy, and Crisis in School Administration and Supervision* (Dubuque, Iowa: Wm. C. Brown Company Publishers, 1972), pp. 302-3.

8. The administrator who wishes further information about administrative competencies should subscribe to *CCBC Notebook*, University of Utah, Salt Lake City, Utah.

9. See, for example, John Hemphill et al., *Administrative Performance and Personality* (New York: Bureau of Publications, Teachers College, Columbia University, 1972). Also see Russell T. Gregg, "Preparation of Administrators," in *Encyclopedia of Educational Research*, ed. Robert L. Ebel (New York: Macmillan Co., 1969), pp. 993-1002. For an interesting personal report, see Earl C. Kelley, "What Makes a Good Administrator?" *School Executive* (September 1945):58-59.

10. National Association of Secondary School Principals and National Association of Elementary School Principals, *Ethical Standards for School Administrators* (Washington, D.C.: NASSP and NAESP, 1973).

11. Some practical advice on planning for the opening of school is given by John A. McKay, "To Experience It Is to Know It," *Bulletin of the National Association of Secondary School Principals* 57 (November 1973):55-59.

12. Edwin J. Brown, "Experienced Schoolman Talks to Beginners," *Phi Delta Kappan* 47 (Feburary 1966):320-21.

13. James M. Lipham, "Leadership and Administration," in *Behavioral Science and Educational Administration,* ed. Daniel Griffiths, Sixty-third Yearbook of the National Society for the Study of Education (Chicago: University of Chicago Press, 1964), p. 122.

14. Ibid.

15. Ibid.

16. For a discussion of prerequisites for leadership, see Richard A. Gorton, *Conflict, Controversy and Crisis*, pp. 302-3.

20
Need for Continuing
Professional Development

This book has recommended a number of principles and concepts which, if appropriately utilized, should improve the administration of a school. The competencies that the school administrator will need to perform effectively have been suggested at various points and the many challenges confronting the administrator have been stressed. Certainly it should be clear to the reader by now that the job of the school administrator is not an easy one.

In order to demonstrate further the nature of the administrator's problem-filled job and the consequent need for continuous professional growth, the following two sections will discuss the problems of the new administrator and report on the types of problems faced by all administrators—new and experienced. The latter half of the chapter will then focus on several approaches to continued professional development for the school administrator.

THE NEW ADMINISTRATOR

FIRST YEAR PROBLEMS

It is difficult to generalize about the types of problems that the beginning administrator may encounter, because these problems will vary according to the administrator's background, training, personality, and school situation. However, discussions with and observations of new administrators suggest that there are several problems which many of them faced during the first year.* It should be pointed out that a majority of these same problems are also encountered to a certain degree by experienced administrators who move to a new situation.

The Acceptance Problem

Many beginning administrators are initially concerned about how students, parents, and particularly teachers will react to them. As beginning administrators in a new situation, they naturally hope to gain acceptance by the groups with whom they will be working. But what type of acceptance should they be seeking? They want to be respected, but they wonder, "Is it impor-

*Surprisingly, very little has been researched or written on the problems of the beginning administrator.

tant to be liked? And if you seek the personal approval of the people with whom you work, will they still respect you?''

These are normal questions for any beginning administrator to ask. In fact, many experienced administrators who change jobs feel some concern about being accepted in a new environment. However, the beginning administrator usually is new, not only to the work environment, but to the job itself, so being concerned about other people's reactions is understandable. Whether a beginning administrator will actually encounter difficulty in gaining the acceptance of others will depend in large part on the type of acceptance that is sought.

If the administrator decides that people must like him/her, or must approve all decisions before action can be initiated, there are likely to be problems. One frequently may have to make decisions or take actions which will result in a reduction of one's popularity, but it is better to do what seems right in a situation rather than what may be popular. Any administrator who makes a decision or initiates action based *primarily* on its potential for generating a favorable response from those who will be affected by the decision or action will soon learn that it is virtually impossible to please everyone. He/she will also discover that a decision or action which elicits an immediate, favorable response from those affected may not always lead to the best results in the long run.

On the other hand, the administrator who never makes any attempt to secure the approval or acceptance of a proposed decision by the persons whom it will affect cannot expect their continuing cooperation. While people may not need to *like* the administrator personally, or approve of all administrative actions, they generally must find the administrator or a majority of administrative acts acceptable, if they are going to implement fully what that individual wants done in the school. Therefore, if people's feelings and reactions toward the administrator and his/her decisions are not taken into consideration, a growing wave of discontent may emerge.

Probably the most appropriate response for a beginning administrator in regard to the ''acceptance problem'' is to concentrate during the first year on administering a well-organized, smoothly running school. The achievement of this goal will favorably influence most people's acceptance of the administrator, perhaps more than any other factor. Of course, he/she should also try to develop a warm and helping relationship with the staff, students, and parents. However, in all likelihood, their judgment of the administrator will depend primarily on whether the school is being administered effectively, and will be based only secondarily on personal considerations. Both factors may be influential but the former is the most important.

The Problem of Insufficient Time

During the first year the beginning administrator may frequently have the feeling that there is never enough time to do everything that needs to be accomplished. But the problem of lack of time is not limited to new administrators; it also frustrates experienced administrators, although perhaps to a lesser degree.[1]

The problem of having too little time can generally be attributed to four factors: (1) inexperience, (2) the absence of a system for organizing time, (3) the administrative job itself, which by its very nature is demanding and time-consuming, and (4) failure to delegate responsibility. Since there is little probability that the job of the administrator will become less demanding, and since most beginning administrators are initially employed in situations where the opportunity for delegating responsibility may be limited, we shall concentrate on analyzing the first two factors.

Due to inexperience, the new administrator usually takes longer to perform most administrative tasks. Despite having received excellent university training for the new role, and even having acquired previous experience as an intern, the administrator will be performing many tasks for the first time. These duties will take longer to accomplish until, with practice, shortcuts can be identified and errors eliminated. Therefore, until the beginning administrator gains more experience, the time problem will not be significantly ameliorated.

However, as indicated earlier, inexperience is not the only cause of a fledgling administrator's problem of seemingly never having enough time. Another major factor is the absence of a system for organizing time. Unless the administrator utilizes such a system, he/she will reach the end of many days and weeks, wondering why more wasn't achieved. The administrator may have been busy while at school, but at the end of the work period there may be little to show for the efforts.

One approach the administrator might use to organize time more effectively is to keep a time log each day for a week or two, and then analyze how the time is being spent and how it might be utilized more efficiently. According to a study by Weldy, administrators spend a certain portion of their time on activities which might be better organized or restructured, and a time log may be helpful in spotlighting possible problems.[2] In the publication *Time: A Valuable Resource for the School Administrator,* Weldy makes a number of practical recommendations for improving the administrator's use of time, including saving time in meetings, using clerical services more judiciously and planning work to save time.[3]

Another approach which could be helpful to the administrator who is trying to utilize time better is Management by Objectives (MBO).[4] Originating in the business sector but now being adopted by many school districts, Management by Objectives is a system by which an administrator defines objectives, establishes priorities, plans a course of action for achieving the objectives, and evaluates success. By requiring a beginning administrator to define what needs to be achieved and to establish priorities,

MBO can help to organize time more efficiently. And by requiring the administrator to evaluate whether or not objectives have been achieved, MBO can be helpful in ascertaining effectiveness and making changes where desirable and feasible.

Although MBO has more frequently been used in connection with semester or yearly objectives, it can also profitably be employed by a beginning administrator to organize time on a daily and weekly basis. An example of a daily MBO format is presented in figure 20.1.*

Name _____ Date _____ School _____

Objectives for Today:

Plan of Action for Accomplishing Each Objective:

Evaluation Plan for Ascertaining Success:

Figure 20.1. Daily MBO Format.

It should be pointed out that, until the beginning administrator becomes proficient in using MBO, it may take *more* time rather than less.[5] However, the time spent in thinking and planning is an investment which should pay dividends in better decision making, even it it doesn't immediately save any time. In the final analysis, the administrator may never entirely eliminate the feeling of having insufficient time to accomplish all the responsibilities, but MBO should be helpful in utilizing time more productively.

The Authority Problem
Many beginning administrators seem to experience difficulty in exercising authority during their first year. They either try to exert authority they don't

*The format described in figure 20.1 can also be adapted for use on a weekly basis.

possess, or fail to utilize the authority they do possess and which needs to be employed for the successful resolution of a problem. The consequence of exercising authority that one doesn't possess can be resistance and even outright noncompliance; failure to exercise authority which the individual possesses and which circumstances require can result in a deteriorating situation and loss of respect or confidence in the individual who is supposed to exercise the authority. In either case a general eroding of the perceived authority vested in an administrator's position can occur.

One reason why many beginning administrators encounter problems in the exercise of authority is that they have not examined carefully the nature and scope of their authority. Administrators should recognize that their basic authority is delegated to them by the school board and the superintendent of schools; therefore, they should understand clearly the policies and directives of the school board and the superintendent.

Unfortunately, in too many situations the authority of the administrator is not formally delegated or explicitly stated because it is believed to be inherent in the position or associated with the responsibilities which have been assigned. Therefore, a beginning administrator should attempt to secure as clear a reading as possible on the extent of authority actually possessed in the situation.

A second reason why many beginning administrators experience difficulty in exercising authority is that they don't seem to understand the limitations of authority or the conditions under which it is best employed.[6] Authority is not power. The administrator possesses *power* if people can be forced to do what he/she wants them to do, even when they resist or refuse to accept that individual's authority in a situation. The beginning administrator will soon discover that he/she has very little power in most circumstances.

Authority, on the other hand, is based on people's acceptance of an administrator's initiatives because they believe the administrator has the right to direct them by virtue of his/her position in the school organization and the authority vested in that position by the school board and/or the superintendent of schools. While this type of authority, typically referred to as "legitimate authority," has been severely eroded in recent years,[7] it still exists in large measure if appropriately utilized.

In exercising authority, the beginning administrator should keep in mind the following guidelines, based on Barnard's analysis of the authority problem in organizations:[8]

1. In deciding on the need for an order and in its formulation, presentation, and execution, the administrator should take into consideration how the order will affect the recipients personally, recognizing that people are likely to question or resist orders which they feel are not in their best interest.
2. The administrator should take into consideration the strengths and

limitations of those who will be expected to implement an order, and should avoid, if possible, issuing orders for which people lack the necessary motivation, skill, or training to carry out.

3. The administrator should explain thoroughly the rationale behind each order and its relationship to the goals of the organization, and should not assume that people understand the reasons for an order or that they will necessarily see the logic or value of an order.

4. The administrator should leave room for modifying the original order or its method of implementation. Flexibility and a willingness to compromise when appropriate are key factors in exercising administrative authority successfully.

5. The administrator should issue only those orders that will with relative surety be obeyed, or that can be enforced if they are resisted. Orders which cannot be enforced in one situation weaken the administrator's authority for successfully issuing orders in other circumstances.

By following these guidelines and working within the authority limitations of his/her position, the beginning administrator should be able to avoid most of the difficulties associated with the "authority problem." In working with students, teachers and other school related groups the beginning administrator will probably find that the best approach is to utilize his/her expertise to *influence* or persuade people to take a particular course of action, rather than relying on his/her authority to direct them.[9]

The Effectiveness Problem

It is understandable that a beginning administrator may experience some concern about his/her effectiveness during the first year. After all, it is natural for an administrator who is new to the job, and to the school situation itself, to wonder how effectively he/she is performing in the new role. In spite of this concern, however, the administrator may encounter difficulty in ascertaining that effectiveness.

In the first place, there may not be general agreement on the criteria to be used in evaluating an administrator's effectiveness. Superiors may make the evaluation based on one set of criteria, the teachers may use another set of criteria, the students another, and the parents still a different set. There may be a great deal of overlap in the criteria utilized by these groups, but the value they ascribe to each criterion may differ significantly. For example, both the teachers and the administrator's superiors might agree that maintaining "good school-community relations" should be considered in evaluating the administrator's effectiveness but may differ greatly on the importance they attach to this aspect.

A second difficulty that the beginning administrator may encounter is that, although the superiors and the other groups with whom he/she interacts may be constantly making evaluative conclusions, they may not explicitly communicate these conclusions to him/her. For example, it is still not unusual for an administrator to receive no *formal* evaluation from superiors. The latter may either fail to recognize the importance of yearly, formal administrator evaluation, or have no system for implementing it. In addition, unless the administrator actively seeks feedback from students, teachers, and parents, they also are unlikely to give their evaluation of his/her effectiveness. Most of these groups are in a subordinate role to the administrator, and there is little if any tradition of subordinates' *initiating* an evaluation of their administrator.

For these reasons then, many administrators receive little substantive feedback on their effectiveness. If an administrator is in this kind of a situation, however, there are certain steps that should be considered. First of all, administrator evaluation criteria and approaches *are* being used in a number of school systems, and that information should be brought to the attention of the administrator's superiors.[10] If administrator and superiors can agree upon appropriate criteria and on an evaluation approach, then perhaps periodic assessment of the administrator by superiors can occur.*

Secondly, an administrator should initiate some type of effectiveness evaluation by teachers, students, and parents. He/she might try to adapt the evaluation form used by superiors, or develop a new evaluation form to be used specifically by teachers, students, and parents. A form which the author employed with the latter groups when he was a beginning administrator is presented in figure 20.2; a form which has been used in another situation is presented in figure 20.3.

Date _____

Instructions: Please be as candid and complete as possible. I am very much interested in your perceptions of my effectiveness as an administrator, particularly your suggestions for improvement. You need not sign your name to this evaluation.

Strengths (please identify three characteristics, or actions that I have taken this year which you view as positive, and which you would like to see me continue).

Weaknesses (please identify three characteristics or actions that I have taken this year which you think I should work on in terms of self-improvement, or which you think I should eliminate).

Figure 20.2. Evaluation of Administrator's Effectiveness.

*An instrument which has been extensively researched and field tested, and should be considered, is entitled PEEL—Performance Evaluation of the Education Leader. More information about the instrument can be obtained by writing Howard I. Demeke at Arizona State University.

As a professional staff member, you are being asked by your principal for your evaluation. The purpose of this evaluation is to give your principal information about how others see him, and such information will be used only by your principal for his benefit. Please give careful and professional consideration to each item and return the form unsigned in the envelope provided. Your contribution is viewed as professional evaluation and is appreciated as such.

Place a check mark (√) on the scale following each statement to show your reaction or view of your principal. Mark the answer scale at that point you feel most closely represents your view.

Principal-Staff Relations

	Always	Usually	Frequently	Seldom	Never	No Opinion
1. My principal backs me in situations where students misbehave and lets me know what action was taken.						
2. I am able to talk to my principal freely and openly.						
3. My principal is consistent and practices what he preaches.						
4. My principal makes me feel that the work I do is important and that my contribution is worthwhile.						
5. If my principal delegates a responsibility to me, I know he will let me handle the job and that he will back me.						
6. My principal is receptive to constructive criticism.						
7. My principal will—and can—make a decision. When I go to him, I get an answer.						
8. My principal is available, or accessible, whenever I need to see him.						
9. The evaluation of teachers by my principal is fair.						
10. I get adequate encouragement and praise from my principal.						
11. All departments or areas of interest receive equal treatment by my principal.						
12. My principal represents our building staff fairly and adequately with the Central Administration staff.						
13. My principal is fair in assigning duties to staff members.						
14. My principal respects me as a human being.						

Comments_____

Figure 20.3. Principal Evaluation Form. [14]

Organization and Building Management

My principal plans and conducts faculty meetings that are:

	Always	Usually	Frequently	Seldom	Never	No Opinion
15. a. worthwhile . . .						
16. b. well organized . . .						
17. c. interesting . . .						
18. My principal plans, organizes, and communicates regarding schedule adjustments and building organization.						
19. My principal demonstrates the ability to provide items necessary in conducting my class, i.e., materials and supplies.						
20. Building policies and regulations are written and clearly understood.						

Comments_____

_____

_____

Student Relationships

21. My principal is accessible to students.						
22. My principal knows how to communicate with students.						
23. My principal is viewed by students as being fair.						
24. Students can talk to my principal and he will listen.						
25. My principal uses positive reinforcement as well as punishment with students.						
26. My principal is effective and fair in handling student discipline.						

Comments_____

_____

_____

Curriculum and Program Development

27. My principal provides adequate leadership to our staff in developing and understanding our philosophy and objectives.						
28. My principal can build an adequate schedule which accommodates all curricular areas and student needs.						
29. My principal encourages staff to improve curriculum content.						
30. My principal fosters and supports change						
31. My principal supports innovation at the building and system levels.						

(continued)

Figure 20.3. Continued.

Comments_____

_____

_____

_____

_____

	Always	Usually	Frequently	Seldom	Never	No Opinion

Community and Parent Relations

My principal knows and functions effectively within the power structure of our:

32. a. school district . . .
33. b. community . . .
34. My principal communicates well with parents as individuals or groups.
35. My principal knows when and how to involve parents in the life of the school.
36. My principal understands and has empathy with the social-economic-ethnic character of this community.

Classify your principal on the following scales:

|_____|

37. Provides a management function which fosters the status quo.   Provides a leadership role with emphasis on instructional improvement and change.

|_____|

38. Demonstrates a concern and emphasis for district policy and rules. Doesn't want the boat rocked.   Displays an interest in people and interprets rules to accommodate individual needs. Is not afraid to break a rule.

39. What do you consider to be the single most worthwhile effort made by your principal this year, in terms of better education for students?

_____

_____

40. What single thing could your principal do to improve education for students in your school in the coming year?

_____

_____

_____

Figure 20.3. Continued.

418

Whether the administrator uses the types of evaluation forms presented in figures 20.2 and 20.3, or a different one, he should initiate some form of evaluation by students, teachers, and parents each school year. These are important groups to the administrator, and their effectiveness perceptions can provide excellent feedback on performance, with suggestions for improvement.

The Socialization Problem

Many, if not most beginning administrators finish their university course work and start their first job in administration with a certain degree of idealism. Once on the job, however, they are typically exposed to a socialization process which, in many cases, diminishes much of the idealism they may have acquired. [11]

Although this process starts on the day that the administrator is employed, it will most clearly be felt when he/she makes the first effort to introduce change in the school. In many situations the bureaucratic red tape that the administrator must overcome before change can be introduced will discourage him/her from implementing the improvements envisioned. He/she will quickly discover that there are few incentives and sometimes considerable personal risk for trying to initiate school improvements. The new administrator who attempts to introduce procedures that differ from those employed in the other schools in the district may be viewed as a maverick by the central office, and as a "loner" by colleagues. Informal pressures by both may be brought to bear in order to make the new administrator and the school become "a part of the district." The result may be a conflict between the personal needs of the administrator and the expectations of the school district or, even more likely, a compromise of the administrator's idealism. [12]

That the socialization process is important was demonstrated in a study by Bridges, who found that the longer an administrator was exposed to the role expectations of the school district, the more his/her behavior was influenced by those expectations rather than by personal needs. [13]

In essence, the socialization process that beginning administrators will be exposed to in a district is designed to encourage them to emphasize institutional expectations rather than personal needs. Regrettably, these expectations often don't leave much room for idealism or for different approaches to administering a school.

In spite of its potentially negative effects, the socialization process of the school district should not be completely rejected by beginning administrators. The process can be a positive one in acquainting them with the role expectations, norms, and sanctions of the district, and several factors may minimize the possibly negative consequences of the socialization process. First of all, simply recognizing that the process does exist should be helpful. Secondly, if beginning administrators follow an earlier recommendation to delay introducing change until they learn more about their job and their new situation, they probably will not be exposed to the negative aspects of the socialization process until they are more secure, and therefore will be in a better position to withstand certain pressures when they are ready to introduce change.

Finally, new administrators should not assume that there is no flexibility in the role expectations, norms, and sanctions operating in a school district. There may be room in the district for an idealistic administrator who wants to do things differently in the school, if he knows how to "bend" the role expectations, norms, and sanctions without breaking them. This will require knowledge, understanding, and, perhaps most important, risk taking to find out what is possible— but it can be done. [15] And, if beginning administrators hope to retain the idealism that they possessed when they started in administration, that effort will indeed need to be made.

CONTINUING PROBLEMS OF MIDDLE MANAGEMENT

While the problems reported by one administrator may not be perceived as problems by another, attempts have been made to identify a common set of problems faced by most school administrators—both new and experienced.

For example, in research by the Center for the Advanced Study of Educational Administration, elementary school principals identified lack of time for supervision, a disinterested and uninformed public, a lack of highly qualified staff to make provisions for individual student differences, inflexible physical facilities, an ambiguous principal role definition, and personnel selection and placement as their most critical problems. [16] A survey for the National Association of Elementary School Principals, conducted by Educational Research Services, [17] found that elementary principals were most concerned about

1. the district administration's failure to represent principals' interests.
2. the increased paper work and other administrative problems which have made their role more one of educational manager than instructional leader.
3. declining student enrollments which have led to cutbacks in staff and have handicapped the principals in trying to improve the faculty by hiring new staff.
4. parents' demands for decision making, social problems of lower income neighborhoods, and the implementation of guidance procedures.

When one turns to an examination of concerns of secondary school principals, the problems are reported in more detail but for the most part they seem similar to those of elementary school principals. In Norton's study of problems of the high school principal, 100 principals were asked to complete an open-ended questionnaire which had them identify four categories of problems: (1) routine problems, (2) routinized problems that often recur, (3) difficult and pressing problems, and (4) problems with no solution. [18] The problems reported by the principals for each of these four categories are presented in figure 20.4.

Figure 20.4 shows a rather complete picture of the types and severity of problems experienced by the high school principal. It should be noted that problems of pupil personnel seemed to be more serious at the secondary school level than at the elementary school level. While Norton's study was conducted in only one state, results from a nation-wide survey by the National Association of Secondary School Principals are generally consistent with his findings. [19]

The information presented thus far strongly indicates that the problems of administration are not confined to the first year, and that anyone who is thinking about a career in middle management in education should be competent in problem solving. [20] However, the fact that administrators face many problems need not discourage those considering a career in school administration. Any position has problems associated with it, and if a person can become an effective problem-solver, administration could become a rewarding and successful career. However, a key to achieving that objective will be the extent to which an individual administrator is willing to pursue continued professional development. The alternative can be professional stagnation or regression.

CONTINUING PROFESSIONAL DEVELOPMENT

After a person has completed a preparation program, obtained state certification, and secured a position as a vice-principal or principal, there is a natural tendency to feel that he/she has "arrived." At this point the administrator has probably invested considerable time and effort in preparation for school administration, and now, having a job, continued professional development may be one of the least attractive things to contemplate. The administrator may realize that there are still a few remaining deficiencies in his/her background and may acknowledge the need to keep up-to-date on new approaches in education. But the administrator thinks, *"More* education or professional development? Never! At least, not for the moment. There are too many things going on in school and there just isn't time to engage in further professional development."

Fortunately, most school administrators eventually recognize and accept the fact that they must engage in continuing professional development in

| Question 1 | Question 2 | Question 3 | Question 4 |
Routine	*Routine and Reoccurring*	*Difficult and Pressing*	*No Solutions More Than Expediencies*

1. Records and Reports
  a. Attendance
  b. Record keeping
  c. Reports
	Problems of Pupil Personnel
	  a. General discipline
	  b. Tardiness and absence
	  c. Student dress code
		Problems of Pupil Personnel
		  a. Discipline considerations
		  b. Teacher-student relationships
		  c. Student activism and dress code for students
			Problems of Pupil Personnel
			  a. Drug abuse
			  b. Student activism
			  c. Student dress code

2. Scheduling and Organization
  a. Class scheduling
  b. Scheduled co-curricular activities
  c. Lunch arrangements and dismissals
	Scheduling and Organization
	  a. Co-curricular activities and sponsorship
	  b. Class sheduling
	  c. Lunch program
		Curriculum Development and Instruction
		  a. Curriculum planning and development
		  b. Effecting change innovation
		  c. Extracurricular program
			General Problems
			  a. Crowded conditions and poor facilities
			  b. Interference by board of education
			  c. Work overload and superintendent interference

3. Problems of Pupil Personnel
  a. Tardiness and absences
  b. Minor discipline
  c. Make-up absences
	Teacher Personnel
	  a. Student relationships
	  b. Teacher attitude
	  c. In-service program
		Teacher Personnel
		  a. Staff evaluation and supervision
		  b. Teacher-to-teacher relationships
		  c. Teacher apathy
			Curriculum and Development and Instruction
			  a. Nonmotivated learner
			  b. Curriculum development
			  c. Slow learners

4. Teacher Personnel
  a. Teachers' meetings
  b. Class assignments
  c. Teacher-administrator relationships
	Parental Relations
	  a. Public relations
	  b. Cooperation
	  c. Discontent
		Scheduling and Organization
		  a. Class schedule
		  b. Extracurricular assignments
		  c. Placement of low ability students
			Parental Relations
			  a. Public relations
			  b. Community involvement
			  c. Parental expectations

5. General Problems
  a. Transportation problems
  b. Custodial problems
	Business Affairs
	  a. Budget utilization
	  b. Purchasing and distribution
	  c. Need for funds
		Parental Relations
		  a. Public relations
		  b. Cooperation
		  c. Others
			Teacher Personnel
			  a. Teacher-student relations
			  b. Others

(Reprinted by permission from the April 1972 issue of *The Clearing House*.)

Figure 20.4. The Five Ranking Problems of High School Principals with Three Leading Sub-Problems.[21]

order to remain effective in their schools, and they find ways to organize their time better so that they can pursue such activities. Finding enough time will always be a problem for the practitioner. But an individual who feels strongly about the need for self-improvement will somehow find time for it, while the person without such strong convictions will "never seem to have the time" for continued professional growth.

For the administrator who is sincerely interested in continuing professional development, a variety of opportunities exist. Too often professional development has been perceived as representing only more course work. Although additional courses can make a contribution toward the further professional growth of an administrator, there are other kinds of activities that are equally valuable. These can range from membership on committees of state and national professional associations to a planned program of reading certain of the professional journals and books published during the year.

Identified below and discussed briefly are a number of professional growth activities, including additional course work, which are recommended for the administrator's consideration.

PARTICIPATION IN PROFESSIONAL ORGANIZATIONS

Every school administrator should belong to and participate in local, state, and national professional administrator organizations.* These organizations can offer many opportunities for professional growth and development, and the administrator can benefit greatly from active participation.

At the district level, a forward-looking local school administrators' association will organize in-service meetings for its members, sponsor trips and visitations to schools where innovative programs are being implemented, and involve its members extensively in making recommendations for the improvement of education in the district. All of these activities can contribute to the continuing professional development of an administrator.

If, for some reason, an administrator's local professional association does not have a professional improvement program similar to the one described, the administrator can exercise leadership in the interest of initiating such a program. Professional improvement activities should not be left solely to universities or to the state or national administrators' associations. There should be an ongoing program of professional development for

---

*At the national level the professional association to which most elementary school administrators belong is the National Association of Elementary School Principals; most secondary school principals belong to the National Association of Secondary School Principals.

administrators within every district, and the local administrators' association should play a large role in planning for and implementing this program.*

At the state and national association levels, an administrator will find a wide variety of opportunities for professional growth. While the administrator may not feel either ready or possessing enough available time to become an officer of a state or national association, there is no reason why that individual shouldn't be able at least to try to participate in one or more of the committee activities of the professional associations.

Most school administrators' state and national associations have standing committees for the areas of curriculum, student personnel, and research, among others, and are frequently anxious to involve members of the association in these activities. By participating on a committee, the administrator will have an opportunity to develop leadership skills and to exchange ideas with colleagues. From such involvement the administrator should be able to broaden his/her perspective beyond the local situation, and at the same time make a useful contribution to the professional associations.

In addition to office-holding and committee work, the state and national professional associations offer potentially significant opportunities for the professional development and improvement of any administrator through annual conventions. At each convention there are presentations and discussions about problems, issues, and new approaches in education, and there is considerable time for school administrators to interact informally. Certainly the chance to "get away from it all" and to recharge one's emotional and professional batteries before facing again the trials and tribulations of the job are a legitimate part of the need to attend a convention.

But whether attendance at state or national conventions will result in the further professional development of an administrator will depend primarily on the extent to which he/she actively pursues the available opportunities. If the administrator spends most of the time socializing, he/she may "enjoy" the convention, but probably will not derive much professional growth. This is not to say that there should be no socializing at a convention or that such activities are without value. Quite the contrary.

However, if the administrator is to benefit fully from the convention in terms of professional growth, he/she will need to plan and organize time judiciously so that it will be possible to attend and participate in meetings covering a wide range of professional topics, as well as to examine the various convention hall exhibits of new materials or technology which could be uti-

---

*An excellent in-service program for school administrators which utilizes an individualized, personal approach has been developed by the Kettering Foundation and has been implemented in a number of school districts. For more information, see Edward Brainard, *Individualizing Administrator Continuing Education* (Englewood, Colo.: A CFK Ltd. Occasional Paper 1973); also see Daniel A. Salmon, "In-service Programs." An ERIC Report: Ed-089-425, 1974.

lized in the school. A state or national convention represents a tremendous opportunity for additional professional development and improvement, if the administrator capitalizes on it.

As a supplement to their annual conventions, the national associations and many of the state administrator associations have recently initiated a series of professional development seminars or institutes which appear to offer considerable opportunity for the continuing education of administrators. At the state level these seminars or institutes frequently take the form of a workshop scheduled for two consecutive weekends, and may be cosponsored by the state association and a cooperating university. Participants are usually able to obtain university credit for their work, and the topics explored at the meetings are typically very timely and relevant. Because the practitioner doesn't have to spread such activities over an entire semester, as is generally the case in university courses, he/she is better able to arrange a schedule in order to participate in the kinds of programs sponsored by the administrators' associations.

The format and advantages of the institutes offered by the national associations are similar in many respects to the state associations' programs. The main differences lie in the greater variety of topics explored, greater availability of nationally renowned speakers and resource people, and more numerous options in regard to the time schedule of the institutes. Figure 20.5 shows the kind of topics that have been explored in institutes sponsored by national administrators' associations.

---

2 1/2-Day Institutes—The Principal and the Press and Other Mass Media; Techniques for Role Playing and Interaction Analysis; Changing the Report Card System; Coping with Student Unrest; Planning a Mini-Course Program; the Principal's Role in Teacher Negotiations; First Steps in Planning a Research and Development Program in a School; Organizing a School for Curriculum (Including Co-curriculum) Study; Recent Developments in School Law and Court Decisions; Planning a Public Relations Program for a Specific Goal; plus others.

5-Day Institutes—Desegregating Schools; Creating Open Environments in Teaching and Learning; Development and Quality Control of Learning Packages and Performance Objectives; Individual Scheduling, Including the Teacher-Adviser Role; Continuous Progress, Year-Round Schools; Evaluating Staff Performance; Involving Students, Staff, and Community in Decision Making; Realizing Better Results for Expenditures of School Funds; Developing a Management-by-Objectives System for a Secondary School.

15-Day Institutes (First Session: 10 days; Second Session: 5 days; with 2 to 3 weeks interim)—Planning the NASSP Model School Concept: "Total Commitment to Total Change;" Mobilizing the School and Community to Plan a New Building or Remodel Existing Plan (Issues, Options, Guidelines, etc.)

Figure 20.5. Professional Development Institutes.[22]

As figure 20.5 shows, the national institutes represent a significant opportunity for the continuing professional development of an administrator. The topics are relevant and cover a wide range of professional issues and new approaches. The institutes are scheduled so that the administrator is seldom away from the job for too long a period of time, with perhaps the exception of the fifteen-day institute. Even in the latter case, most administrators could, with the right kind of advance planning, rearrange their schedules so that they could occasionally attend a two-week institute. Without a doubt, the national institutes offer the school administrator a tremendous opportunity to continue professional development with a minimum of disruption to the everyday work schedule.

PROFESSIONAL READING

Most school administrators usually work a ten- to twelve-hour day, and many of their evenings are occupied with various kinds of school-related meetings. School administration is a demanding job and seldom is the evening when the administrator does not arrive home weary and fatigued. Therefore, when an administrator finally gets a rare evening or weekend free from the demands of the position, professional reading may be the last activity that person would like to pursue. It isn't that the administrator doesn't realize the benefits of professional reading. It's just that he/she has neither the energy or the motivation to do so, and other alternatives may seem more attractive.

While it will not be easy for a school administrator to engage in a program of professional reading, he/she must make the effort in order to keep informed and avoid falling into a "professional rut." Although an administrator may find the summer months more convenient for reading, particularly books, there should also be an attempt to set aside three or four hours a week during the regular school year, perhaps on weekends, for reading professional journals. A planned program and regular schedule of reading journals during the school year and summer months is a "must" for the administrator who is serious about maintaining professional growth and development.

In addition to professional journals, the administrator should try to read several books each year that are concerned with education or related matters. A book can provide a deeper understanding of a subject than would a journal article, and will frequently contain data and information that one could not easily derive from an article.

The problem for the administrator who contemplates reading a book is that the task may require an extended period of concentration and time that is not normally available during the regular school year. However, the winter and spring holidays and the summer months should be convenient times for the administrator to delve into several books. By setting a goal of reading one book during each holiday period and at least one each month during the summer, the administrator could maintain a program of reading five to six books a year. Although such a program cannot be represented as extensive, it is at least a beginning upon which the administrator can expand, depending on available time and developing interest.

The types of books an administrator should read will vary, of course, according to interests and needs. But insofar as possible, the attempt should be made to read broadly, rather than only books on education. The administrator who is unsure about which books to select for reading, can consult the book review section of *The Kappan* for books on education and the book review section of the *New York Times* for those dealing with various aspects of our society. The important factor, though, is not *how* the administrator makes the selection, but that he/she does become committed to scheduling some time during the school vacation periods and the summer months for reading books which will provide professional and personal benefits.

RESEARCH

Many administrators shudder at the sound or sight of the word, *research.* They may have gone through a preparatory program in which they were required to read research articles or to undertake a research study. In pursuing these activities administrators have sometimes had experiences with research which were not pleasant. As a result, many administrators are "gun-shy" about research and certainly do not perceive it as a means of furthering their professional growth and development.

This is regrettable, since research is only a systematic method for seeking an answer to a question or a possible cause of a problem. Although some methods are more complex and sometimes more difficult to understand than others, research—reduced to its essential elements—is simply a means of investigating something about which one would like to learn more. It is true that the utilization of research procedures will force an administrator to become more systematic and objective in investigating a question or problem, but the primary advantage of using research methods is that the information ultimately obtained is likely to be more valid and trustworthy than if such methods were not used.

At this point, the reader may be thinking, "But what kind of research could I do in my school?" Actually, the school setting doesn't lend itself to conducting all types of research studies, and it must be remembered that the administrator's main job is not that of researcher. However, the four examples presented below illustrate the kinds of research studies that are usually possible in a school and which an administrator might consider initiating or becoming involved in at some stage:

Follow-up Studies. Combination questionnaire-personal interview studies to gather information from graduates on career and further training patterns and their recommendations for improving the school program.

Feedback Studies. Combination questionnaire-personal interview studies to obtain information from students, teachers, and/or parents on their perceptions of the effectiveness of some aspect of the school program, e.g., the curriculum, and their recommendations for improvement.

Current Status Studies. Standardized testing and/or questionnaire studies to obtain current information, on, for example, student achievement and ability, dropout rate, or percentage of students participating in student activities.

Diagnostic Studies. Studies designed to shed light on why, for instance, some students underachieve and are truant; why some teachers aren't as effective as they should be; or why certain curricular programs aren't working the way they should be. The research methodology would depend on the area being investigated, the availability of instruments, and the flexibility of the school in permitting such research to be conducted.

Each of the types of studies identified above can generally be conducted within a school setting, and should provide the administrator and others with useful information for improving the educational program of the school. It might be further emphasized that these kinds of research studies may be *necessary* if the school program is to be improved in any substantial sense. As a result of participating in research studies, the administrator will not only make a contribution toward improving the school program, but should also become more knowledgeable about the school and ways to improve it, thereby increasing his/her own professional growth and development.

PROFESSIONAL WRITING AND PUBLIC SPEAKING

Most textbooks on school administration and supervision recommend professional writing and public speaking as means of continuing professional development. However, the observable evidence shows that relatively few administrators engage in these activities. [23]

There is little doubt that an administrator can further develop professionally through writing and public speaking. The self-discipline, concentration, planning, and organizing required for professional writing and public speaking are valuable for the school administrator. But many administrators lack not only time to engage in writing and speaking, but also the confidence or skill for performing these tasks. Neither their undergraduate nor graduate training has prepared them well for professional writing or public speaking. Therefore, although they may recognize the need to do more professional writing and public speaking and may even feel remiss, many administrators simply choose to avoid these tasks when opportunities present themselves.

In light of the problems previously discussed, it may not be realistic to recommend that an administrator engage in professional writing and public speaking as means of further professional development. Still, these are useful activities if an administrator is willing to invest the extra time and effort necessary for accomplishing them. An administrator who lacks confidence or skill in public speaking should consider joining a "Toastmasters" group or taking a speech course. The way for an administrator to start professional writing may be by describing an aspect of the school program which would be of interest to other administrators in the state and could be included in a state publication. Later, as skill and confidence develop, the administrator can try to write articles for national publications.

Writing and speaking well are difficult tasks for most people, not just for administrators. But if an administrator has ideas, convictions—in other words, something to say—an attempt should be made to communicate those thoughts to people through professional writing and public speaking.

ADVANCED COURSEWORK

Most administrators quickly discover after they take a job that their initial administrator preparation program did not prepare them for every aspect of school administration.* The preservice preparation program is usually designed to meet state certification requirements for administrators (which are minimum standards) and to provide a foundation of knowledge and skills on which they can continue to develop building blocks of competency. Some of these building blocks can be achieved through on-the-job experience and others as a result of pursuing the activities already discussed in this section on continuing professional development.

One important way in which a person can continue to develop professionally is by taking additional courses. By this means an administrator can fill in gaps in his preparation program and become better informed about some of the newer approaches and ideas in education.

If an administrator would like to develop further professionally by taking additional course work at a university, the first step might be to write or call the chairperson of a department of educational administration for an appointment. Before conferring with the chairperson however, the administrator should spend some time analyzing his/her particular strengths and limitations, and the challenges currently confronting the school. As a

---

*For a review of criticisms of the preservice training of administrators see John Merrow et al., "A White Paper on the Preparation of School Administrators," *National Elementary Principal* 53 (July-August 1974): 108-18.

result of this analysis, the administrator will be better able to identify and define his/her special needs for further professional development, and the university department chairperson or an assigned adviser will be in a much better position to help plan an appropriate program of course work and related learning experiences.

The administrator might also give some consideration to whether or not the course work is to lead to an advanced degree or certificate. For many administrators, the main reason for seeking additional university course work seems to be to obtain an advanced degree. Actually, there is no evidence that possession of a doctor's degree or specialist's certificate will make it any easier to obtain, hold, or succeed in a job in school administration. Although some school districts prefer that applicants possess a doctorate or specialist's degree, the final decision on candidates is usually based on factors other than their degree, as long as they have been certified by the state. Many if not most school districts include provision for an increase in salary for those who obtain a specialist's certificate or doctor's degree, but the increase is usually slight and hardly justifies the time, effort, and money invested by the individual.

The only truly legitimate reason for an administrator's taking advanced course work is that he/she wants to increase professional knowledge and skills. If this is the main motivation, it is perfectly reasonable to plan a program in such a way that it leads to an advanced degree. The primary goal of an administrator, though, should be to increase his/her learning so that a more effective leadership contribution can be made toward improving the school program.

A FINAL NOTE

Throughout the book and particularly in this chapter the problem dimensions of school administration have been emphasized. The school administrator who is not able to anticipate and prevent or resolve problems successfully is not likely to perform effectively as an administrator nor provide the leadership needed to improve educational opportunities. However, if an individual possesses or can acquire and maintain through continuous professional development the personal qualities and competencies discussed in various places in this book, he/she should be able to respond effectively to present and future challenges and opportunities for leadership. [24]

Review

1. Define the nature of each of the five typical problems which many new administrators face during their first year. Describe how each of the problems might be avoided or resolved.

2. Analyze the similarities and differences between the problems of the elementary school principal and the problems of the secondary school principal. What are the implications of these problems for the school administrator?
3. Identify and define the possible obstacles that an individual may encounter in the contemplation of a need for continuing professional development.
4. Describe the kinds of professional growth opportunities that are possible by participating in the following activities and indicate what the administrator needs to do to capitalize on these opportunities:
   a. membership in professional organizations
   b. professional reading
   c. research
   d. professional writing and public speaking
   e. advanced course work.

Notes

1. Gilbert R. Weldy, *Time: A Resource for the School Administrator* (Reston, Va.: National Association of Secondary School Principals, 1974.)

2. Ibid., pp. 3-5.

3. Ibid., pp. 13-53.

4. The credit for the origination of the concept of MBO is usually given to Peter F. Drucker, *The Practice of Management* (New York: Harper & Row, Publishers, 1954).

5. For an excellent review of the concepts of MBO and their practical application, see Anthony P. Raia, *Managing by Objectives* (Glenview, Ill.: Scott, Foresman & Co., 1974).

6. For an extensive discussion of the ideas in this section, see Richard A. Gorton, *Conflict, Controversy and Crisis in School Administration and Supervision* (Dubuque, Iowa: Wm. C. Brown Company Publishers, 1972), chap. 11.

7. For an analysis of this problem, see ibid., pp. 307-8.

8. See Chester Barnard, *The Functions of the Executive* (Cambridge: Harvard University Press, 1948), p. 165.

9. For a further discussion of this type of influence, see Gorton, *Conflict, Controversy and Crisis,* pp. 312-20.

10. The best source for such information is Educational Research Service, Washington, D.C. This agency periodically surveys the practices of school districts in regard to administrator evaluation, and publishes the results of the surveys as well as sample administrator evaluation forms, of which this (figure 20.3) is one.

11. For an interesting discussion of the effects of the problem, see Thomas W. Wiggens, "What's in the Script for Principal Behavior?" An ERIC Report: Ed-057-445, 1971.

12. Jacob W. Getzel, "Conflict in Role Behavior in the Educational Setting," in *Readings in the Social Psychology of Education*, ed. W. W. Charters, Jr., and N. L. Gage (Boston: Allyn and Bacon, 1963).

13. Edwin M. Bridges, "Bureaucratic Role and Socialization: The Influence of Experience on the Elementary Principal," *Educational Administration Quarterly* 1 (Spring 1965):19-29.

14. Washington, D.C.: Educational Research Service.

15. Evidence for this was reported in a study by Joseph L. Ferreira, "The Administrative Internship and Role Change: A Study of the Relationship between Interaction and Attitudes," *Educational Administration Quarterly* 6 (Winter 1970):77-90.

16. Gerald Becker et al., *Elementary School Principals and Their Schools: Beacons of Brilliance and Potholes of Pestilence* (Eugene, Ore.: Center for the Advanced Study of Educational Administration, 1971), pp. 27-67. For a more recent discussion of problems of the

elementary school principalship, see *The National Elementary School Principal,* May-June 1974, which summarizes several viewpoints on problems of the principalship.

17.   William Pharis report at the 1975 Annual Meeting of the National Association of Elementary School Principals.

18.   M. Scott Norton, "Current Problems of the High School Principal," *The Clearing House* 41 (April 1972):451-57.

19.   Findings of 1974 R and D Questionnaire, National Association of Secondary School Principals.

20.   Ron Iannone, "What Motivates Principals?" *Journal of Educational Research* 66, no. 6 (February 1973):260-62.

21.   Ibid., p. 455.

22.   Excerpt from promotional material distributed by the National Association of Secondary School Principals.

23.   For example, see *The Elementary School Principal in 1968 . . . A Research Study* (Washington, D.C.: Department of Elementary School Principals, 1968), p. 31.

24.   For additional information on inservice training for administrators, see Jerry Huglen, *Inservice Training for Staff and Administrators* (Washington, D.C.: National Association of Elementary School Principals, 1974.) See also *Inservice Programs for Educational Administrators and Supervisors* (Arlington, Virginia: Educational Research Service, 1974).

Index